ECONOMIC ISSUES, PROBLEMS AND PERSPECTIVES

# THE STOCK MARKET FLASH CRASH OF 2010

## ECONOMIC ISSUES, PROBLEMS AND PERSPECTIVES

Additional books in this series can be found on Nova's website under the Series tab.

Additional E-books in this series can be found on Nova's website under the E-books tab.

ECONOMIC ISSUES, PROBLEMS AND PERSPECTIVES

# THE STOCK MARKET FLASH CRASH OF 2010

EMMA G. PETERSON
AND
LOUISE S. WEBER
EDITORS

Nova Science Publishers, Inc.
*New York*

For permission to use material from this book please contact us:
Telephone 631-231-7269; Fax 631-231-8175
Web Site: http://www.novapublishers.com



**LIBRARY OF CONGRESS CATALOGING-IN-PUBLICATION DATA**
The stock market flash crash of 2010 / editors, Emma G. Peterson and Louise S. Weber.
p. cm.
Includes index.
ISBN 978-1-61122-959-2 (hbk.)
1. Stocks--United States. 2. Stocks--Prices--United States. 3. Stock exchanges--United States. I. Peterson, Emma G. II. Weber, Louise S.
HG4910.S6884 2010
332.63'273090511--dc22
2010047102

*Published by Nova Science Publishers, Inc. † New York*

# CONTENTS

# PREFACE

On May 6th, 2010, the prices of many U.S.-based equity products experienced an extraordinarily rapid decline and recovery. That afternoon, major equity indices in both the futures and securities markets, each already down over 5% from their prior-day close, suddenly plummeted a further 5-6% in a matter of minutes before rebounding almost as quickly. This new book examines the findings of the staffs of the Commodity Futures Trading Commission and the Securities and Exchange Commission regarding the market events, background discussions and analyses of this turbulent day for the markets

Chapter 1- On May 6, 2010, the prices of many U.S.-based equity products experienced an extraordinarily rapid decline and recovery. That afternoon, major equity indices in both the futures and securities markets, each already down over 4% from their prior-day close, suddenly plummeted a further 5-6% in a matter of minutes before rebounding almost as quickly.

Many of the almost 8,000 individual equity securities and exchange traded funds ("ETFs") traded that day suffered similar price declines and reversals within a short period of time, falling 5%, 10% or even 15% before recovering most, if not all, of their losses. However, some equities experienced even more severe price moves, both up and down. Over 20,000 trades across more than 300 securities were executed at prices more than 60% away from their values just moments before. Moreover, many of these trades were executed at prices of a penny or less, or as high as $100,000, before prices of those securities returned to their "pre-crash" levels.

By the end of the day, major futures and equities indices "recovered" to close at losses of about 3% from the prior day.

Chapter 2- On May 6, 2010, the financial markets experienced a brief but severe drop in prices, falling more than 5% in a matter of minutes, only to recover a short time later. Since that day, the staffs of the Securities and Exchange Commission and the Commodity Futures Trading Commission have been collecting and reviewing massive amounts of information in order to understand the events and to recommend appropriate measures.

In: The Stock Market Flash Crash of 2010
Editor: Emma G. Peterson and Louise S. Weber

ISBN: 978-1-61122-959-2


*Chapter 1*

# FINDINGS REGARDING THE MARKET EVENTS OF MAY 6, 2010: REPORT OF THE STAFFS OF THE CFTC AND SEC TO THE JOINT ADVISORY COMMITTEE ON EMERGING REGULATORY ISSUES*

***U.S. Commodity Futures Trading Commission and U.S. Securities and Exchange Commission***

## EXECUTIVE SUMMARY

On May 6, 2010, the prices of many U.S.-based equity products experienced an extraordinarily rapid decline and recovery. That afternoon, major equity indices in both the futures and securities markets, each already down over 4% from their prior-day close, suddenly plummeted a further 5-6% in a matter of minutes before rebounding almost as quickly.

Many of the almost 8,000 individual equity securities and exchange traded funds ("ETFs") traded that day suffered similar price declines and reversals within a short period of time, falling 5%, 10% or even 15% before recovering most, if not all, of their losses. However, some equities experienced even more severe price moves, both up and down. Over 20,000 trades across more than 300 securities were executed at prices more than 60% away from their values just moments before. Moreover, many of these trades were executed at prices of a penny or less, or as high as $100,000, before prices of those securities returned to their "pre-crash" levels.

By the end of the day, major futures and equities indices "recovered" to close at losses of about 3% from the prior day.

---

* This is an edited, reformatted and augmented edition of a United States Commodity Futures Trading Commission and United States Securities & Exchange Commission, dated September 30, 2010.

## What Happened?

May 6 started as an unusually turbulent day for the markets. As discussed in more detail in the Preliminary Report, trading in the U.S opened to unsettling political and economic news from overseas concerning the European debt crisis. As a result, premiums rose for buying protection against default by the Greek government on their sovereign debt. At about 1 p.m., the Euro began a sharp decline against both the U.S Dollar and Japanese Yen.

Around 1:00 p.m., broadly negative market sentiment was already affecting an increase in the price volatility of some individual securities. At that time, the number of volatility pauses, also known as Liquidity Replenishment Points ("LRPs"), triggered on the New York Stock Exchange ("NYSE") in individual equities listed and traded on that exchange began to substantially increase above average levels.

By 2:30 p.m., the S&P 500 volatility index ("VIX")was up 22.5 percent from the opening level, yields of ten-year Treasuries fell as investors engaged in a "flight to quality," and selling pressure had pushed the Dow Jones Industrial Average ("DJIA") down about 2.5%.

Furthermore, buy-side liquidity[1] in the E-Mini S&P 500 futures contracts (the "E-Mini"), as well as the S&P 500 SPDR exchange traded fund ("SPY"), the two most active stock index instruments traded in electronic futures and equity markets, had fallen from the early-morning level of nearly $6 billion dollars to $2.65 billion (representing a 55% decline) for the E-Mini and from the early-morning level of about $275 million to $220 million (a 20% decline) for SPY.[2] Some individual stocks also suffered from a decline their liquidity.

At 2:32 p.m., against this backdrop of unusually high volatility and thinning liquidity, a large fundamental[3] trader (a mutual fund complex) initiated a sell program to sell a total of 75,000 E-Mini contracts (valued at approximately $4.1 billion) as a hedge to an existing equity position.

Generally, a customer has a number of alternatives as to how to execute a large trade. First, a customer may choose to engage an intermediary, who would, in turn, execute a block trade or manage the position. Second, a customer may choose to manually enter orders into the market. Third, a customer can execute a trade via an automated execution algorithm, which can meet the customer's needs by taking price, time or volume into consideration. Effectively, a customer must make a choice as to how much human judgment is involved while executing a trade.

This large fundamental trader chose to execute this sell program via an automated execution algorithm ("Sell Algorithm") that was programmed to feed orders into the June 2010 E-Mini market to target an execution rate set to 9% of the trading volume calculated over the previous minute, but without regard to price or time.

The execution of this sell program resulted in the largest net change in daily position of any trader in the E-Mini since the beginning of the year (from January 1, 2010 through May 6, 2010). Only two single-day sell programs of equal or larger size – one of which was by the same large fundamental trader – were executed in the E-Mini in the 12 months prior to May 6. When executing the previous sell program, this large fundamental trader utilized a combination of manual trading entered over the course of a day and several automated execution algorithms which took into account price, time, and volume. On that occasion it took more than 5 hours for this large trader to execute the first 75,000 contracts of a large sell program.[4]

However, on May 6, when markets were already under stress, the Sell Algorithm chosen by the large trader to only target trading volume, and neither price nor time, executed the sell program extremely rapidly in just 20 minutes. [5]

This sell pressure was initially absorbed by:

- high frequency traders ("HFTs")and other intermediaries[6] in the futures market;
- fundamental buyers in the futures market; and
- cross-market arbitrageurs[7] who transferred this sell pressure to the equities markets by opportunistically buying E-Mini contracts and simultaneously selling products like SPY, or selling individual equities in the S&P 500 Index.

HFTs and intermediaries were the likely buyers of the initial batch of orders submitted by the Sell Algorithm, and, as a result, these buyers built up temporary long positions. Specifically, HFTs accumulated a net long position of about 3,300 contracts. However, between 2:41 p.m. and 2:44 p.m., HFTs aggressively sold about 2,000 E-Mini contracts in order to reduce their temporary long positions. At the same time, HFTs traded nearly 140,000 E-Mini contracts or over 33% of the total trading volume. This is consistent with the HFTs' typical practice of trading a very large number of contracts, but not accumulating an aggregate inventory beyond three to four thousand contracts in either direction.

The Sell Algorithm used by the large trader responded to the increased volume by increasing the rate at which it was feeding the orders into the market, even though orders that it already sent to the market were arguably not yet fully absorbed by fundamental buyers or crossmarket arbitrageurs. In fact, especially in times of significant volatility, high trading volume is not necessarily a reliable indicator of market liquidity.

What happened next is best described in terms of two liquidity crises – one at the broad index level in the E-Mini, the other with respect to individual stocks.

## Liquidity Crisis in the E-Mini

The combined selling pressure from the Sell Algorithm, HFTs and other traders drove the price of the E-Mini down approximately 3% in just four minutes from the beginning of 2:41 p.m. through the end of 2:44 p.m. During this same time cross-market arbitrageurs who did buy the E-Mini, simultaneously sold equivalent amounts in the equities markets, driving the price of SPY also down approximately 3%.

Still lacking sufficient demand from fundamental buyers or cross-market arbitrageurs, HFTs began to quickly buy and then resell contracts to each other – generating a "hot-potato" volume effect as the same positions were rapidly passed back and forth. Between 2:45:13 and 2:45:27, HFTs traded over 27,000 contracts, which accounted for about 49 percent of the total trading volume, while buying only about 200 additional contracts net.

At this time, buy-side market depth in the E-Mini fell to about $58 million, less than 1% of its depth from that morning's level. As liquidity vanished, the price of the E-Mini dropped by an additional 1.7% in just these 15 seconds, to reach its intraday low of 1056. This sudden decline in both price and liquidity may be symptomatic of the notion that prices were moving so fast, fundamental buyers and cross-market arbitrageurs were either unable or unwilling to supply enough buy-side liquidity.

In the four-and-one-half minutes from 2:41 p.m. through 2:45:27 p.m., prices of the E-Mini had fallen by more than 5% and prices of SPY suffered a decline of over 6%. According to interviews with cross-market trading firms, at this time they were purchasing the E-Mini and selling either SPY, baskets of individual securities, or other index products.

By 2:45:28 there were less than 1,050 contracts of buy-side resting orders in the E-Mini, representing less than 1% of buy-side market depth observed at the beginning of the day. At the same time, buy-side resting orders in SPY fell to about 600,000 shares (equivalent to 1,200 E-Mini contracts) representing approximately 25% of its depth at the beginning of the day.

Between 2:32 p.m. and 2:45 p.m., as prices of the E-Mini rapidly declined, the Sell Algorithm sold about 35,000 E-Mini contracts (valued at approximately $1.9 billion) of the 75,000 intended. During the same time, all fundamental sellers combined sold more than 80,000 contracts net, while all fundamental buyers bought only about 50,000 contracts net, for a net fundamental imbalance of 30,000 contracts. This level of net selling by fundamental sellers is about 15 times larger compared to the same 13-minute interval during the previous three days, while this level of net buying by the fundamental buyers is about 10 times larger compared to the same time period during the previous three days.

At 2:45:28 p.m., trading on the E-Mini was paused for five seconds when the Chicago Mercantile Exchange ("CME") Stop Logic Functionality was triggered in order to prevent a cascade of further price declines. In that short period of time, sell-side pressure in the E-Mini was partly alleviated and buy-side interest increased. When trading resumed at 2:45:33 p.m., prices stabilized and shortly thereafter, the E-Mini began to recover, followed by the SPY.

The Sell Algorithm continued to execute the sell program until about 2:51 p.m. as the prices were rapidly rising in both the E-Mini and SPY.

## Liquidity Crisis with Respect to Individual Stocks

The second liquidity crisis occurred in the equities markets at about 2:45 p.m. Based on interviews with a variety of large market participants, automated trading systems used by many liquidity providers temporarily paused in reaction to the sudden price declines observed during the first liquidity crisis. These built-in pauses are designed to prevent automated systems from trading when prices move beyond pre-defined thresholds in order to allow traders and risk managers to fully assess market conditions before trading is resumed.

After their trading systems were automatically paused, individual market participants had to assess the risks associated with continuing their trading. Participants reported that these assessments included the following factors: whether observed severe price moves could be an artifact of erroneous data; the impact of such moves on risk and position limits; impacts on intraday profit and loss ("P&L"); the potential for trades to be broken, leaving their firms inadvertently long or short on one side of the market; and the ability of their systems to handle the very high volume of trades and orders they were processing that day. In addition, a number of participants reported that because prices simultaneously fell across many types of securities, they feared the occurrence of a cataclysmic event of which they were not yet aware, and that their strategies were not designed to handle.[8]

Based on their respective individual risk assessments, some market makers and other liquidity providers widened their quote spreads, others reduced offered liquidity, and a significant number withdrew completely from the markets. Some fell back to manual trading but had to limit their focus to only a subset of securities as they were not able to keep up with the nearly ten-fold increase in volume that occurred as prices in many securities rapidly declined.

HFTs in the equity markets, who normally both provide and take liquidity as part of their strategies, traded proportionally more as volume increased, and overall were net sellers in the rapidly declining broad market along with most other participants. Some of these firms continued to trade as the broad indices began to recover and individual securities started to experience severe price dislocations, whereas others reduced or halted trading completely.

Many over-the-counter ("OTC") market makers who would otherwise internally execute as principal a significant fraction of the buy and sell orders they receive from retail customers (*i.e.*, "internalizers") began routing most, if not all, of these orders directly to the public exchanges where they competed with other orders for immediately available, but dwindling, liquidity.

Even though after 2:45 p.m. prices in the E-Mini and SPY were recovering from their severe declines, sell orders placed for some individual securities and ETFs (including many retail stop-loss orders, triggered by declines in prices of those securities) found reduced buying interest, which led to further price declines in those securities.

Between 2:40 p.m. and 3:00 p.m., approximately 2 billion shares traded with a total volume exceeding $56 billion. Over 98% of all shares were executed at prices within 10% of their 2:40 p.m. value. However, as liquidity completely evaporated in a number of individual securities and ETFs,[9] participants instructed to sell (or buy) at the market found no immediately available buy interest (or sell interest) resulting in trades being executed at irrational prices as low as one penny or as high as $100,000. These trades occurred as a result of so-called stub quotes, which are quotes generated by market makers (or the exchanges on their behalf) at levels far away from the current market in order to fulfill continuous two-sided quoting obligations even when a market maker has withdrawn from active trading.

The severe dislocations observed in many securities were fleeting. As market participants had time to react and verify the integrity of their data and systems, buy-side and sell-side interest returned and an orderly price discovery process began to function. By approximately 3:00 p.m., most securities had reverted back to trading at prices reflecting true consensus values. Nevertheless, during the 20 minute period between 2:40 p.m. and 3:00 p.m., over 20,000 trades (many based on retail-customer orders) across more than 300 separate securities, including many ETFs,[10] were executed at prices 60% or more away from their 2:40 p.m. prices. After the market closed, the exchanges and FINRA met and jointly agreed to cancel (or break) all such trades under their respective "clearly erroneous" trade rules.

## Lessons Learned

The events summarized above and discussed in greater detail below highlight a number of key lessons to be learned from the extreme price movements observed on May 6.

One key lesson is that under stressed market conditions, the automated execution of a large sell order can trigger extreme price movements, especially if the automated execution algorithm does not take prices into account. Moreover, the interaction between automated execution programs and algorithmic trading strategies can quickly erode liquidity and result in disorderly markets. As the events of May 6 demonstrate, especially in times of significant volatility, high trading volume is not necessarily a reliable indicator of market liquidity.

May 6 was also an important reminder of the inter-connectedness of our derivatives and securities markets, particularly with respect to index products. The nature of the cross-market trading activity described above was confirmed by extensive interviews with market participants (discussed more fully herein), many of whom are active in both the futures and cash markets in the ordinary course, particularly with respect to "price discovery" products such as the E-Mini and SPY. Indeed, the Committee was formed prior to May 6 in recognition of the continuing convergence between the securities and derivatives markets, and the need for a harmonized regulatory approach that takes into account cross-market issues. Among other potential areas to address in this regard, the staffs of the CFTC and SEC are working together with the markets to consider recalibrating the existing market-wide circuit breakers – none of which were triggered on May 6 – that apply across all equity trading venues and the futures markets.

Another key lesson from May 6 is that many market participants employ their own versions of a trading pause – either generally or in particular products – based on different combinations of market signals. While the withdrawal of a single participant may not significantly impact the entire market, a liquidity crisis can develop if many market participants withdraw at the same time. This, in turn, can lead to the breakdown of a fair and orderly price-discovery process, and in the extreme case trades can be executed at stub-quotes used by market makers to fulfill their continuous two-sided quoting obligations.

As demonstrated by the CME's Stop Logic Functionality that triggered a halt in E-Mini trading, pausing a market can be an effective way of providing time for market participants to reassess their strategies, for algorithms to reset their parameters, and for an orderly market to be re-established.

In response to this phenomenon, and to curtail the possibility that a similar liquidity crisis can result in circumstances of such extreme price volatility, the SEC staff worked with the exchanges and FINRA to promptly implement a circuit breaker pilot program for trading in individual securities. The circuit breakers pause trading across the U.S. markets in a security for five minutes if that security has experienced a 10% price change over the preceding five minutes. On June 10, the SEC approved the application of the circuit breakers to securities included in the S&P 500 Index, and on September 10, the SEC approved an expansion of the program to securities included in the Russell 1000 Index and certain ETFs. The circuit breaker program is in effect on a pilot basis through December 10, 2010.

A further observation from May 6 is that market participants' uncertainty about when trades will be broken can affect their trading strategies and willingness to provide liquidity. In fact, in our interviews many participants expressed concern that, on May 6, the exchanges and

FINRA only broke trades that were more than 60% away from the applicable reference price, and did so using a process that was not transparent.

To provide market participants more certainty as to which trades will be broken and allow them to better manage their risks, the SEC staff worked with the exchanges and FINRA to clarify the process for breaking erroneous trades using more objective standards.[11] On September 10, the SEC approved the new trade break procedures, which like the circuit breaker program, is in effect on a pilot basis through December 10, 2010.

Going forward, SEC staff will evaluate the operation of the circuit breaker program and the new procedures for breaking erroneous trades during the pilot period. As part of its review, SEC staff intends to assess whether the current circuit breaker approach could be improved by adopting or incorporating other mechanisms, such as a limit up/limit down procedure that would directly prevent trades outside of specified parameters, while allowing trading to continue within those parameters. Such a procedure could prevent many anomalous trades from ever occurring, as well as limit the disruptive effect of those that do occur, and may work well in tandem with a trading pause mechanism that would accommodate more fundamental price moves.

Of final note, the events of May 6 clearly demonstrate the importance of data in today's world of fully-automated trading strategies and systems. This is further complicated by the many sources of data that must be aggregated in order to form a complete picture of the markets upon which decisions to trade can be based. Varied data conventions, differing methods of communication, the sheer volume of quotes, orders, and trades produced each second, and even inherent time lags based on the laws of physics add yet more complexity.

Whether trading decisions are based on human judgment or a computer algorithm, and whether trades occur once a minute or thousands of times each second, fair and orderly markets require that the standard for robust, accessible, and timely market data be set quite high. Although we do not believe significant market data delays were the primary factor in causing the events of May 6, our analyses of that day reveal the extent to which the actions of market participants can be influenced by uncertainty about, or delays in, market data.

Accordingly, another area of focus going forward should be on the integrity and reliability of market centers' data processes, especially those that involve the publication of trades and quotes to the consolidated market data feeds. In addition, we will be working with the market centers in exploring their members' trading practices to identify any unintentional or potentially abusive or manipulative conduct that may cause system delays that inhibit the ability of market participants to engage in a fair and orderly process of price discovery.

## About This Chapter

Findings for this chapter are presented in four sections. The first section explores the nature and sources of the selling pressure at various points during the day on May 6. The second section analyzes the impact this selling pressure had on key market participants, focusing in particular on their withdrawal from the markets and the consequent evaporation of liquidity. The third section studies additional factors that may have had a role in the events of the day. Finally, the fourth section concludes with a detailed examination of the aggregate order books for selected stocks and ETFs, illustrating how reductions in liquidity led some securities to trade at absurd prices.

# I. Trading in Broad Market Indices on May 6

The events of May 6 can be separated into 5 phases (shown in Figures 1.1 and 1.2):

- During the first phase, from the open through about 2:32 p.m., prices were broadly declining across markets, with stock market index products sustaining losses of about 3%.
- In the second phase, from about 2:32 p.m. through about 2:41 p.m., the broad markets began to lose more ground, declining another 1-2%.
- Between 2:41 p.m. and 2:45:28 p.m. in the third phase lasting only about four minutes or so, volume spiked upwards and the broad markets plummeted a further 5-6% to reach intra-day lows of 9-10%.
- In the fourth phase, from 2:45 p.m. to about 3:00 p.m. broad market indices recovered while at the same time many individual securities and ETFs experienced extreme price fluctuations and traded in a disorderly fashion at prices as low as one penny or as high as $100,000.[12]
- Finally, in the fifth phase starting at about 3:00 p.m., prices of most individual securities significantly recovered and trading resumed in a more orderly fashion.

In order to better understand the dramatic price fluctuations of broad-market indexes in phases two and three, as well as extraordinary price movements in individual securities in phase four, we begin with a brief description of the overall market conditions in the morning and early afternoon on May 6.

## I.1. Market Conditions on May 6 Prior to the Period of Extraordinary Volatility

As discussed in the Preliminary Report, the morning of May 6 opened to unsettling political and economic news from overseas concerning the European debt crisis. In this environment, many market participants demanded higher premiums to bear additional risk.

The broad-based increase in risk on May 6 was evidenced by a number of indicators. Premiums on credit default swaps increased for a number of European sovereign debt securities, including debt from Greece, Portugal, Spain, Italy, and Ireland. In addition, the Euro experienced downward pressure in global currency markets.

In the course of the day, the S&P 500 volatility index ("VIX"), a measure of the expected volatility of the S&P 500 Index, increased by 31.7 percent, which was the fourth largest single-day increase in VIX. Prices on gold futures rose 2.5%, while yields of ten-year Treasuries fell nearly 5% as investors engaged in a "flight to quality."

Starting at about 1:00 p.m., an overall increase in risk also began to manifest itself in the price volatility of individual equities. The number of volatility pauses, also known as

Liquidity Replenishment Points ("LRPs"), triggered on the New York Stock Exchange for individual equities listed and traded on that exchange began to substantially increase above average levels.

By 2:30 p.m., selling pressure had pushed the Dow Jones Industrial Average ("DJIA") down about 2.5%. By this time, buy-side liquidity in the E-Mini had fallen from the early-morning level of nearly $6 billion dollars to $2.65 billion (representing a 55% decline). Buy-side liquidity in SPY had also fallen from the early-morning level of about $275 million to $220 million (a decline of 20%). Some individual stocks also suffered a decline in both buy-side and sell-side liquidity by this time.

## I.2. Stock Index Products: the E-Mini Futures Contract and SPY Exchange Traded Fund

The E-Mini and SPY are the two most active stock index instruments traded in the electronic futures and equity markets. Both are derivative products designed to track stocks in the S&P 500 Index, which in turn represents approximately 75% of the market capitalization of U.S.-listed equities. In order to compare trading and liquidity dynamics in these two products it is important to note their differences so that appropriate side-by-side adjustments can be made.

- The E-Mini futures contract was introduced by the CME on September 9, 1997, and trades exclusively on the CME Globex electronic trading platform 24 hours a day with the exception of short technical break periods. SPY is a registered investment company, launched in 1993, that operates as part of the SPDR family of ETFs, and trades on all large equity trading venues, including numerous alternative trading systems ("ATSs").
- The notional value of one E-Mini contract is $50 times the S&P 500 Index, and its minimum price movement (known as "tick") is 0.25 index points or $12.50 per contract. Shares of SPY trade at prices of approximately one tenth of the value of the S&P 500 Index with minimum price movements of one penny per share. One E-Mini contract is therefore approximately equivalent to 500 SPY shares. On May 6 the S&P 500 Index was about 1,100, which equates to $55,000 in notional value for one E-Mini contract, and $110 for one share of SPY.
- The number of outstanding E-Mini contracts is not fixed and there is no limit on how many contracts can be outstanding at any given time. The number of SPY shares outstanding is fixed throughout the trading day but, like other ETFs, SPY may issue its shares to, and redeem them from, specified market participants (known as authorized participants) in large aggregations or blocks (known as creation units) at the end of a trading day.

Limit orders in the E-Mini can be placed only with prices that are effectively within 12 index points (slightly over 1% on May 6) of the last transaction price. There are no bands on the prices for limit orders in SPY.

## I.3. A Loss of Liquidity

Since the E-Mini and SPY both track the same set of S&P 500 stocks, it can be expected that prices of these products would move in tandem during their rapid decline. However, a detailed examination of the order books[13] for each product reveals that in the moments before prices of the E-Mini and SPY both hit their intra-day lows, the E-Mini suffered a significant loss of liquidity during which buy-side market depth[14] was not able to keep pace with sell-side pressure. In comparison, buy-side liquidity in SPY reached its low point for the day a few minutes later, after prices in both the E-Mini and SPY began to recover.

Figures 1.3 and 1.4 present market depth of the E-Mini and SPY. For the E-Mini, depth for the entire CME Globex order book for the June 2010 E-Mini contract is included in the calculation of market depth. For SPY, total market depth includes all resting orders from the trading venues listed in Footnote 15 that are within 500 basis points on either side of the mid-quote of the then-current national best bid and national best offer ("NBBO"). This is equivalent to plus or minus 50 points on each side of the S&P 500 Index.[15] As shown, the divergence between buy-side and sell-side resting orders in the E-Mini began quite early in the day, and already by 2:00 p.m., sell-side depth was twice as large as buy-side depth. For SPY, this divergence did not begin to appear until about 1:30 p.m.

Figure 1.5 compares full buy-side depth for the E-Mini and SPY relative to their respective morning averages: between 9:30 a.m. to 10:00 a.m., the average for the E-Mini is approximately 100,000 contracts (about $5.5 billion), and the average for SPY is approximately 2.5 million shares (about $275 million). By 2:40 p.m., buy-side resting orders in the E-Mini had already declined to less than 20% of their morning average. By way of comparison, at 2:40 p.m. buy-side resting orders in the SPY were about 75% of the morning average. Then, over the next few minutes buy-side resting orders in the E-Mini were rapidly depleted whereas resting orders in SPY remained at between 20% and 40% of its morning average until 2:50 p.m., when they fell to about 9%.

A closer examination of the E-Mini order book offers additional evidence that in the very short term liquidity dynamics in the E-Mini differed somewhat from that in SPY.

Figure 1.6 presents buy-side resting orders for the E-Mini on a second-by-second basis from 2:40 p.m. through 2:46 p.m. At 2:42:40, buy-side resting orders in the E-Mini rapidly went down to 15,000 contracts, and then steadily declined over the next three minutes. By 2:45:28 there were less than 1,050 contracts of buy-side resting orders for the E-Mini, representing less than 1% of buy-side market depth observed at the beginning of the day. In comparison, during that same time, buy-side resting orders in SPY fell to about 600,000 shares (the equivalent of 1,200 E-Mini contracts[16]), representing approximately 25% of its depth at the beginning of the day. Importantly, as illustrated in Figures 1.7 and 1.8, these erosions in buy-side liquidity did not affect near-inside market depth.[17]

Trading in the E-Mini was paused for 5 seconds at 2:45:28, when the CME Stop Logic Functionality was triggered to prevent the execution of the series of stop-loss losses that, if executed, would have resulted in a cascade in prices outside a predetermined "no bust" range.[18] Trading in SPY did not pause during the 5-second pause in the E-Mini.

As the data shows, buy-side liquidity in the E-Mini declined significantly faster than in SPY. However, according to Figures 1.6 and 1.9, buy-side liquidity in the E-Mini order book was quickly refilled during the 5-second pause and aggressive buy-side orders began to lift prices as soon as the trading resumed.

In comparison, it was sell-side depth in SPY that nearly vanished at 2:46 p.m. while the buy-side depth remained steady at about 600,000 shares (see Figure 1.10). Furthermore, SPY buy-side depth within 500 basis points of the mid-quote reached minimums of about 225,000 shares four minutes later at 2:50 p.m. and 2:51 p.m. even though prices in the E-Mini and SPY were recovering.[19] These 225,000 shares in the SPY (equivalent to 450 contracts in the E-Mini) represent approximately 9% of its early morning depth.

In summary, since the E-Mini and SPY both track the same set of S&P 500 stocks, cross-market arbitrage (discussed at the end of this section) between these two products kept their prices closely aligned during their rapid declines. However, as demonstrated above, in the moments before prices of the E-Mini and SPY both hit their intra-day lows, the E-Mini suffered a significant loss of liquidity during which buy-side market depth was not able to keep pace with sell-side pressure. Four minutes later, when prices in the E-Mini and SPY were recovering, buy-side market depth for SPY reached its daily low.

## I.4. Automated Execution of a Large Sell Order in the E –Mini[20]

In order to examine what may have triggered the dynamics in the E-Mini on May 6, over 15,000 trading accounts that participated in transactions on that day were classified into six categories: Intermediaries, HFTs, Fundamental Buyers, Fundamental Sellers, Noise Traders, and Opportunistic Traders.

For classification purposes, both Intermediaries and HFTs were treated as "market makers."[21] As such, these traders would normally be active in the market every day, including the days prior to the events of May 6. Thus, the classification of HFTs and Intermediaries was based on trading data for May 3-5, 2010. Data for May 6, 2010 was used to designate traders into other trading categories.

Intermediaries are defined as "market makers" who follow a strategy of buying and selling a large number of contracts, but hold a relatively low level of inventory. This trading strategy manifests itself in both a low standard deviation of position holdings and a low ratio of overall net holdings to trading volume.

HFTs are defined as "market makers" with very large daily trading frequency. For classification purposes, the top 3% of the Intermediaries sorted by the number of trades were designated as HFTs.

Fundamental Traders are defined as those who were either buying or selling in one direction during the trading day and held a significant net position at the end of the day. Fundamental Traders are further separated into Fundamental Buyers and Sellers depending on both the direction of their trade and the trading volume associated with the accumulation of their net positions.

Noise Traders are defined as those traders who traded fewer than 10 contracts on May 6.

Opportunistic Traders are defined as those traders who do not fall in the other five categories. Traders in this category sometimes behave like the intermediaries (both buying and selling around a target position) and at other times behave like fundamental traders (accumulating a directional long or short position). This trading behavior is consistent with a number of trading strategies, including momentum trading, cross-market arbitrage, and other arbitrage strategies.

The behavior of these categories of trading accounts was examined before and during the period of extreme volatility on May 6. Summary statistics for each category of E-Mini market participants are presented in Table I.1.

Against a backdrop of negative market sentiment and thinning liquidity, at 2:32 p.m., a large Fundamental Seller (a mutual fund complex) initiated a program to sell a total of 75,000 E-Mini contracts (valued at approximately $4.1 billion) as a hedge to an existing equity position.

Generally, a customer has a number of alternatives in how to execute a large trade. First, a customer may choose to engage an intermediary, who would, in turn, execute a block trade or manage the position. Second, a customer may choose to manually enter orders into the market. Third, a customer can execute a trade via an automated execution algorithm, which can meet the customer's needs by taking price, time or volume into consideration.[22] Effectively, a customer must make a choice of how much human judgment is involved while executing a trade.

This large Fundamental Seller chose to execute this sell program via an automated execution algorithm ("Sell Algorithm")that was programmed to feed orders into the June 2010 E-Mini market to target an execution rate set to 9% of the trading volume calculated over the previous minute, but without regard to price or time.

The execution of this sell program resulted in the largest net change in daily position of any trader in the E-Mini since the beginning of the year (from January 1, 2010 through May 6, 2010). Only two single-day sell programs of equal or larger size – one of which was by the same large Fundamental Seller – were executed in the E-Mini in the 12 months prior to May 6. When executing the previous sell program, this large Fundamental Seller utilized a combination of manual trading entered over the course of a day and several automated execution algorithms which took into account price, time, and volume. On that occasion it took more than 5 hours for this large trader to execute the first 75,000 contracts of a large sell program.[23]

However, on May 6, when markets were already under stress, the Sell Algorithm chosen by the large Fundamental Seller to only target trading volume, and not price nor time, executed the sell program extremely rapidly in just 20 minutes.[24]

HFTs and Intermediaries were the likely buyers of the initial batch of orders submitted by the Sell Algorithm, and, as a result, these buyers built up temporary long positions. Specifically, HFTs accumulated a net long position of about 3,300 contracts. HFTs, therefore, initially provided liquidity to the market.

However, between 2:41 p.m. and 2:44 p.m., HFTs aggressively sold about 2,000 E-Mini contracts in order to reduce their temporary long positions. Thus, at this time, HFTs stopped providing liquidity and instead began to take liquidity. At this time, HFTs were competing with the large Fundamental Seller for the liquidity expected to be provided by Fundamental Buyers who would hold their positions, or by Opportunistic Buyers who would trade based on their ability to hedge their positions in the equity markets.

At the same time, HFTs traded nearly 140,000 E-Mini contracts or over 33% of the total trading volume. This is consistent with the HFTs' typical practice of trading a very large number of contracts, but not accumulating an aggregate inventory beyond three to four thousand contracts in either direction.

The Sell Algorithm used by the large Fundamental Seller responded to the increased volume by increasing the rate at which it was feeding the orders into the market, even though orders that it already sent to the market were arguably not yet fully absorbed by fundamental buyers or cross-market arbitrageurs. In fact, especially in times of significant volatility high trading volume is not a reliable indicator of market liquidity.

In a day of very negative market sentiment and high volatility, the combined selling pressure from the Sell Algorithm, HFTs and other traders drove the price of the E-Mini down approximately 3% in just four minutes from the beginning of 2:41 p.m. through the end of 2:44 p.m.

As discussed below, during this price decline, Opportunistic Buyers (and some Fundamental Buyers) were indeed purchasing the E-Mini (and contemporaneously selling SPY or baskets of individual securities), but not in sufficient quantity nor at a fast enough pace to keep up with the selling pressure in the E-Mini.

Furthermore, 16 (out of over 15,000) trading accounts that were classified as HFTs traded over 1,455,000 contracts on May 6, which comprised almost a third of the total daily trading volume. Yet, net holdings of HFTs fluctuated around zero so rapidly that they rarely held more than 3,000 contracts long or short on that day. Moreover, compared to the three days prior to May 6, there was an unusually high level of "hot potato" trading volume– due to repeated buying and selling of contracts – among the HFTs, especially during the period between 2:41 p.m. and 2:45 p.m. Specifically, between 2:45:13 and 2:45:27, HFTs traded over 27,000 contracts, which accounted for about 49 percent of the total trading volume, while buying only about 200 additional contracts net.

At this time, buy-side market depth in the E-Mini fell to about $58 million, less than 1% of its depth from that morning's level. As liquidity vanished, the price of the E-Mini dropped by an additional 1.7% in just these 15 seconds, to reach its intraday low of 1056. In fact, in the four-and-one-half minutes from 2:41 p.m. through 2:45:27 p.m., the prices of the E-Mini had fallen by more than 5%. This sudden decline in both price and liquidity may be symptomatic of the notion that prices were moving so fast, Fundamental or Opportunistic Buyers were either unable or unwilling to supply enough buy-side liquidity.

Between 2:32 p.m. and 2:45 p.m., as prices of the E-Mini rapidly declined, the Sell Algorithm sold about 35,000 E-Mini contracts (valued at approximately $1.9 billion) of the 75,000 intended.[25] During the same time, all Fundamental Sellers combined sold more than 80,000 contracts net, while all Fundamental Buyers bought only about 50,000 contracts net, for a net fundamental imbalance of 30,000 contracts. This level of net selling by Fundamental Sellers is about 15 times larger compared to the same 13-minute interval during the previous three days, while this level of net buying by the Fundamental Buyers is about 10 times larger compared to the same time period during the previous three days.

At 2:45:28 p.m., trading on the E-Mini was paused for five seconds when the CME Stop Logic Functionality was triggered in order to prevent a cascade of further price declines. In that short period of time, sell-side pressure in the E-Mini was partly alleviated and buy-side interest increased. When trading resumed at 2:45:33 p.m., prices stabilized and shortly thereafter, the E-Mini began to recover.

Data from the E-Mini order book reveal that a significant amount of additional orders from Opportunistic and Fundamental buyers began arriving sometime during and after the 5 second pause in trading. These buy orders initially neutralized the fall in prices and then sent prices up. While the HFTs did not significantly alter their trading strategy during the rebound in prices, nearly half of Intermediaries withdrew from the market.

The Sell Algorithm continued to execute the sell program until about 2:51 p.m. as prices were rising in both the E-Mini and SPY. Between 2:45 and 2:51 p.m., the Sell Algorithm sold the remaining 40,000 E-Mini contracts or so (valued at approximately $2.2 billion) of the 75,000 intended.[26]

Between 2:45 p.m. and 3:08 p.m., the 23-minute period during which E-Mini prices rebounded, Fundamental Sellers sold more than 110,000 contracts net and Fundamental Buyers bought more than 110,000 contracts net. The large fundamental trader sold the remaining 40,000 contracts or so of its program during this period. This level of net selling by Fundamental Sellers is about 10 times larger compared to the same 23-minute interval during the previous three days, while this level of buying by the Fundamental Buyers is more than 12 times larger compared to the same time period during the previous three days.

By 3:08 p.m., accelerating demand from both Opportunistic and Fundamental Buyers, attracted by the significant price concessions, and lifted the E-Mini prices back to nearly their pre-drop level.

## I.5. Cross-Market Propagation

In order to assess how the liquidity shock may have propagated across securities and markets on May 6, staff spoke with 15 cross-market trading firms that collectively represented net buying of more than 100,000 June 2010 E-Mini contracts (approximately $5.6 billion in notional value) between 2:00 p.m. and 3:00 p.m. on May 6.

Cross-market strategies primarily focus on the contemporaneous trading of securities-related products in the futures and securities markets. The objective of these strategies is to capture temporary price differences between any two related products, but with limited or no exposure to subsequent price moves in those products.

The specific nature of cross-market trading strategies varies widely. Some firms focus on "one-way" strategies by acting as a liquidity provider (i.e., trading passively by submitting nonmarketable resting orders) primarily in one product, and then hedging by trading another product (often by submitting marketable limit or market orders to trade aggressively in the hedging product). Other firms run "two-way" strategies that provide liquidity in multiple products and then hedge as necessary in another product.

In addition, according to the interviews, some firms focus on derivative index products such as futures, ETFs, and listed options, and do not trade the basket of underlying stocks. Other firms, in contrast, attempt to take advantage of the increased difficulty of trading baskets of underlying stocks by specializing in strategies that trade such baskets. With respect to these basket strategies, some firms engage in "pure" arbitrage by trading/hedging in substantially the full basket of underlying stocks, while other firms use "optimized baskets" that are designed to reduce hedging costs or otherwise improve the profitability of their cross-market strategies.

Although the specific nature of cross-product strategies can vary widely, they all start from the basic objective to "buy low, sell high"– that is, to buy the product (whether futures, ETF, or basket of underlying stocks) that is (relatively) cheap and to sell the product that is (relatively) rich. Moreover, cross-product trading firms reported that they incorporate these relative price differences among products in determining their quoted prices. For example, if the E-Mini moved down in comparison with SPY, they would immediately lower their bids and offers in SPY to reflect the price difference, even prior to those bids and offers being executed by incoming contra side orders.

These firms interviewed reported that the products they most consistently used for cross-market trading strategies on May 6 and other trading days were the E-Mini, SPY, and the basket of underlying stocks in the S&P 500 Index.

Consistent with the E-Mini's very high trading volume, most of the interviewed cross-market trading firms reported that they viewed the E-Mini as the primary price discovery product for the S&P 500 Index. While some firms noted that SPY has increased in importance in recent years as its trading volume has expanded, the firms agreed that price changes in the E-Mini generally lead price changes in SPY and in the basket of underlying stocks. The interviewed firms reported that on May 6, E-Mini prices also led the decline and that they were purchasing the E-Mini during this period.

Moreover, nearly all of the interviewed large net buyers in the E-Mini market, which were engaged in cross-market arbitrage strategies, reported that during the decline in prices of the E-Mini and SPY, the E-Mini was relatively cheaper than either SPY or baskets of individual securities. These same firms reported that they therefore purchased the E-Mini and contemporaneously sold SPY, baskets of individual securities, or other equity index products.

Many cross-market trading firms reported that, by 2:45 p.m., they had ceased operating their cross-market strategies because of the highly abnormal price changes in the market.

Nevertheless, those firms that continued to operate cross-market strategies during this period reported that the E-Mini generally led the recovery of prices across all three products.

## I.6. Liquidity in the Stocks of the S&P 500 Index

In order to control for a possibility of a fundamental liquidity event that may have started in stocks underlying the E-Mini and SPY, thereby affecting their prices, we compared the order books of the E-Mini and SPY to that of a basket of large-cap stocks. To do so, an aggregate order book was re-created for the 500 stocks comprising the S&P 500 Index. To account for the wide range of price levels among these 500 stocks, shares of each were standardized to a split-adjusted price of $50 at the open.

The aggregate order book for the S&P 500 out to 500 basis points is plotted in Figure 1.11. Buy and sell market depth is approximately level and balanced throughout most of the day at about 70 million standardized shares. At 2:00 p.m. both the buy and sell order books begin to decline, and then rapidly fall just after 2:30 p.m. Of note is that the buy and sell order books remained mostly balanced even throughout the decline. At 2:45 p.m., buy-side depth was about 20 million standardized shares, or 28% of its early-afternoon value, reaching a low of 14 million shares, or 20% at 2:49 p.m., before rebounding.

Since the pattern of changes in the order books during the day for the E-Mini, SPY, and S&P 500 are characteristically different we normalized each of their values to 2:30 p.m. for the purposes of comparison.[27] As shown in Figure 1.12, the decline in full-depth buy-side liquidity for the E-Mini precedes that of the SPY and the S&P 500. In addition, E-Mini liquidity recovers sooner than either the SPY (which reached its daily low at 2:50 p.m.) or the S&P 500.

In sum, there does not appear to have been a fundamental liquidity event in S&P 500 stocks that preceded and drove price declines in the E-Mini and SPY.

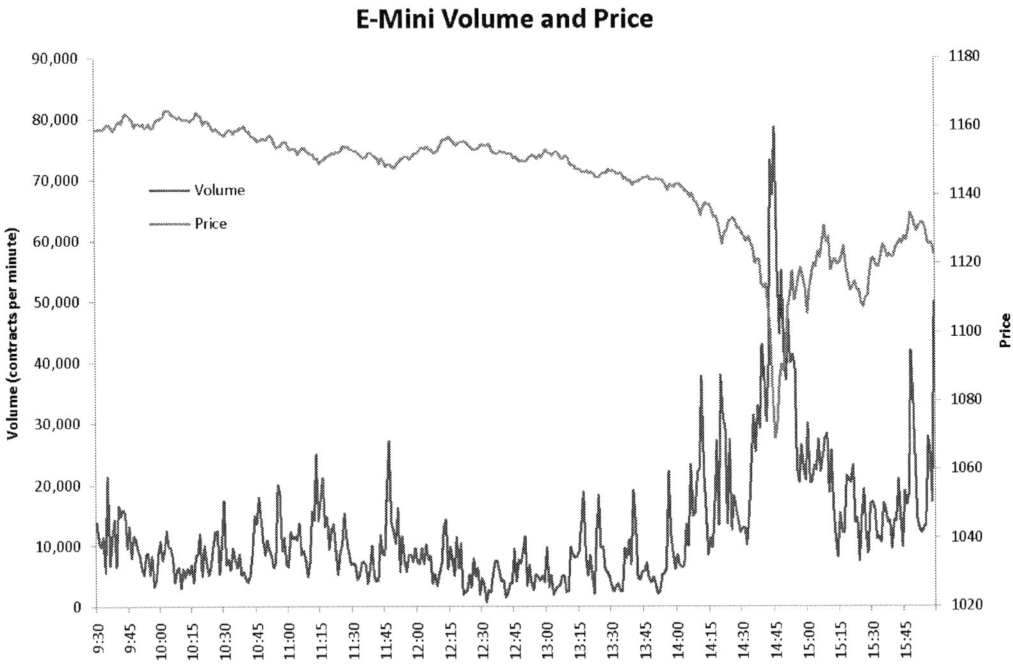


Figure 1.1. E-Mini Volume and Price

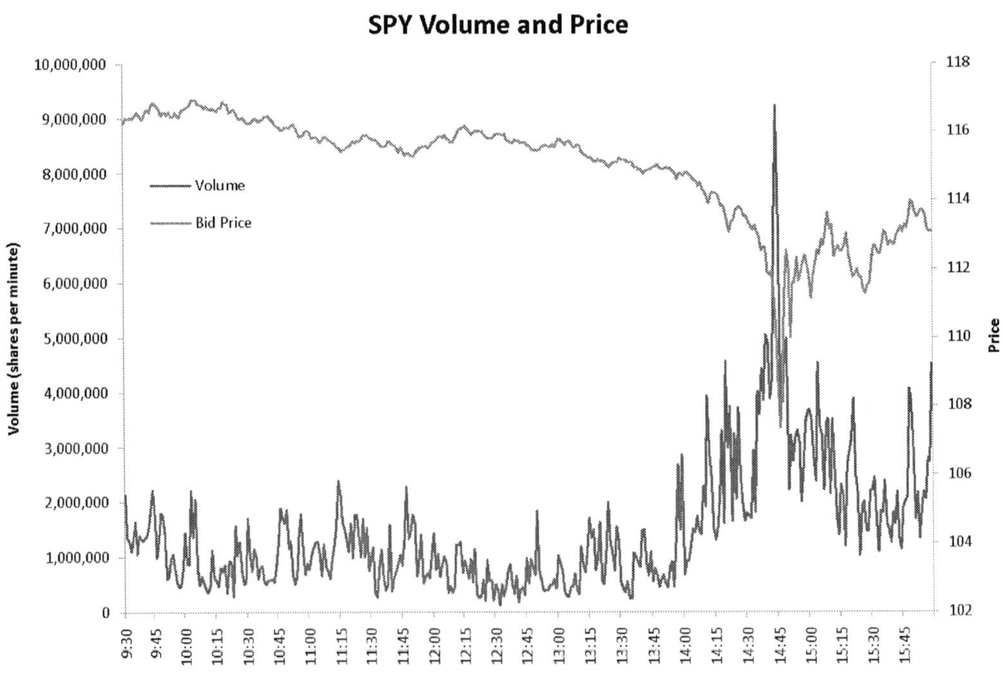


Figure 1.2. SPY Volume and Price

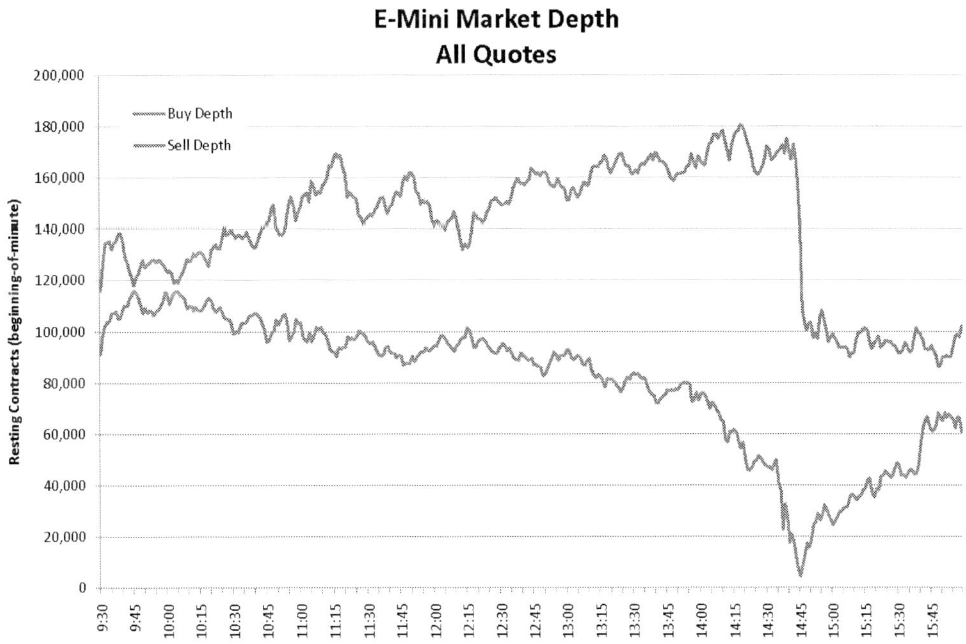


Figure 1.3. E-Mini Buy-Side and Sell-Side Market Depth (all quotes)

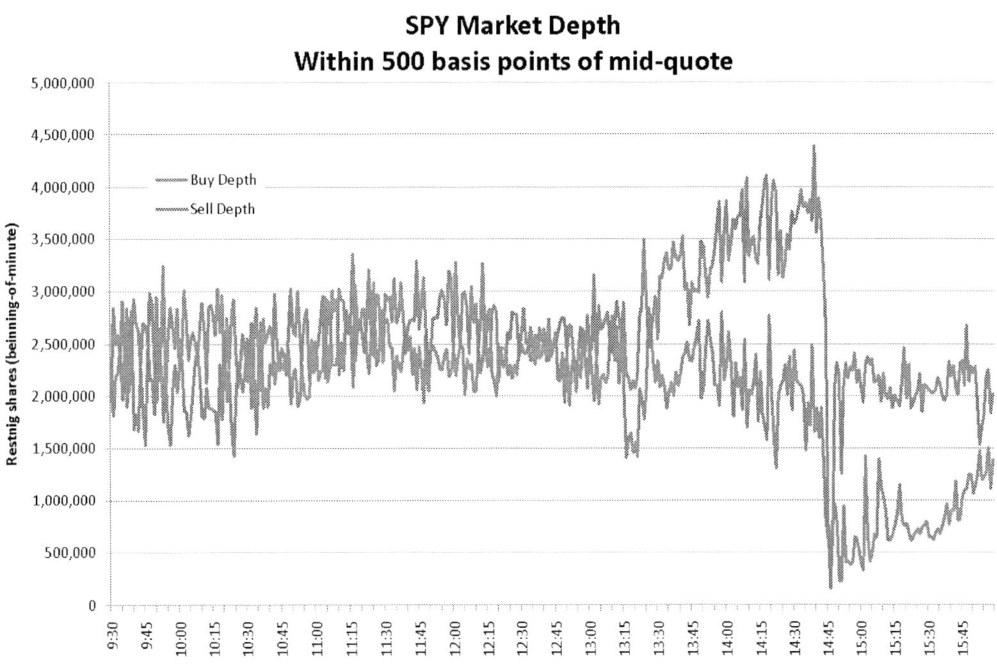


Figure 1.4. SPY Buy-Side and Sell-side Market Depth within 500 basis points of mid-quote

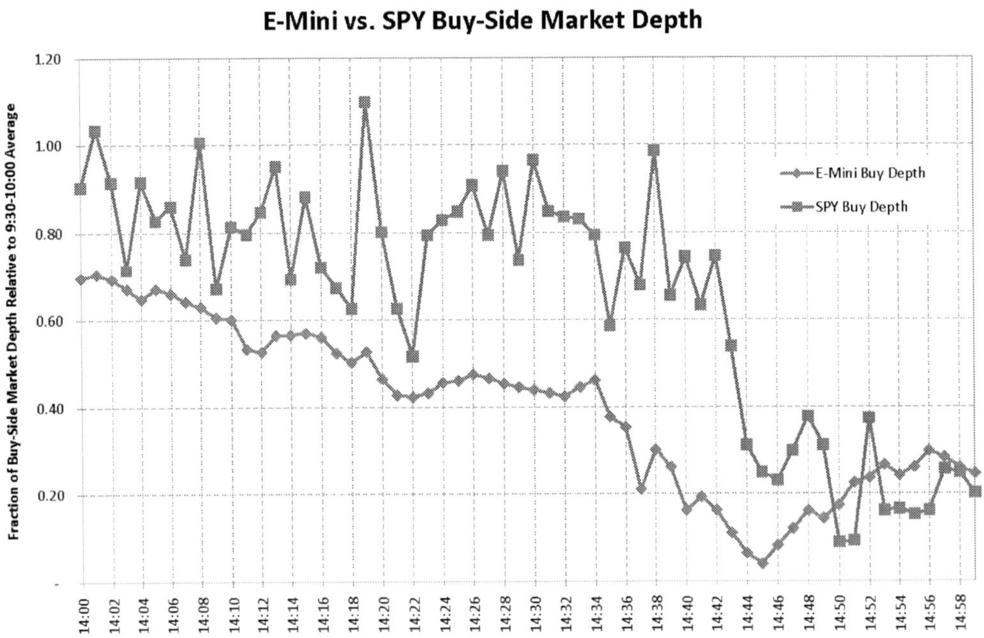


Figure 1.5. Buy-Side Market Depth for E-Mini (all quotes) and SPY (within 500 basis points of mid-quote)

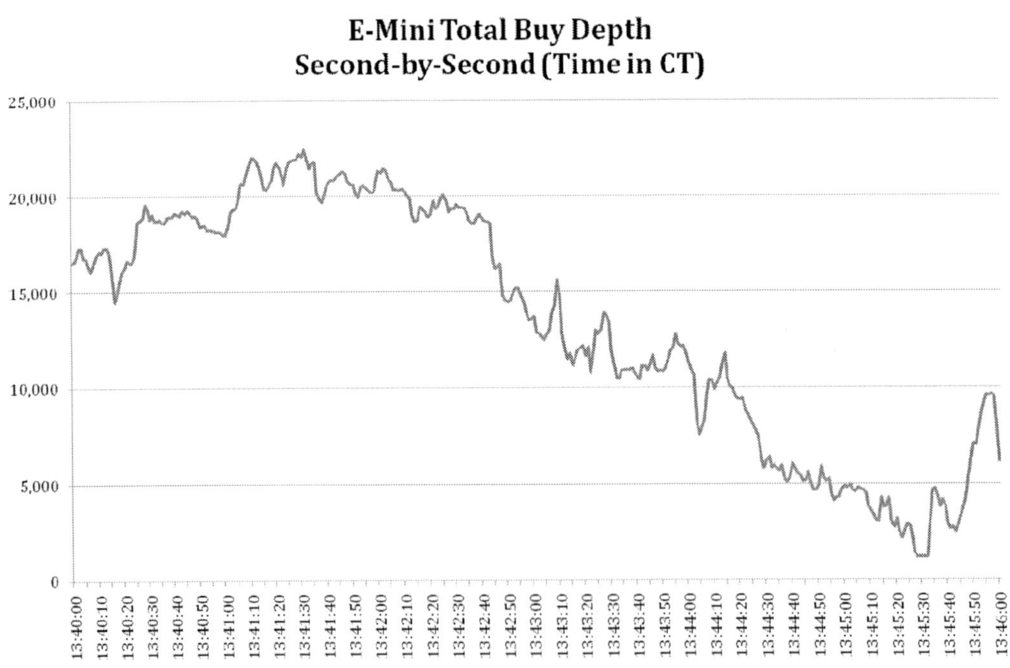


Figure 1.6. E-Mini Buy-Side Market Depth, Second-by-Second (note time is in CT)

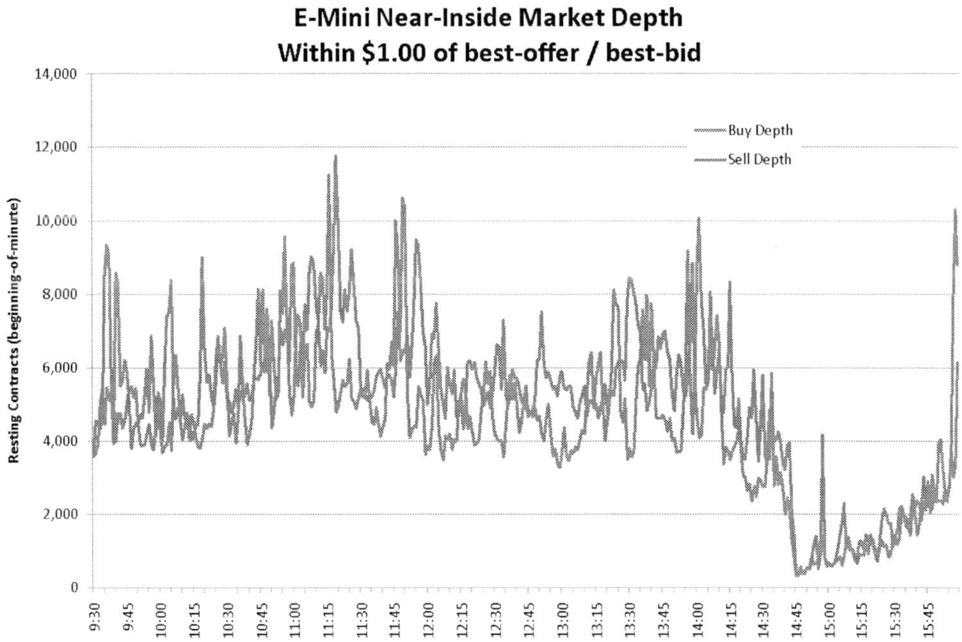


Figure 1.7. E-Mini Buy-Side and Sell-Side "Near-Inside" Market Depth within $1.00 of best-offer and best-bid (approximately 10 basis points from the "mid-quote")

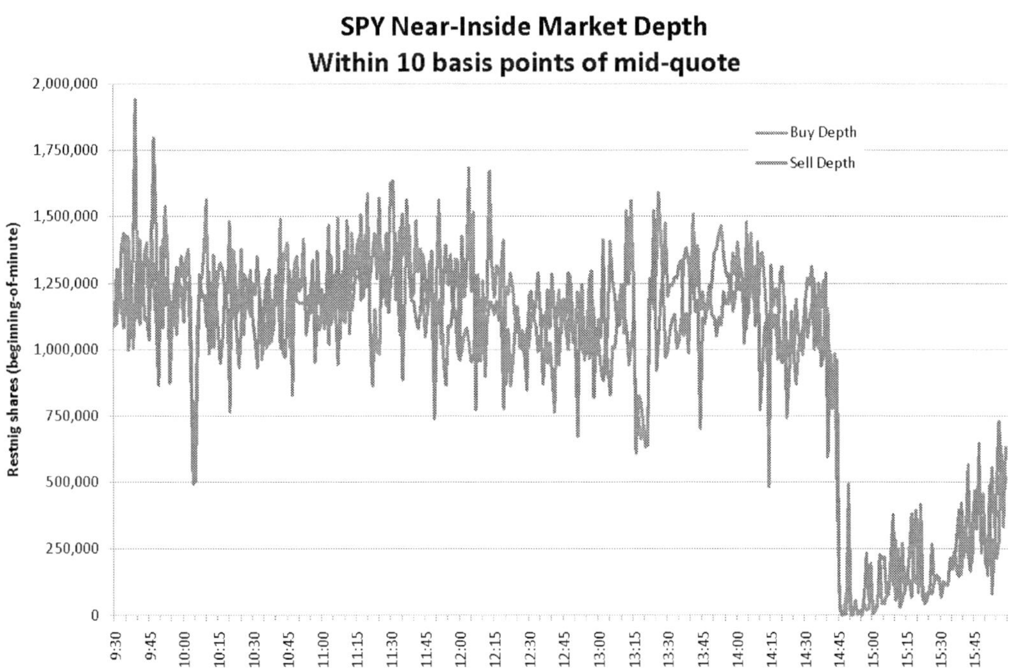


Figure 1.8. SPY Buy-Side and Sell-Side "Near-Inside" Market Depth within 10 basis points of mid-quote

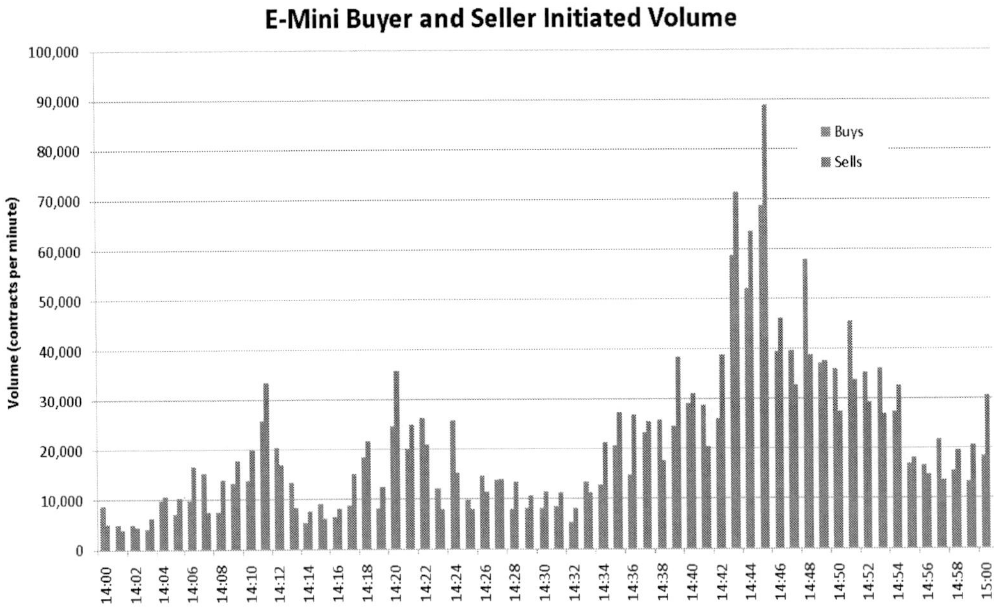


Figure 1.9. E-Mini Buyer and Seller Initiated Volume

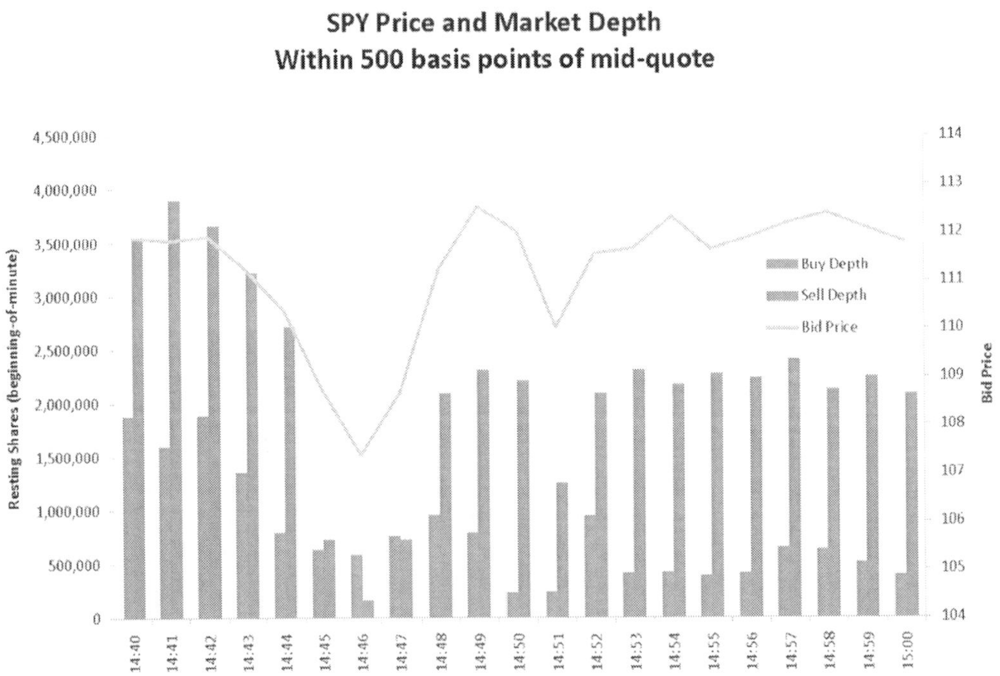


Figure 1.10. SPY Bid Price, and Buy-Side and Sell-side Market Depth within 500 basis points of mid-quote

**Table I.1. Summary Statistics of E-Mini Trader Categories**

| Trader Type | % Volume | % of Trades | # Traders | Avg Trade Size | Limit Orders % Volume | Limit Orders % Trades |
|---|---|---|---|---|---|---|
| **Panel A: May 3-5** | | | | | | |
| High Frequency Trader | 34.22% | 32.56% | 15 | 5.69 | 100.000% | 100.000% |
| Intermediary | 10.49% | 11.63% | 189 | 4.88 | 99.614% | 98.939% |
| Buyer | 11.89% | 10.15% | 1,013 | 6.34 | 91.258% | 91.273% |
| Seller | 12.11% | 10.10% | 1,088 | 6.50 | 92.176% | 91.360% |
| Opportunistic | | | | | | |
| Trader | 30.79% | 33.34% | 3,504 | 4.98 | 92.137% | 90.549% |
| Noise Trader | 0.50% | 2.22% | 6,065 | 1.22 | 70.092% | 71.205% |
| All | 2,397,639 | 446,340 | 11,875 | 5.41 | 95.45% | 94.36% |
| **Panel B: May 6** | | | | | | |
| High Frequency Trader | 28.57% | 29.35% | 16 | 4.85 | 99.997% | 99.997% |
| Intermediary | 9.00% | 11.48% | 179 | 3.89 | 99.639% | 99.237% |
| Buyer | 12.01% | 11.54% | 1,263 | 5.15 | 88.841% | 89.589% |
| Seller | 10.04% | 6.95% | 1,276 | 7.19 | 89.985% | 88.966% |
| **Opportunistic** | | | | | | |
| Trader | 40.13% | 39.64% | 5,808 | 5.05 | 87.385% | 85.352% |
| Noise Trader | 0.25% | 1.04% | 6,880 | 1.20 | 63.609% | 64.879% |
| All | 5,094,703 | 1,030,204 | 15,422 | 4.99 | 92.443% | 91.750% |

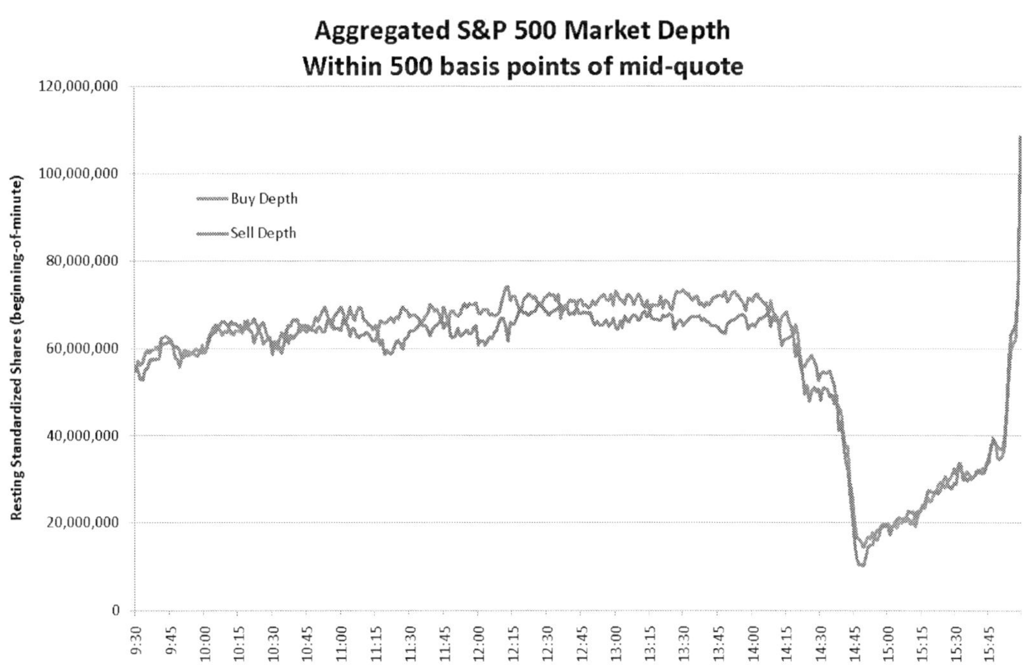


Figure 1.11. Aggregated S&P 500 Buy-Side and Sell-side Market Depth within 500 basis points of mid-quote

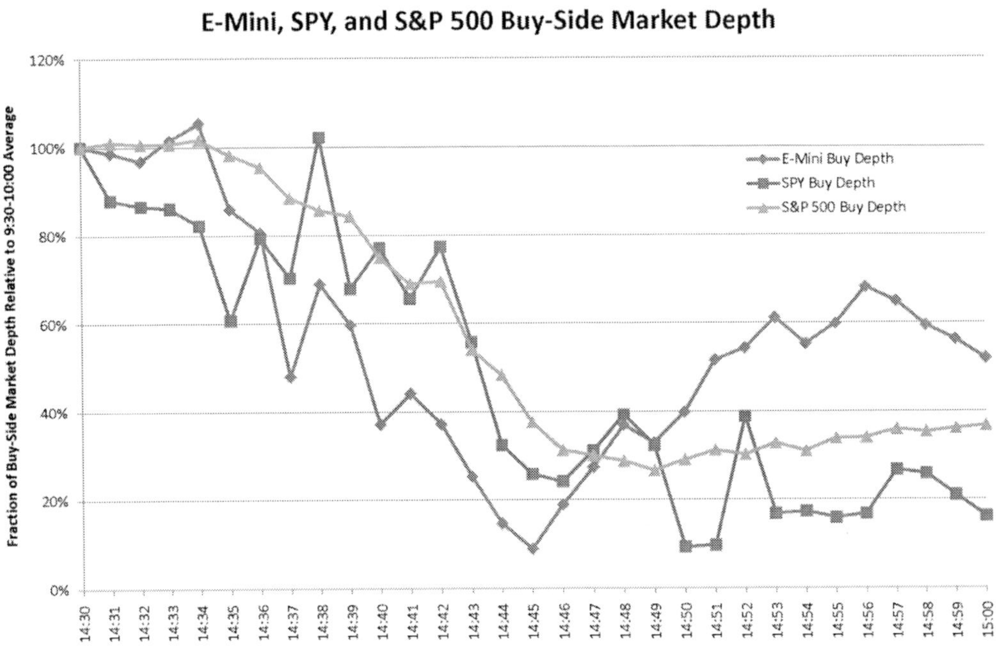


Figure 1.12. Comparison of Buy-side Market Depth for E-Mini (all quotes), and SPY and Aggregate S&P 500 (within 500 basis points of mid-quote)

# II. Market Participants and the Withdrawal of Liquidity

## II.1. Overview

In the previous section we explored the liquidity of the E-Mini and SPY, and discussed the behavior of cross-market arbitrage participants on May 6 during the decline of the broad markets. Among our findings was that even though volume spiked that afternoon, the markets suffered significant reductions in liquidity as prices fell.

Charts 1.A and 1.B on the next two pages illustrate the extent to which large capitalization stocks lost liquidity. The four panels of the first chart display progressively narrower slices of time within which a more detailed view of the aggregate order books for stocks comprising the S&P 500 is shown. This is the same data as plotted in Figure 1.12, but in this case different color bands are used to represent liquidity at different depths from the mid-quote, from 10 basis points through 500 basis points. We note that between 2:35 p.m. and 2:46 p.m., buy-side depth falls to about 25% of its mid-day value, and sell-side depth falls even further to about 15% of its mid-day value. Resting liquidity near the inside of the market at 10 basis points virtually disappears, indicative of spreads widening as liquidity (and prices) fell.

The second chart repeats the data from the first chart but adds additional bars revealing the extent to which resting orders existed beyond 500 basis points from the mid-quote. The graphs show a significant reduction in buy-side market depth, but sell-side depth is only slightly affected. This suggests that resting buy-side interest even beyond 500 basis points was being hit (or canceled) as prices fell.

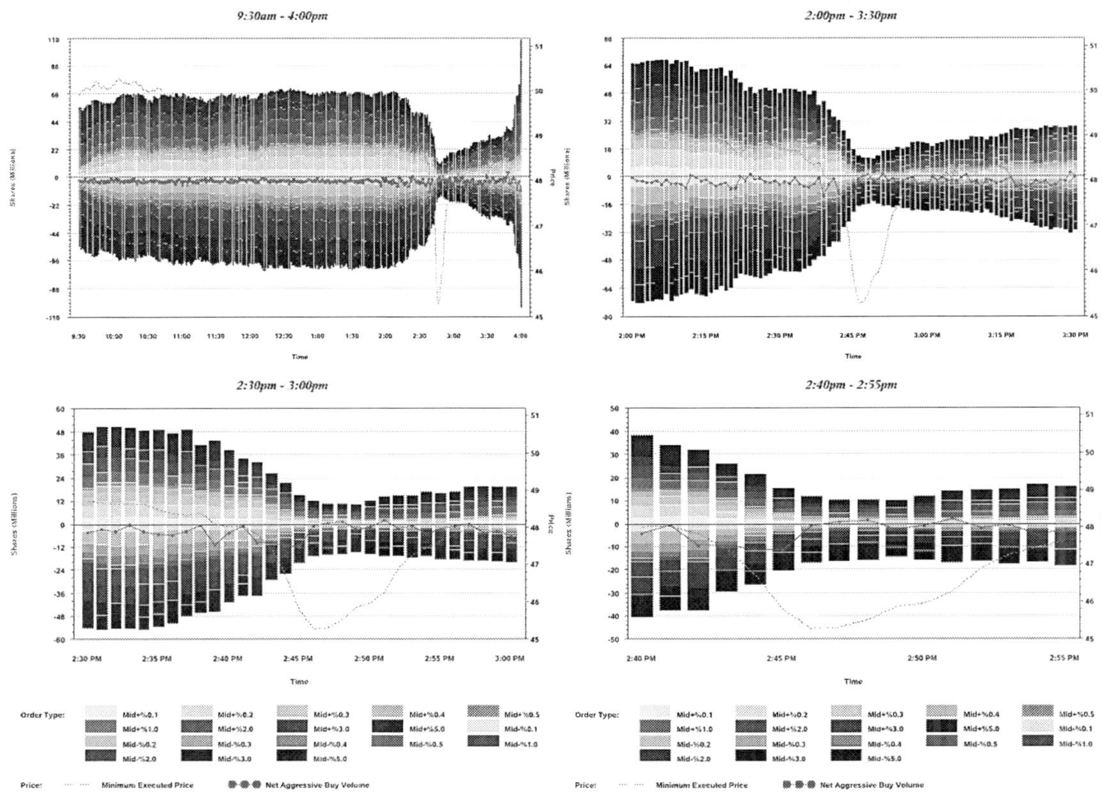


The order book depth reflects the total number of shares in unfilled limit orders, by ticker and minute. The data combines the information from NYSE Openbook, ArcaBook, NASDAQ ModelView, and BATS order book data.

Net Aggressive Buy Volume is defined as executed shares associated with aggressive buy orders minus executed shares associated with aggressive sell orders.

Aggressive buy orders are market buy orders and buy orders at or above the offer price. Aggressive sell orders are market sell orders and sell orders at or below the bid price.

Chart 1.A. S&P 500 Market Depth (within 500 basis points) and Net Aggressive Buy Volume

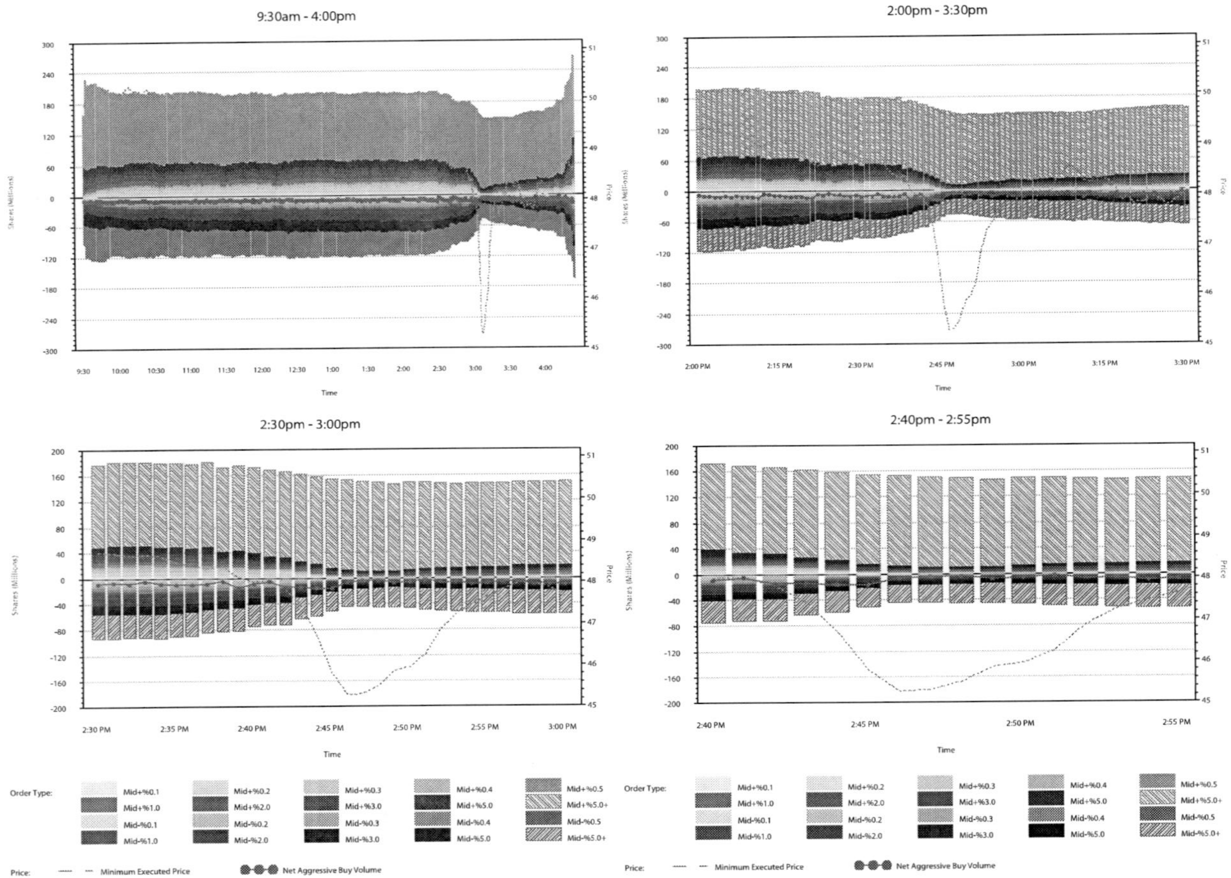


The order book depth reflects the total number of shares in unfilled limit orders, by ticker and minute. The data combines the information from NYSE Openbook, ArcaBook, NASDAQ ModelView, and BATS order book data.

Net Aggressive Buy Volume is defined as executed shares associated with aggressive buy orders minus executed shares associated with aggressive sell orders.

Aggressive buy orders are market buy orders and buy orders at or above the offer price. Aggressive sell orders are market sell orders and sell orders at or below the bid price.

Chart 1.B. S&P 500 Full Market Depth and Net Aggressive Buy Volume

## II.2. Market Participants

To better understand this reduction in liquidity and how it affected market participants, we conducted a series of extensive interviews across a wide range of firms[28] that typically provide market liquidity, beyond those involved in cross-market arbitrage, including:

- traditional equity market makers;
- high-frequency traders;
- internalizers; and
- options market makers.

Each interview was conducted in two parts. In the first half, firms outlined their trading strategies and business models. In the second half, we discussed their actions on May 6, paying special attention to what caused each firm to act in a particular way. Guidelines for the interview process were created to ensure all relevant topics, as applicable to each type of market participant, were covered. In some cases, second rounds of interviews were scheduled to follow-up on specific details not covered during the first interview.

In general we found that many (though not all) firms we interviewed significantly curtailed or completely halted their trading activities at some point during the afternoon of May 6. The specifics of their strategies and the relative size of their trading activities dictated the extent to which this had an impact on the rest of the market. We note that even within the broad categories defined above, each firm has a unique way of trading, and their specific responses to the rapid market changes observed on May 6 are quite nuanced. Nevertheless, a number of common themes emerged that help explain the actions of the day.

### *II.2.a. General Withdrawal of Liquidity*

Almost all of the firms we interviewed use a combination of automated algorithms and human traders to oversee their operations. As such, data integrity was cited by the firms we interviewed as their number one concern. To protect against trading on erroneous data, firms implement automated stops that are triggered when the data received appears questionable.

One way of identifying potentially erroneous data is to screen for large, rapid price moves. For example, it was reported that the rapid decline in prices of the E-Mini, starting around 2:40 p.m. triggered data-integrity pauses in trading across a number of automated algorithms. Rapid declines in individual securities also contributed to data-integrity concerns and triggered trading pauses. Collectively we refer to these as "price-driven integrity pauses." It is important to note these types of pauses are not necessarily the result of erroneous price data, but instead are based on prudential checks into the *possibility* that large, observed price changes are the byproduct of a system error. In fact, the large price declines simultaneously observed across securities and the E-Mini contract during the afternoon of May 6 were indeed real.

Some firms use multiple data sources as inputs to their data-integrity checks, and when those sources do not agree, a pause can be triggered. As discussed in Section 3, latency issues regarding a subset of pricing data on the consolidated market data feeds for NYSE-traded stocks[29] triggered data-integrity checks in the systems of some firms. We refer to these as "feed-driven integrity pauses."

Whenever data integrity was questioned for any reason, firms temporarily paused trading in either the offending security, or in a group of securities. As a firm paused its trading, any liquidity the firm may have been providing to the market became unavailable, and other firms that were still providing liquidity to the markets had to absorb continued order flow. To the extent that this led to more concentrated price pressure, additional rapid price moves would in turn trigger yet more price-driven integrity pauses.

Some firms experienced their own internal system capacity issues due to the significant increase in orders and executions they were initiating that afternoon, and were not able to properly monitor and verify their trading in a timely fashion. When that occurred, trading was paused and sometimes halted for an extended period of time.

Another reason cited for withdrawing from the market was a belief that trades in individual securities at prices representing a 10% or greater short-term move would later be canceled, leaving a firm inadvertently and excessively long or short the market. We note that this particular concern was not necessarily due to uncertainty in whether or not a trade was going to be canceled, but rather the belief that they were indeed going to be canceled.

A number of firms reported on their use of internal risk limits based on a variety of metrics, including intraday P&L, overall volume of executions, price volatility, and absolute long or short exposure to a security, group of securities, or the overall market. Triggers in one or more of these risk limits during the afternoon of May 6 caused some firms to curtail, pause, and sometimes completely halt, their trading activities, thereby depriving the markets of liquidity they otherwise would have been providing.

We also asked firms to comment on three specific external factors first highlighted in the Preliminary Report and in subsequent presentations: (i) delays in consolidated market data for NYSE-traded stocks; (ii) the declarations of self-help by Nasdaq and BATS on NYSE Arca; and (iii) the use of LRPs by NYSE.

Most of the firms we interviewed that are concerned with data latency in the milliseconds (such as market makers, internalizers, and HFTs) subscribe directly to the proprietary feeds offered by the exchanges. These firms do not generally rely on the consolidated market data to make trading decisions and thus their trading decisions would not have been directly affected by the delay in data in this feed. However, some of these firms do use the consolidated market data feeds for data-integrity checks, and delay-induced data discrepancies certainly contributed to the general sense of unease experienced that day.

Other firms that are not concerned with data latency in the milliseconds (such as many asset managers and other lower-frequency traders) tend to rely on the consolidated market data feeds for trading decisions. A number of those interviewed reported pulling back from the market as general volatility increased, and those seeing delays and price-discrepancies on the consolidated market data feeds did report that was a contributing factor in their decision to curtail or halt further trading. The source and potential implications of data delays in the consolidated market data feeds will be explored further in Section 3.

On the afternoon of May 6, Nasdaq and BATS declared self-help against NYSE Arca during which neither Nasdaq nor BATS were required to route orders to NYSE Arca or honor NYSE Arca's quote.[30] However, most of the large market participants we interviewed route orders directly to each individual exchange based on their own algorithms, and told us that they were generally unaffected by these self-help declarations. Furthermore, though these firms noted that Nasdaq and BATS declared self-help on NYSE Arca that afternoon, they continued to route their own orders to NYSE Arca based on NYSE Arca's quotes and trades.

At the end of this section and in Section 3 we further explore the issue of self-help and conclude that, consistent with our interview findings, self-help was not a significant factor on May 6, nor did it contribute to the severe price dislocations observed in many securities.

As discussed in the Preliminary Report, NYSE's LRP mechanism effectively banded the trading range on NYSE for many NYSE-listed securities during the periods of extreme volatility observed on the afternoon of May 6. Market participants we interviewed had mixed reactions to NYSE's use of LRPs. Since most of the firms we spoke with route their own orders, they were able to make their own real-time decisions on whether to include or exclude NYSE in their routing algorithms. Thus these firms did not think LRPs had a direct impact on their ability to trade. Rather, firms reported that they were more concerned with general market volatility and the integrity of prices.

However, a number of firms did report that they considered the triggering of a relatively large number of LRPs indicative of system-wide liquidity issues, which added to their sense of unease, and perhaps influenced decisions to withdraw from trading. A detailed discussion of the role of LRPs on the events of May 6 is provided in Section 3.

### *II.2.b. Traditional Equity and ETF Market Makers*

In general, the rules of national securities exchanges allow a member to voluntarily register as a market maker on a security-by-security basis and subject to certain obligations. These exchange rules require members to maintain a continuous two-sided quotation in the security or securities for which they are registered as a market maker. While the strategies of equity and ETF market making firms may differ, we classify "traditional" market makers as firms with business models that attempt to profit primarily from trading passively by submitting nonmarketable "resting" limit orders and capturing a bid-ask spread. Typically, traditional market makers are "non-directional" or "market neutral" with respect to the securities for which they post quotations; however, a number of market makers utilize ETFs and other securities in order to hedge market exposure they may accumulate during imbalances in buy and sell order flow.[31]

On May 6, market makers reported that rapid price movements and market volatility occurring at about 2:45 p.m. caused internal risk limits to be breached. This in turn triggered their automated trading systems to widen the bid-ask spread of their quotes, as well as reduce the number of shares offered at these levels. For some market makers, self-imposed limits to trading during rapid market moves led to an immediate pause in providing liquidity in lieu of – or soon after – widening quotes.

Most market makers cited data integrity as a primary driver in their decision as to whether to provide liquidity at all, and if so, the manner (size and price) in which they would do so. On May 6, a number of market makers reported that rapid price moves in the E-Mini and individual securities triggered price-driven integrity pauses. Some, who also monitor the consolidated market data feeds, reported feed-driven integrity pauses. We note that even in instances where a market maker was not concerned (or even knowledgeable) about external issues related to feed latencies, or declarations of self-help, the very speed of price moves led some to question the accuracy of price information and, thus, to automatically withdraw liquidity. According to a number of market makers, their internal monitoring continuously triggered visual and audio alarms as multiple securities breached a variety of risk limits one after another.

Some market makers also experienced internal systems problems on May 6. Such problems tended to stem from difficulties in processing "overwhelming" external information wrought by the unique conditions of the day. In some cases, market makers that would have otherwise manually overridden their systems and continued providing liquidity were simply incapable of doing so in a timely manner due to the tremendous pressure caused by a flood of orders, executions, and market data that needed to be manually checked. As the majority of market makers required some form of human intervention to reenter the marketplace once automatic pauses were triggered, the time needed by the various market participants to reenter the market ranged from as short as a few seconds to as long as several hours.

In order to comply with their obligation to maintain continuous two-sided quotations, market makers utilize stub quotes if they choose to discontinue actively quoting.[32] Thus, on May 6, while in the process of reassessing whether to reenter the market, some market maker quotations had extended to stub quote levels – for market makers on Nasdaq or NYSE Arca such stub quotes could be automatically generated upon a market maker's withdrawal from the market.[33] When available liquidity for an ETF or stock was exhausted, marketable orders executed against stub quotes, and such executions ultimately represented a significant proportion of broken trades. We discuss market participants' use of stub quotes and their experience with broken trades in greater detail at the end of this section.

### *II.2.c. ETFs and May 6*

In our Preliminary Report, we noted that many of the securities experiencing the most severe price dislocations on May 6 were equity-based ETFs.[34] We therefore spent considerable time with ETF market makers to understand why this was the case. Some ETF market makers and liquidity providers treat ETFs as if they were the same as corporate stocks and do not track the prices of the individual securities underlying the ETF. Instead, this group bases its market making on immediate buy and sell interest, subject to trends in broad market indicators, including the E-Mini, that may affect a bias in their bids and offers. Others heavily depend upon the tracking of underlying securities as part of their ETF pricing and algorithmic modeling. And yet others trade in individual securities at the same time they trade ETFs. For the latter two categories, changes in the prices of individual securities that are components of an ETF directly affect the manner in which such market makers trade those ETFs.

For instance, market makers that track the prices of securities that are underlying components of an ETF are more likely to pause their trading if there are price-driven, or data feed-driven, integrity questions about those prices.[35] Moreover, extreme volatility in component stocks makes it very difficult to accurately value an ETF in real-time. When this happens, market participants who would otherwise provide liquidity for such ETFs may widen their quotes or stop providing liquidity (in some cases by using stub quotes) until they can determine the reason for the rapid price movement or pricing irregularities.[36] A large majority of ETF market makers with whom we spoke, and particularly those that value underlying stocks as part of their normal market making activities, paused their market making for considerable periods of time starting at about 2:45 p.m. on May 6. We believe this is one of the reasons equity-based ETFs were disproportionately affected by the extreme price volatilities of that afternoon. We further note that ETFs that do not derive their value from the prices of domestic equity securities were not disproportionately affected.

Anecdotally, market makers in ETFs reported that ETFs trade distinctly from individual securities, which often results in more concentrated liquidity on exchange order books.

Specifically, they considered ETFs a "professional's market," where depth of book is more limited compared to individual stocks, and there are little, if any, resting retail orders far from the mid-quote. Sell pressure that overwhelms immediately-available near-inside liquidity is less likely to be "caught" by resting orders farther from the mid-quote in an ETF versus an individual stock.

To test this hypothesis we aggregated the liquidity books for the 100 largest ETFs (by market capitalization) into a single order book and compared that with an aggregate order book for the largest 100 individual stocks. These order books are presented in Charts 2.A, 2.B, 3.A, and 3.B.

The differences are significant. Market depth for the top 100 individual stocks is well-distributed from 10 through 500 basis points (Chart 2.A). In contrast, market depth for the top 100 ETFs is highly concentrated - approximately half of all liquidity is within 30 basis points of the mid-quote (Chart 3.A). At the peak of the decline, buy-side liquidity for the ETFs seems to suffer more severely, falling to 10% of their mid-day value compared to 20% for stocks.

When depth beyond 500 basis points is added to the charts the results are even more striking. For stocks, market depth at those levels doubles on the buy side and triples on the sell side (Chart 2.B). For ETFs the increase is much more modest (Chart 3.B). These results are consistent with the hypothesis that relative to the liquidity of large-cap stocks, much more of the liquidity in ETFs is provided by market professionals, such as market makers and HFTs, who tend to quote much closer to the inside of the market than do non-professional investors who may have price targets much further from the mid-quote. Therefore, when professionals pulled out because of data-integrity concerns, ETFs may not have had the same level of resting liquidity far from the mid-quote as did large-cap stocks, allowing a disproportionate number of ETF orders to hit stub-quote levels.

Of final note, several market makers indicated that they experienced some form of data latency from one or more of the exchanges, most notably NYSE Arca. However, though most ETFs are listed on NYSE Arca, only a few of the ETF market makers we interviewed raised this latency, or the declaration of self-help by other exchanges against NYSE Arca because of this latency, as an issue of concern on May 6. We explore this topic in further detail at the end of this section and in Section 3.

### *II.2.d. Equity-Based High Frequency Traders*

HFTs are proprietary trading firms that use high speed systems to monitor market data and submit large numbers of orders to the markets. HFTs utilize quantitative and algorithmic methodologies to maximize the speed of their market access and trading strategies.[37] Some HFTs are hybrids, acting as both proprietary traders and as market makers. In addition, some HFT strategies may take "delta-neutral" approaches to the market (ending each trading day in a flat position), while others are not delta-neutral and sometimes acquire net long and net short positions.

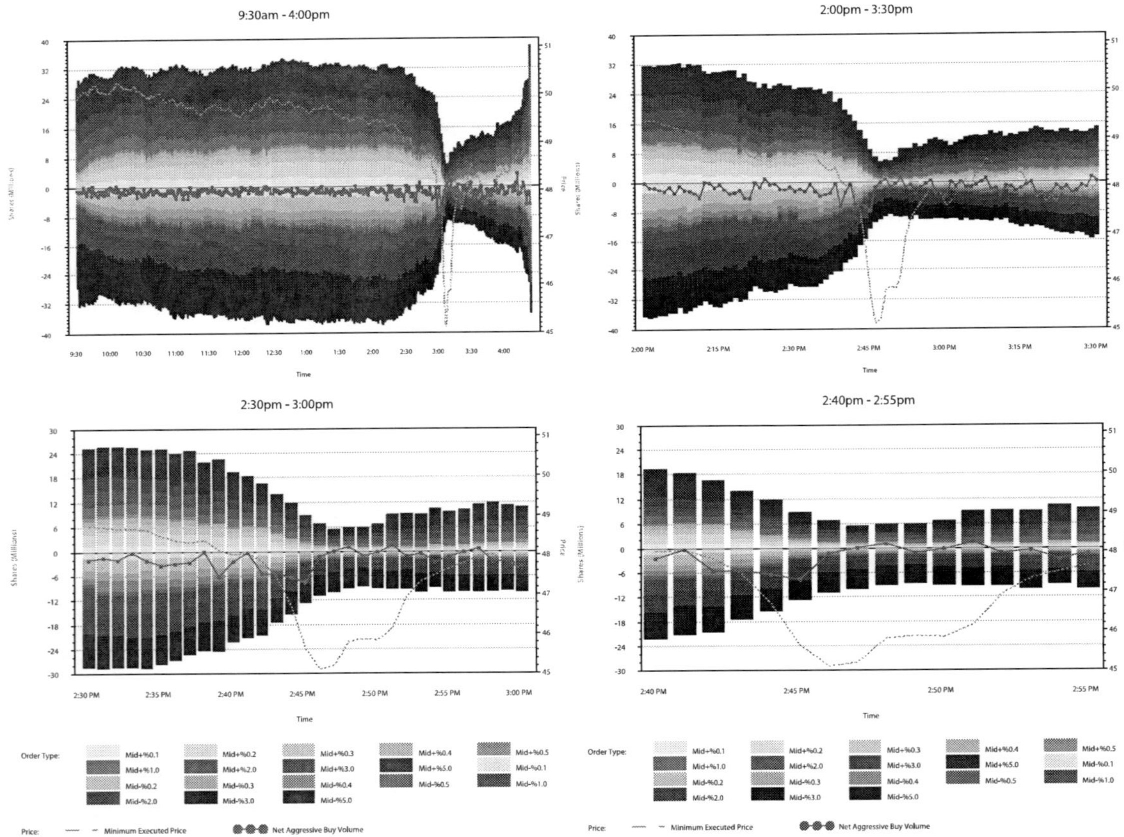


The order book depth reflects the total number of shares in unfilled limit orders, by ticker and minute. The data combines the information from NYSE Openbook, ArcaBook, NASDAQ ModelView, and BATS order book data.

Net Aggressive Buy Volume is defined as executed shares associated with aggressive buy orders minus executed shares associated with aggressive sell orders.

Aggressive buy orders are market buy orders and buy orders at or above the offer price. Aggressive sell orders are market sell orders and sell orders at or below the bid price.

Chart 2.A. Non-ETF Top 100 Market Depth (within 500 basis points) and Net Aggressive Buy Volume

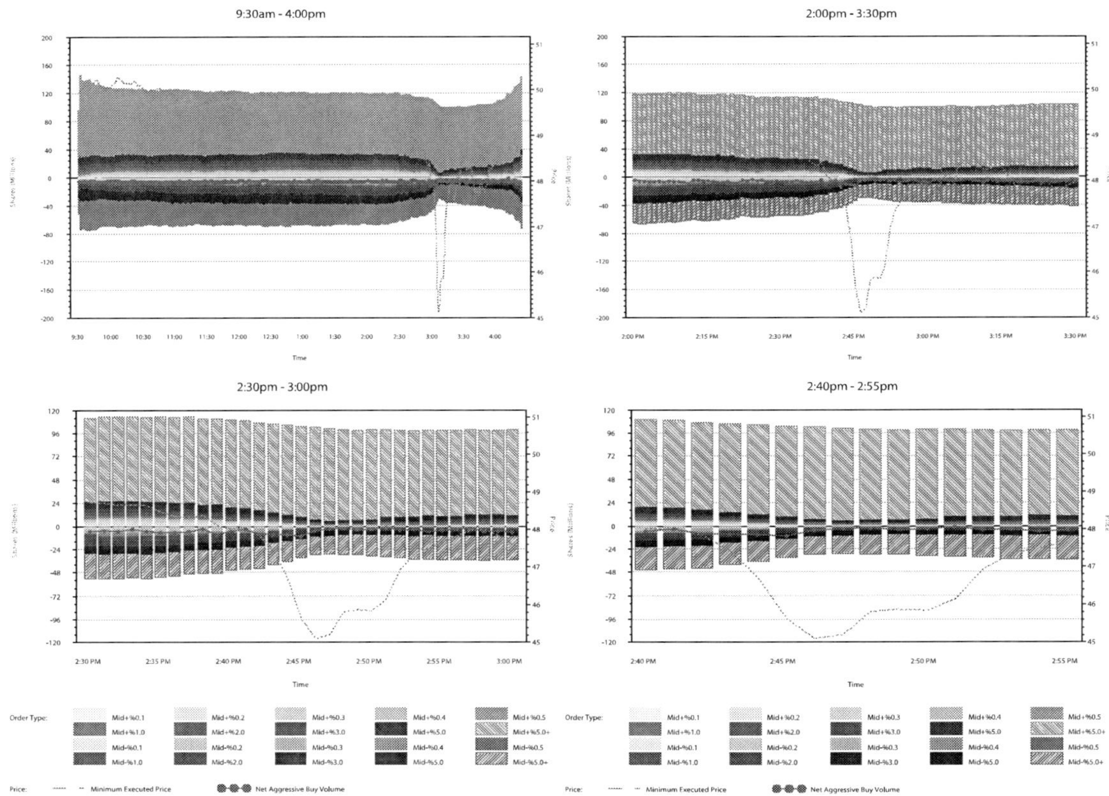


The order book depth reflects the total number of shares in unfilled limit orders, by ticker and minute. The data combines the information from NYSE Openbook, ArcaBook, NASDAQ ModelView, and BATS order book data.

Net Aggressive Buy Volume is defined as executed shares associated with aggressive buy orders minus executed shares associated with aggressive sell orders.

Aggressive buy orders are market buy orders and buy orders at or above the offer price. Aggressive sell orders are market sell orders and sell orders at or below the bid price.

Chart 2.B. Non-ETF Top 100 Full Market Depth and Net Aggressive Buy Volume

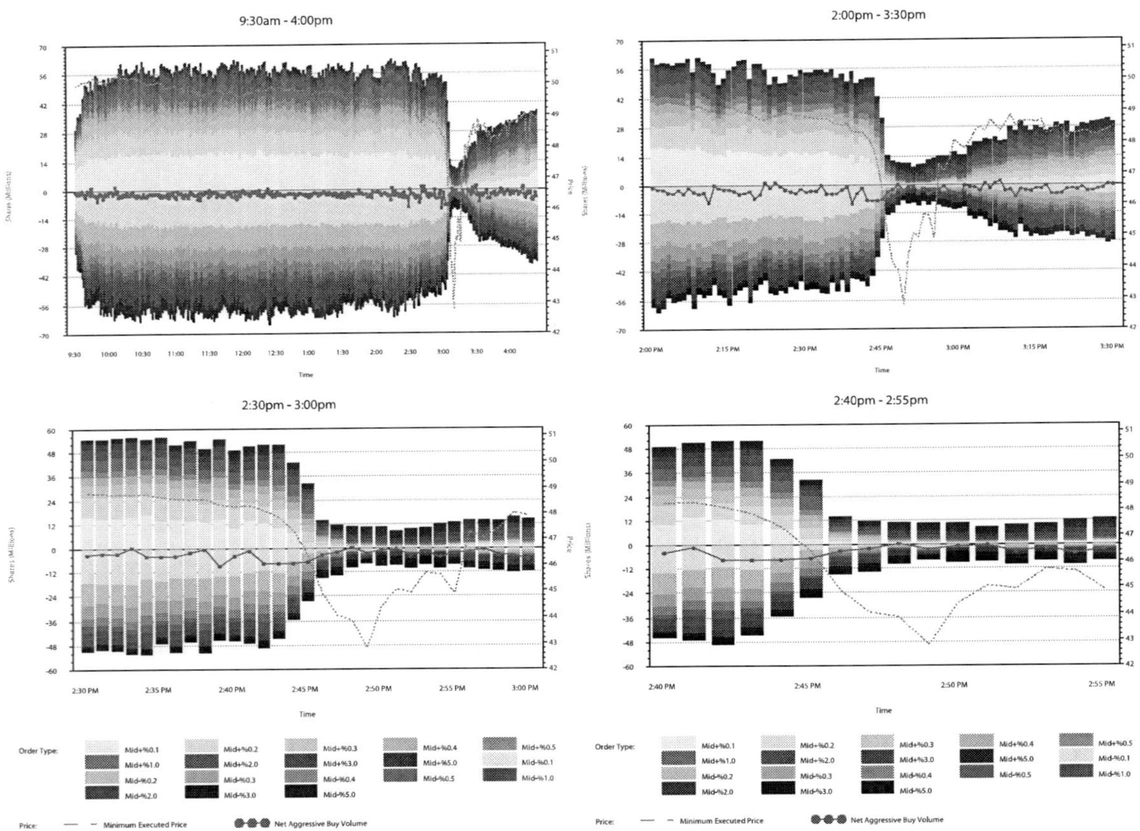


The order book depth reflects the total number of shares in unfilled limit orders, by ticker and minute. The data combines the information from NYSE Openbook, ArcaBook, NASDAQ ModelView, and BATS order book data.

Net Aggressive Buy Volume is defined as executed shares associated with aggressive buy orders minus executed shares associated with aggressive sell orders.

Aggressive buy orders are market buy orders and buy orders at or above the offer price. Aggressive sell orders are market sell orders and sell orders at or below the bid price.

Chart 3.A. ETF Top 100 Market Depth (within 500 basis points) and Net Aggressive Buy Volume

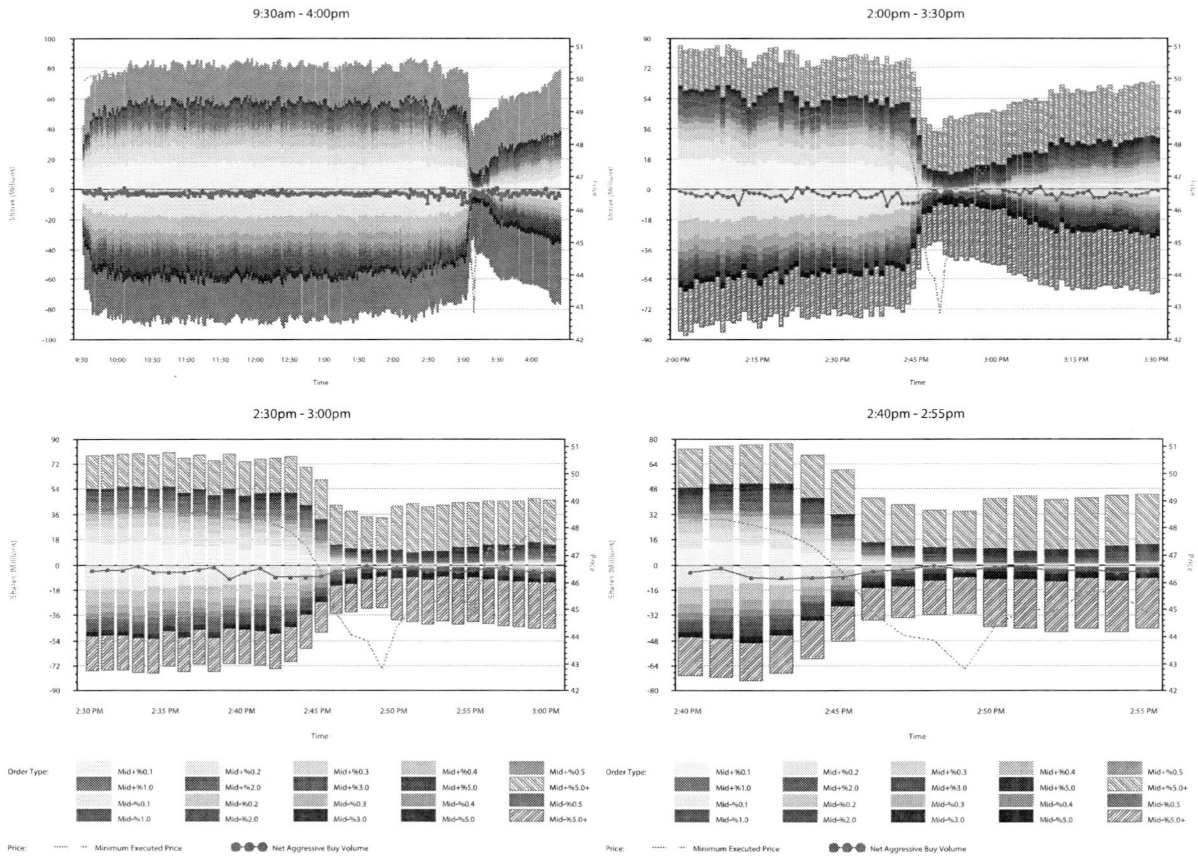


The order book depth reflects the total number of shares in unfilled limit orders, by ticker and minute. The data combines the information from NYSE Openbook, ArcaBook, NASDAQ ModelView, and BATS order book data.

Net Aggressive Buy Volume is defined as executed shares associated with aggressive buy orders minus executed shares associated with aggressive sell orders.

Aggressive buy orders are market buy orders and buy orders at or above the offer price. Aggressive sell orders are market sell orders and sell orders at or below the bid price.

Chart 3.B. ETF Top 100 Full Market Depth and Net Aggressive Buy Volume

Of the HFTs we interviewed, we did not find uniformity in response to market conditions on May 6. Although some HFTs exited the market for reasons similar to other market participants, such as the triggering of their internal risk parameters due to rapid price moves and subsequent data-integrity concerns, other HFTs continued to trade actively. Among those HFTs that continued to trade, motivations varied, but were in part based on whether they thought their algorithms would be able to operate successfully (profitably) under the extreme market conditions observed that afternoon.

We examined the aggregate minute-by-minute dollar volume of trading by the 12 largest HFTs as reflected in audit trail data reported to FINRA[38] for securities listed on NYSE, NYSE Arca (which are primarily ETFs), and Nasdaq. This audit trail data includes trades reported by Nasdaq, reported to the Nasdaq TRF, and the ADF. It does not include trades executed on any other exchanges, including the NYSE, NYSE Arca, and BATS, or reported to any other exchange's trade reporting facility. Accordingly, the data encompasses less than half of the trading volume during the most volatile period on May 6. Moreover, HFTs generally are understood to be less active in the OTC market than in exchange markets. However, we believe that the data provides a useful means to evaluate the extent to which large HFTs participated, and withdrew from participation, in the combined Nasdaq and OTC markets on May 6. This data should not be used, however, to estimate total HFT participation across all markets. .

Based on analysis of FINRA data, we found that 6 of the 12 HFTs scaled back their trading during some point after the broad indices hit their lows at about 2:45 p.m. Two HFTs largely stopped trading at about 2:47 p.m. and remained inactive through the rest of the day. Four other HFTs appear to have each significantly curtailed trading for a short period of time, ranging from as little as one minute (from 2:46 p.m. to 2:47 p.m.) to as long as 21 minutes (from 2:57 p.m. to 3:18 p.m.).

Figures 2.1, 2.2, and 2.3 show that aggregate trading activity of these 12 HFTs picked up just after 2:30 p.m. and increased significantly during the period in which the broad indices were rapidly declining from 2:43 p.m. through 2:46 p.m. Table II.1 shows that HFT trading activity during those three minutes increased by over 250% for NYSE Arca-listed securities, which we note are predominately ETFs.

These figures also show that as the broad markets recovered after 2:46 p.m., HFT activity in Nasdaq-listed stocks returned to prior (pre-2:43 p.m.) levels, activity in NYSE-listed stocks declined slightly, but activity in NYSE Arca-listed securities fell more dramatically. Since over two-thirds of the securities with broken trades were ETFs listed on NYSE Arca, we compared HFT trading activity in all securities with broken trades against those without broken trades.

**Table II.1 HFT Trading Activity Per Minute of 12 HFTs (FINRA Data Set)**

| Market | 2:43 to 2:46 p.m. ($ Mil.) | 2:00 to 3:00 p.m., ex 2:43 to 2:46 p.m. ($ Mil.) | Percent Change |
|---|---|---|---|
| NYSE | 368.8 | 168.0 | 117% |
| NYSE Arca | 1,011.7 | 285.6 | 254% |
| Nasdaq | 310.9 | 134.7 | 131% |

As shown in Figures 2.4, 2.5, and 2.6, for securities listed at NYSE, NYSE Arca, and Nasdaq, participation rates of the 12 HFTs with and without broken trades were approximately equal from about 2:00 p.m. through 2:40 p.m. More notable, average participation rates for securities listed on NYSE Arca are higher than for NYSE or Nasdaq securities. The figures also show that at about 2:50 p.m., participation rates for securities with broken trades and those without broken trades diverge for securities listed on each of the three exchanges, but most noticeably in NYSE Arca-listed securities (particularly when compared to the previously high rate of participation in NYSE Arca-listed securities).

The data suggests that for at least the period from 2:00 p.m. through 2:40 p.m. on May 6, HFTs were relatively more active in ETFs (listed primarily NYSE Arca) than corporate stocks (listed primarily on NYSE and Nasdaq). Furthermore, their reduced participation in NYSE Arca-securities with broken trades reveals that they too were part of the general withdrawal of liquidity seen in those products.

Lastly, we examined the FINRA data set for HFT buying and selling activity to see if HFTs traded more heavily on one side or the other during the rapid decline of the broad market indices. In general, the FINRA data set indicates that HFTs were primarily sellers of securities on May 6. As an example, Figure 2.7 plots buys versus sells over the course of the day for all three types of listed securities. Prior to 2:00 p.m., HFT sells accounted for about 52.4% of their total activity in these stocks. Between 2:00 p.m. and 2:45 p.m., HFTs increased selling to 53.5% of their activity, and from 2:46 p.m. to 4 p.m., HFT selling activity dropped back to 52.0% of their activity. As discussed in Section 1 above, a portion of this selling of securities could be attributable to cross-market strategies in which one or more of the HFTs were contemporaneously buying a futures product and selling ETFs or stocks. In addition, one or more HFTs may have engaged in cross-product strategies of buying ETFs and contemporaneously selling stocks (or vice versa).

To assess HFT trading during the market decline in a more comprehensive fashion, we also examined a data set obtained from the largest public quoting markets on May 6 – each of the equities exchanges and Direct Edge (EDGA and EDGX). This data included total dollar volume on those markets across all securities by 15-minute increments, and was further categorized according to liquidity-taking and liquidity-providing buys and sells. Specific participant data was also provided for each executing broker-dealer that was among the top 20 aggressive sellers on each market during the rapid price decline on May 6. From this list of aggressive sellers, we aggregated data for 17 executing broker-dealers that appear to be primarily associated with HFT firms in order to compare trading patterns of these firms with the rest of the market. The group should not be used to extrapolate the overall percentage of trading volume of HFTs because it does not include, for example, the proprietary trading desks of multi-service broker-dealers that may engage in HFT strategies. Moreover, this data set does not include trading in the OTC market (except for Direct Edge).

For the 6-business-day period of May 3 through May 10, these 17 HFT firms averaged 43.8% of total dollar volume on the public quoting markets. Their trading was divided between 51.5% liquidity-taking buys and sells (aggressive trading – generally taking bids and lifting offers) and 48.5% liquidity-providing buys and sells (passive trading – generally posting bids and offers). Figure 2.8 plots the net aggressive dollar volume (total aggressive buys minus total aggressive sells – a positive figure means that the HFT firms were aggressively buying more than they were aggressively selling, and a negative number means that the HFT firms were aggressively selling more than they were aggressively buying), along with the dollar trading volume of the 17 HFT firms as a percentage of the total dollar trading volume on the public quoting markets. In addition, Table II.2 below sets forth the volume of their trading in each of four categories (aggressive selling, aggressive buying, passive selling, and passive buying) during 15 minute periods over the course of May 6, along with the percentage of the public quoting markets in each of those categories.

As a percentage of total market dollar volume, the activity for these 17 HFT firms increased in the period from 2:00 p.m. through 2:45 p.m. to a high of 50.3%, before sharply falling to 36.6% in the period from 2:46 through 3:00 p.m. This pattern is consistent with some HFT firms reducing or pausing trading during that time. Notably, the 17 HFT firms escalated their aggressive selling more significantly (reaching a total of $9.3 billion) than any other category of trading during the rapid price decline in the period ending 2:45 p.m. As noted above, a portion of this aggressive selling could be attributable to cross-market strategies in which the firms were contemporaneously buying futures products. In general, however, it appears that the 17 HFT firms traded with the price trend on May 6 and, on both an absolute and net basis, removed significant buy liquidity from the public quoting markets during the downturn.

### *II.2.e. Internalizers*

Internalizers, composed of both OTC market makers and block positioners, handle orders of their own customers or customers of other broker-dealers. Those acting as OTC market makers appear to handle a very large percentage of marketable (immediately executable) order flow of individual investors. Internalizers tend to use their own capital to trade opposite of retail customers. Normally, they match or provide price improvement compared to the NBBO that customers would receive if their order were sent directly to an exchange. If an internalizer is unwilling to match or improve the NBBO for a particular order, it will route the order to other trading centers. In doing so, it will generally prefer trading centers that do not charge an access fee, including dark pools[39] and even other internalizers, but if the order is not filled within a short time it will be routed directly to an exchange displaying the best available price.[40]

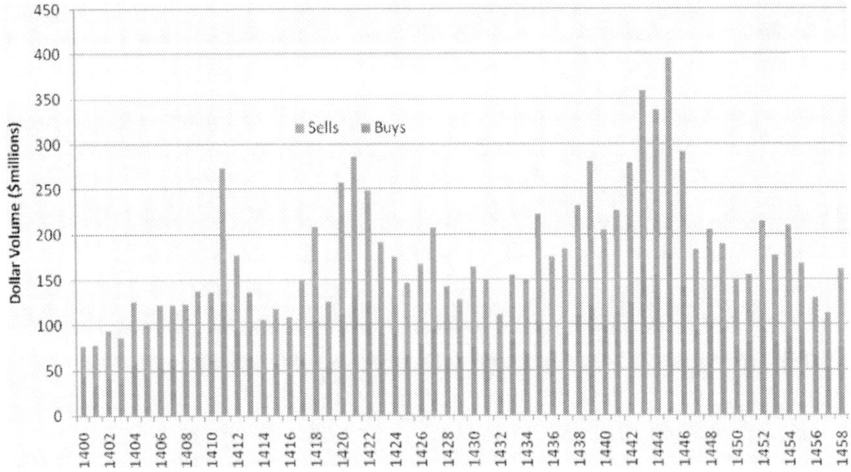


Figure 2.1. Dollar Volume of High Frequency Traders for NYSE-Listed Securities

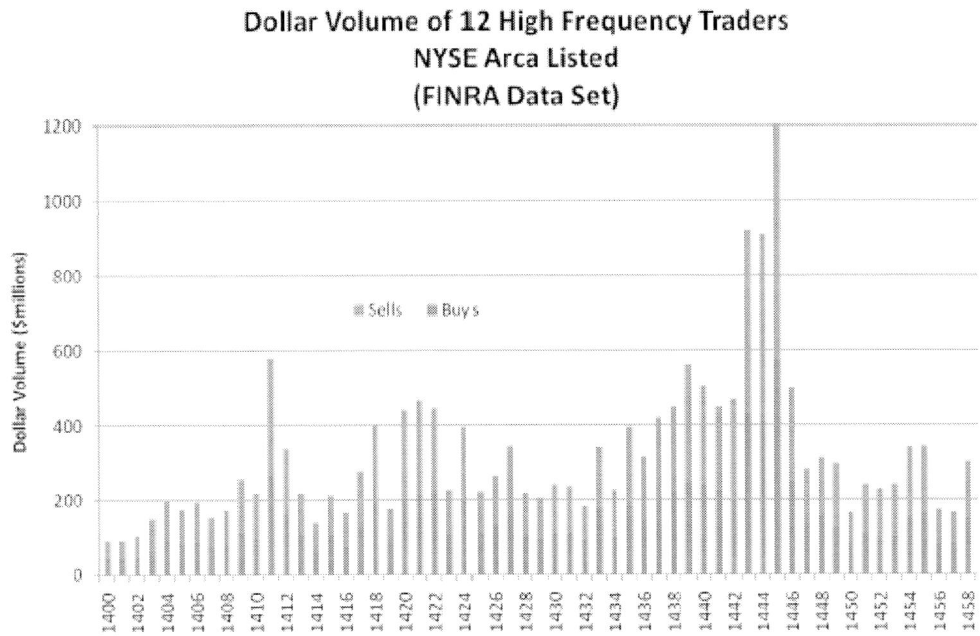


Figure 2.2. Dollar Volume of High Frequency Traders for NYSE Arca-Listed Securities

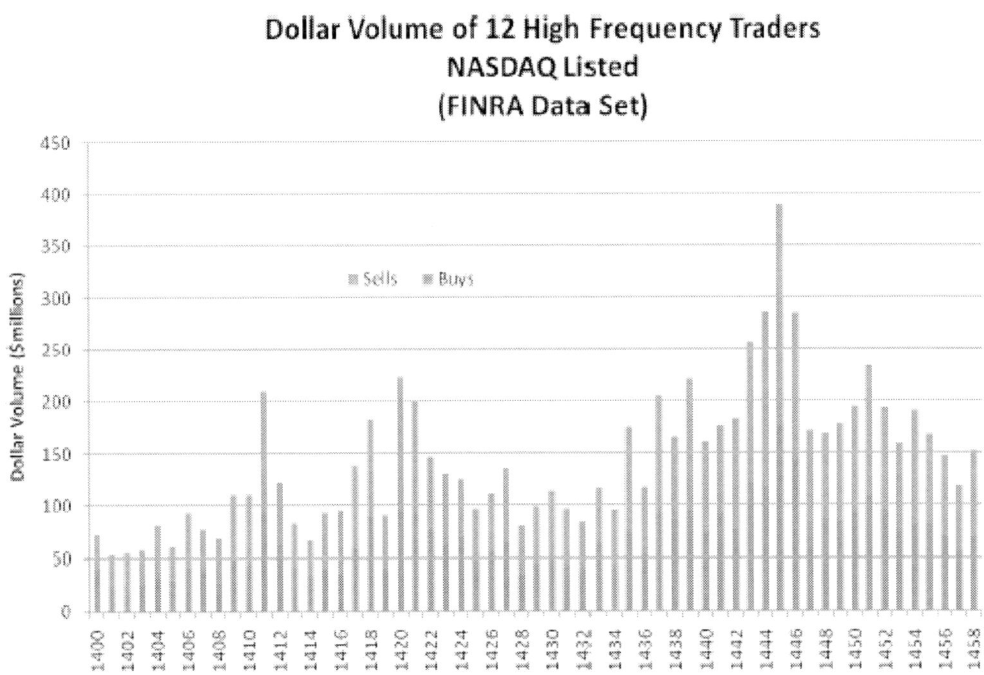


Figure 2.3. Dollar Volume of High Frequency Traders for Nasdaq-Listed Securities

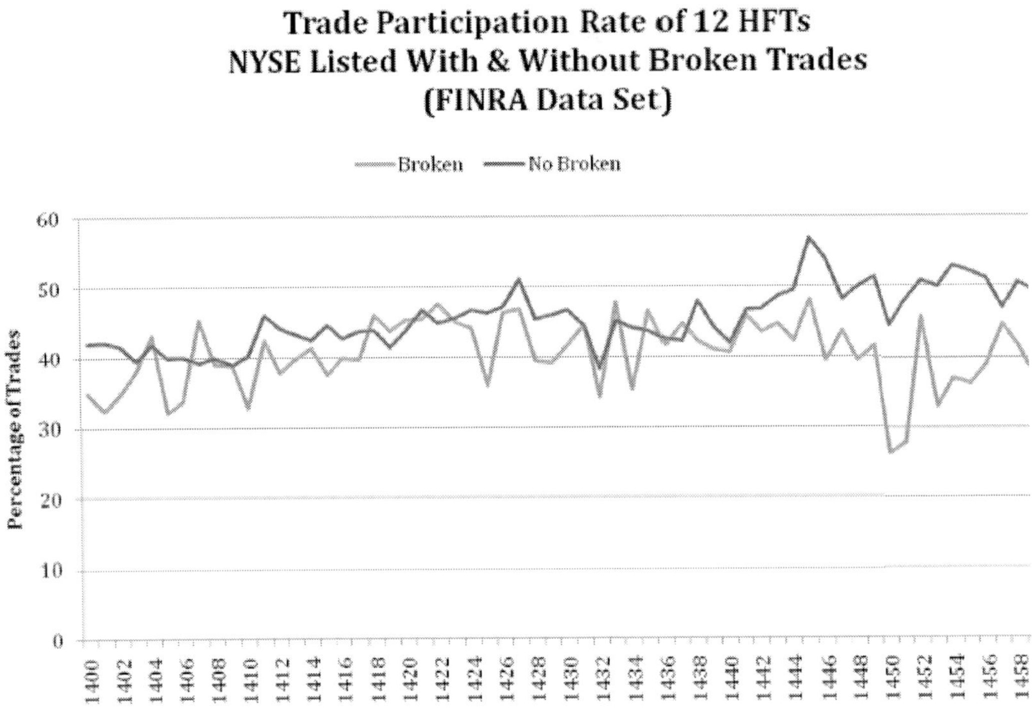


Figure 2.4. HFT Participation Rates for NYSE-Listed Securities

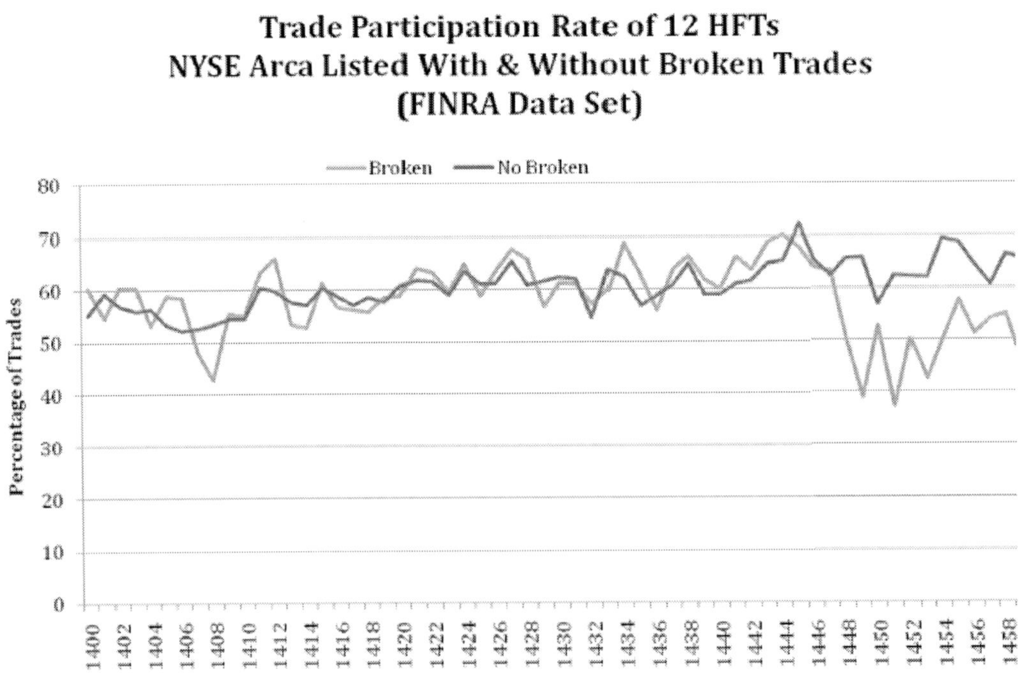


Figure 2.5. HFT Participation Rates for NYSE Arca-Listed Securities

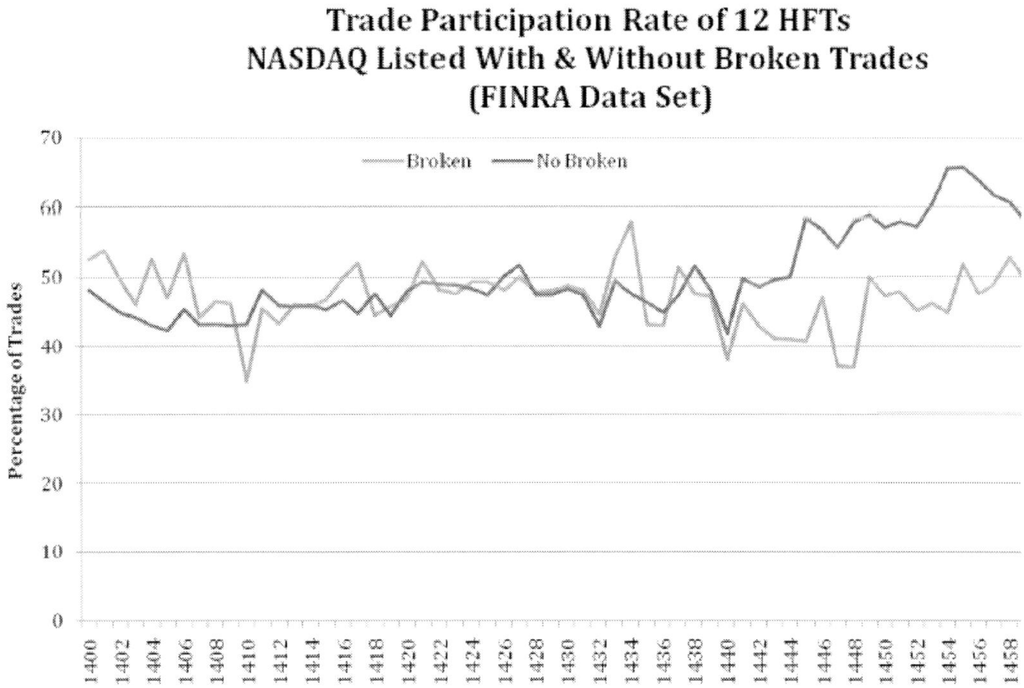


Figure 2.6. HFT Participation Rates for Nasdaq-Listed Securities

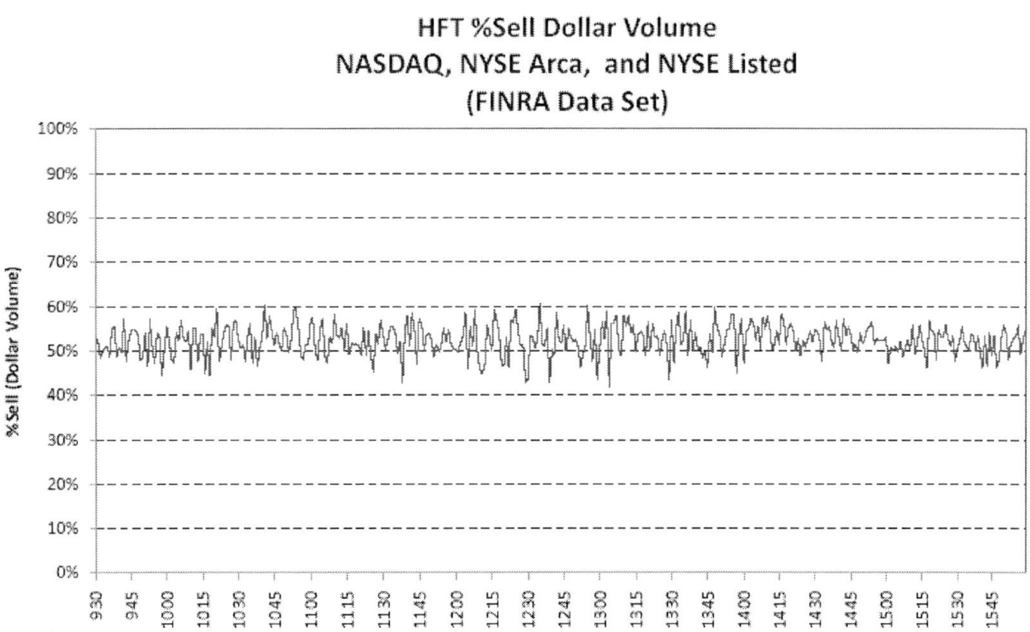


Figure 2.7. HFT Buying and Selling Ratios for Securities Listed on Nasdaq, NYSE Arca, and NYSE

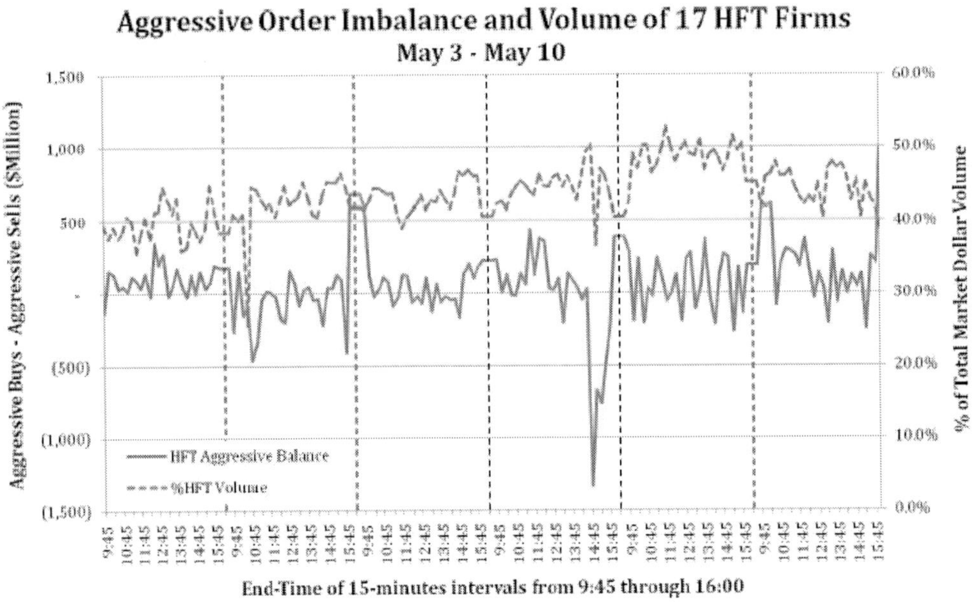


Figure 2.8. Aggressive Order Imbalance and Volume of 17 HFT Firms in Public Quoting Markets

Internalizer behavior varied on May 6. For example, block positioners – with primarily institutional customers – presented a very different view than OTC market makers. Block positioners indicated that they were indirectly affected by the extreme volatility of May 6, since many of their clients backed away from the market in order to give themselves time to digest and make sense of events. On the other hand, OTC market makers indicated that their behavior was directly affected by market events and that they paused or halted internalization for some period of time.

For instance, some OTC internalizers reduced their internalization on sell-orders but continued to internalize buy-orders, as their position limit parameters were triggered. Other internalizers halted their internalization altogether. Among the rationales for lower rates of internalization were: very heavy sell pressure due to retail market and stop-loss orders, an unwillingness to further buy against those sells, data integrity questions due to rapid prices moves (and in some cases data latencies), and intra-day changes in P&L that triggered predefined limits. In some instances, when internalizers attempted to route some of their order flow to a dark pool or other internalizer, orders were rebuffed. Partly, this was due to internal systems issues at some entities, and partly this was because each internalizer was experiencing the same events and making the same decisions to reduce or halt internalization. Data on total volume by exchange clearly shows where internalizers and (though not extensively interviewed) dark pools stopped providing liquidity for incoming orders. Internalizers instead routed orders to the exchanges, putting further pressure on the liquidity that remained in those venues.

Table II.2. Dollar Volume of 17 High Frequency Trading Firms in Public Quoting Markets on May 6

| | HFT ($ Millions) | | | | | | | % of Total Market | | | | |
|---|---|---|---|---|---|---|---|---|---|---|---|---|
| | Aggressive | | | Passive | | | Long/ Short | Aggressive | | Passive | | Total |
| | Sell | Buy | Net | Sell | Buy | Net | | Sell | Buy | Sell | Buy | |
| **9:45 AM** | 2,674 | 2,904 | 230 | 3,044 | 2,723 | 322 | -92 | 39.2% | 37.8% | 40.5% | 40.9% | 42.2% |
| **10:00 AM** | 2,449 | 2,447 | -2 | 2,278 | 2,331 | 53 | 51 | 38.8% | 41.3% | 39.5% | 37.8% | 42.6% |
| **10:15 AM** | 2,046 | 2,170 | 123 | 2,000 | 1,918 | -82 | 42 | 39.8% | 40.2% | 37.9% | 38.2% | 41.5% |
| **10:30 AM** | 2,141 | 2,128 | -13 | 1,879 | 1,828 | -51 | -64 | 41.0% | 44.1% | 40.0% | 36.0% | 43.4% |
| **10:45 AM** | 2,085 | 2,063 | -22 | 1,789 | 1,790 | 1 | -21 | 41.9% | 45.1% | 40.2% | 36.9% | 44.3% |
| **11:00 AM** | 2,654 | 2,785 | 131 | 2,432 | 2,424 | -9 | 122 | 40.4% | 47.0% | 42.1% | 37.7% | 45.3% |
| **11:15 AM** | 2,667 | 2,728 | 61 | 2,443 | 2,396 | -47 | 15 | 39.4% | 47.1% | 43.2% | 36.2% | 44.8% |
| **11:30 AM** | 2,224 | 2,659 | 435 | 2,669 | 2,214 | -454 | -19 | 38.9% | 40.8% | 41.8% | 39.6% | 43.9% |
| **11:45 AM** | 1,683 | 1,805 | 122 | 1,631 | 1,612 | -19 | 103 | 38.0% | 44.4% | 41.2% | 37.3% | 43.3% |
| **12:00 PM** | 2,316 | 2,695 | 379 | 2,549 | 2,274 | -275 | 104 | 40.3% | 45.5% | 44.1% | 40.6% | 46.2% |
| **12:15 PM** | 1,790 | 2,145 | 355 | 2,010 | 1,792 | -218 | 137 | 41.2% | 41.7% | 40.0% | 42.4% | 44.6% |
| **12:30 PM** | 1,390 | 1,422 | 32 | 1,276 | 1,230 | -46 | -14 | 41.0% | 45.4% | 42.0% | 37.3% | 44.5% |
| **12:45 PM** | 1,324 | 1,339 | 15 | 1,115 | 1,136 | 20 | 35 | 43.2% | 47.4% | 40.8% | 38.2% | 45.8% |
| **1:00 PM** | 1,624 | 1,720 | 96 | 1,560 | 1,437 | -123 | -27 | 42.8% | 47.1% | 44.0% | 38.9% | 45.2% |
| **1:15 PM** | 1,642 | 1,434 | -208 | 1,233 | 1,318 | 85 | -123 | 42.9% | 45.8% | 40.6% | 35.5% | 44.4% |
| **1:30 PM** | 2,294 | 2,425 | 131 | 2,269 | 2,139 | -130 | 1 | 39.9% | 46.6% | 44.8% | 38.1% | 45.0% |
| **1:45 PM** | 1,834 | 1,919 | 85 | 1,811 | 1,688 | -123 | -38 | 39.0% | 45.5% | 44.2% | 36.8% | 44.6% |
| **2:00 PM** | 1,834 | 1,871 | 37 | 1,879 | 1,651 | -228 | -191 | 38.2% | 41.8% | 43.3% | 35.4% | 42.6% |
| **2:15 PM** | 4,002 | 3,955 | -47 | 3,739 | 3,517 | -221 | -268 | 41.2% | 47.6% | 46.4% | 37.1% | 45.0% |
| **2:30 PM** | 5,786 | 5,814 | 28 | 5,571 | 5,294 | -277 | -249 | 44.6% | 49.0% | 48.2% | 41.8% | 49.3% |
| **2:45 PM** | 9,302 | 7,959 | -1,343 | 7,528 | 7,714 | 185 | -1,158 | 47.1% | 51.8% | 50.2% | 39.9% | 50.3% |
| **3:00 PM** | 5,748 | 5,071 | -677 | 5,575 | 5,480 | -95 | -772 | 34.0% | 32.9% | 37.8% | 33.5% | 36.6% |

**Table II.2. (Continued)**

| | HFT ($ Millions) | | | | | | | % of Total Market | | | | |
|---|---|---|---|---|---|---|---|---|---|---|---|---|
| | Aggressive | | | Passive | | | Long/ Short | Aggressive | | Passive | | Total |
| | Sell | Buy | Net | Sell | Buy | Net | | Sell | Buy | Sell | Buy | |
| **3:15 PM** | 5,820 | 5,054 | -765 | 5,515 | 5,428 | -86 | -852 | 46.3% | 42.2% | 47.3% | 44.3% | 47.0% |
| **3:30 PM** | 5,220 | 4,732 | -488 | 4,823 | 4,984 | 160 | -328 | 43.2% | 45.0% | 47.0% | 42.2% | 46.0% |
| **3:45 PM** | 4,763 | 4,547 | -216 | 4,677 | 4,324 | -353 | -568 | 42.6% | 41.0% | 43.4% | 39.8% | 43.7% |
| **4:00 PM** | 6,173 | 6,561 | 388 | 7,658 | 7,194 | -465 | -76 | 33.3% | 37.8% | 45.7% | 40.1% | 40.6% |

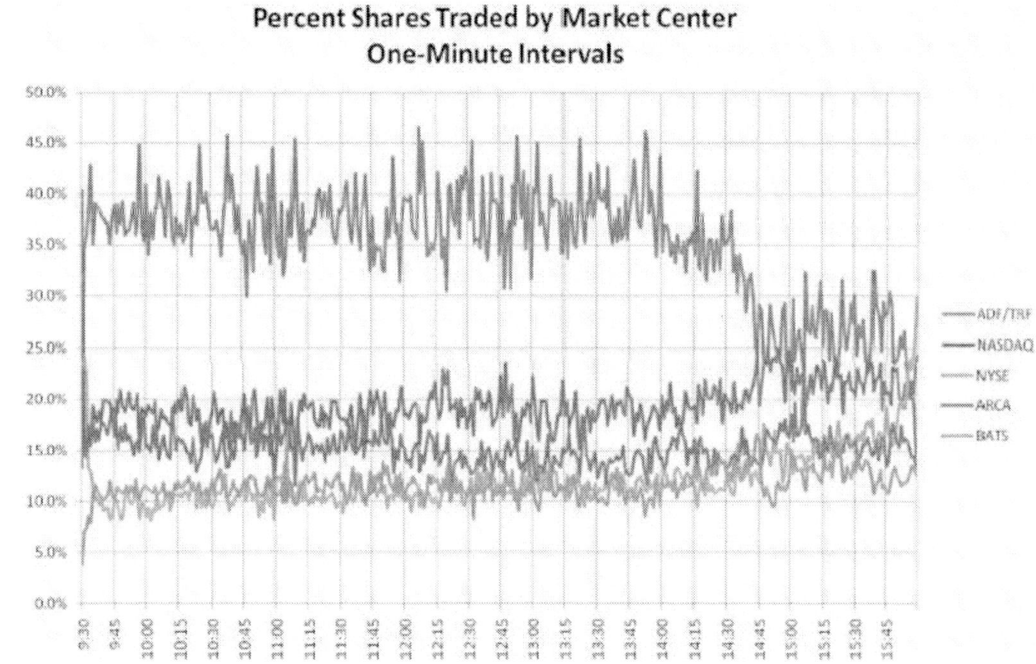


Figure 2.9. Volume across each large market venue

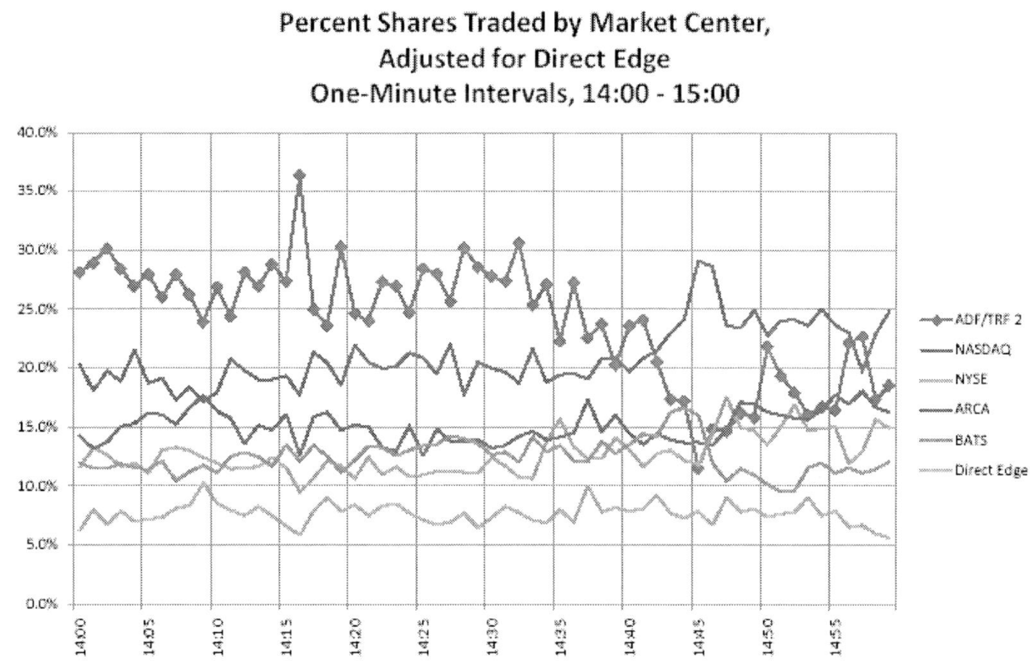


Figure 2.10. Volume across each large market venue adjusted for Direct Edge

Trading volume across all markets reflects this withdrawal of liquidity. OTC trades are reported to a FINRA facility: the ADF or a TRF. The primary sources of ADF/TRF trades are OTC market makers and other internalizers, dark pools (alterative trading systems) that do not display quotations in the consolidated quotation data), and ECNs. On May 6, the ECNs with the most volume were EDGA and EDGX, operated by Direct Edge, and now operated as national securities exchanges. As shown in Figures 2.9 and 2.10, ADF/TRF trades as a percentage of overall trading volume declined rapidly after the price decline began at approximately 2:30 p.m. The first chart sets forth the total volume of ADF/TRF trades. The second chart focuses on the period from 2:00 p.m. to 2:30 p.m., and removes the volume of ADF/TRF trades attributable to EDGA and EDGX.[41]

As can be seen in Figure 2.10, ADF/TRF volume percentages (excluding EDGA and EDGX) declined from 25-30% prior to the market disruption on May 6 to approximately 11% at approximately 2:45 p.m. This is consistent with a general reduction of internalization by OTC market makers and an increase in the number of transactions that were executed in the public markets as riskless principal. As discussed at the end of this section, orders that were part of this surge account for about half of the trades that were executed at the most depressed and extreme prices.

### *II.2.f. Options Market Makers*

Liquidity on options exchanges is derived from orders to buy or sell particular options series and quotations submitted by members of an exchange that are registered as options market makers ("OMMs"). Generally, however, the market for listed options depends upon the liquidity supplied by professional liquidity providers, such as market makers, to a greater extent than in the market for NMS stocks. This is due in part to the greater dispersion of trading interest across the thousands of series of listed options.[42]

The options exchanges allow a member, on a voluntary basis, to register as an OMM. All of the options exchanges, except BATS and NOM, require that at least one market maker be registered in a class in order for trading to occur in that class. As a practical matter, because equity options are multiply-traded across the options exchanges, a particular options class generally would not trade without a market maker on at least one exchange. Pursuant to the options exchanges' rules, the transactions of an OMM in its market making capacity generally must constitute a course of dealings reasonably calculated to contribute to the maintenance of a fair and orderly market, including maintaining two-sided quotations.[43]

We spoke with several of the options exchanges and OMMs regarding how the options markets and its participants functioned on May 6. In general, the options markets and participants reported that trading in options did not experience similar disruptions as in the underlying securities markets. However, because OMMs' behavior is heavily influenced by underlying market conditions, some OMMs widened their quotes or exited the options market on May 6.

OMMs reported that they make markets in options by calculating the value of the underlying security or basket of securities and then quoting slightly above and below this price, profiting from the bid-ask spread. Due to the derivative nature of options, OMMs adjust their quotes in response to price changes in the underlying security, typically via proprietary "auto-quote" systems that generate a theoretical price.

On May 6, while OMMs reported that they generally did not have problems receiving data from proprietary data feeds from the individual stock exchanges, OMMs considered the incoming data unreliable due to extreme volatility in underlying securities. Thus, in order to mitigate risk, OMMs began to widen their quotes, decreased their quotation size or temporarily withdrew from the market consistent with their quoting obligations. Some

OMMs' systems automatically took their quotes $5 wide once they determined that the information they were receiving from the underlying exchanges was unreliable, while some other OMM's systems were programmed to go wide in a more graduated fashion upon certain triggers, while others did not widen to the $5 maximum.[44]

OMMs that widen their quotes do so with the expectation that their quotes will not be executed against. However, on May 6, at least one OMM reported that despite going wide, its quotations continued to be executed against.

Generally, there were no significant liquidity shortages reported in the options markets and very few trades were broken or adjusted. In addition, several relatively insignificant systems issues were noted. For instance, NYSE Arca experienced a system outage related to outbound order routing which resulted in the other options exchanges declaring self-help against that exchange. Some OMMs reported having problems with their internal quoting systems that required them to pull out of the market temporarily; however, they described these problems as existing "bugs" in their systems that came to light on May 6, but were not caused by the market activities that day. These OMMs reported that they were able to fix their systems and re-enter the market in a timely manner.

## II.3. Analysis of Broken Trades

### *II.3.a. Stub Quotes*

As part of our interview process, we asked market participants about their use and interaction with stub quotes. Pursuant to exchange rules, registered market makers are required to engage in a course of dealing for their own account to assist in the maintenance, insofar as reasonably practicable, of fair and orderly markets. On equities markets, these exchange rules generally require a market maker to maintain a continuous two-sided quotation in the security or securities for which the member is registered as a market maker. However, such rules do not generally dictate the prices at which a market maker must quote.[45] When a market maker's liquidity has been exhausted, or if it is unwilling to provide liquidity, it may on some markets submit what is called a stub quote – an offer to buy or sell a given stock at a price so far away from the prevailing market that it is not intended to be executed, such as an order to buy at a penny or less or sell at $100,000 – to comply with its obligation to maintain a continuous two-sided quotation.[46]

Some equities exchanges provide for the automatic generation of stub quotes, and a subset require their market makers to use such a mechanism to ensure compliance with continuous two-sided quoting rules. Some allow for flexibility in specifying how auto-generated quotes cascade upwards or downwards as market prices move, though floors of 1 penny or 1/100$^{th}$ of a penny on the bid-side, and a ceiling of $99,999.99 on the ask-side are common. One reason that auto-generated quotes are implemented is to ensure market makers can "technically" meet their continuous two-sided quoting obligations even if they have temporarily disconnected from the exchange. A cancelled ("broken") trade priced at $0.01 may have been the result of an exchange-generated stub quote or an active market maker quoting at that same level. However, quotes of 15 cents or 22 cents for example, are most likely not exchange-generated, but instead represent stub-like quotes posted by a market maker. A market maker actively quoting at the "higher" price of 15 cents will have many more broken trades than a market maker who disconnected from trading and relied on exchange-generated stub quotes of one penny.

Some equities market makers told us that in the normal course of business they do not generally use stub quotes, but acknowledged that their systems, or their exchanges' systems used on their behalf, would have quoted at stub levels after their active quotes were exhausted in any particular security, or in all securities if they completely halted trading. In turn, some market participants responsible for routing orders reported that because they believed they had a firm obligation to fulfill customer market orders at the NBBO, they sent orders to be filled even though prices were at stub quote levels. Others reported that they assumed executions at stub quote prices would likely be broken, and sent orders seeking to hit stub quotes to prevent the piling up of orders in their internal systems. Additionally, some firms reported that their algorithmic trading systems attempted to execute against declining prices all the way down to stub quotes – either because such trading was consistent with the parameters for that system, or because the system did not necessarily recognize that it was hitting stub quotes (just that it was hitting the NBBO). These reported practices are consistent with the findings discussed below with respect to the types of orders involved in the broken trades that day.

### *II.3.b. Broken Trades*

As discussed in the Preliminary Report, the vast majority of the almost 2 billion shares traded on May 6 between 2:40 p.m. and 3:00 p.m. were at prices within 10% of their 2:40 p.m. value.[47] For most of the trades executed at a loss on May 6, their declines were consistent with the general declines in the broad market indices. We note that many of the securities that suffered rapid price moves found their prices reverting to their former levels nearly as quickly. This suggests that immediately-available liquidity was not able to fully absorb the considerable demand to sell (and in some cases buy) shares, and that prices recovered as soon as this pressure was reduced and the imbalance alleviated (*see* S&P 500 order book charts 1.A and 1.B at the beginning of this section).

Above, we discussed the behavior of market participants and the reasons for the general withdrawal of liquidity. As shown, spreads in securities rapidly widened as market makers and other providers of liquidity pulled back. Some market makers completely stopped quoting for all securities and, if required, relied on exchange-generated bids of one penny or less to fulfill their market making obligations – "stub quotes," as previously described. In some cases, stub quotes were continuously refreshed pursuant to functionality offered by the host exchange, whereas in other cases they were only refreshed up to a certain size after which point automatic quoting stopped. Other equities market makers generated their own unrealistically-low stub-like bids for securities that were at or near the same level as exchange-generated stub quotes. In all cases, the market maker providing the stub quote generally did so with the assumption that its quotes would not be hit by incoming orders.

Executions against stub quotes represented a significant proportion of broken trades on May 6. Though the type of volatility experienced that day is very unusual, even more extraordinary was the fact that over 20,000 trades representing 5.5 million shares were executed at prices more than 60% away from their 2:40 p.m. value. These trades were subsequently broken by the exchanges and FINRA under their clearly erroneous rules because they were executed at clearly unrealistic prices under severe market conditions.[48] Almost two-thirds of shares in cancelled trades were executed at prices of less than $1.00, and about 5% were executed at prices above $100.

On May 6, both market orders and limit orders traded against stub quotes. A market order submitted to an exchange immediately seeks the best available liquidity, regardless of price. If the only liquidity available is a stub quote, the market order will execute against that price. Similarly, if a limit order is submitted with a limit price that represents the then-current NBBO and the NBBO at that time is a stub quote due to a lack of other available liquidity, it too would receive a stub quote execution. And since stub quotes are often generated in an automated fashion, as soon as one is lifted another is quickly posted and available to receive the next market or limit order. Analysis of the order routing by internalizers, discussed below, reflects such activity.

As noted previously, many internalizers of retail order flow stopped executing as principal for their customers that afternoon, and instead sent orders to the exchanges, putting further pressure on the liquidity that remained in those venues. Many trades that originated from retail customers as stop-loss orders or market orders were converted to limit orders by internalizers prior to routing to the exchanges for execution. If that limit order could not be filled because the market continued to fall, then the internalizer set a new lower limit price and resubmitted the order, following the price down and eventually reaching unrealistically-low bids. Since internalizers were trading as riskless principal, many of these orders were marked as short even though the ultimate retail seller was not necessarily short.[49] This partly helps explain the data in Table 7 of the Preliminary Report in which we had found that 70-90% of all trades executed at less than five cents were marked short.

Detailed analysis of trade and order data revealed that one large internalizer (as a seller) and one large market maker (as a buyer) were party to over 50% of the share volume of broken trades, and for more than half of this volume they were counterparties to each other (i.e., 25% of the broken trade share volume was between this particular seller and buyer). Furthermore, in total, data show that internalizers were the sellers for almost half of all broken trade share volume. Given that internalizers generally process and route retail trading interest, this suggests that at least half of all broken trade share volume was due to retail customer sell orders.

The data also provides important information regarding the extent to which declarations of self-help against NYSE Arca by Nasdaq and BATS may have exacerbated the issues on May 6. For example, the large market maker mentioned above specialized in ETFs and was registered as a market maker in ETFs on NYSE Arca. The internalizer had directly routed approximately 2,400 sell orders to NYSE Arca for about 1.7 million shares that resulted in broken trades. This same internalizer had also routed approximately 2,900 sell orders for a total of about 400,000 shares to BATS and Nasdaq that resulted in broken trades. If this example is typical of the price patterns at that time, and given that the internalizer would have routed to the exchange with the best available price, it seems that the general withdrawal of liquidity that led to broken trades was at least as prevalent on NYSE Arca as it was on Nasdaq and BATS. This suggests that if Nasdaq or BATS had re-routed orders to NYSE Arca, then these orders would have also been executed at unrealistically-low prices on NYSE Arca and subsequently broken. From this example it does not seem that self-help led to orders "routing around" liquidity at NYSE Arca, but rather that liquidity had been withdrawn across all exchanges, including NYSE Arca.[50]

The fact that a single market maker on NYSE Arca represented so many broken trades suggests that this market maker was one of the last providers of liquidity for those securities in that market. Other market makers had either stopped quoting or were quoting at even lower prices, demonstrating the extent to which liquidity had virtually evaporated.

An analysis of order types reveals that almost 90% of all broken trades were sold with a limit price. Given the assumption that a large number of sell orders were due to retail customers, we would have expected a higher percentage of market orders. However, as previously discussed, internalizers often convert market orders to other order types (such as marketable limit orders at the current NBBO) when they route customer orders to the exchanges for execution. On the buy-side we find that market orders were used in less than 1% of all broken trades.

In summary, our analysis of trades broken on May 6 reveals they were concentrated primarily among a few market participants. A significant number of those trades were driven by sell orders from retail customers sent to internalizers for immediate execution at then-current market prices. Internalizers, in turn, routed these orders to the public exchanges for execution at the NBBO. However, for those securities in which market makers had withdrawn their liquidity, there was insufficient buy interest, and many trades were executed at very low (and sometimes very high) prices, including stub quotes.

# III. Potential Impact of Additional Factors

In this section we explore the potential impacts of three additional factors on the events of May 6: the use of LRPs by the NYSE, in which trading is effectively banded on the NYSE in NYSE-listed stocks exhibiting rapid price moves; declarations of self-help by Nasdaq against NYSE Arca under which Nasdaq temporarily stopped routing orders to NYSE Arca; and delays in NYSE quote and trade data disseminated over the CQS and CTS data feeds.

## III.1. NYSE Liquidity Replenishment Points

NYSE utilizes a hybrid floor/electronic trading model, unlike most other markets today which are fully electronic. Within this model NYSE has implemented price-bands known as "liquidity replenishment points." LRPs are intended to act as a "speed bump" and to dampen volatility in a given stock by temporarily converting from an automated market to a manual auction market when a price movement of sufficient size is reached. In such a case, trading on NYSE in that stock will "go slow" and automatic executions will cease for a time period ranging from a fraction of a second to a minute or two to allow the Designated Market Maker ("DMM") to solicit and/or contribute additional liquidity before returning to an automated market. LRP limits vary according to each security's share price and average daily volume within specified ranges, generally falling between 1% and 5% of share price.[51] It is worth noting that hitting a LRP does *not* cause trading in the security to completely halt or pause, but only to go slow on the opposite side of the market that hit the LRP (or both sides if the quote has locked or crossed the market), thereby preventing the automatic execution of trades at prices beyond the LRP limit.

A LRP may be triggered even when there is additional interest on NYSE's order book beyond the LRP price point. In these cases NYSE will suspend automated quotations in the security, and will identify its quote on the consolidated tape with a "non-firm" indicator. This is referred to as a "slow market" or "going slow" in the security. Other markets are permitted to bypass NYSE's quote when it is identified as "non-firm."

Most LRPs either resolve themselves within a second, when additional buy or sell interest brings prices back within the LRP limits, or are resolved just as quickly by a DMM's algorithm that automatically sets a new resumption price according to buy and sell interest. Once the LRP is resolved the quotes are no longer labeled as "slow" and automated executions resume. In some cases a DMM's algorithm will be used to determine the resumption price at which automated quoting and executions can continue. In other cases, when additional liquidity is needed beyond what the DMM's algorithm is programmed to supply, the resumption price is determined manually by the DMM in a process that can take from a few seconds to a minute or more.

Upon resumption of automatic executions, a new LRP is calculated for the security. On days of extraordinary market volatility, stocks with significant and/or continual declines may cause NYSE trading to remain in the "slow" mode for extended periods or to intermittently return to automated execution status before quickly again hitting an LRP and thereby "going slow" again. However, even in cases of prolonged or recurring LRPs in a particular security, customer interest in the security is not "trapped" by the LRP(s) or the slow market state. Customers may cancel their interest at any time prior to execution, regardless of the state of the market.

As discussed in the Preliminary Report,[52] many securities triggered LRPs multiple times on the afternoon of May 6, and though 75% of all events were resolved in less than 1 second, others lasted many seconds, or were in an extended period of multiple sub-second LRPs. Between 2:30 p.m. and 3:00 p.m., more than 1000 securities triggered LRP events lasting more than 1 second, compared to a "normal" day average of only 20-30 such events.[53]

According to the market participants we interviewed, their systems are programmed to automatically adjust for slow quotes on NYSE and will route orders to other exchanges as needed. And, as mentioned, participants have the option of automatically cancelling existing orders on NYSE if so desired. Participants did not report they had difficulty routing or felt their orders were "trapped" as a result of LRP events.

However, a number of market participants told us that the fact so many LRPs were being triggered further underscored the severity of market conditions as they were unfolding, and that this additional "evidence" played into their decisions to reduce liquidity, pause trading, or withdraw from the markets.

Though market participants told us they were able to route their orders as needed, it is nevertheless possible that residual liquidity could have been trapped on NYSE during the LRP events, and that this liquidity could have absorbed some of the sell pressure of securities with the most severe price dislocations. In this regard, we note that over 80% of the 326 securities having broken trades were not listed on NYSE and therefore not subject to the LRP events.[54] For those listed on NYSE we found 42 of the 56 stocks for which broken trades occurred on other exchanges were, in aggregate, subject to 180 LRPs lasting 10 seconds or longer.[55]

With this sample, we addressed two questions: first, is there evidence that a substantial percentage of trades executed elsewhere might have been otherwise executed against liquidity that appeared on NYSE during the LRP; and second, during the LRP and when other exchanges were permitted to route around the NYSE, is there evidence of liquidity flowing into NYSE. That is, does NYSE appear to be drawing away and "trapping" additional liquidity from other exchanges during the LRP?

As an indicator of "trapped" liquidity, we compared the estimated "available" bid depth during the LRP for each stock to the number of executions on other exchanges.[56] Based on our sample, it does not appear that a substantial number of executions might have benefited from access to NYSE liquidity. For over half of the LRPs, there was no possibility of "trapped" liquidity because either no executions were reported on other exchanges during the LRP event (36 cases) or available bid depth at NYSE itself was zero (61 cases).

For 83 LRPs in 29 stocks, executions occurred on other exchanges at the same time there was available liquidity on NYSE. Figure 3.1 presents each of these events on a grid comparing the number of shares executed by other exchanges on the vertical axis (from 100 to 1 million shares) with the number of shares of available liquidity on NYSE during the LRP on the horizontal axis (from 100 to 100,000 shares). The dotted red line indicates the threshold above which there were significantly more shares executed at other exchanges than there was liquidity at NYSE, and below which there was more liquidity available on NYSE than there were shares executed at other exchanges. It is important to note that the data includes all of the shares executed on other exchanges, and is not limited to executions that resulted in broken trades. In this respect our impact estimate is quite conservative, and even so, we see that there were only 19 LRP events affecting 12 stocks in which available liquidity on NYSE within 500 basis points of the NBBO may have been able to absorb the sell pressure.

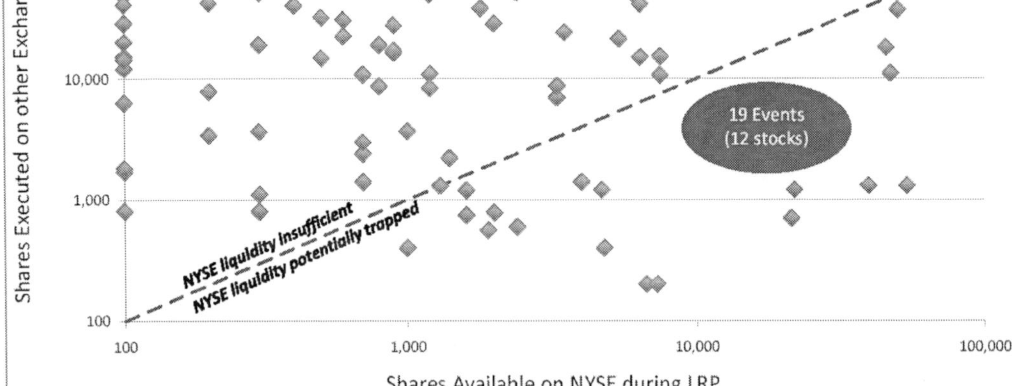


Figure 3.1. Shares available on NYSE (within 500 basis points of the NBBO) compared to shares executed on other exchanges during LRPs lasting 10 seconds or longer

The data also do not suggest that significant liquidity was being attracted to the NYSE during the LRP. We measured the total number of bid shares gained (lost) from the second prior to the LRP to the second after the conclusion of the LRP. Only one third of the LRPs (59 cases) were associated with any increase in bid depth within 500 basis points of the NBBO during the LRP. For the entire sample, the average increase in available liquidity was only 133 shares. Further exploration of the data did not evidence a pattern that suggests an increase in bid depth is associated with the length of the LRP, which would be expected if unexecutable bids were being drawn into NYSE during the LRP.

Taken as a whole:

- the actions of market participants, including their ability to route around "slow" quotes and cancel orders if desired;
- the fact that the majority of securities with broken trades were not subject to LRPs; and
- that for those stocks subject to lengthy LRPs, only 12 may have had sufficient liquidity on NYSE to absorb some of the sell pressure that was executed on other exchanges;

we conclude that NYSE LRPs did not cause or create the broad-based liquidity crisis on May 6.

Nonetheless, as stated above, market participants reported that the increasing number of LRPs being triggered on NYSE underscored the severity of market conditions as they were unfolding, and that this additional "evidence" played into their decisions to reduce liquidity, pause trading, or withdraw from the markets.

## III.2. Declarations of Self-Help Against NYSE Arca

We have examined whether the declarations of "self-help" against NYSE Arca by Nasdaq at 2:36:59 p.m. and by Nasdaq OMX BX at 2:38:40 p.m. ("Self-Help Declarations") affected the availability of liquidity on May 6 and thereby contributed to imbalances between liquidity supply and demand.[57] As discussed below, self-help is an exception to Rule 611 of Regulation NMS that permits (but does not require) a trading center to bypass the quotations of an exchange that is experiencing a systems problem. The exception is intended to assure that market participants are not required by rule to route orders to execute against quotations that are not immediately accessible. By declaring self-help against NYSE Arca, Nasdaq and Nasdaq OMX BX executed trades, and Nasdaq routed orders,[58] without regard to the protected quotations displayed by NYSE Arca. The discussion below first gives an overview of Rule 611 and the self-help exception and then evaluates the effect of the Self-Help Declarations on May 6.

### *III.2.a. Overview of Rule 611 and the Self-Help Exception*

In general, Rule 611(a) requires trading centers[59] to establish, maintain, and enforce written policies and procedures reasonably designed to prevent "trade-throughs"[60] – the execution of trades at prices inferior to "protected quotations."[61] To be protected, a quotation must, among other things, be immediately and automatically accessible and be an exchange's best (highest) bid or best (lowest) offer (also referred to as "top-of-book" quotations). An exchange's additional quotations at prices above or below its best-priced quotations ("depth-of-book" quotations) are not protected quotations.[62] As a result, market participants are entitled to make their own determination, based on best execution and other factors, of whether to route orders to execute against an exchange's depth-of-book quotations.

Rule 611(b) provides a number of exceptions from the general requirement to prevent trade-throughs of protected quotations, all of which must be implemented through policies and procedures that are reasonably designed to comply with the terms of the exception. One of the exceptions is commonly referred to as "self-help." Specifically, Rule 611(b)(1) provides an exception for a trade-through that "was effected when the trading center displaying the protected quotation that was traded through was experiencing a failure, material delay, or malfunction of its systems or equipment." The Regulation NMS Adopting Release interpreted this rule language to mean that "trading centers should be entitled to bypass another trading center's quotations if it repeatedly fails to respond within one second to incoming orders attempting to access its protected quotations," and noted that, as a result, "trading centers will have the necessary flexibility to respond to problems at another trading center as they occur throughout the trading day."[63] The Regulation NMS Adopting Release also discussed the policies and procedures that are reasonably required to comply with the self-help exception. Among other things, it indicated that the declarer of self-help must adopt objective parameters for use of the exception, must immediately notify the exchange that is the subject of the self-help declaration, and must assess whether the cause of a problem lies with its own systems rather than such exchange's systems. [64]

Two additional exceptions from Rule 611 are relevant to an evaluation of the effect of the Self-Help Declarations on May 6. Both exceptions are based on the use of intermarket sweep orders ("ISOs"). As defined in Rule 600(b)(30) of Regulation NMS, all ISOs must, among other things, specify a limit price indicating that additional ISOs, as necessary, have been routed to execute against all protected quotations with better prices than such limit price. As a result, all ISOs must be limit orders, and the router of the ISO must assume responsibility for any protected quotation with better prices than the limit price. Rule 611(c), in turn, requires that the trading center or broker-dealer responsible for the routing of an ISO take reasonable steps to assure that the ISO meets the requirements of Rule 611(b)(30). All ISOs must have a trading center or broker-dealer that is responsible for their routing.

Rule 611(b) provides two types of ISO exceptions. One type (set forth in Rule 611(b)(6)) allows a trading center to execute an order at a price if it simultaneously routes ISOs to execute against the full displayed size of any protected quotations with better prices than the execution price. Another type of ISO exception (set forth in Rule 611(b)(5)) allows order routers to control the execution of their limit orders by routing ISOs themselves and directly assuming responsibility for preventing trade-throughs. When a trading center receives an incoming order marked ISO, Rule 611(b)(5) provides an exception that allows the trading center to execute the ISO immediately without regard to better-priced protected quotation at other trading centers.

When an ISO exception is used in conjunction with the self-help exception, the trading center or broker-dealer responsible for routing an ISO is entitled to use the self-help exception to bypass the protected quotations of an exchange that is experiencing systems problems.

Such trading center or broker-dealer must implement the self-help exception through the reasonable policies and procedures that were noted above.

In assessing the effect of the self-help exception on May 6 or any other day, it is important to recognize what use of the exception does not do. In particular, the declaration of self-help by a trading center or broker-dealer against an exchange does not automatically remove such exchange's quotations from the montage of protected quotations, nor does the declaration of self-help entitle any other market participant (beyond the declarer of self-help) to bypass such exchange's quotations when it executes trades itself or routes ISOs to other venues. In this regard, the limited scope of the self-help exception reflects the variable nature of systems problems that can affect the routing and execution of orders. In some instances, an exchange may be experiencing problems that affect all routers, but, in other instances, an exchange's problems may affect only a single order router or group of order routers (such as with an isolated connectivity problem). Use of the self-help exception is limited to those trading centers and broker-dealers that have a reasonable basis to believe that the orders they route to an exchange will be affected by that exchange's systems problem.

### *III.2.b. Evaluation of Self-Help Declarations on May 6*

Nasdaq declared self-help against NYSE Arca at 2:35:59 p.m., and Nasdaq OMX BX declared self-help against NYSE Arca at 2:38:40 p.m. The Nasdaq declaration was revoked at 3:01:09 p.m., and the Nasdaq OMX BX exception was revoked at 3:01:55 p.m. Data indicate that for a subset of securities NYSE Arca repeatedly did not respond to orders from these exchanges within one second. Consistent with Rule 611, Nasdaq and Nasdaq OMX BX notified NYSE Arca directly concerning their use of the self-help exception. They also publicly disclosed their Self-Help Declarations by, among other things, publishing them on their Internet website. As a result, many market participants were aware of the Self-Help Declarations soon after they were made.

As discussed above, the Self-Help Declarations entitled only Nasdaq and Nasdaq OMX BX to execute trades and route ISOs without regard to NYSE Arca quotations.[65] Our discussions with market participants indicate that many knew of the Self-Help Declarations, but, with one exception noted below, all market participants stated that they continued routing orders to NYSE Arca despite the Self-Help Declarations. In addition, no market participants indicated that they programmed their trading systems to include the declaration of self-help against one or more exchanges as a risk control that could affect their trading behavior, which is consistent with the fact that most participants route their trades directly.

The single exception was a market participant that did not declare self-help itself, but rather simply removed NYSE Arca from its routing table at approximately the same time that Nasdaq declared self-help. This market participant did not, however, execute any trades internally that traded through the NYSE Arca quotations, nor did it route any ISOs. Accordingly, the effect of this course of action was limited to orders that the market participant routed to Nasdaq and Nasdaq OMX BX (i.e., the only exchanges that bypassed NYSE Arca during the general market disruption on May 6).

A potential concern about the effect of the Self-Help Declarations on May 6 is that they could have led to inaccessible liquidity at NYSE Arca when Nasdaq and Nasdaq OMX BX began bypassing the quotations of NYSE Arca. If a significant volume of liquidity demanding order flow bypassed NYSE Arca, it could have exacerbated the overall imbalance between the liquidity supply and demand during the general market disruption. For the Self-Help

Declarations to have caused such a result, however, a significant volume of order flow would need to have been diverted away from NYSE Arca to Nasdaq and Nasdaq OMX BX (at which point, Nasdaq or Nasdaq OMX BX would either have executed the orders themselves or routed them away as ISOs to exchanges other than NYSE Arca).

To assess quantitatively the extent to which the Self-Help Declarations may have caused a bypassing of liquidity at NYSE Arca, we have examined two types of data: (i) the percentage of trading volume executed on NYSE Arca before and after the Self-Help Declarations; and (ii) the volume of liquidity demanding sell orders that were executed at NYSE Arca during the general price decline compared with the volume of liquidity demanding sell orders that Nasdaq routed away to other exchanges during the same time period.

First, NYSE Arca executed a comparable volume of trading before and after the Self-Help Declarations. From 2:00 p.m. through 2:36 p.m., NYSE Arca's percentage of total share volume across all NMS stocks was approximately 14.7%. From 2:37 p.m. till 3:00 p.m., NYSE Arca's share volume was approximately 15.4%. The comparable volume of percentage of total trading indicates that NYSE Arca liquidity continued to be accessible after the Self-Help Declarations.

Second, during the period of the general price decline in individual securities from 2:30 p.m. to 2:47 p.m., NYSE Arca executed approximately 162 million shares in liquidity taking sell and sell short orders across all NMS stocks. By comparison, Nasdaq routed away to other quoting markets approximately 22 million shares in liquidity taking sell and sell short orders across all NMS stocks, or only 13.6% of the volume of liquidity taking sell orders that were routed directly to and executed on NYSE Arca during that time frame.

Additionally, as discussed above in Section 2, the data with respect to broken trades on May 6, suggests that liquidity was not trapped on NYSE Arca.

In sum, we do not find that the Self-Help Declarations directly contributed to the severe imbalances between liquidity supply and demand on May 6. However, the Self-Help Declarations likely contributed more generally to concerns among many market participants about abnormal trading and data reliability. Nonetheless, nearly all market participants appear to have continued routing orders directly to NYSE Arca when it displayed the best priced quotations. This order flow caused NYSE Arca trading and prices to remain closely aligned with trading and prices at other markets.

## III.3. Market Data Issues

Rule 603(b) of Regulation NMS requires equity exchanges and FINRA to act jointly to disseminate consolidated information, including an NBBO, on quotations for and transactions in NMS stocks. The consolidated information is disseminated through securities information processors that collect, process, and prepare for publication such information including the price, size, and symbol of quotations and executions. In addition, many exchanges offer proprietary data feeds directly to customers that include details of trades and orders on that exchange only. These proprietary data feeds must be offered on terms that are fair and reasonable, and cannot be sent to customers any sooner than the data provided to the processors. However, because the proprietary data feeds are not consolidated, such data feeds may reach the end user faster than the consolidated feeds.

On the afternoon of May 6, NYSE set quote traffic records and experienced significant delays in its dissemination of certain execution and quotation information. At the time, NYSE was in the middle of upgrading its systems that publish information to the processors. NYSE explained that the sustained high volume of market data delayed the dissemination of quotation and execution information to the processors in 1,665 NYSE listed symbols (A – HEZ, KC – MGZ) (the "1665 Symbols") that were traded on NYSE servers that had not been upgraded.[66]

Between 2:44:45 p.m. and 2:46:29 p.m. on May 6, NYSE quotes in the 1665 Symbols had average delays to the CQS of over 10 seconds. Between 2:45 p.m. and 2:50 p.m., over 40 of the 1665 Symbols had an average delay to CQS of more than 20 seconds, and the average delay for all of the 1665 Symbols was just over 5 seconds. During the same five-minute period, however, NYSE disseminated quotation information for the 1665 Symbols through one of its proprietary data feeds with an average delay of just over 8 milliseconds, or 0.008 seconds.

NYSE also experienced delays disseminating transaction information to the consolidated feed and through at least one of its proprietary data feeds. Between 2:45 p.m. and 2:50 p.m., NYSE transactions in the 1665 Symbols had average delays to the CTS of over five seconds (with some delays lasting as long as 35 seconds) and average delays through one of its proprietary data products of over seven seconds. We are unaware of any other delays NYSE may have experienced on other proprietary data products.

SEC rules require that the exchanges and FINRA provide timely and accurate data to the CTS and CQS systems to inform all participants of the trading and quoting activities occurring in the market place. At the time of this chapter, there has been considerable attention in the public media regarding these data delays, and we agree that this is an important topic that should be addressed. However, it is equally important that we explore the extent to which these delays may have impacted trading on May 6.

The CTS and CQS systems represent a consolidated view of trading and top-of-book quoting[67] across all national exchanges and ECNs, and trading at internalizers and dark pools. As such, the relative timing of trades and quotes within these systems are subject to some aggregation delays, which generally are less than 10 milliseconds. As discussed in Section 2, many large market participants route orders directly to exchanges and subscribe to the proprietary feeds from each exchange in order to minimize aggregation delays and receive depth-of-book quotes. Accordingly, automated systems making trading decisions based on these feeds should not have been directly affected by delays in the CTS and CQS system. It is important to note that retail order flow is generally handled by internalizers who are also among those participants that use proprietary exchange feeds to make trading and routing decisions.

However, firms that use proprietary feeds to make trading decisions may still have been impacted by delays on the CTS and CQS feeds. As discussed, concerns about data integrity contributed to pauses or halts in many automated trading systems, which in turn led to a reduction in general market liquidity. Most firms reported to us that the primary drivers of their integrity-based halts were observed, rapid changes in the E-Mini and *observed*, rapid changes in individual securities. But data-integrity checks based on the CTS and CQS feeds would have been directly affected by delays in the consolidated market data, and firms using those integrity-checks reported that this influenced, and to some extent supported, their decisions to pause or halt trading.

For firms employing trading strategies that are less time-sensitive, and whose automated systems rely solely on data from the CQS and CTS, data delays on these feeds could have directly triggered integrity-pauses. Some such firms reported that delays on the CQS and CTS were a more significant part, though not the sole reason, for their decision to curtail or halt trading on the afternoon of May 6. We note, however, that while these types of firms are not generally market makers or liquidity providers, they can be significant fundamental buyers and sellers.

A number of other hypotheses regarding the causes and implications of these data delays have been offered. One specific concern is that traders could take advantage of the timing delay between data reported to the consolidated feed and data reported on the proprietary feeds by buying securities at prices on one feed and selling securities at prices on the other. It generally is not possible to do this, however, since the consolidated feeds do not reflect a separate trading market from the exchanges. One cannot "buy" or "sell" at an exchange's prices as shown on the consolidated data feeds separately from the exchange's prices as shown on its proprietary data feed. All orders attempting to execute against an exchange quote in the consolidated data feed must be routed to that exchange where they will be matched in real-time based on then-available quotes at that exchange. These real-time exchange matching system prices may be different from the quotes in the consolidated data feeds if, as on May 6, the exchange is experiencing latencies in transmitting its data to the consolidated data processors. The exchange's prices in the consolidated data feeds are quite literally inaccurate – they do not in fact reflect prices that are currently available to anyone at the exchange.

One potential exception would be a dark pool that executes trades based on exchange prices, but uses the consolidated data feeds to reference those prices rather than subscribing to the exchanges' proprietary data feeds. In such a case, it could be possible for a trader to route an order to the dark pool hoping for an execution at a stale price and, if it received such an execution, to then route an order to an exchange to capture the differential between the current price and the stale price. We believe, however, that dark pools representing the great majority of dark pool volume subscribe to the proprietary data feeds so that the opportunity for this trading tactic is limited.

Moreover, if there are latencies in transmitting exchange data to the consolidated data processors, investors who make real-time decisions to buy or sell based on observed prices in the consolidated feeds (as do most individual investors) are likely to find that their orders are not filled in the manner expected, and these investors will be at a disadvantage compared to those making decisions based on proprietary feeds. This is one of the reasons data delays on the consolidated feed should be kept to an absolute minimum.

Some market participants and firms in the market data business have analyzed the CTS and CQS data delays of May 6, as well as the quoting patterns observed on a variety of other days. It has been hypothesized that these delays are due to a manipulative practice called "quote-stuffing" in which high volumes of quotes are purposely sent to exchanges in order to create data delays that would afford the firm sending these quotes a trading advantage.

Our investigation to date reveals that the largest and most erratic price moves observed on May 6 were caused by withdrawals of liquidity and the subsequent execution of trades at stub quotes. We have interviewed many of the participants who withdrew their liquidity, including those who were party to significant numbers of buys and sells that occurred at stub quote prices. As described throughout this chapter each market participant had many and varied reasons for its specific actions and decisions on May 6. For the subset of those liquidity providers who rely on CTS and CQS data for trading decisions or data- integrity checks, delays in those feeds would have influenced their actions. However, the evidence does not support the hypothesis that delays in the CTS and CQS feeds triggered or otherwise caused the extreme volatility in security prices observed that day.

Nevertheless, as discussed in the Executive Summary, the events of May 6 clearly demonstrate the importance of data in today's world of fully-automated trading strategies and systems. The SEC staff will therefore be working closely with the market centers to help ensure the integrity and reliability of their data processes, especially those that involve the publication of trades and quotes to the consolidated tape. In addition, the SEC staff will be working with the market centers in exploring their members' trading practices to identify any unintentional or potentially abusive or manipulative conduct that may cause such system delays that inhibit the ability of market participants to engage in a fair and orderly process of price discovery.

# IV. Analysis of Order Books

As stated in the Preliminary Report, "The temporary nature of the decline in prices in the broader market may be indicative of a failure in liquidity."[68] Based on the limited data available at that time, we observed only that temporary price dislocations could have been associated with an unusually high demand for liquidity, or an unusually weak supply of liquidity, or some combination of these factors.

In this chapter we have extended our analyses to include the full order books of many thousands of securities and ETFs. To do so we obtained NYSE OpenBook Ultra and NYSE ArcaBook data, Nasdaq ModelView and similar data from BATS. These sources provided minute-by-minute "snapshots" of the order book, for all listed securities.[69] These data allowed us to calculate the number of shares represented by buy and sell limit orders on these exchanges at a wide range of price points. We measured the price points in terms of the relative distance from the midpoint of the NBBO. These data provide a detailed picture of the available liquidity for each security, throughout the day.

In addition, we obtained order audit trail files from several sources, including NYSE, NYSE Amex, NYSE Arca, Nasdaq and BATS, each containing detailed data on orders received, modified, canceled, and executed. In total, this data contained 5.3 billion records.

## IV.1. Analysis of Changes in Liquidity and Price Declines

In addition to the analyses of specific order books presented in Sections I and II, order book and order audit trail data were used to look for a general relationship between price-changes and liquidity-changes for approximately 5,000 non-ETF securities.

**Table IV.1. Average and median intra-day price declines for 4,920 corporate stocks as a function of buy-side liquidity lost on May 6**

| | Typical Buy-Order Depth (thousands of standardized shares) | | | | | | |
|---|---|---|---|---|---|---|---|
| **Lowest Remaining Liquidity** | **Less than 0.5** | **0.5 to 2.2** | **2.2 to 7.4** | **7.4 to 28.3** | **More than 28.3** | **Total** | |
| **More than 17%** | -3.76% | -5.27% | -5.83% | -5.65% | -6.35% | -5.24% | mean |
| | *-2.69%* | *-4.45%* | *-5.20%* | *-5.79%* | *-6.50%* | *-4.89%* | *median* |
| | 238 | 244 | 198 | 153 | 151 | 984 | # obs |
| **10–17%** | -5.24% | -6.65% | -8.03% | -8.45% | -8.31% | -7.83% | mean |
| | *-4.59%* | *-5.72%* | *-7.14%* | *-7.95%* | *-8.15%* | *-7.41%* | *median* |
| | 65 | 156 | 165 | 246 | 352 | 984 | # obs |
| **6–10%** | -6.94% | -8.57% | -9.19% | -9.36% | -9.36% | -9.06% | mean |
| | *-5.65%* | *-7.08%* | *-8.16%* | *-8.55%* | *-9.02%* | *-8.45%* | *median* |
| | 69 | 116 | 190 | 291 | 318 | 984 | # obs |
| **2–6%** | -8.27% | -9.82% | -11.88% | -12.78% | -12.33% | -11.36% | mean |
| | *-7.52%* | *-8.21%* | *-9.88%* | *-9.71%* | *-9.58%* | *-9.21%* | *median* |
| | 92 | 224 | 282 | 245 | 141 | 984 | # obs |
| **Less than 2%** | -7.26% | **-11.64%** | **-15.97%** | **-23.20%** | **-39.78%** | -11.18% | mean |
| | *-5.43%* | *-8.36%* | *-12.35%* | *-12.97%* | *-26.31%* | *-7.51%* | *median* |
| | 520 | 244 | 149 | 49 | 22 | 984 | # obs |

Notes: Typical buy order depth is measured as the median number of standardized shares bid within 500 basis points of the mid-quote on a minute-by-minute basis during May 6. Lowest remaining liquidity equals the minimum of these values divided by the median. Price declines are measured from the opening to the intra-day low. Results are bucketed by quintile. Shares are standardized across securities to a value of $50/share (bid price) at 9:30am.

To look at liquidity changes, we sorted each of the securities into quintiles based on the extent to which the buy-side order book for that security contracted on May 6. As a measure of the extent of the contraction, we used the minimum buy-side depth observed in any minute on that day, divided by its median depth on that day. In addition, because of possible systematic differences between securities with typically different sized order books we sorted these securities into quintiles based on the respective median of their buy-side depths within 500 basis points ("bp") of the mid-quote, as measured in one minute increments on May 6.

Crossing the quintiles based on the typical depth of the order book with quintiles based on the contraction of the order book creates 25 categories spanning 4,920 non-ETF securities. For the securities in each of these categories, Table IV.1 presents the average and the median intraday stock price drop, measured as the open to low, and the number of securities in the category.

The results in Table IV.1 show that, except for securities in the lowest 20% of typical buy-side depth (far left column), drops in price become increasingly more severe with ever-larger drops in liquidity. The most severe average price drop of 39.8% occurred in the 22 securities that had both the greatest intraday average of buy-side depth and the worst decline in that depth.

## IV.2. Detailed Order Book Data for Selected Securities

Charts for seven selected securities[70] presenting a detailed look at minute-by-minute changes in order book depth, aggressive executed orders, and price changes, are discussed below. Data presented on each chart includes:

- **ORDER DEPTH**. The blue bars show the market depth for resting buy-side orders, and the green bars show the depth for resting sell-side orders. There is a separate bar for each minute during trading hours, and the height of the bars in the lightest shades show the number of shares available for purchase/sale within 10 basis points of the midpoint of the NBBO. As the shades get darker, the range of prices expands, initially by increments of 10 bp (to 20 bp, 30 bp, 40 bp, and 50 bp), and then by larger increments (to 100 bp, 200 bp, 300 bp, and finally to 500 bp). It is important to note that the range of prices reflected by darker colors is associated with non-linear price increments. For each security there are two sets of charts: the first presents liquidity limited to within 500 bp of the NBBO midpoint, and the second presents all available liquidity.[71]
- **PRICES**. The dotted yellow lines show the minimum executed price for each minute, obtained from the NYSE Trades and Quotes database ("TAQ").
- **NET AGGRESSIVE BUY VOLUME**. The charts also include a solid red line that shows the number of executed shares characterized as Net Aggressive Buy Volume. This is computed by summing the number of executed shares in any given minute resulting from buy market orders and buy limit orders priced at or above the national best offer, and subtracting the number of executed shares in that same minute resulting from sell market orders and sell limit orders priced at or below the national best bid.

The charts show a consistent pattern of liquidity rapidly shrinking at approximately 2:45 p.m. for each security. For some securities liquidity declines faster than others, and in some cases the extent of the decline is more dramatic than others, but the pattern is remarkably consistent across both corporate stocks and ETFs.

***Accenture plc (ACN): Charts 4.A and 4.B***

As described in the Preliminary Report, share prices of Accenture fell from nearly $40 to one cent and recovered all of their value within a matter of seconds. The bids for ACN rapidly declined in seven seconds from about $30 at 2:47:47 p.m. to $0.01 by 2:47:54 p.m. ACN had 112 broken trades, all of which occurred between 2:47:51 p.m. and 2:48:01 p.m.

Charts 4.A and 4.B show that, prior to 2:20 p.m., there were approximately 200,000 shares available as selling liquidity and 120,000 to 140,000 shares for purchase within 500 bp of the NBBO midpoint. Outside of this price range, there are an additional 400,000 to 600,000 shares associated with sell orders, and prior to 2:30 p.m., an additional 50,000 to 100,000 shares associated with buy orders. In aggregate, the number of sell orders accounted for up to, and in some cases, more than, twice the number of buy orders. Although there are some fluctuations, the book of limit orders remains fairly stable until around 2:20 p.m.

After 2:20 p.m., liquidity began to disappear, gradually getting smaller on both the buy side and the sell side. Until 2:40 p.m., the amount of sell liquidity within 500 bp continued to exceed the amount of buy liquidity within 500 bp by almost 100%, and outside of the 500 bp range, the disparity was even greater. Within the next few minutes, the amount of sell liquidity fell rapidly until by 2:43 p.m. there were only 50,000 shares available for either selling liquidity or buying liquidity. From 2:43 p.m. through 2:44 p.m., selling liquidity fell sharply, perhaps as orders were executed, and buying liquidity declined less, so that at 2:44 p.m., there were approximately 33,000 shares with orders to purchase within 500 bp of the NBBO midpoint, but only approximately 22,000 shares with orders to sell within 500 bp.

Over the period, the amount of buy-side liquidity actually increased, so that in the minute prior to the drop in the stock price, the amount of buy limit orders was approximately 45,000 shares, more than four times the number of sell limit orders. By the end of minute when the broken trades occurred (shown on the chart as 2:48 p.m., representing a snapshot of the order book at 2:48:00 p.m. exactly), we did not observe any shares available as either buy or sell limit orders within 5% of the NBBO. Outside of this price range, there are many sell orders, but no buy orders. Orders were executed against stub quotes during that minute. In the next minute, share prices recovered, and liquidity reappeared. However, the full depth of the order book does not return to pre-2:20 p.m. levels until just before the close of the markets at 4 p.m.

The charts also include information about order flow, specifically the net number of executed aggressive buy orders per minute. The data indicate that there were more aggressive sell orders than buy orders throughout the day, with a few exceptions. In addition, the net number of aggressive buy orders per minute indicates some potentially significant increases in selling pressure. These downward spikes do not approach the number of shares available for purchase within 500 bp of the mid-quote, however, until 2:43 p.m. and 2:46 p.m. Based on these data, it appears that the drop in price was associated with the decline in liquidity that was concurrent with an observed increase in selling pressure.

***Proctor & Gamble Co. (PG), Charts 5.A and 5.B***

Procter & Gamble is another company whose stock price decline was discussed in the Preliminary Report. PG declined from more than $60 to a low of $39.37 in approximately three and a half minutes (a 36.14% decline from the 2:40 p.m. price), then recovered above $60 in approximately one minute. We observed that the decline in PG did not begin until 2:44 p.m., well after the broader market indices, which began their precipitous drop at approximately 2:40 p.m.

Charts 5.A and 5.B indicate that PG had far more absolute market depth than ACN during the morning and early afternoon of May 6. The amount of shares in sell limit orders within 500 bp is nearly ten times the comparable number of shares for ACN. The difference is not as dramatic for buy limit orders, where the ratio is closer to four times the comparable number for ACN. Throughout the day, the number of shares in the selling limit order book strongly exceeded the number of shares in the buying limit order book. The ratio appears to be steady, at approximately four-to-one, between the open and 2:39 p.m., either within the 500 bp range or outside of that range.

At 2:40 p.m., the amount of selling liquidity within the 500 bp range dropped from approximately 1,200,000 shares to approximately 500,000 shares, while the amount of buying liquidity was roughly unchanged at approximately 230,000 shares. Liquidity continued to disappear until 2:47 p.m., when PG hit its lowest price, and the amount of buy and sell liquidity within 500 bp was less than 50,000 shares on each side. It is noticeable that the amount of liquidity within 500 bp did not return to its earlier levels at any time after this drop. After 3 p.m. it remains fairly steady at approximately 250,000 shares of selling liquidity and 100,000 shares of buying liquidity. It is also apparent that the total liquidity, which includes the full range of quotes, did not decline on the sell side, but the total buying liquidity was dramatically reduced at 2:47 p.m.

The charts also indicate that the net aggressive selling executed orders exceeded the amount of available buy limit orders within 500 bp at 2:45 p.m. However, the balance shifted toward aggressive buy executions, so that by 2:47 p.m., the number of aggressive buys exceeded the number of aggressive sells.

### *3M Co. (MMM), Charts 6.A and 6.B*

The Preliminary Report also discussed 3M, another large capitalization stock that declined substantially. We observed that the bid-ask spread for MMM stayed quite narrow, and volume remained significant, even as the price declined from about $82 at 2:44 p.m. to a low of approximately $68 at 2:46 p.m. Prior to reaching this low, the bid-ask spread over any given second dramatically widened and remained erratic before beginning a slow and choppy recovery.

In addition, we noted that MMM first declined from approximately $82.50 at 2:44 p.m. to approximately $71.00, then slowly began to recover. Though this 14% decline was substantial, at approximately 2:46 p.m., the price declined sharply for a second time and hit a daily low of $67.98, resulting in a total decline from its 2:40 p.m. price of 18.39%, second only to PG among DJIA stocks. The price then suddenly climbed within a few seconds to approximately $77.

As shown in Charts 6.A and 6.B, MMM is closer in magnitude of available liquidity to Accenture than PG, with selling liquidity within 500 bp ranging from 340,000 shares to 150,000 shares prior to 2:15 p.m. As with both PG and ACN, MMM had more selling liquidity during the morning hours than buying liquidity, with a ratio that was close to two-to-one for most of the day. Also, throughout most of the day, aggressive selling volume exceeded aggressive buying volume. There was a pronounced decline in selling liquidity of approximately 100,000 shares just before 2 p.m. Selling liquidity within 500 bp continued to decline, and buying liquidity also fell, between 2:00 p.m. and 2:45 p.m. Like both PG and ACN, the available liquidity in MMM was very low between 2:45 and 2:50 p.m. Also, like PG, there was no substantial decline in selling liquidity in the range beyond 500 bp, between 2:45 p.m. and 2:50 p.m., despite the large decline in buying liquidity in this wider price range.

The observed second dip in MMM prices, discussed in the Preliminary Report, appears to coincide with a small increase in net aggressive selling volume, and at the time of the second downward spike in prices, it is clear that there is still very little liquidity within 500 bp of the NBBO midpoint.

### *International Business Machines Corp (IBM), Charts 7.A and 7.B*

In the Preliminary Report, we observed that IBM was a security with a much smaller price decline than the securities described above. In light of the observed differences in price patterns for executions, it is interesting to note many common features with regards to the patterns of liquidity availability and aggressive selling pressure. Charts 7.A and 7.B show that, similar to ACN, PG, and MMM, liquidity was much higher prior to 2:00 p.m., and it declined with increasing speed until it hit its low point at 2:47 p.m. The available liquidity at 2:47 p.m. was approximately 10,000 shares within 500 bp in selling liquidity and approximately 30,000 shares within 500 bp in buying liquidity, far less than the roughly 250,000 shares of comparable selling and buying liquidity available between 11:00 a.m. and 2:10 p.m.

A difference between IBM and ACN, PG, and MMM is that the net aggressive selling orders exceeded the number of shares available in the limit order book at 2:45 p.m., even though the overall price decline of IBM was modest by comparison to those other securities. This may indicate that incoming buy-orders were replenishing the order book at a pace that was fast enough to prevent a further erosion of prices. Even so, we note that buy-side market depth declined to a minimum of approximately 12% of its median value on May 6. Based on the data summarized in Table IV.1, IBM was therefore in the second lowest quintile of liquidity-contraction. This is consistent with the premise that relative market-depth declines are a reasonable indicator of the magnitude of corresponding price declines.

***Apple Inc. (AAPL), Charts 8.A and 8.B***

In contrast to the stocks discussed above, the depth of the buy order book for AAPL (within 500 bp of the mid-quote) exceeded the depth of its sell order book throughout most of the day until 2:39 p.m. However, just as for the other securities, the available liquidity dropped rapidly between 2:30 p.m. and 2:45 p.m., reaching a minimum where very few shares were available at 2:47 p.m., when its price rapidly declined.

Unlike ACN, PG, MMM, and IBM, AAPL showed spikes of executed aggressive buying orders throughout the day that exceeded the number of contemporaneous executed aggressive selling orders. In addition, the data shows three large spikes in net aggressive executed selling orders, at 2:35 p.m., 2:37 p.m., and 2:45 p.m. However, it does not appear that these spikes created significant imbalances between the buy-order book and the sell-order book. Rather, these imbalances were manifest starting at 2:48 p.m., when the price of AAPL was recovering. We also note that there were two broken trades in APPL occurring at approximately 3:29 p.m. when 895 shares were executed at high stub-quote prices of $100,000.

***General Electric Co. (GE), Charts 9.A and 9.B***

The data on liquidity and aggressive net executed orders for GE does not indicate a dramatically different pattern than what was observed for ACN, PG, MMM, IBM, and AAPL. First, GE had a substantially deeper book, compared to PG at approximately 1,800,000 to 2,500,000 shares of buying liquidity and 1,200,000 to 1,800,000 shares of selling liquidity. Second, like AAPL, within the 500 bp range, its buy liquidity exceeded its sell liquidity, but outside of that range, GE had more sell liquidity than buy liquidity. Like each of the other securities, both buy and sell liquidity declined dramatically around 2:30 p.m. Compared to PG, GE had more liquidity available at 2:47 p.m. and 2:48 p.m., reaching a minimum of approximately 200,000 shares of selling liquidity and 250,000 shares of buying liquidity within the 500 bp range. It also had large spikes in aggressive net executed selling orders, similar to AAPL, PG and IBM.

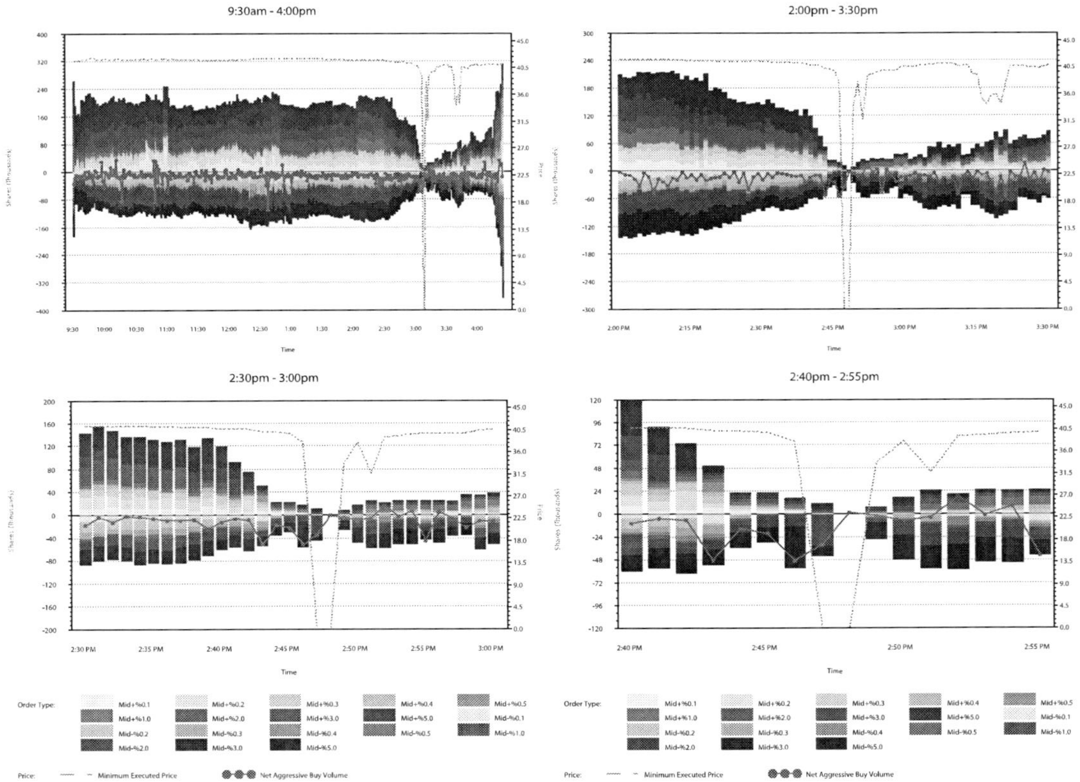


The order book depth reflects the total number of shares in unfilled limit orders, by ticker and minute. The data combines the information from NYSE Openbook, ArcaBook, NASDAQ ModelView, and BATS order book data.

Net Aggressive Buy Volume is defined as executed shares associated with aggressive buy orders minus executed shares associated with aggressive sell orders.

Aggressive buy orders are market buy orders and buy orders at or above the offer price. Aggressive sell orders are market sell orders and sell orders at or below the bid price.

The traded price fell 99.98% from $41.52 at 2:30PM to $0.01 at 2:47PM (based on TAQ data).

There were 112 broken trades with 10,790 shares from 2:36pm to 3:02pm. There were 112 broken trades with 10,790 shares throughout the day.

Chart 4.A. Accenture plc. (ACN) Market Depth (within 500 basis points) and Net Aggressive Buy Volume

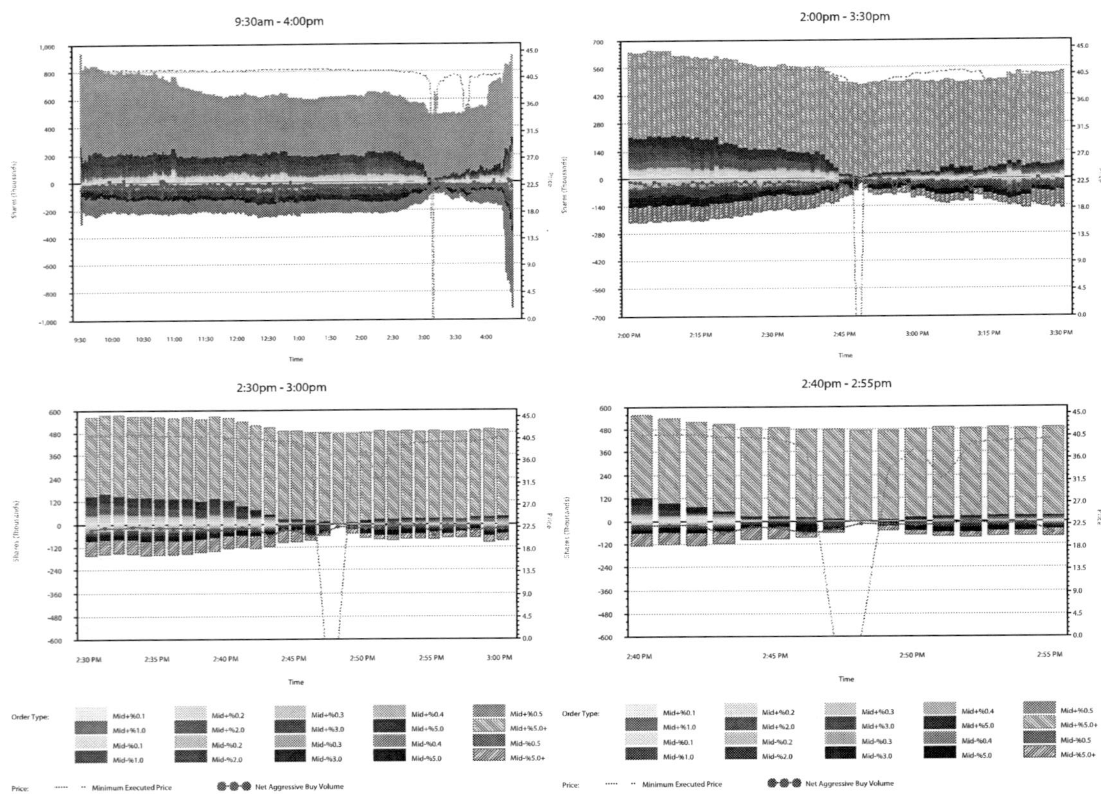


The order book depth reflects the total number of shares in unfilled limit orders, by ticker and minute. The data combines the information from NYSE Openbook, ArcaBook, NASDAQ ModelView, and BATS order book data.

Net Aggressive Buy Volume is defined as executed shares associated with aggressive buy orders minus executed shares associated with aggressive sell orders.

Aggressive buy orders are market buy orders and buy orders at or above the offer price. Aggressive sell orders are market sell orders and sell orders at or below the bid price.

The traded price fell 99.98% from $41.52 at 2:30PM to $0.01 at 2:47PM (based on TAQ data).

There were 112 broken trades with 10,790 shares from 2:36pm to 3:02pm. There were 112 broken trades with 10,790 shares throughout the day.

Chart 4.B. Accenture plc. (ACN) Full Market Depth and Net Aggressive Buy Volume

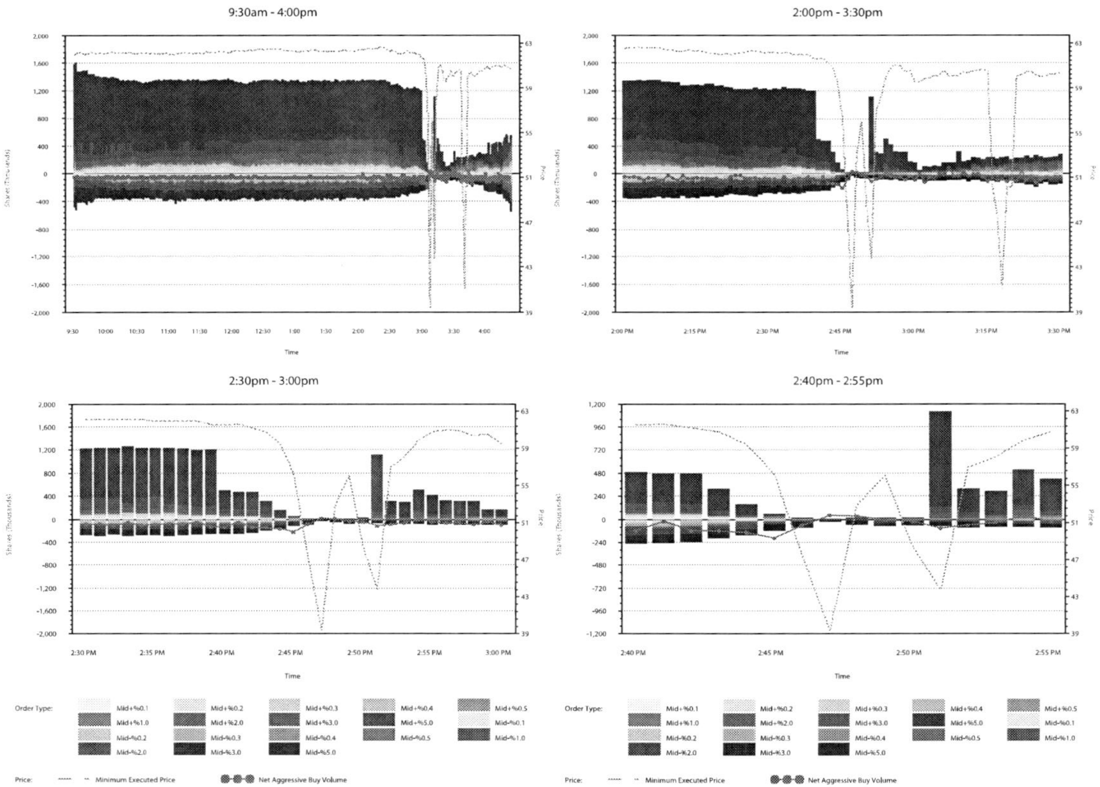


The order book depth reflects the total number of shares in unfilled limit orders, by ticker and minute. The data combines the information from NYSE Openbook, ArcaBook, NASDAQ ModelView, and BATS order book data.

Net Aggressive Buy Volume is defined as executed shares associated with aggressive buy orders minus executed shares associated with aggressive sell orders.

Aggressive buy orders are market buy orders and buy orders at or above the offer price. Aggressive sell orders are market sell orders and sell orders at or below the bid price.

The traded price fell 36.69% from $62.19 at 2:30PM to $39.37 at 2:47PM (based on TAQ data).

There were no broken trades on May 6, 2010.

Chart 5.A. Procter & Gamble Company (The) (PG) Market Depth (within 500 basis points) and Net Aggressive Buy Volume

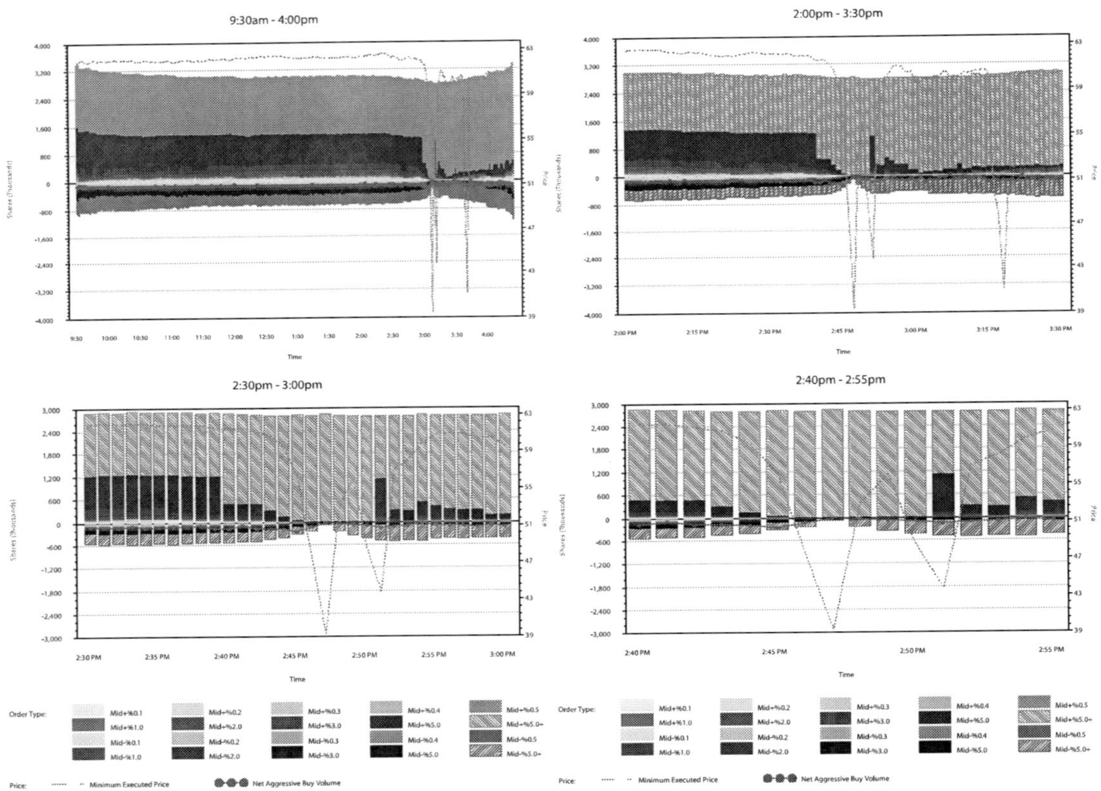


The order book depth reflects the total number of shares in unfilled limit orders, by ticker and minute. The data combines the information from NYSE Openbook, ArcaBook, NASDAQ ModelView, and BATS order book data.

Net Aggressive Buy Volume is defined as executed shares associated with aggressive buy orders minus executed shares associated with aggressive sell orders.

Aggressive buy orders are market buy orders and buy orders at or above the offer price. Aggressive sell orders are market sell orders and sell orders at or below the bid price.

The traded price fell 36.69% from $62.19 at 2:30PM to $39.37 at 2:47PM (based on TAQ data).

There were no broken trades on May 6, 2010.

Chart 5.B. Procter & Gamble Company (The) (PG) Full Market Depth and Net Aggressive Buy Volume

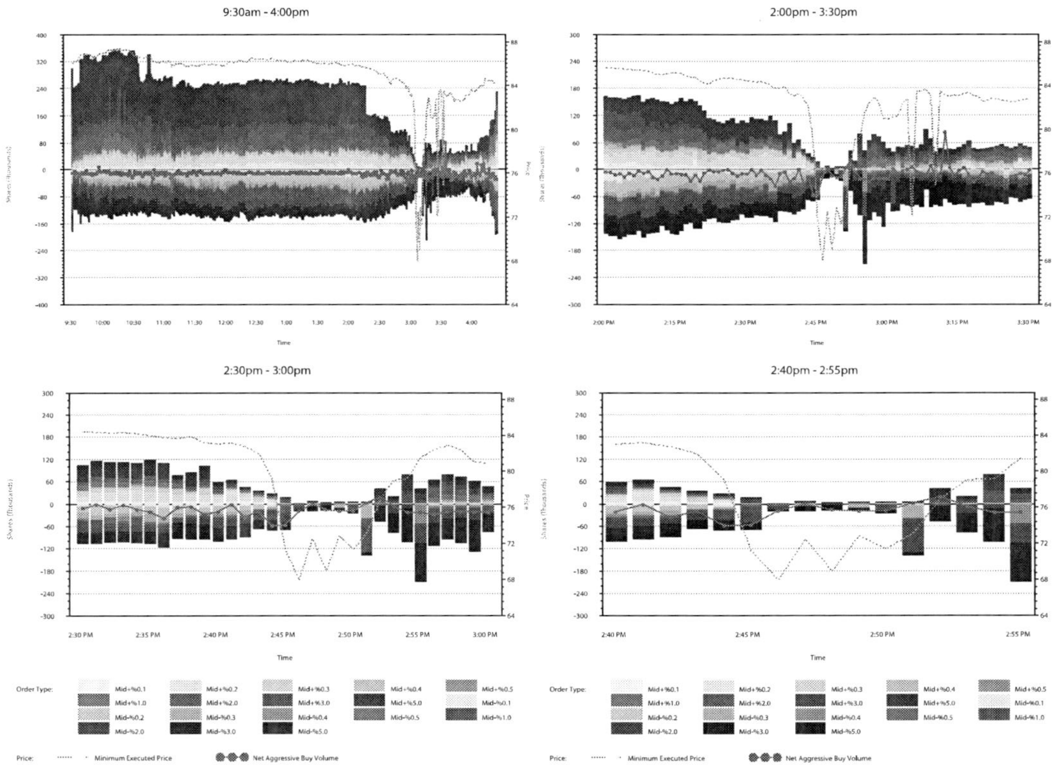


The order book depth reflects the total number of shares in unfilled limit orders, by ticker and minute. The data combines the information from NYSE Openbook, ArcaBook, NASDAQ ModelView, and BATS order book data.

Net Aggressive Buy Volume is defined as executed shares associated with aggressive buy orders minus executed shares associated with aggressive sell orders.

Aggressive buy orders are market buy orders and buy orders at or above the offer price. Aggressive sell orders are market sell orders and sell orders at or below the bid price.

The traded price fell 19.65% from \$84.61 at 2:30PM to \$67.98 at 2:46PM (based on TAQ data).

There were no broken trades on May 6, 2010.

Chart 6.A. 3M Company (MMM) Market Depth (within 500 basis points) and Net Aggressive Buy Volume

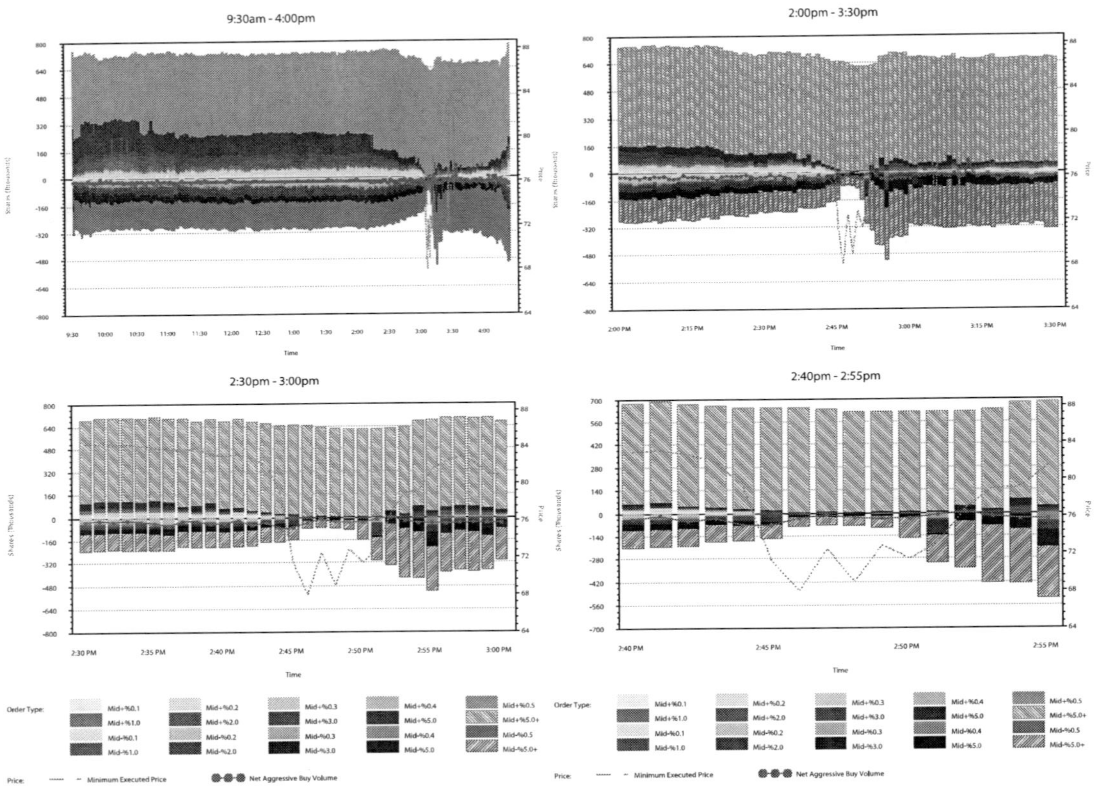


The order book depth reflects the total number of shares in unfilled limit orders, by ticker and minute. The data combines the information from NYSE Openbook, ArcaBook, NASDAQ ModelView, and BATS order book data.

Net Aggressive Buy Volume is defined as executed shares associated with aggressive buy orders minus executed shares associated with aggressive sell orders.

Aggressive buy orders are market buy orders and buy orders at or above the offer price. Aggressive sell orders are market sell orders and sell orders at or below the bid price.

The traded price fell 19.65% from $84.61 at 2:30PM to $67.98 at 2:46PM (based on TAQ data).

There were no broken trades on May 6, 2010.

Chart 6.B. 3M Company (MMM) Full Market Depth and Net Aggressive Buy Volume

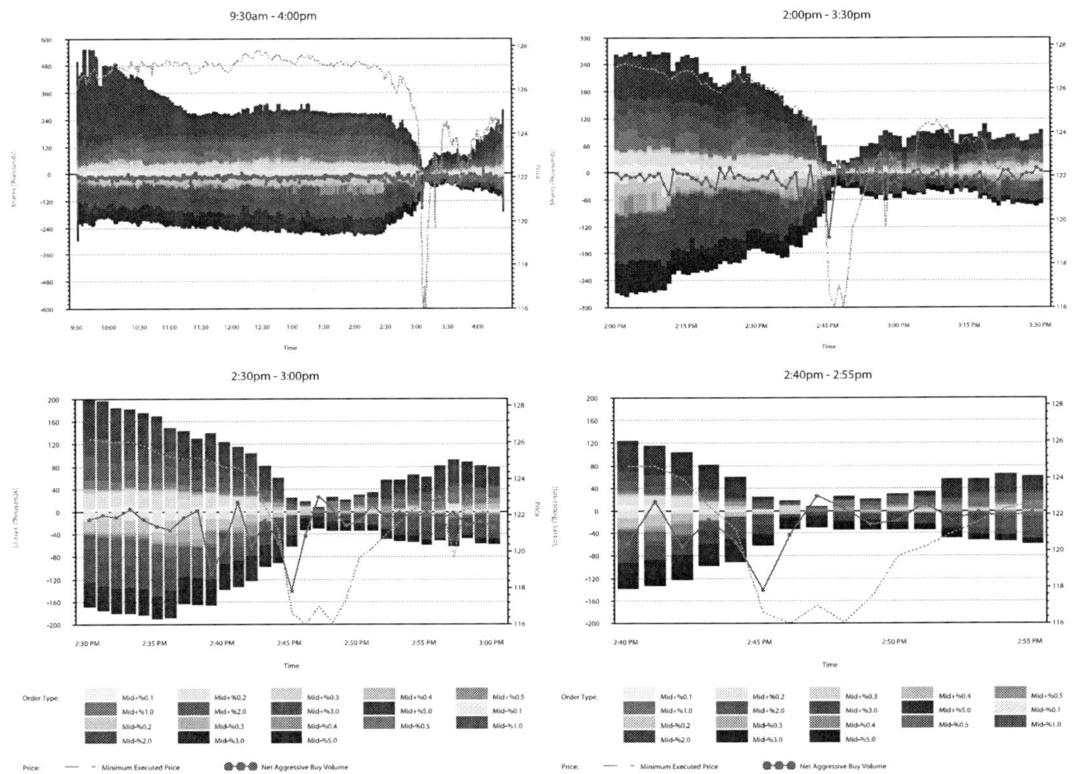


The order book depth reflects the total number of shares in unfilled limit orders, by ticker and minute. The data combines the information from NYSE Openbook, ArcaBook, NASDAQ ModelView, and BATS order book data.

Net Aggressive Buy Volume is defined as executed shares associated with aggressive buy orders minus executed shares associated with aggressive sell orders.

Aggressive buy orders are market buy orders and buy orders at or above the offer price. Aggressive sell orders are market sell orders and sell orders at or below the bid price.

The traded price fell 8.31% from $126.52 at 2:30PM to $116.00 at 2:46PM (based on TAQ data).

There were no broken trades on May 6, 2010.

Chart 7.A. International Business Machines Corporation (IBM) Market Depth (within 500 basis points) and Net Aggressive Buy Volume

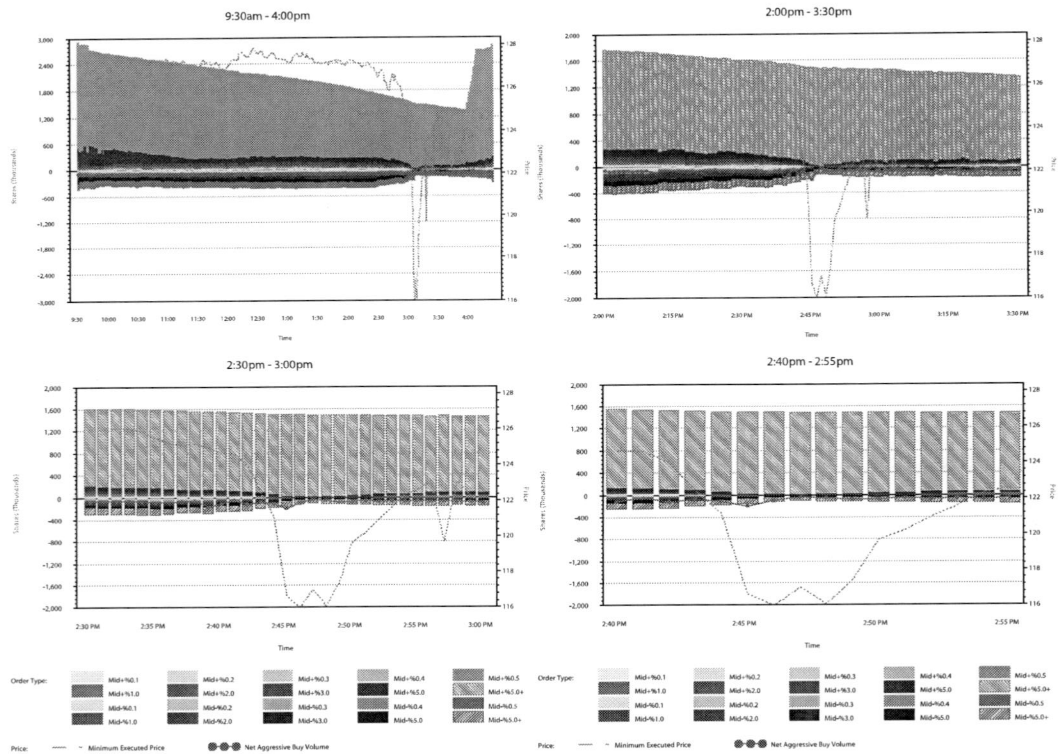


The order book depth reflects the total number of shares in unfilled limit orders, by ticker and minute. The data combines the information from NYSE Openbook, ArcaBook, NASDAQ ModelView, and BATS order book data.

Net Aggressive Buy Volume is defined as executed shares associated with aggressive buy orders minus executed shares associated with aggressive sell orders.

Aggressive buy orders are market buy orders and buy orders at or above the offer price. Aggressive sell orders are market sell orders and sell orders at or below the bid price.

The traded price fell 8.31% from $126.52 at 2:30PM to $116.00 at 2:46PM (based on TAQ data).

There were no broken trades on May 6, 2010.

Chart 7.B. International Business Machines Corporation (IBM) Full Market Depth and Net Aggressive Buy Volume

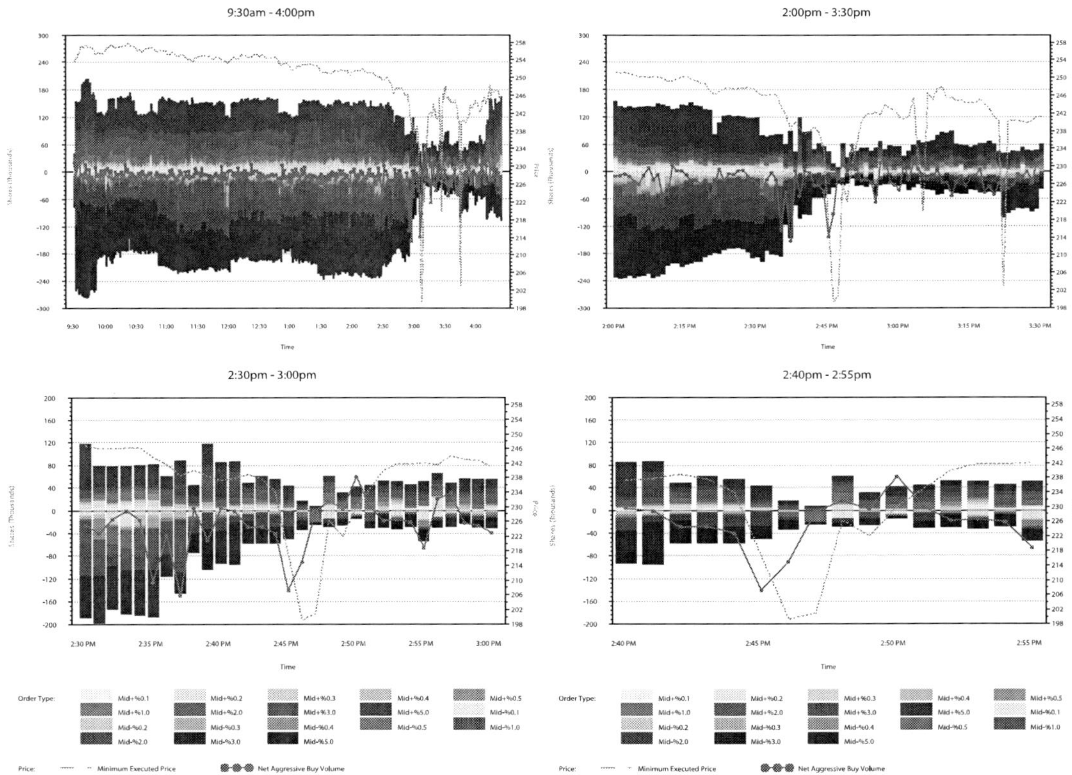


The order book depth reflects the total number of shares in unfilled limit orders, by ticker and minute. The data combines the information from NYSE Openbook, ArcaBook, NASDAQ ModelView, and BATS order book data.

Net Aggressive Buy Volume is defined as executed shares associated with aggressive buy orders minus executed shares associated with aggressive sell orders.

Aggressive buy orders are market buy orders and buy orders at or above the offer price. Aggressive sell orders are market sell orders and sell orders at or below the bid price.

The traded price fell 19.55% from $247.65 at 2:30PM to $199.25 at 2:46PM (based on TAQ data).

There were no broken trades between 2:36pm to 3:02pm. There were 2 broken trades with 895 shares throughout the day.

Chart 8.A. Apple Inc. (AAPL) Market Depth (within 500 basis points) and Net Aggressive Buy Volume

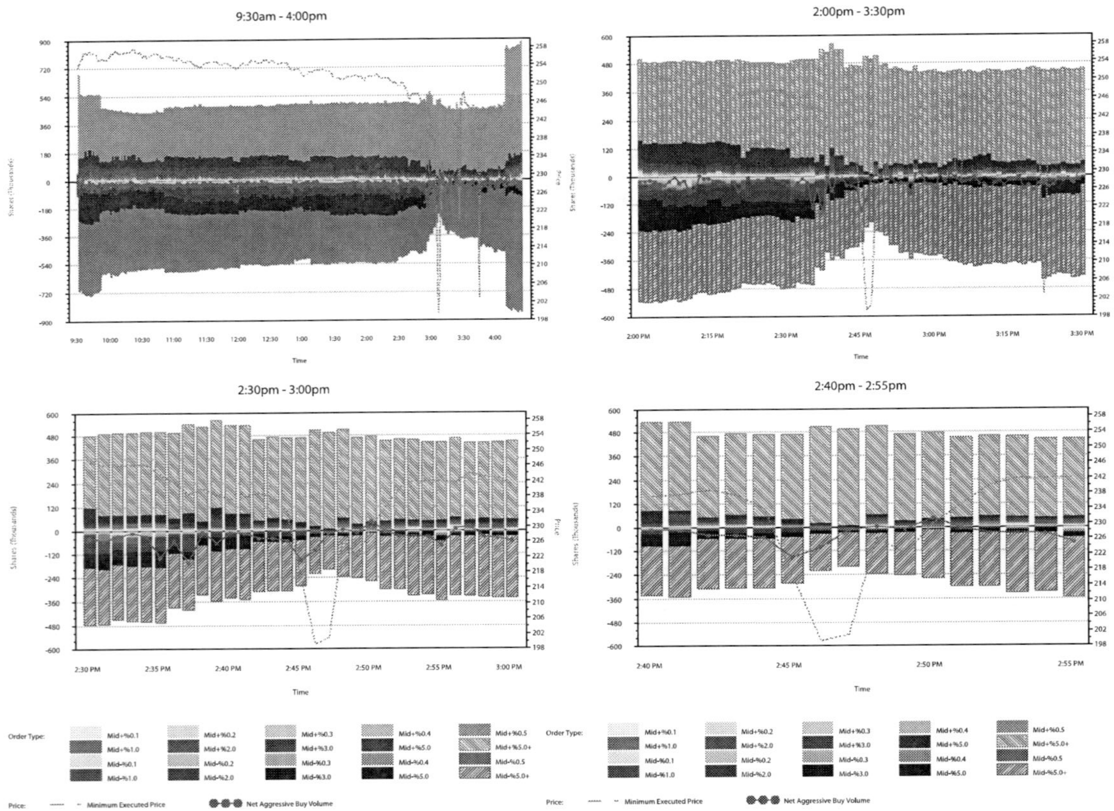


The order book depth reflects the total number of shares in unfilled limit orders, by ticker and minute. The data combines the information from NYSE Openbook, ArcaBook, NASDAQ ModelView, and BATS order book data. Net Aggressive Buy Volume is defined as executed shares associated with aggressive buy orders minus executed shares associated with aggressive sell orders.

Aggressive buy orders are market buy orders and buy orders at or above the offer price. Aggressive sell orders are market sell orders and sell orders at or below the bid price. The traded price fell 19.55% from $247.65 at 2:30PM to $199.25 at 2:46PM (based on TAQ data).

There were no broken trades between 2:36pm to 3:02pm. There were 2 broken trades with 895 shares throughout the day.

Chart 8.B. Apple Inc. (AAPL) Full Market Depth and Net Aggressive Buy Volume

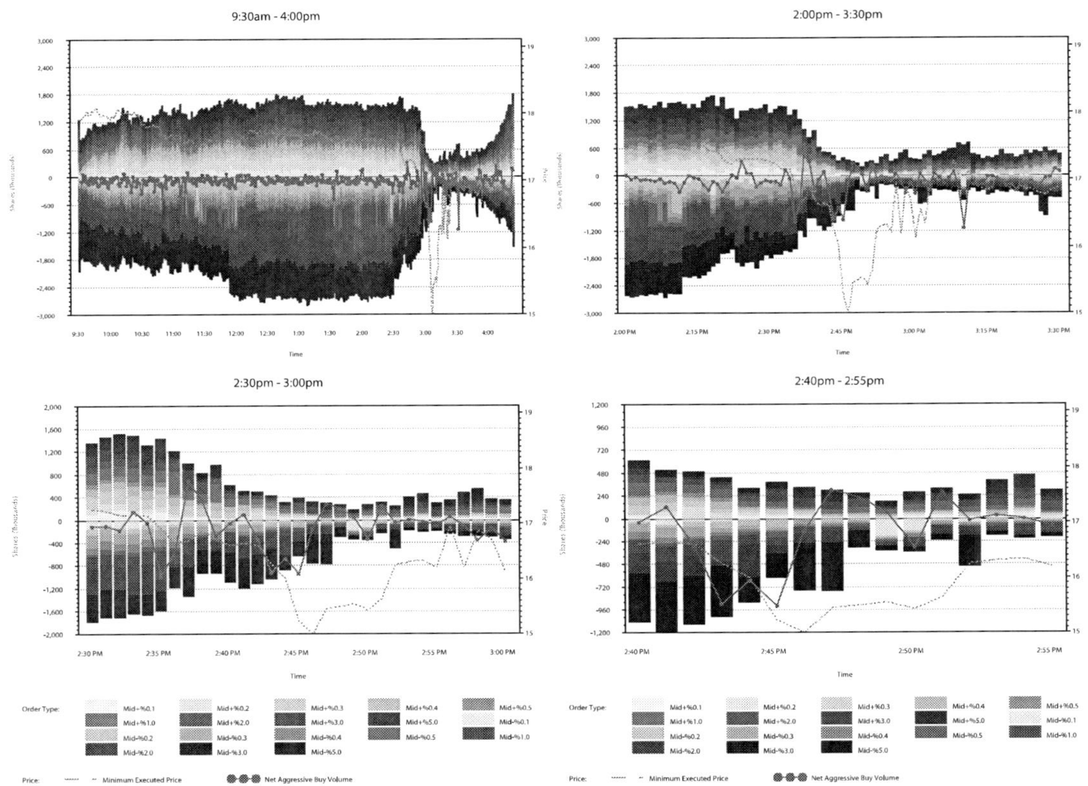


The order book depth reflects the total number of shares in unfilled limit orders, by ticker and minute. The data combines the information from NYSE Openbook, ArcaBook, NASDAQ ModelView, and BATS order book data.

Net Aggressive Buy Volume is defined as executed shares associated with aggressive buy orders minus executed shares associated with aggressive sell orders.

Aggressive buy orders are market buy orders and buy orders at or above the offer price. Aggressive sell orders are market sell orders and sell orders at or below the bid price.

The traded price fell 13.29% from $17.30 at 2:30PM to $15.00 at 2:46PM (based on TAQ data).

There were no broken trades on May 6, 2010.

Chart 9.A.General Electric Company (GE) Market Depth (within 500 basis points) and Net Aggressive Buy Volume

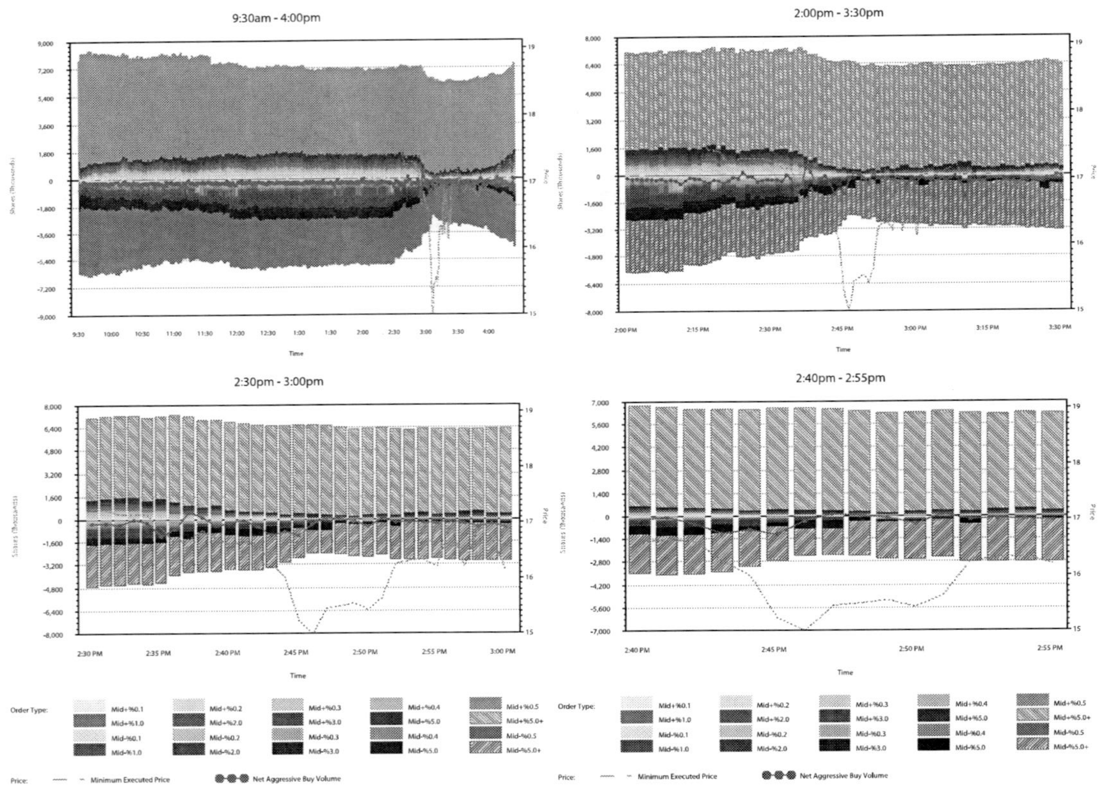


The order book depth reflects the total number of shares in unfilled limit orders, by ticker and minute. The data combines the information from NYSE Openbook, ArcaBook, NASDAQ ModelView, and BATS order book data. Net Aggressive Buy Volume is defined as executed shares associated with aggressive buy orders minus executed shares associated with aggressive sell orders.

Aggressive buy orders are market buy orders and buy orders at or above the offer price. Aggressive sell orders are market sell orders and sell orders at or below the bid price. The traded price fell 13.29% from $17.30 at 2:30PM to $15.00 at 2:46PM (based on TAQ data).

There were no broken trades on May 6, 2010.

Chart 9.B. General Electric Company (GE) Full Market Depth and Net Aggressive Buy Volume

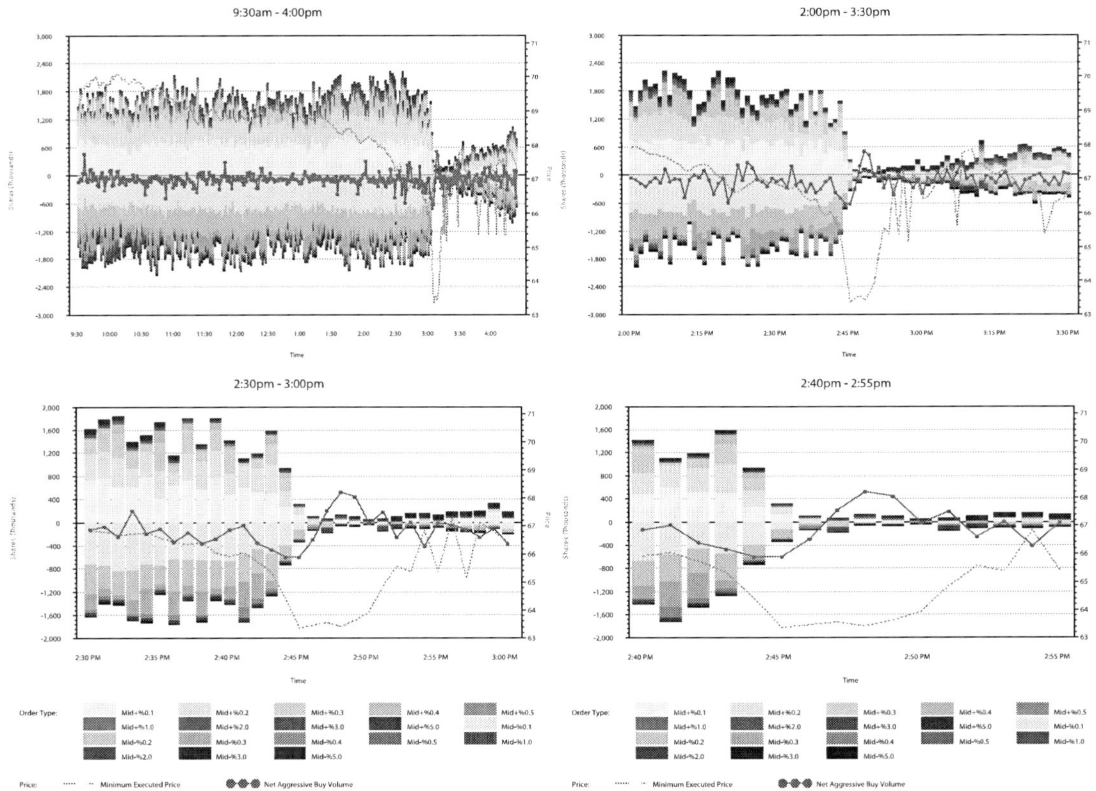


The order book depth reflects the total number of shares in unfilled limit orders, by ticker and minute. The data combines the information from NYSE Openbook, ArcaBook, NASDAQ ModelView, and BATS order book data.

Net Aggressive Buy Volume is defined as executed shares associated with aggressive buy orders minus executed shares associated with aggressive sell orders.

Aggressive buy orders are market buy orders and buy orders at or above the offer price. Aggressive sell orders are market sell orders and sell orders at or below the bid price. .

The traded price fell 5.36% from $66.95 at 2:30PM to $63.36 at 2:45PM (based on TAQ data).

There were no broken trades between 2:36pm to 3:02pm. There were 5 broken trades with 1,300 shares throughout the day.

Chart 10.A. Russell 2000 Index (Barclays) (IWM) Market Depth (within 500 basis points) and Net Aggressive Buy Volume

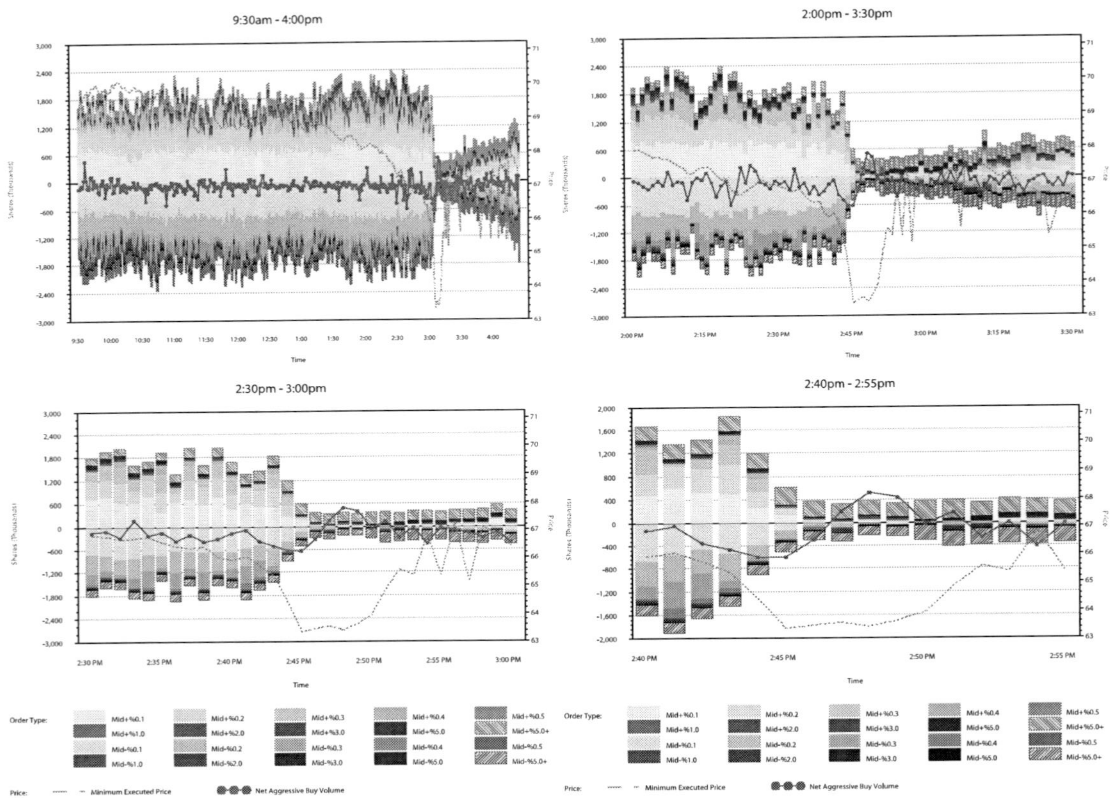


The order book depth reflects the total number of shares in unfilled limit orders, by ticker and minute. The data combines the information from NYSE Openbook, ArcaBook, NASDAQ ModelView, and BATS order book data.

Net Aggressive Buy Volume is defined as executed shares associated with aggressive buy orders minus executed shares associated with aggressive sell orders.

Aggressive buy orders are market buy orders and buy orders at or above the offer price. Aggressive sell orders are market sell orders and sell orders at or below the bid price.

The traded price fell 5.36% from \$66.95 at 2:30PM to \$63.36 at 2:45PM (based on TAQ data).

There were no broken trades between 2:36pm to 3:02pm. There were 5 broken trades with 1,300 shares throughout the day.

Chart 10.B. Russell 2000 Index (Barclays) (IWM) Full Market Depth and Net Aggressive Buy Volume

***iShares Russell 2000 Index (IWM), Charts 10.A and 10.B***

As observed in the Preliminary Report, a disproportionate number of the stocks with substantial stock price declines and recoveries were ETFs. The patterns of liquidity and aggressive order imbalance for the iShares Russell 2000 Index in Charts 10.A and 10.B show many common elements, but also some differences when compared with the non-ETF securities.

For most of the day there was very significant buy order and sell order market depth of approximately 1.8 million shares. Starting at 2:44 p.m. there was a dramatic contraction both buy depth and sell depth, and by 2:50 p.m. liquidity within 500 bp from the mid-quote had all but vanished. However, price declines were modest throughout the time period.

Also of note is that quotes were highly concentrated within about 30 bp from the mid-quote, with relatively almost no market depth beyond 500 bp. As liquidity declined after 2:45 p.m., a greater fraction of total market depth only existed beyond 500 bp of the mid-quote.

## End Notes

[1] We use the term "liquidity" throughout this chaptergenerally to refer to buy-side and sell-side market depth, which is comprised of resting orders that market participants place to express their willingness to buy or sell at prices equal to, or outside of (either below or above), current market levels. Note that for SPY and other equity securities discussed in this chapter, unless otherwise stated, market depth calculations include only resting quotes within 500 basis points of the mid-quote. Additional liquidity would have been available beyond 500 basis points. *See* Section 1 for further details on how market depth and near-inside market depth are defined and calculated for the E-Mini, SPY, and other equity securities.

[2] However, these erosions did not affect "near-inside" liquidity – resting orders within about 0.1% of the last transaction price or mid-market quote.

[3] We define fundamental sellers and fundamental buyers as market participants who are trading to accumulate or reduce a net long or short position. Reasons for fundamental buying and selling include gaining long-term exposure to a market as well as hedging already-existing exposures in related markets.

[4] Subsequently, the large fundamental trader closed, in a single day, this short position.

[5] At a later date, the large fundamental trader executed trades over the course of more than 6 hours to offset the net short position accumulated on May 6.

[6] *See* Section 1 for the context in which high-frequency trading and market intermediaries are defined for the E-Mini.

[7] Cross-market arbitrageurs are opportunistic traders who capitalize on temporary, though often small, price differences between related products by purchasing the cheaper product and selling the more expensive product.

[8] Some additional factors that may have played a role in the events of May 6 and that are discussed more fully in Sections 2 and 3 include: the use of LRPs by the NYSE, in which trading is effectively banded on the NYSE in NYSE-listed stocks exhibiting rapid price moves; declarations of self-help by The Nasdaq Stock Market, LLC ("Nasdaq") against NYSE Arca, Inc. ("NYSE Arca") under which Nasdaq temporarily stopped routing orders to NYSE Arca; and delays in NYSE quote and trade data disseminated over the Consolidated Quotation System ("CQS") and Consolidated Tape System ("CTS") data feeds. Our findings indicate that none of these factors played a dominant role on May 6, but nonetheless they are important considerations in forming a complete picture of, and response to, that afternoon.

[9] Detailed reconstructions of order books for individual securities are presented at the end of this chapter, exploring the relationship between changes in immediately available liquidity and changes in stock prices. This rich data set highlights both the broad theme of liquidity withdrawal on May 6, as well as some of the nuanced differences between securities that may have dictated why some stocks fell only 10% while others collapsed to a penny or less.

[10] Section 2 discusses the disproportionate impact the market disruption of May 6 had on ETFs.

[11] For stocks that are subject to the circuit breaker program, trades will be broken at specified levels depending on the stock price:

- For stocks priced $25 or less, trades will be broken if the trades are at least 10% away from the circuit breaker trigger price.

- For stocks priced more than $25 to $50, trades will be broken if they are 5% away from the circuit breaker trigger price.
- For stocks priced more than $50, the trades will be broken if they are 3% away from the circuit breaker trigger price.

Where circuit breakers are not applicable, the exchanges and FINRA will break trades at specified levels for events involving multiple stocks depending on how many stocks are involved:

- For events involving between five and 20 stocks, trades will be broken that are at least 10% away from the "reference price," typically the last sale before pricing was disrupted.
- For events involving more than 20 stocks, trades will be broken that are at least 30% away from the reference price.

[12] *See* Preliminary Report, Figure 10.

[13] Order book data for the E-Mini is from the CME and is comprised of the total number of shares across all orders at a given price point. Order book data for SPY aggregates individual order books from Nasdaq ModelView, NYSE Openbook Ultra, NYSE ARCABook, and BATS Exchange, Inc. ("BATS"). These exchanges, combined, reflect approximately 90% of the executions on exchanges on May 6. We note that BATS data is limited to five price points on either side of the mid-quote and as a result our analysis can understate the total available liquidity for SPY.

[14] We use the term market depth throughout this chapter to refer to resting orders that market participants place to express their willingness to buy or sell at prices equal to, or outside of (either below or above), current market levels. These orders are referred to as "buy interest" and "sell interest", and the number of shares of each type of order interest represent "buy-side market depth" and "sell-side market depth." Collectively, buy-side and sell-side resting orders form a "liquidity pool" against which incomingsell or buy orders can be executed.

Normally, the rate at which resting orders within a liquidity pool are being depleted by incoming orders requiring immediate execution is approximately the same as the rate at which new buy and sell interests replenish the pool. However, imbalances can develop if the rate at which incoming orders requiring immediate execution outpaces the rate buy and sell interest is replenished, or if market participants reduce, or even halt, their replenishment thereby withdrawing their liquidity. A liquidity crisis can ensue if this imbalance becomes so severe that new orders requiring immediate execution cannot be matched with resting orders at near-market prices, which in turn can lead to extreme prices moves and volatility.

[15] Additional liquidity in SPY existed at even wider levels but was not included in analyses that compare SPY market depth to E-Mini market depth since, as discussed above, limit orders in the E-Mini are price-banded to within about 100 basis points of the last transaction price.

[16] Recall that additional liquidity in SPY existed at even wider levels but was not included in analyses.

[17] For SPY, near-inside market depth includes all resting quotes within 10 basis points on either side of the mid-quote of the then-current NBBO. For the E-Mini, near-inside market depth includes all resting quotes within $1.00 on either side of the last transaction price. On May 6 this was approximately equivalent to 10 basis points.

[18] The "no bust" range is currently setat six index points for the E-Mini, or about 0.6% (60 basis points) of price on May 6.

[19] After 2:45 p.m., as prices in the E-Mini and SPY were recovering from their rapid declines, severe reductions in the liquidity of many individual securities and ETFs, triggered by these rapid declines, were causing even more severe price dislocations in those individual securities and ETFs – a topic that will be discussed in detail throughout subsequent sections of this chapter.

[20] This section is based in part on a paper by Kirilenko, Kyle, Samadi, and Tuzun (2010).

[21] For the purpose of this chapter the term "market maker," when used only in the context of the E-Mini, reflects a style of trading, not a formal registration requirement.

[22] Specifically, automated execution algorithms generally target execution profiles defined in terms of time, price or volume (or any combination of the three). For example, some traders feed orders into the market based on volume-weighted average price ("VWAP") algorithms that are designed to obtain an average price over a specified period of time and therefore have a built-in time throttle that prevents an unexpectedly fast execution that can cause significant market impact. Other such throttles include a limit price that would prevent executions at unfavorable prices.

[23] Subsequently, the large Fundamental Seller closed, in a single day, this short position.

[24] At a later day, it took the large Fundamental Seller more than 6 hours to offset the net short position accumulated on May 6.

[25] Approximately 18,000 out of the 35,000 orders (or about 51 percent) were executed aggressively, i.e., removed resting liquidity from the market, while about 17,000 were executed passively (i.e. provided resting liquidity to the market).

[26] Approximately 24,000 out of the 40,000 orders (or about 60 percent) were executed aggressively and the remaining 16,000 or so passively.

[27] In particular, 2:30 p.m. represents reasonably level points for the E-Mini, SPY, and S&P 500 order books.

[28] The staff held extensive interviews with over three dozen firms who traded in significant size on May 6, ranging from liquidity providers to traders, and asset managers. We believe this sample contains a sufficiently large number of key firms to reliably represent the behavior and actions of most of the large market participants that afternoon. We also held extensive interviews with exchanges that inform other sections of this chapter. Note that a number of market participants engage in multiple strategies throughout the course of a trading day and the discussions that follow are therefore based on strategy type as opposed to firm.

[29] The consolidated market data feeds disseminate real-time quotation and trade information for exchange-listed stocks, as required by the federal securities laws and rules. The data reflected on the consolidated market data feeds derives from various market centers, including all securities exchanges, ECNs, and OTC broker-dealers. There are three different networks that distribute information for exchange-listed stocks: Network A for stocks primarily listed on the NYSE; Network C for stocks primarily listed on Nasdaq; and Network B for stocks primarily listed on exchanges other than the NYSE and Nasdaq.

[30] Nasdaq declared self-help against NYSE Arca at approximately 2:37 p.m. (5 minutes prior to the main market disruption). BATS declared self-help against NYSE Arca at approximately 2:49 p.m. (after the E-Mini and SPY had reached their intra-day lows at 2:45 p.m.). *See* Section 3 for further details.

[31] Some market makers reported that they did not commonly use futures for equity hedging purposes.

[32] Stub quotes are quotes at unrealistically low or high prices that fulfill a market maker's obligation to provide continuous bids and offers, but at levels that the market maker does not expect to be reached under ordinary market conditions.

[33] *See infra* at Section 2.C for a discussion of generation of and executions against stub quotes.

[34] *See* Preliminary Report, at Figure 18 and accompanying text.

[35] The design of ETFs is intended to ensure that the market price of an ETF's shares generally track the ETF's net asset value (the value of its assets minus its liabilities), which can often be represented by a basket of securities. *See* Preliminary Report, Overview of ETFs, Appendix A at A-23.

[36] The sensitivity of a market maker's model to an underlying stock movement will dictate the speed at which a firm widens and/or pauses its quotations.

[37] As noted in the Preliminary Report, other characteristics often attributed to proprietary firms engaged in high frequency trading are: (1) the use of high-speed and sophisticated computer programs for generating, routing, and executing orders; (2) use of co-location services and individual data feeds offered by exchanges and others to minimize network and other types of latencies; (3) very short time-frames for establishing and liquidating positions; (4) the submission of numerous orders that are cancelled shortly after submission; and (5) ending the trading day in as close to a flat position as possible (that is, not carrying significant, unhedged positions overnight). *See* Preliminary Report.

[38] These firms were identified by FINRA as either engaging in high frequency trading strategies (such as electronic market making or statistical arbitrage), or providing trading access to other HFT firms. The FINRA Equity Trade Journal data contains information on reported trades from Nasdaq, the Nasdaq Trade Reporting Facility (TRF), and the Alternative Display Facility (ADF). As noted in the text, the FINRA data contains only a subset of all trading activity. If a market participant identifier of these high frequency trading firms is on either side of the trade report, we count that trade as a HFT trade. During the period from 9:31 a.m. to 2:45 p.m., the 12 HFTs were involved in 46% of the trades in the FINRA Equity Trade Journal data.

[39] Dark pools are alternative trading systems that do not provide their best-priced orders for inclusion in the consolidated quotation data. In general, dark pools offer trading services to institutional investors and others that seek to execute large trading interest in a manner that will minimize the movement of prices against their trading interest and thereby reduce trading costs.

[40] An OTC market maker will rarely route an actual customer order. Instead it will route a corresponding principal order and when it is executed, the market maker will execute the customer order on a riskless principal basis.

[41] EDGA and EDGX usually account for about 10% of consolidated volume. The other ECNs that report to a TRF account for a very small percentage of total volume.

[42] For a more in depth discussion of the options markets and OMM obligations, *see* Preliminary Report, at Appendix A-18.

[43] Exchange rules dictate that OMMs provide continuous two-sided quotations throughout the trading day in thousands of individual series. Although BATS and NOM permit trading in an options class without a registered market maker, if a market maker is registered in a class, that market maker is subject to continuous quoting obligations as prescribed by the exchange. *See id.*

[44] Most of the options exchanges have rules that impose a maximum bid/ask spread of $5, although NOM and BATS do not have maximum limits. Unlike the underlying markets, the options markets genrally do not allow for the publishing of stub quotes.

[45] *See* Preliminary Report at Appendix A-9 to A-10 for a historical discussion of stub quotes. In addition, the Exchange Act does not require a national securities exchange to have market makers. *See, e.g.* Securities Exchange Act Release Nos. 61698 (March 12, 2010), 75 FR 13151 (March 18, 2010) (order granting the exchange registration of EDGX and EDGA)

[46] *See, e.g.* Nasdaq Rule 4613; NYSE Arca Equities Rules 7.23 and 7.31(k); and BATS Rule 11.8.

[47] *See* Preliminary Report, at Tables 1 and 2.

[48] On September 10, 2010, the SEC approved new rules submitted by the national exchanges and FINRA that clarify the process for breaking erroneous trades. *See* Securities Exchange Act Release os. 62330 (June 21, 2010), 75 FR 36725 (June 28, 2010); 62331 (June 21, 2010), 75 FR 36746 (June 28, 2010); 62332 (June 21, 2010), 75 FR 36749 (June 28, 2010); 62333 (June 21, 2010), 75 FR 36759 (June 28, 2010); 62334 (June 21, 2010), 75 FR 36732 (June 28, 2010); 62336 (June 21, 2010), 75 FR 36743 (June 28, 2010); 62337 (June 21, 2010), 75 FR 36739 (June 28, 2010); 62338 (June 21, 2010), 75 FR 36762 (June 28, 2010); 62339 (June 21, 2010), 75 FR 36765 (June 28, 2010); 62340 (June 21, 2010), 75 FR 36768 (June 28, 2010); and 62342 (June 21, 2010), 75 FR 36752 (June 28, 2010); 62335 (June 21, 2010), 75 FR 37494 (June 29, 2010); and 62341 (June 21, 2010), 75 FR 36756 (June 28, 2010). The comment period for each of these proposals has been extended to September 10, 2010. *See* Securities Exchange Act Release Nos. 62797 (Aug. 30, 2010) and 62798 (Aug. 30, 2010).

[49] Reg. SHO imposes uniform order marking requirements for sales of all equity securities. Pursuant to Reg. SHO, an order can be marked "long" when the seller owns the security being sold and the security either is in the physical possession or control of the broker-dealer, or it is reasonably expected that the security will be in the physical possession or control of the broker or dealer no later than settlement. If a person does not own the security being sold, or owns the security sold but does not reasonably believe that the security will be in the possession or control of the broker-dealer prior to settlement, the sale must be marked "short." In the case of an internalizing broker-dealer that is facilitating a customer sell order where the customer is net long and the broker-dealer is net short, but is effecting the sale as principal or riskless principal, the broker-dealer must mark the principal leg of the transaction as short.

[50] *See* Section 3 for further details on the timing and potential effects of self-help declarations.

[51] LRPs are triggered much more frequently than the recently approved inter-market volatility trading pauses in individual stocks, which are triggered by a price movement of 10% or more over a five-minute period. *See* Securities Exchange Act Release No. 34-62252 (June 10, 2010), 75 FR 34186 (June 16, 2010).

[52] *See* Preliminary Report, Figure 9 and accompanying text.

[53] We note that spikes in the number of LRPs have also occurred in the past during periods of "ordinary" high market volatility in September-October 2008 and October-December 2009.

[54] *See* Preliminary Report, Table 4.

[55] There were no broken trades on NYSE because executions were not permitted outside the LRP bands.

[56] We estimated the available bid depth during the LRP by reference to the minimum of the bid depth resting on NYSE within 500 basis points from the mid-quote of the NBBO in the second prior to the LRP and a similar bid depth in the second after the conclusion of the LRP. We chose the minimum to account for orders being cancelled or executed during the LRP, in which case these quotes were not trapped.

[57] There were other declarations of self-help on May 6. Earlier in the day, several exchanges declared self-help against CBSX (the equity trading facility of the Chicago Board Options Exchange), but all of the declarations were revoked by 1:15 p.m. Subsequent to the Self-Help Declarations, National Stock Exchange ("NSX") declared self-help against the NYSE at 2:48:11 p.m. and against NYSE Arca at 2:51:11 p.m., BATS declared self-help against NYSE Arca at 2:49:17 p.m., and three broker-dealers declared self-help against NYSE Arca at 2:50:51 p.m. and after. We have not discussed these self-help declarations because they occurred before or after the general market disruption on May 6.

[58] The equities trading facility of Nasdaq OMX BX does not route equities to other market centers. *See* Securities Exchange Act Release No. 59154 (December 23, 2008), 73 FR 80468 (December 31, 2008).

[59] The term "trading center" is defined in Rule 600(b)(78) of Regulation NMS. It is broadly defined to include exchanges, alternative trading systems (including dark pools), exchange market makers, OTC market makers, and any other broker-dealers that execute trades internally.

[60] The term "trade-through" is defined in Rule 600(b)(77) of Regulation NMS as "the purchase or sale of an NMS stock during regular trading hours, either as principal or agent, at a price that is lower than a protected bid or higher than a protected offer."

[61] "Protected quotation" is defined in Rule 600(b)(58) as a protected bid or protected offer, and those terms are defined in Rule 600(b)(57) of Regulation NMS as, among other things, automated quotations (as defined in Rule 600(b)(3)) in NMS stocks that are displayed by a national securities exchange or a national securities association. On May 6, 2010, ten such entities were entitled to display protected quotations – BATS, CBSX, Chicago Stock Exchange, International Securities Exchange LLC, Nasdaq, Nasdaq OMX BX, NSX, NYSE, NYSE Amex, and NYSE Arca.

[62] Prior to adopting Regulation NMS, the SEC requested comment on whether to require protection of certain depth-of-book quotations. A large majority of commenters did not support depth-of-book protection because they believed it would unduly restrict competition among markets and be significantly more costly to implement than top-of-book protection. *See* Securities Exchange Act Release No. 51808 (June 9, 2005), 70 FR 37496, 37529-37530 (June 29, 2005) ("Regulation NMS Adopting Release").

[63] *See* Regulation NMS Adopting Release, *supra* note 64, at 37521.

[64] *See id.*, at 37521-37522.

[65] Although Nasdaq OMX BX does not route equities, its Self-Help Declaration still entitled it to trade-through NYSE Arca's quotation.

[66] NYSE informed us that it has since completed the upgrade to its systems.

[67] The CQS provides only the best bid and best offer per exchange. Bids and offers deeper in each exchange's books are not disseminated through CQS.

[68] *See* Preliminary Report, at 22.

[69] These exchanges, combined, reflect approximately 90% of the executions on exchanges on May 6. We note that BATS data is limited to five price points on either side of the mid-quote and as a result our analysis may understate the total available liquidity.

[70] These seven securities were chosen as typical examples representing patterns of liquidity observed in many individual stocks and ETFs on May 6. Some of these securities were previously discussed in the Preliminary Report. The data and discussions presented in the section are limited only to trading and liquidity on May 6, and no meaning should be construed about the companies themselves or their trading patterns on days other than May 6.

[71] It is important to note that limit orders that are more than 500 bp from the NBBO midquote include a very wide range of prices (including stub-quotes), and were probably viewed as unlikely to be executed. These orders may have been placed months prior to May 6.

In: The Stock Market Crash of 2010
Editor: Emma G. Peterson and Louise S. Weber
ISBN: 978-1-61122-959-2


*Chapter 2*

# PRELIMINARY FINDINGS REGARDING THE MARKET EVENTS OF MAY 6, 2010: REPORT OF THE STAFFS OF THE CFTC AND SEC TO THE JOINT ADVISORY COMMITTEE ON EMERGING REGULATORY ISSUES*

***U.S. Commodity Futures Trading Commission***

## I. INTRODUCTION

The Commodity Futures Trading Commission ("CFTC") and the Securities and Exchange Commission ("SEC" and collectively, the "Commissions") have established a Joint CFTC-SEC Advisory Committee on Emerging Regulatory Issues (the "Committee"). The establishment of the Committee was one of 20 recommendations included in the agencies' joint ization report issued last year.[1]

The first item on the agenda of the Committee will be to conduct a review of the market events of May 6 and to make recommendations related to market structure and liquidity issues that may have contributed to the volatility experienced on that day, as well as disparate trading conventions and rules across various markets.

This chapter to the Committee reflects the preliminary findings of the Commissions' their ongoing review of the events of Mayrespective staffs 6. The report is intended to brief the Committee regarding the May 6 events and to provide certain context regarding the current structure of the equity and futures markets and the regulatory framework for those markets.

This chapter includes: (a) an executive summary; (b) an overview providing general market context with respect to the events of May 6; (c) preliminary findings with respect to those events; and (d) areas for further analysis and initial next steps. In addition, this chapter contains several appendices providing relevant background regarding the market structure of the securities and futures markets.

---

* This is an edited, reformatted and augmented edition of a United States Commodity Futures Trading Commission and United States Securities & Exchange Commission, dated May 18, 2010.

It is important to emphasize that the review of the events of May 6 is in its preliminary stages and is ongoing. The reconstruction of even a few hours of trading during an extremely active trading day in markets as broad and complex as ours— involving thousands of products, millions of trades and hundreds of millions of data points—is an enormous undertaking. Although trading now occurs in microseconds, the framework and processes for creating, formatting, and collecting data across various types of market participants, products and trading venues is neither standardized nor fully automated. Once collected, this data must be carefully validated and analyzed. Such further data and analysis may substantially alter the preliminary findings presented in this chapter. The staffs of the Commissions therefore expect to supplement this chapter with further additional findings and analyses.

## II. Executive Summary

On May 6, 2010, the financial markets experienced a brief but severe drop in prices, falling more than 5% in a matter of minutes, only to recover a short time later. Since that day, the staffs of the Securities and Exchange Commission and the Commodity Futures Trading Commission have been collecting and reviewing massive amounts of information in order to understand the events and to recommend appropriate measures.

### Securities Markets

#### *Preliminary Findings*

May 6 started with unsettling political and economic news from overseas concerning the European debt crisis that led to growing uncertainty in the financial markets. Increased uncertainty during the day is corroborated by various market data: high volatility; a flight to quality among investors; and the increase in premiums for buying protection against default by the Greek government. This led to a significant, but not extraordinary, down day in early trading for the securities and futures markets.

Beginning shortly after 2:30 p.m.,[2] however, this overall decline in the financial markets suddenly accelerated. Within a matter of a few minutes, there was an additional decline of more than five percent in both the equity and futures markets. This rapid decline was followed by a similarly rapid recovery. This extreme volatility in the markets suggests the occurrence of a temporary breakdown in the supply of liquidity across the markets.

The decline and rebound of prices in major market indexes and individual securities on May 6 was unprecedented in its speed and scope. The whipsawing prices resulted in investors selling at losses during the decline and undermined confidence in the markets. Although evidence concerning the behavior of the financial markets on May 6, 2010 continues to be collected and reviewed, a preliminary picture is beginning to emerge.

At this point, we are focusing on the following working hypotheses and findings–

(1) possible linkage between the precipitous decline in the prices of stock index products such as index ETFs and the E-mini S&P 500 futures, on the one hand, and

simultaneous and subsequent waves of selling in individual securities, on the other, and the extent to which activity in one market may have led the others;

(2) a generalized severe mismatch in liquidity, as evinced by sharply lower trading prices and possibly exacerbated by the withdrawal of liquidity by electronic market makers and the use of market orders, including automated stop-loss market orders designed to protect gains in recent market advances;

(3) the extent to which the liquidity mismatch may have been exacerbated by disparate trading conventions among various exchanges, whereby trading was slowed in one venue, while continuing as normal in another;

(4) the need to examine the use of "stub quotes", which are designed to technically meet a requirement to provide a "two sided quote" but are at such low or high prices that they are not intended to be executed;

(5) the use of market orders, stop loss market orders and stop loss limit orders that, when coupled with sharp declines in prices, for both equity and futures markets, might have contributed to market instability and a temporary breakdown in orderly trading; and

(6) the impact on Exchange Traded Funds (ETFs), which suffered a disproportionate number of broken trades relative to other securities.

We have found no evidence that these events were triggered by "fat finger" errors, computer hacking, or terrorist activity, although we cannot completely rule out these possibilities.

### *Key Avenues for Further Investigation*

Much work is needed to determine all of the causes of the market disruption on May 6. At this stage, however, there are a number of key themes that we are investigating.

***Futures and Cash Market Linkages***. The first relates to the linkages between trading in equity index products, including stock index futures and the equity markets. About 250 executing firms processed transactions for thousands of accounts during the hour 2:00 p.m. – 3:00 p.m. in the E-Mini S&P 500 futures contract. Of these accounts, CFTC staff has more closely focused their examination to date on the top ten largest longs and top ten shorts. The vast majority of these traders traded on both sides of the market, meaning they both bought and sold during that period. One of these accounts was using the E-Mini S&P 500 contract to hedge and only entered orders to sell. That trader entered the market at around 2:32 and finished trading by around 2:51. The trader had a short futures position that represented on average nine percent of the volume traded during that period. The trader sold on the way down and continued to do so even as the price level recovered. This trader and others have executed hedging strategies of similar size previously.[3]

Data from the CME order book indicates that, although trading volume in E-mini S&P 500 futures was very high on May 6, there were many more sell orders than there were buy orders from 2:30 p.m. to 2:45 p.m. The data also indicate that the bid ask spread widened significantly at or about 2:45 p.m. and that certain active traders partially withdrew from the market. Considerable selling pressure at this vulnerable period in time may have contributed to declining prices in the E-Mini S&P 500 – and other equivalent products such as the SPY (an ETF that tracks the S&P 500).

All of these markets are closely linked by a complex web of traders and trading strategies. The precipitous decline in price in one market on May 6 may have influenced a sustained series of selling in other financial markets. The rapid rebound in price in one market could similarly have been linked to a rebound in price in another.

***Implications for the Equity Markets.*** The great majority of securities experienced declines that are generally consistent with the decline in value of the large indexes. Some were less than the approximately 5% decline in the E-mini S&P 500 during that period, and some were greater. Approximately 86% of securities, however, reached lows for the day that were less than 10% away from the 2:40 p.m. price.

The other 14% of securities suffered greater declines than the broader market, with some trading all the way down to one penny. The experience of these securities exposed potential weaknesses in the structure of the securities markets that must be addressed.

One hypothesis as to why the prices of some securities declined by abnormally large amounts on May 6 is that they were affected by disparate practices among securities exchanges. In the U.S. securities market structure, many different trading venues, including multiple exchanges, alternative trading systems and broker-dealers all trade the same stocks simultaneously. Disparate practices potentially could have hampered linkages among these trading venues and led to fragmented trading in some securities. Two types of disparate practices on May 6 relate to the NYSE's liquidity replenishment points ("LRPs") and the self-help remedy in Regulation NMS. These and other practices merit significant ongoing review:

- *LRPs and Similar Practices.* The NYSE's trading system incorporates LRPs that are intended to dampen volatility. When an LRP is triggered, trading on the NYSE will "go slow" and pause for a time to allow additional liquidity to enter the market. Some have suggested that LRPs actually exacerbated, rather than dampened, price volatility on May 6 by causing a net loss of liquidity, as orders were routed to other trading venues for immediate execution rather than waiting on the LRP mechanism. If this occurred, it potentially could have caused some NYSE securities to decline further than the broad market decline. However, others believe that the LRP mechanism indeed dampened volatility by rebuilding additional buy side liquidity that soaked up some of the excess selling interest in these securities on May 6. LRPs and other types of exchange procedures for handling or executing orders will be closely examined to determine whether they inappropriately impede liquidity.
- *Self-Help Remedy.* Another disparate exchange practice potentially relevant to the thinning of liquidity is the self-help remedy. Two exchanges declared self-help against NYSE Arca in the minutes prior to 2:40 p.m. Exchanges are entitled to exercise the self-help remedy when another exchange repeatedly fails to provide a response to incoming orders within one second. A declaration of self-help frees the declaring exchanges from their obligation to route orders to the affected exchange. Some have suggested the exercise of self-help led to a net loss of liquidity as the declaring exchanges stopped routing orders to NYSE Arca.

- *Stop Loss Market Orders.* An additional hypothesis as to why some securities suffered more severe declines than the broader market on May 6 is that they were particularly affected by stop loss market orders. These orders have stop prices that, for sell orders, are lower than current prices. When the stop price is reached, such orders turn into market orders to sell. In fast-falling market conditions, stop loss market orders could potentially trigger a chain reaction of automated selling if they are in place in significant quantity for a particular stock. We are investigating whether such a chain reaction led to abnormally large declines for some stocks on May 6.
- *Short Sales and Stub Quotes.* We also are examining the use of short sales and stub quotes on May 6. Our analysis thus far of broken trades has found that short sales accounted for approximately 70 % of executions against stub quotes between 2:45 p.m. and 2:50 p.m., and approximately 90 % of executions against stub quotes between 2:50 p.m. and 2:55 p.m. Notably, short sale executions against stub quotes would be subject to the alternative uptick rule (Rule 201) adopted by the SEC in February 2010, with a compliance date in November 2010.

In addition, we will evaluate the use of stub quotes by market makers. As noted above, stub quotes are not intended to be executed and effectively indicate that the market maker has pulled out of the market. Their presence at the bottom and top of order books on May 6 may have led to a very large number of broken trades. We will examine the extent to which market makers used stub quotes to nominally meet their market making obligations on May 6.

***Exchange-Traded Funds.*** Of the U.S.-listed securities with declines of 60% or more away from the 2:40 p.m. transaction prices, which resulted in their trades being cancelled by the exchanges, approximately 70% were ETFs. This suggests that ETFs as a class were affected more than any other category of securities.

Based on our analysis to date, we are focused on a number of issues that may have contributed to the ETFs' experience, including:

- Because ETFs generally track securities market indices, the extraordinary price declines in certain individual securities likely contributed to the ETF price declines. For the most part, the severe ETF price declines followed, in time, the sharp decline in the broad markets. ETFs that track bond indices generally did not experience severe price declines. We therefore are considering the linkages between ETF price declines and the declines in the equity market.
- The role of market makers and authorized participants in ETFs, and whether an inability to hedge their ETF positions during periods of severe volatility may have contributed to a lack of liquidity in ETF shares.
- The use of ETFs by institutional investors as a way to quickly acquire (or eliminate) broad market exposures and whether this investment strategy led to substantial selling pressure on ETFs as the market began to decline significantly.
- The impact of ETF stop loss market orders, particularly from retail investors, on the overall ETF market price declines.

- Given that NYSE Arca is the primary listing exchange for almost all ETFs, whether the declaration of "self-help" against NYSE Arca by other exchanges may have impacted NYSE Arca-listed stocks generally and ETFs in particular. The loss of access to NYSE Arca's liquidity pool may have had a greater impact on market liquidity and trading for ETFs.

## Futures Markets

### *Preliminary Findings*

Economic evidence from the futures markets is also consistent with the conclusion that a liquidity drain likely played a role in the dramatic and sudden movements in the price of stock index futures.

As noted above, preliminary data indicates that, although trading volume in E-mini S&P 500 futures was very high on May 6, there were many more sell orders than there were buy orders from 2:30 p.m. to 2:45 p.m. The data also indicate that the bid ask spread widened significantly at or about 2:45 p.m. and that certain active traders partially withdrew from the market.

Starting at 2:45:28 p.m., CME's Globex stop logic functionality initiated a brief pause in trading in the E-mini S&P 500 futures. This functionality is initiated when the last transaction price would have triggered a series of stop loss orders that, if executed, would have resulted in a cascade in prices outside a predetermined 'no bust' range (6 points in either direction in the case of the E-mini). The purpose of this functionality is to prevent sudden, cascading declines (or increases) in price caused by order book imbalances.

The stop logic functionality has been activated previously for a variety of instruments. In the case of the E-mini S&P 500 futures, the stop logic functionality has been triggered a number of times in the past few years, including several times during the financial crisis in the Fall of 2008, when market data indicates similar conditions as those seen on May 6.

On May 6, activation of the stop logic functionality initiated a five second pause in trading on the E-mini S&P 500 futures contract. The price of the E-mini S&P 500 futures rebounded after the five second pause imposed by the stop logic functionality.

Staff analysis of market performance measures is consistent with the conclusion that a very temporary, but serious liquidity shortage occurred across the securities and futures markets.

## Next Steps

### *Securities Markets*

SEC staff will continue our ongoing investigation of the nature of the overall market liquidity dislocation and the impact on individual stocks. Where appropriate we are moving quickly to prevent a recurrence of the harm that investors suffered on May 6.

- We anticipate that the self-regulatory organizations (exchanges and FINRA) will propose circuit breakers for individual stocks that are designed to address temporary liquidity dislocation. Specifically, a pause in trading should provide an opportunity for all available sources of liquidity (both manual and automated) to be mobilized to meet sudden surges in demand for liquidity.

- The procedures for breaking trades that occur at off-market prices should be improved to provide investors greater consistency, transparency and predictability.
- We are also continuing to review a range of other policy options, including addressing the use of stub quotes, reviewing the obligations of professional liquidity providers and evaluating the use of various order types (market orders, stop loss orders).

### *Futures Markets*

CFTC staff will continue its analysis into the events of May 6. Specifically, CFTC staff is carefully reviewing the activity of the largest traders in stock index futures.

CFTC staff will also continue its analysis, already begun by our Office of Chief Economist, of liquidity provision in futures markets, with a particular focus on electronic trading. The subjects to be reviewed here include high frequency and algorithmic trading, automatic execution innovations on trading platforms, market access issues, and co-location.

CFTC staff is considering a proposed rulemaking with respect to exchange co-location and proximity hosting services. The purpose of the proposed rule would be to ensure that all otherwise qualified and eligible market participants that seek co-location or proximity hosting services offered by futures exchanges have equal access to such services without barriers that exclude access, or that bar otherwise qualified third-party vendors from providing co-location and/or proximity hosting services. Another purpose of the proposal would be to ensure that futures exchanges that offer co-location or proximity hosting services disclose publically the latencies for each available connectivity option, so that participants can make informed decisions.

CFTC staff will also be considering possible rules to enhance the CFTC's surveillance capabilities. These measures include automation of the statement of reporting traders in the large trader reporting system and obtaining account ownership and control information in the exchange trade registers.[4] These initiatives would increase the timeliness and efficiency of account identification, an essential step in data analysis.

### *Joint Actions*

- Staff also intends to pursue a joint study to examine the linkages between correlated assets in the equities (single stocks, mutual funds and ETFs), options and futures markets. The study could partly focus on examining cross-market linkages by analyzing trading in stock index products such as equity index futures, ETFs, equity index options, and equity index OTC derivatives using, to the extent practicable, market data, special call information, and order book data.
- Existing cross-market circuit breaker provisions should be re-examined to ensure they continue to be effective in today's fast paced electronic trading environment. Although the coordinated circuit breakers between futures and equities were not triggered, the events of May 6 reinforce the importance of having communication

links between futures and equity markets so that there is meaningful and appropriate coordination of trading pauses and halts.

## Process of Analysis

Over the last ten days, the SEC and the CFTC have collected and analyzed a wide range of data from many different sources in order to prepare this preliminary report. Specifically:

- The SEC has sourced and analyzed price, time, and volume data on over 19 billion shares executed on May 6, and quote data representing the best bid and best offer for over 7,800 securities, for each exchange, for each millisecond during the trading day. Our goal is to gather data necessary to create a complete order book showing snap-shots of the full displayable depth on a particular market and audit trail data containing detailed information on all orders submitted.
  - Analysis of the complete order book is necessary to examine how changes in the provision of liquidity below the best bid, and above the best offer, led to rapid changes in execution prices, with some trades hitting high and low "stub quotes."
  - Analysis of order audit trail data is necessary to examine what types of orders were driving these price swings (e.g., market, limit, etc).
  - The audit trail contains information on introducing brokers but does not include details regarding the trading activity of specific market participants. Currently, such data is only available directly from broker-dealers through "blue sheet" requests. Furthermore, even in this data participants are identified only in the way that they are known to the broker-dealer, as there are currently no uniform standards[5]
  - The order book and order audit trail are maintained at exchanges, FINRA, broker-dealers and other market centers. In some cases this information must be collected by the SROs, and then must be compiled and organized by the SEC. Every exchange has established its own requirements for what constitutes an audit trail, including what items are captured, how they are named, and the structure of the data file.
- The SEC has sourced and analyzed aggregate data on the volume and type of liquidity, provided and taken, by the largest liquidity providers and takers on various exchanges.
- The SEC has worked extensively with the relevant securities exchanges and FINRA to assess the circumstances of the market events on May 6. In addition, the SEC is analyzing detailed data for all *NYSE LRPs* occurring on May 6th, as well as over the last 5 months.
- CFTC staff has analyzed transaction and order book data on stock index futures, including the E-Mini S&P 500 futures contract.
- CFTC staff has been reviewing information from a special call on over 40 large traders for their trading activity in the E-mini S&P 500 and Russell 2000 futures contracts on May 6, 2010. A special call is a CFTC directive to a trader holding a

reportable position to furnish any pertinent information concerning the trader's positions, transactions, or activities.

- CFTC staff also has been reviewing information from a special call to swap dealers about their activity in over-the-counter broad-based security index derivatives markets on May 6, 2010. In addition, staff has been engaged in a detailed review of trader activity on May 6 through a comprehensive examination of trade-register data. To date, staff has received over 25 gigabytes of data in over 307,000 files, with more data expected.

Both the CFTC and the SEC have had extensive conversations with a wide variety of market participants (investors, hedge funds, exchange traded funds, dealers, high frequency traders, etc.) to better understand their trading activities throughout May 6, and to gather *anecdotal evidence* from which common themes and/or trends can be identified to inform further areas of investigation.

## III. General Market Context

This section provides general market context for the trading activity on May 6.

Throughout the day on Thursday, May 6, many financial news outlets were reporting on political and economic events that were creating uncertainty in the financial markets. This increased uncertainty during that day is evidenced by patterns observable in financial market data. There is evidence of increasing volatility throughout the day, a "flight to quality"[6] (as seen in the rise in the price of gold and decline in U.S. Treasury yields), an increase in the price of premiums on credit default swaps to protect against the risk of default on European sovereign debt, and downward pressure on the Euro in global currency markets.

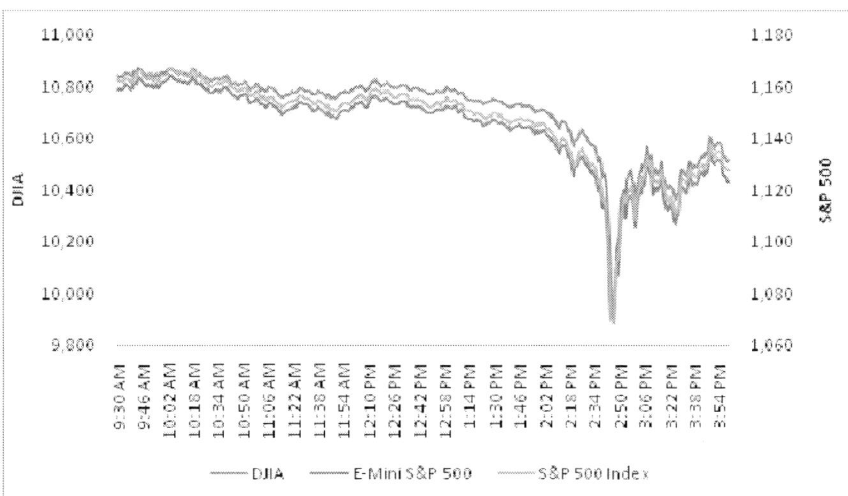


Source: Bloomberg

Figure 1. Select Equity Indices and Equity Index Futures, May 6, 2010

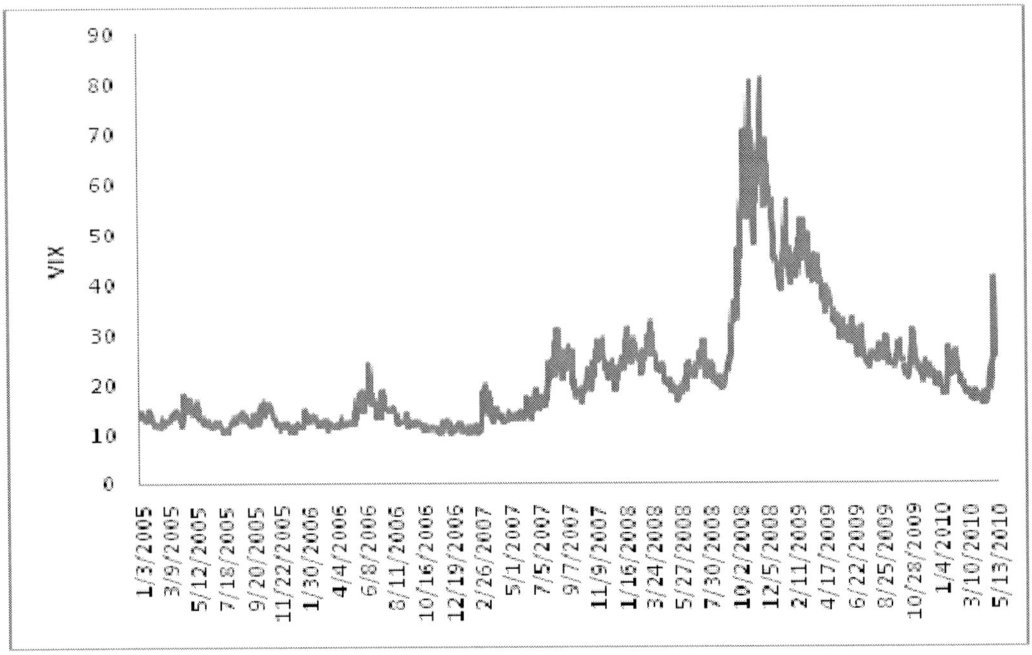


Source: Bloomberg

Figure 2. Historical Daily VIX Values, January 2005 to May 2010

All major broad-based equity indices and equity index futures spent much of the morning and early afternoon in negative territory (see chart below). For example, between 9:30 a.m. and 2:00 p.m., the Dow Jones Industrial Average (DJIA) declined 161 points to 10,712 (-1.5%), the S&P 500 Index declined 33 points to 1,145 (-2.9%), and the E-mini S&P 500 Index June futures declined 15 points to 1,143 (-1.3%).

## Indicators of Market Uncertainty

*Market Volatility*

A general indicator of market uncertainty is the Chicago Board Options Exchange SPX Volatility Index ("VIX"). The VIX is a measure of the expected volatility of the S&P 500 index, based on options prices, and is sometimes colloquially referred to as the "fear index." The VIX provides a picture of the expected range of S&P 500 index returns in the next 30 days. Higher values of the VIX imply a greater range of returns, both positive and negative. Thus, increases in the VIX signal increased uncertainty about possible stock returns.

As seen in Figure 2, in 2010 the VIX prior to May 6 has averaged 19.58, a level that indicates much lower expected market volatility when compared to the VIX averages of 2008 (32.69) and 2009 (31.48). The elevated VIX levels from 2008 and 2009 were associated with a broader financial market crisis. Since then, the average level of the VIX has returned to levels that are consistent with the pre-2008 period. For example, in April the VIX averaged 17.42. For the month of May through May 14 the VIX has averaged28.33.

On May 6, the VIX opened at 25.88. This represents a 15.5% increase from when the trading week began on Monday, May 3 at 22.41. After staying level for most of the day, the VIX began to rise around 1:30 p.m. At 2:00 p.m. the VIX had increased 2.72 points or 10.5%

from its opening level, signaling increasing expected volatility in the S&P 500 Index. Over the next half-hour, the VIX steadily increased an additional 3.11 points to 31.71, up 22.5% from the open. A nearly continuous rise in the VIX signals higher levels of expected market risk and uncertainty going forward. The increase in the VIX then accelerated and the index reached 40.26 by 2:46 p.m. Had markets closed at the 2:46 p.m. level of 40.26, it would have represented a 61.6% increase from the previous day's close and would represent the fourth largest single-day increase in market volatility. Ultimately, the VIX closed at 32.80, a 31.7% increase from the previous day's close.[7]

*Flight to Quality*

Gold and U.S. Treasuries are assets that have historically been in high demand during periods of market uncertainty. On May 6, the COMEX nearby gold futures contract rose steadily from approximately $1,180 to $1,210 per troy ounce from the market open to its close at 1:30 p.m. Additionally, the ten-year Treasury yield fell from 3.58% on May 5 to an intraday low of 3.26% before settling at 3.41% (see Figure 4).

Source: Bloomberg

Figure 3. CBOE SPX Volatility Index Intraday Levels

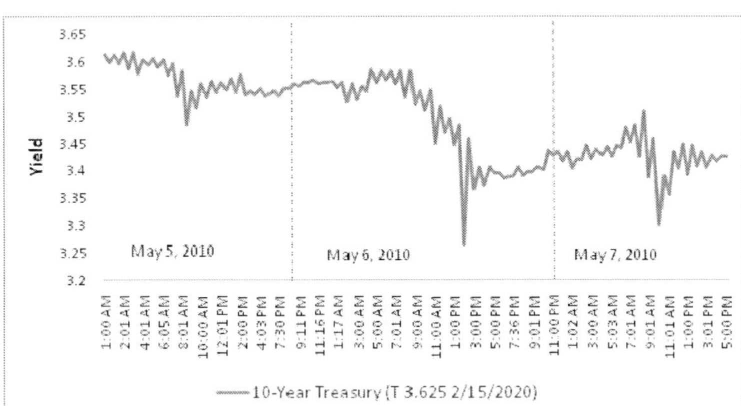


Source: Bloomberg

Figure 4. TenYear U.S. Treasury Note Yield

*Credit Default Swaps*

The credit derivatives markets indicated increased uncertainty over the ability of the government of Greece to service its debt. Spreads on CDS protecting against the default of debt securities issued by Greece widened on May 6 to 937.9 basis points, up from 844.2 basis points the previous day.[8] This essentially meant that the price of premiums to protect against a default by Greece had increased. This widening coincided with the European Central Bank's press conference, beginning at 8:30a.m., in which the Bank did not address the possibility of purchasing Greek government bonds. Figure 5 shows CDS spreads on Greek sovereign debt over the past five years.

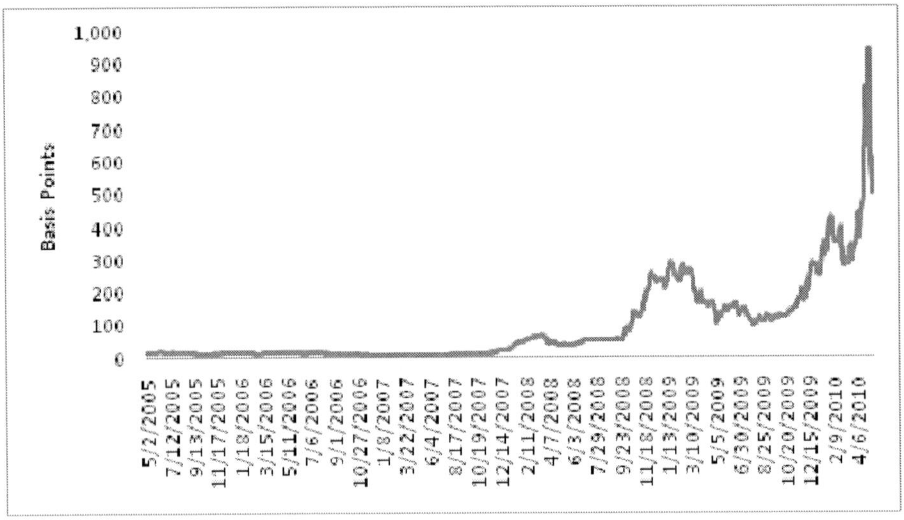


Source: Bloomberg

Figure 5. Credit Default Spreads on Greek Sovereign Debt

Source: Bloomberg

Figure 6. EuroDollar and Euro Yen Exchange Rates on May 6, 2010

*Euro Declines Against the Dollar and Yen*

In addition, global currency markets were indicating concern over the financial stability of the European Union. Shortly after 1:00 p.m., the Euro began a sharp decline against both the U.S. Dollar and the Japanese Yen (see Figure 6).

*Events During the Afternoon of May 6*

By approximately 2:45 p.m. over 200 securities had fallen 50% or more from their 2:00 p.m. levels. Between 2:45 p.m. and 2:47p.m., the DJIA, S&P 500, and NASDAQ100 all reached daily lows. During this same period, all 30 DJIA components reached their intraday minima, representing a range from -4% to -36% from their opening levels. The DJIA bottomed at 9,872.57, the S&P 500 at 1,065.79, and the NASDAQ100 at 1,752.31. The E-mini S&P 500 index futures contract bottomed at 1,056.

After bottoming, equity and equity index futures markets began to rebound. At 2:50 p.m. the DJIA was trading at 10,232 and the E-mini S&P 500 was trading at 1,096. The E-mini S&P 500 climbed further to 1,118 by 2:53 p.m. The DJIA closed at 10,520.32, down 347.68 points, or 3.2%, from the prior day's close. The E-mini S&P 500 settled at 1,122.5, down 41.5 points, or 3.6%, from the prior day's settlement.

# IV. Preliminary Findings

## A. Securities Markets

The market events of May 6, 2010 included a surge in trading in the stock markets, with total trading volume on that day of 19.4 billion shares, approximately 2.2 times the average daily trading volume in the 4th quarter of 2009. The trading volume in NYSE-listed stocks across all trading venues on May 6 represented the second highest daily volume on record, while May 6 volume in NASDAQ-listed stocks across all trading venues was the highest on record.

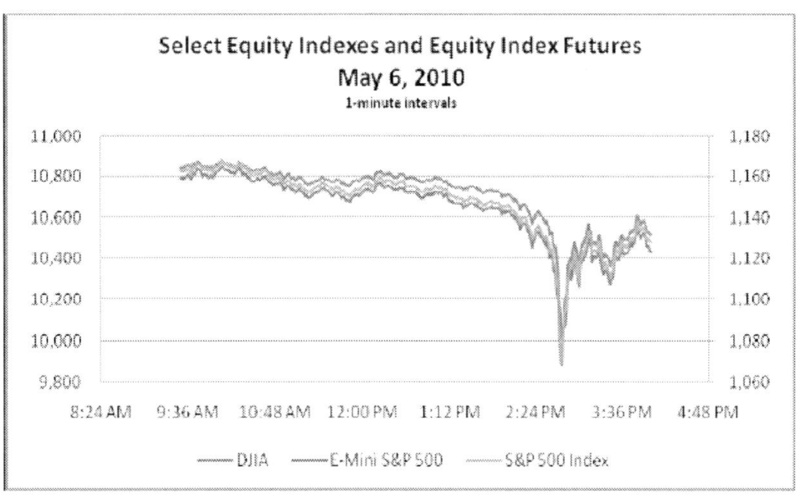


Figure 7. Equity Indices and Equity Index Futures

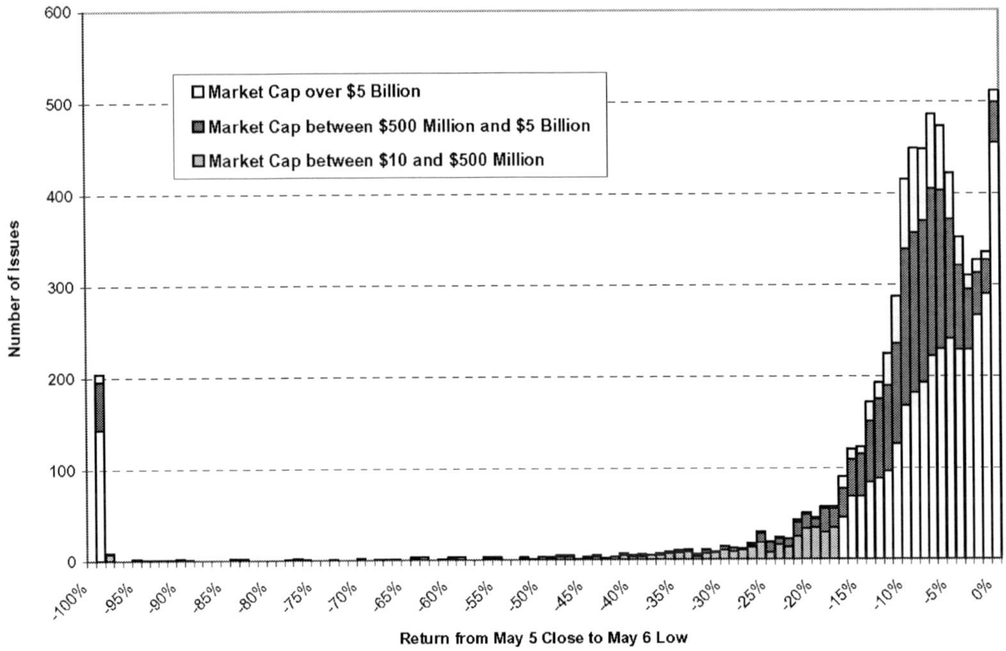


Sources: Thomson Financial Datastream and NYSE Trades and Quotes.

Figure 8. Distribution of May 6 Daily Lows[9]

The severe price decline and recovery that occurred during a period of approximately 20 minutes on the afternoon of May 6 can usefully be described in terms of two broad but related themes: (1) a precipitous drop in value of more than 5% followed immediately by a rapid recovery, both of which occurred consistently across various broad market indices and products; and (2) extreme price fluctuations – mostly losses – that occurred for certain individual securities, followed relatively promptly by reversions to price levels consistent with the broader market. These two themes are discussed below.

### *1. Broader Market Drop and Recovery*

On May 6, a wide variety of broad market indices and products displayed similar behavior – a severe price decline immediately followed by a rapid recovery during a 20-minute period. This phenomenon is illustrated by the following price chart of the DJIA, the S&P 500 Index, and the E-mini S&P 500 futures (Figure 7).

Until approximately 2:40 p.m., the figure reflects a significant, but not extraordinary, down day that was influenced by multiple negative economic factors, as noted in the previous section. At approximately 2:40 p.m., however, prices declined with extraordinary velocity. Each of the indices fell in excess of 5% within 5 minutes, and then immediately began a recovery that exceeded 5% within 10 minutes.

Most individual stocks declined by amounts that were generally consistent with the broader market decline. Approximately 86% of U.S.-listed securities reached lows for the day that were less than 10% away from the 2:40 p.m. price (a useful benchmark for the market price before the rapid market decline and recovery). The remaining 14% of U.S.-listed securities reached lows that exceeded 10% (these securities are discussed in greater detail in section IV.A.2 below).

Figure 8 illustrates in more detail the behavior of these two groups of individual securities. It shows that, for the day, there is a concentration of daily lows at a point near 7% below the May 5 close, on the right-hand side of the graph. The distribution of lows for individual securities around this point is consistent with a day where the ETF that tracks the S&P 500 Index transacted 8.5% below the previous day's close. The figure notably also shows that some securities exhibited substantially more pronounced daily lows than the decline in the broad market would imply. In particular, approximately 200 securities traded, at their lows, almost 100% below their previous day's values, as represented by the spike at the left-hand side of the graph. The incidence of extreme daily lows for large capitalization stocks (depicted on the graph in yellow) appears to be lower than for smaller capitalization stocks (depicted in the graph in purple).

An examination of individual trades during the 2:40 p.m. - 3:00 p.m. period reveals a similar pattern. Table 1 and Table 2 below report the total number of trades, the total share volume and total dollar volume for trades executed between 2:40 p.m. and 3:00 p.m., for losses and gains, respectively. The losses/gains are computed as the difference between the trade price and the 2:40 p.m. price, divided by the 2:40 p.m. price, for each stock. The data do not include out-of-sequence trades.[10] Table 1 indicates that most investors that sold during this period transacted at prices that were within -10% away from the 2:40 p.m. price. Approximately 4.9 million, or 98%, of the trades that were executed during this period at prices less than the 2:40 p.m. price were within -10% of the 2:40 p.m. price. Approximately 102,000 trades were executed during the decline and recovery at prices that were -10% or more away from the 2:40 p.m. price; these trades are discussed in section IV.A.2 below. We see a similar pattern in Dow stocks. Four out of 30 (about 13%) had returns that were less (more negative) than -10%. Table 3 indicates the lowest trade price executed for each of the Dow Jones Industrial Average component stocks and the return computed against the stock's 2:40 p.m. trade price. Of these stocks, four, Proctor& Gamble (PG), 3M (MMM), Hewlett-Packard (HPQ), and General Electric (GE), traded at a loss of over 10%, relative to the 2:40 p.m. price.

**Table 1. Trades Executed at a Loss**

| | Total # trades | Total volume | Total volume ($) |
|---|---|---|---|
| All trades | 7,135,104 | 1,995,000,637 | 56,651,582,692 |
| Losses | 5,013,724 | 1,358,709,226 | 38,047,617,508 |
| 0% to -10% | 4,912,125 | 1,324,448,213 | 37,383,122,363 |
| -10% to -20% | 63,890 | 22,171,745 | 522,444,343 |
| -20% to 30% | 12,923 | 4,077,881 | 85,328,519 |
| -30% to -40% | 6,112 | 2,317,245 | 30,461,333 |
| -40% to -50% | 2,519 | 767,393 | 9,641,261 |
| -50% to -60% | 1,682 | 472,624 | 8,334,944 |
| -60% to -70% | 1,056 | 370,920 | 4,328,898 |
| -70% to -80% | 798 | 292,061 | 2,245,851 |
| -80% to -90% | 1,109 | 237,259 | 1,152,480 |
| -90% to -100% | 11,510 | 3,553,885 | 557,516 |

Both aspects of the 20-minute phenomenon—the effects on the broad market and the even more extreme effects on a minority of securities—warrant serious analysis, given the potential harm to investor confidence and the realized losses of investors. Although the state of our fact-gathering makes any analysis at this time too preliminary to draw firm conclusions—or even many tentative ones—about how and why the events of May 6 occurred, the facts we have and the analysis we have completed thus far do offer a few clues to the origins of the May 6 event.

We are in the process of obtaining and reviewing the order book and the data necessary to reconstruct the order audit trail for the various equity exchanges and electronic communications networks ("ECNs") in the hope of being able to determine whether order book liquidity substantially thinned immediately prior to 2:40 p.m. For example, based on some preliminary data, there may be reason to believe that there may have been a thinning of order book liquidity at one significant exchange at around 2:00 p.m.

The temporary nature of the decline in prices in the broader market may be indicative of a failure in liquidity. As we will show, many individual securities exhibited more extreme temporary price movements than the broad market, consistent with a broader set of liquidity failures. The discussion that follows focuses on a key issue on May 6 – the interaction between liquidity demand and supply. A temporary price dislocation could be caused by an unusually high demand for liquidity, by an unusually weak supply of liquidity, or by some combination of these factors. Our preliminary analysis indicates that both of these factors may be at play. In this section, we focus on questions that bear on this central issue.

NYSE's trading system incorporates LRPs that are intended to dampen volatility in a given stock by temporarily converting from an automated market to a manual auction market when a price movement of a sufficient size is reached. In such case, trading on the NYSE will "go slow" and pause for a time period to allow an opportunity for additional liquidity to enter the market. During an LRP, the NYSE will display a quotation that is not immediately accessible and can be bypassed, but is not required to be bypassed, by other trading venues and order routers.

**Table 2 Trades Executed at a Gain**

| | Total # trades | Total volume | Total volume ($) |
|---|---:|---:|---:|
| All trades | 7,135,104 | 1,995,000,637 | 56,651,582,692 |
| Gains | 2,121,380 | 636,291,411 | 18,603,965,183 |
| 0% to 10% | 2,108,076 | 632,378,310 | 18,079,956,948 |
| 10% to 20% | 10,075 | 3,039,456 | 53,123,704 |
| 20% to 30% | 927 | 281,383 | 8,589,789 |
| 30% to 40% | 517 | 167,439 | 1,827,449 |
| 40% to 50% | 106 | 32,866 | 536,641 |
| 50% to 60% | 45 | 19,188 | 358,048 |
| 60% to 70% | 67 | 14,466 | 387,321 |
| 70% to 80% | 184 | 46,456 | 1,147,215 |
| 80% to 90% | 178 | 44,075 | 1,143,755 |
| > 90% | 1,205 | 267,772 | 456,894,313 |

Figure 9 compares the May 6 LRP profile on the NYSE with the average profile of such events during 2010. The figure indicates the number of securities that triggered an LRP event lasting more than 1 second during any given 30-minute period. The blue blocks, reported first in the series, represent the average number of securities meeting this criterion from January 4, 2010 through May 6, 2010. The yellow blocks, reported second in the series, represent the LRP events on May 6, 2010 itself.

Figure 9 shows a substantial increase in the number of securities with LRPs on the NYSE starting in the period from 1:00 p.m. to 1:30 p.m. and rising to more than 200 in the period from 2:00 p.m. to 2:30 p.m. Between 2:30 and 3:00 pm, the level rose to approximately 1,000. This significant rise in LRPs could be indicative of a thinning of order book liquidity at the NYSE.

**Table 3. Maximum Trade Loss for Dow 30 Stocks**

| Company | Return | Low Price | Time |
|---|---|---|---|
| The Proctor& Gamble Company | -36.14% | $39.37 | 2:47:15 PM |
| 3M Company | -18.39% | $67.98 | 2:46:06 PM |
| Hewlett-Packard Company | -11.81% | $41.94 | 2:46:13 PM |
| General Electric Company | -10.23% | $15.00 | 2:46:11 PM |
| Merck & Company Incorporated | -9.23% | $30.70 | 2:46:11 PM |
| Exxon Mobil Corporation | -8.74% | $58.46 | 2:46:52 PM |
| E.I. Du Pont De Nemours | -8.13% | $33.66 | 2:46:29 PM |
| Cisco Systems Incorporated | -7.52% | $23.23 | 2:45:33 PM |
| The Walt Disney Company | -7.49% | $31.00 | 2:45:45 PM |
| United Technologies Corporation | -7.42% | $65.17 | 2:46:38 PM |
| International Business Machines Corporation | -7.20% | $116.00 | 2:46:33 PM |
| Chevron Corporation | -7.18% | $71.50 | 2:47:03 PM |
| Intel Corporation | -6.09% | $19.90 | 2:47:30 PM |
| The Boeing Company | -5.89% | $62.00 | 2:45:42 PM |
| Verizon Communications | -5.73% | $26.49 | 2:45:48 PM |
| Johnson & Johnson | -5.70% | $60.03 | 2:46:10 PM |
| Kraft Foods Incorporated | -5.21% | $27.49 | 2:47:59 PM |
| Home Depot Incorporated | -5.06% | $32.07 | 2:45:57 PM |
| Pfizer Incorporated | -4.64% | $15.85 | 2:46:06 PM |
| Caterpillar Incorporated | -4.50% | $58.00 | 2:45:33 PM |
| American Express Company | -4.47% | $40.16 | 2:45:52 PM |
| Alcoa Incorporated | -4.34% | $11.25 | 2:47:35 PM |
| Microsoft Corporation | -4.16% | $27.91 | 2:46:39 PM |
| AT&T Incorporated | -3.88% | $24.04 | 2:46:04 PM |
| Wal-Mart Stores Incorporated | -3.74% | $51.53 | 2:45:29 PM |
| Bank of America Corporation | -3.55% | $15.50 | 2:46:36 PM |
| The Coca Cola Company | -3.47% | $51.21 | 2:47:23 PM |
| McDonalds Corporation | -3.43% | $67.49 | 2:47:53 PM |
| JP Morgan Chase & Company | -2.51% | $39.29 | 2:45:45 PM |
| The Travelers Companies Incorporated | -2.31% | $48.53 | 2:45:46 PM |

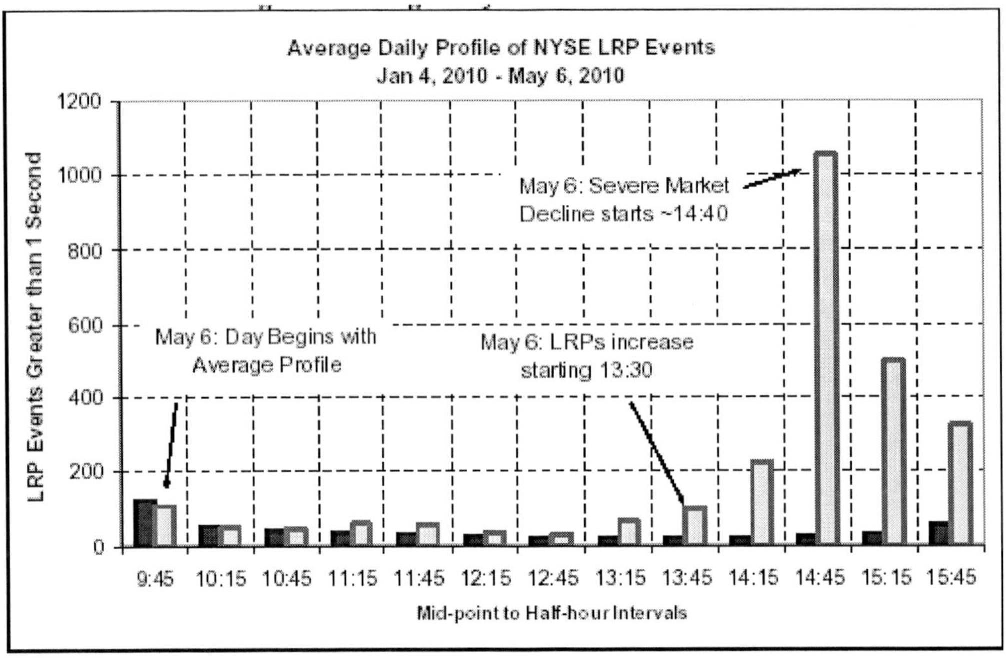


Source: NYSE

Figure 9. Average Daily Profile of NYSE LRP Events

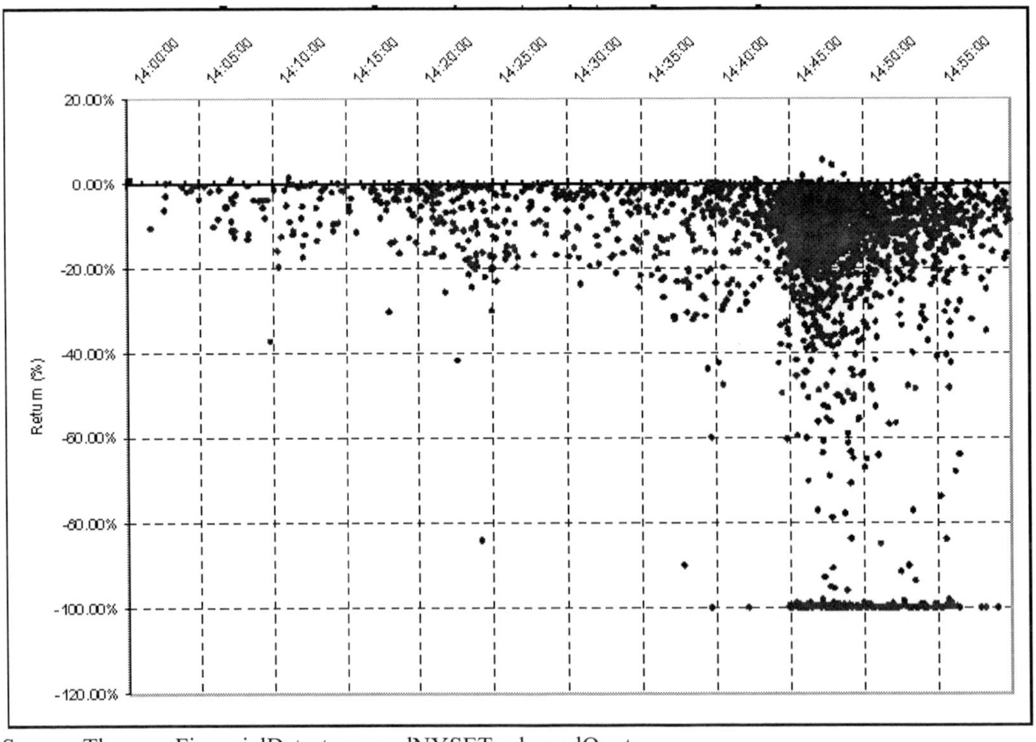


Source: ThomsonFinancialDatastreamandNYSETradesandQuote

Figure10. Timing of Daily Lows, May 6, 2:00pm to 3:00pm[11]

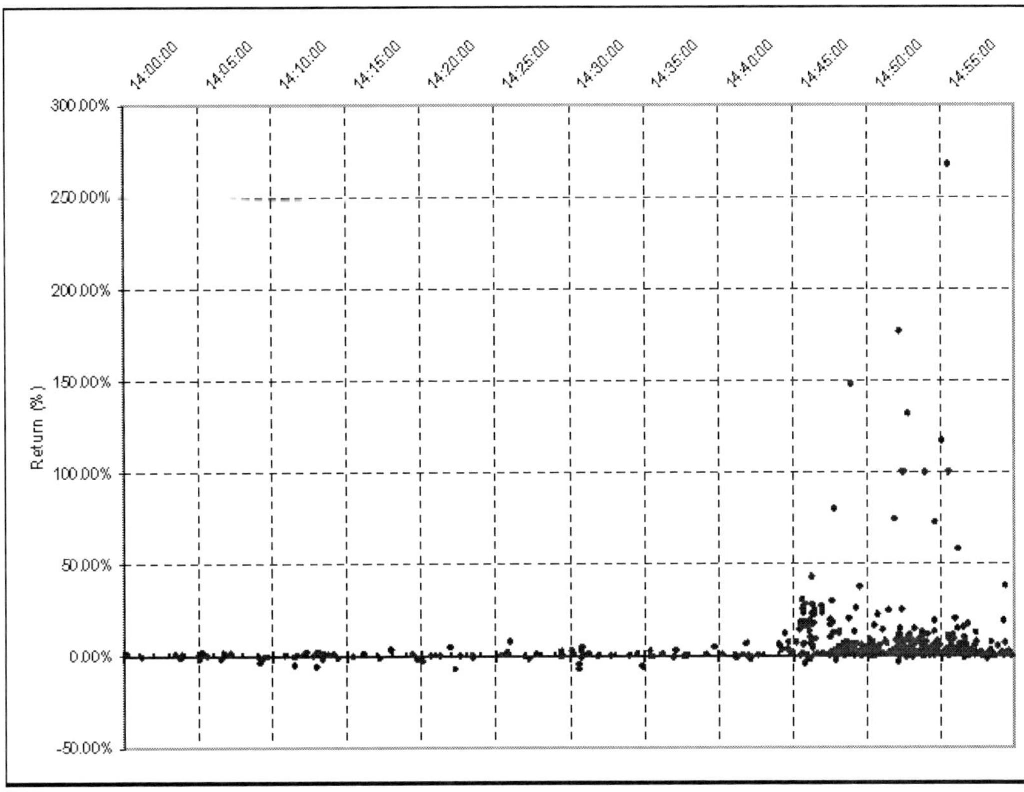


Sources: Thomson Financial Datastream and NYSE Trades and Quote

Figure 11. Timing of Daily Highs, May 6, 2:00 p.m. to 3:00 p.m.[12]

Finally, Figure 10 shows a scatter plot of the time and percentage decline for all securities that realized their daily low measured from May 5 close to their May 6 low during the period between 2:00 p.m. and 3:00 p.m. Each point on the plot represents one stock, the time of day it executed a trade at its lowest trade price of the day, and the return from the previous night's close to that trade price. It shows a steady increase in the number of securities with daily lows throughout the hour.

While a large number of securities experienced extreme low trades during the 2:00 p.m. to 3:00 p.m. interval, a smaller but still significant number of securities experienced extreme highs. Figure 11 indicates positive returns on May 6, excluding a few stocks for scaling reasons. The figure shows that a significant number of securities experienced daily highs more than 25% higher than their close on May 5. These extreme highs were concentrated after 2:44 p.m. Unlike the lows depicted in Figure 10, which began to occur in the early part of the hour, there appear to be no extreme highs occurring prior to 2:44 p.m.

Another factor potentially relevant to the thinning of liquidity is the declaration of self-help by NASDAQ against NYSE Arca at 2:37 p.m., and by NASDAQ OMX BX against NYSE Arca at 2:38 p.m. We have not yet evaluated the basis for the exercise of self-help against NYSE Arca. Under Regulation NMS, exchanges are entitled to exercise self-help when another exchange repeatedly fails to provide a response to incoming orders within one second. The direct effect of a declaration of self-help is that the declaring exchanges will no longer route orders to the affected exchange. We are not aware, however, that any broker-dealer or any other exchange declared self-help against NYSE Arca prior to the time the broad market indexes reached their daily lows.[13] Consequently, the broker-dealers and other exchanges that wished to access NYSE Arca quotes would have been likely to route orders directly to NYSE Arca (and therefore would not have been affected by a self-help declaration), rather than trying to access those quotes indirectly through NASDAQ or NASDAQ OMX BX. Accordingly, we are evaluating the extent to which the declaration of self-help by the two exchanges against NYSE Arca prior to 2:40 p.m. could have caused a significant thinning of available liquidity.

Another interesting question remains as to whether electronic liquidity providers pulled back during the relevant timeframe. At approximately 2:40 p.m. on May 6, prices declined rapidly across many trading venues and products. The activities of electronic liquidity providers are important subjects for analysis. These proprietary trading firms have come to be the dominant type of liquidity provider in the U.S. equity markets. Consequently, we are analyzing their activities on May 6. As noted above, we are in the process of obtaining and reviewing the order book data of exchanges and ECNs. We have, in the meantime, obtained other data from the exchanges concerning the activity of their top ten liquidity providing firms from 2:00 p.m. to 3:00 p.m. We continue to analyze these data to assess the activity of these liquidity providing firms. Some initial findings based on these data are set forth in Figure 12 and Figure 13below.[14]

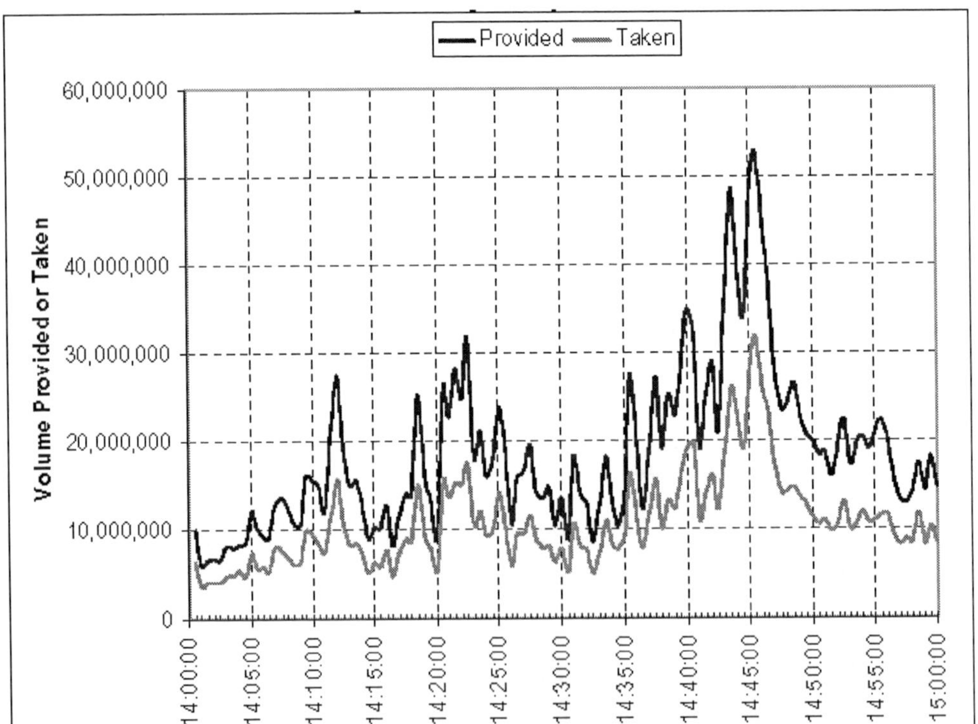


Source: All data was provided by the exchanges

Figure 12. Liquidity Provided/Taken by Top 10 Liquidity Providers Across All Equity Markets2:00 p.m. -3: 00 p.m. May 6, 2010[15]

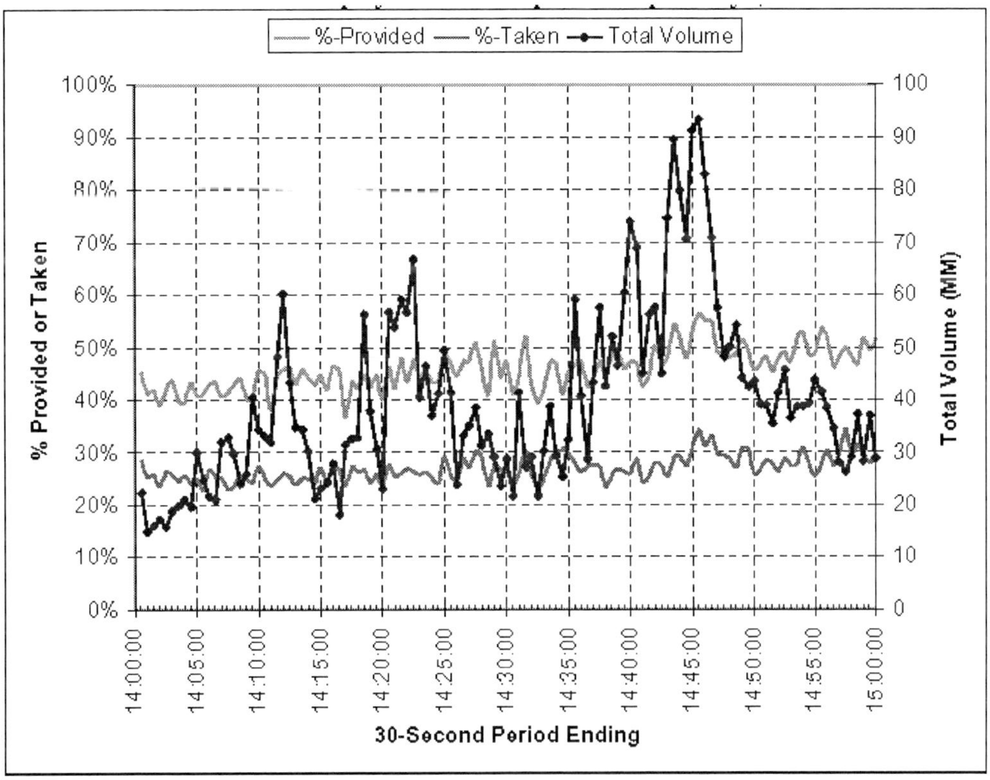


Sources: Liquidity data provided by the exchanges; total volume from NYSE Trades and Quotes.

Figure 13. Percent of Liquidity Provided/Taken by Top 10 Liquidity Providers against Total Volume Across all Equity Markets 2:00 p.m. – 3:00 p.m. May 6, 2010[16]

Figure 12 shows the share volume of aggregate liquidity provided and removed for all stocks by the top 10 firms for all of the exchanges between 2:00 p.m. and 2:59 p.m. Figure 13 shows the percentage of liquidity provided and removed against the total volume across all equity markets. Figure 12 and Figure 13 could indicate that, collectively, these particular firms appear to have remained net liquidity providers throughout this period and that they increased their liquidity provision, both in terms of share volume and percentage of total volume, when total volume increased at approximately 2:40 p.m. We note, however, that the underlying data provided by the exchanges as the source for these figures are also consistent with significant variations in the activities of different liquidity providers during this period. In addition, it should be noted that Figure 12 and Figure 13 represent only the number and percentage of shares of liquidity, and not the prices of the transactions which, of course, are important to a complete understanding of liquidity provider behavior. Anecdotal evidence, moreover, indicates that at least some large electronic liquidity providers and other liquidity providers did withdraw from the market during this time. We continue to analyze the conduct of these and other primary liquidity providing firms.

### *2. Securities that Suffered Declines Disproportionate to the Broader Market*

As noted above, the great majority of individual securities traded at prices that were consistent with the broader market decline during the day, while approximately 14% of U.S.-listed securities reached lows for the day that were more than 10% away from the 2:40 p.m.

price. Table 1 and Figure 8 above show that a similar proportion of trades in securities hit lows for the day that were more than 10% from the previous day's close.[17] This section discusses the individual securities that suffered declines that are out of proportion to the broader market. We first focus on broken trades, including ETFs in particular. The actual dollar volume of these broken trades was of course small, due to artificially low share prices involved, but the shares involved in those trades would have been valued at $212.4 million, at their 2:40 p.m. benchmark price. (See Table 7 below). We then address securities that otherwise experienced unusually severe declines without reaching the threshold for broken trades.

**a) Securities with Broken Trades**

The securities exchanges and FINRA have adopted "clearly erroneous execution rules" that are designed to permit them to cancel trades that in their determination were clearly entered into in error.[18] On May 6, under these rules, the SROs broke trades that were effected from 2:40 p.m. to 3:00 p.m. at prices 60%[19] away from the last trade at or before 2:40 p.m. Table 4 below provides certain information regarding the securities in which trades were broken.[20]

A total of 7,878 securities were traded during this period. Trades were broken in 326 individual securities, consisting of those that experienced a very severe price move of 60% or greater from the 2:40 p.m.[21] No trades were broken in any of the stocks that comprise the DJIA. Trades were broken in only 12 stocks that are included in the S&P 500 Index and in only 30 stocks included in the smaller capitalization Russell 2000 Index. Trades were broken in 227 of the 838 ETFs, however. These ETFs represent 69.6% of all securities with broken trades.

The 99 securities[22] with broken trades that are not ETFs include securities of a wide variety of issuers, both large and small (including 10 exchange-traded products, or ETPs, that are not ETFs) and there may be a variety of explanations for their aberrant behavior. We continue to investigate the trading in these securities on May 6 to determine whether there is a common cause or causes for the trading anomalies, such as a particular susceptibility to liquidity withdrawal or an unusually large number of stop loss market orders.

Tables 5 and 6 below provide certain information regarding the distribution of trades that were broken, both by trading venue and by time period. These tables show that 20,761 trades were broken on May 6, with 12,306 (59.3%) broken by NASDAQ, 4,903 (23.6%) broken by NYSE Arca, 1,816 (8.7%) broken in the OTC market, and 1,094 (5.3%) broken by BATS. No trades were broken by NYSE.

Table 5 and Table 6 show the distribution of securities in which broken trades occurred by markets.[23]

We continue to analyze the distribution of broken trades across markets to determine whether differences in market structure may have had an impact. Because NYSE pauses or slows trading in volatile periods when a LRP is triggered, this likely explains why NYSE had no broken trades on May 6. Some have suggested that LRPs exacerbated price volatility on May 6 by causing a net loss of liquidity as orders were routed to other trading venues for immediate execution rather than wait on the LRP mechanism. If accurate, this potentially could cause some NYSE securities to decline further than the broad market decline. Others believe that the LRP mechanism served to attract additional liquidity that helped soak up some the excess selling interest in these securities on May 6. In any event, nearly 83% of the securities with broken trades do not trade on NYSE, as NYSE trades only NYSE-listed stocks, and thus could not have been directly affected by NYSE LRPs. A determination of the extent to which the use of LRPs by NYSE contributed to the volatility on May 6 requires further study.

Also worth noting is the relatively low number of broken trades on BATS, relative to its share of trading volume. Although more study is required, one explanation for this could be that BATS does not refresh "stub quotes." The SEC staff is reviewing the extent to which the use of stub quotes contributed to the volatility on May 6, and is considering possible policy responses.

**Table 4. Distribution of Securities and Securities with Broken Trades**

| | Market | | Broken | |
|---|---|---|---|---|
| | **Total** | **%** | **Total** | **%** |
| **Securities** | 7,878 | 100.0% | 326 | 100.0% |
| **Primary Listing on NYSE** | 3,277 | 41.6% | 56 | 17.2% |
| **Primary Listing on NASDAQ** | 2,946 | 37.4% | 42 | 12.9% |
| **Primary Listing on ARCA** | 1,088 | 13.8% | 225 | 69.0% |
| **Primary Listing on Amex** | 567 | 7.2% | 3 | 0.9% |
| **Component of DJIA** | 30 | 0.4% | 0 | 0.0% |
| **Component of S&P 500** | 500 | 6.3% | 12 | 3.7% |
| **Component of Russell 2000** | 2,000 | 25.4% | 30 | 9.2% |
| **Exchange-Traded Fund** | 838 | 10.6% | 227 | 69.6 |

The distribution of all stocks and stocks that had broken trades on May 6, 2010 by primary listingexchange, inclusion in key stock indices and the number of Exchange Traded Funds

*Sources: NYSE, NYSEAmex, NYSE Arca, NASDAQ, BATS, CBOE Stock Exchange, ISE, NASDAQBX, National Stock Exchange, Chicago Stock Exchange and FINRA.*

**Table 5. Number of Trades Executing on Each Market**

| | **2:20-2:40p.m.** | **2:40-3:00p.m.** | **Number ofBrokenTrades** |
|---|---|---|---|
| **Total Trades** | 5,721,383 | 7,318,675 | 20,761 |
| **Average Trade Size** | 286.68 | 282.03 | 270.33 |
| On NYSE | 667,368 | 1,039,233 | 0 |
| On Amex | 4,154 | 6,965 | 4 |
| On ARCA | 886,899 | 1,110,765 | 4,903 |
| On NASDAQ | 1,482,761 | 2,052,647 | 12,306 |
| On BATS | 988,252 | 1,177,318 | 1,094 |
| On CBOE | 2,902 | 4,743 | 138 |
| On ISE | 87,313 | 171,978 | 403 |
| On NASDAQ-BX | 271,119 | 401,549 | 63 |
| On National | 35,386 | 58,085 | 27 |
| On Chicago | 5,845 | 10,748 | 7 |
| On ADF/TRF | 1,287,489 | 1,101,252 | 1,816 |

Sources: NYSE, NSYEAmex, NYSEARCA, NASDAQ, BATS, CBOE Stock Exchange, ISE, NASDAQBX, National Stock Exchange, Chicago Stock Exchange and FINRA

**Table 6. Percentage of Trades Executing on Each Market**

| | 2:20-2:40p.m. | 2:40-3:00p.m. | Percentage of Broken Trades |
|---|---|---|---|
| **Total Trades** | 5,721,383 | 7,318,675 | 20,761 |
| **Average Trade Size** | 286.68 | 282.03 | 270.33 |
| On NYSE | 11.70% | 14.60% | 0.00% |
| On Amex | 0.10% | 0.10% | 0.00% |
| On ARCA | 15.50% | 15.60% | 23.60% |
| On NASDAQ | 25.90% | 28.80% | 59.30% |
| On BATS | 17.30% | 16.50% | 5.30% |
| On CBOE | 0.10% | 0.10% | 0.70% |
| On ISE | 1.50% | 2.40% | 1.90% |
| On NASDAQ-BX | 4.70% | 5.60% | 0.30% |
| On National | 0.60% | 0.80% | 0.10% |
| On Chicago | 0.10% | 0.20% | 0.00% |
| On ADF/TRF | 22.50% | 15.40% | 8.70% |

Sources: NYSE, NSYEAmex, NYSEARCA, NASDAQ, BATS, CBOE Stock Exchange, ISE, NASDAQBX, National Stock Exchange, Chicago Stock Exchange and FINRA

**Table 7. Broken Trades by Time Period -May 6, 2010**

| Description | Before 2:40 | 2:40 - 2:45 | 2:45 - 2:50 | 2:50 - 2:55 | 2:55 - 3:00 | After 3:00 | Total |
|---|---|---|---|---|---|---|---|
| **Panel A: All Broken Trades** | | | | | | | |
| # of Broken Trades | 209 | 91 | 11,446 | 4,703 | 2,011 | 2,301 | 20,761 |
| > 14:40 price | 20 | 1 | 156 | 1,130 | 95 | 2,158 | 3,560 |
| < 14:40 price | 189 | 90 | 11,290 | 3,573 | 1,914 | 143 | 17,201 |
| > 160% of 14:40 price | 13 | 0 | 156 | 1,130 | 93 | 1,011 | 2,403 |
| < 40% of 14:40 price | 186 | 90 | 11,290 | 3,572 | 1,914 | 143 | 17,195 |
| < 5¢ | 148 | 6 | 5,158 | 1,928 | 175 | 1 | 7,416 |
| Share Volume (x000) | 37 | 57 | 3,165 | 1,136 | 636 | 582 | 5,612 |
| $ Volume (by 14:40 pm price inv $MM) | 1.3 | 2.1 | 132.4 | 29.3 | 17.6 | 29.7 | 212.4 |
| Return from 14:40 price (weighted) | 245% | -97% | -93% | -41% | 119% | 2976% | 262% |
| **Panel B: Broken Trades that are Short Sales** | | | | | | | |
| % of Broken Trades | 16.3% | 4.4% | 42.0% | 52.6% | 12.1% | 54.2% | 42.4% |
| > 14:40 price | 20.0% | 0.0% | 4.5% | 45.1% | 2.1% | 57.7% | 49.7% |
| < 14:40 price | 15.9% | 4.4% | 42.5% | 55.0% | 12.6% | 1.4% | 40.9% |
| > 160% of 14:40 price | 15.4% | 0.0% | 4.5% | 45.1% | 2.2% | 50.0% | 42.7% |
| < 40% of 14:40 price | 16.1% | 4.4% | 42.4% | 54.7% | 12.6% | 1.4% | 40.8% |
| < 5¢ | 20.3% | 0.0% | 70.9% | 90.1% | 39.4% | 0.0% | 74.0% |
| Share Volume (% of Broken Trades) | 9.8% | 3.0% | 19.0% | 36.7% | 12.2% | 50.4% | 24.9% |
| $ Volume (% of Broken Trades) | 6.0% | 1.8% | 14.5% | 30.3% | 9.5% | 54.8% | 21.7% |
| Return from 14:40 price (weighted) | -76% | -97% | -92% | -21% | -95% | 81% | -35% |

Source: All trade data from SROs. Price data from NYSE Trades and Quotes.

Table 7 shows that, during the core 2:40 p.m. to 3:00 p.m. period, broken trades peaked between 2:45 p.m. and 2:55 p.m., with 11,446 broken trades executed from 2:45 p.m. to 2:50 p.m. and 4,703 broken trades executed between 2:50 p.m. and 2:55 p.m. As expected, this corresponds with the period of peak volatility and trading volume in the securities markets.

Table 7also shows the number of trades that occurred at extraordinarily low prices – five cents or less – which indicates an execution against a "stub" quote of a market maker. A total of 7,416 of these trades took place during the core 2:40 p.m. to 3:00 p.m. period, with the highest levels occurring, as expected, between 2:45 p.m. and 2:50 p.m. (5,158) and 2:50 p.m. and 2:55 p.m. (1,928).

Table 7 further shows the number of broken trades identified as short sales. During the period of peak market volatility, 2:45 p.m. to 2:55 p.m., the broken trades executed at five cents or less were primarily short sales. Short sales account for approximately 70.1% of executions against "stub" quotes between 2:45 p.m. and 2:50 p.m., and approximately 90.1% of executions against "stub" quotes between 2:50 p.m. and 2:55 p.m. It is worth noting that short sale executions against stub quotes at or below the prevailing national best bid would be subject to the alternative uptick rule (Rule 201) adopted by the SEC on February 24, 2010, with a compliance date of November 10, 2010.[24] The SEC staff is continuing to review short selling activity on May 6, including the apparent high level of short selling against "stub" quotes during the period of peak market volatility.

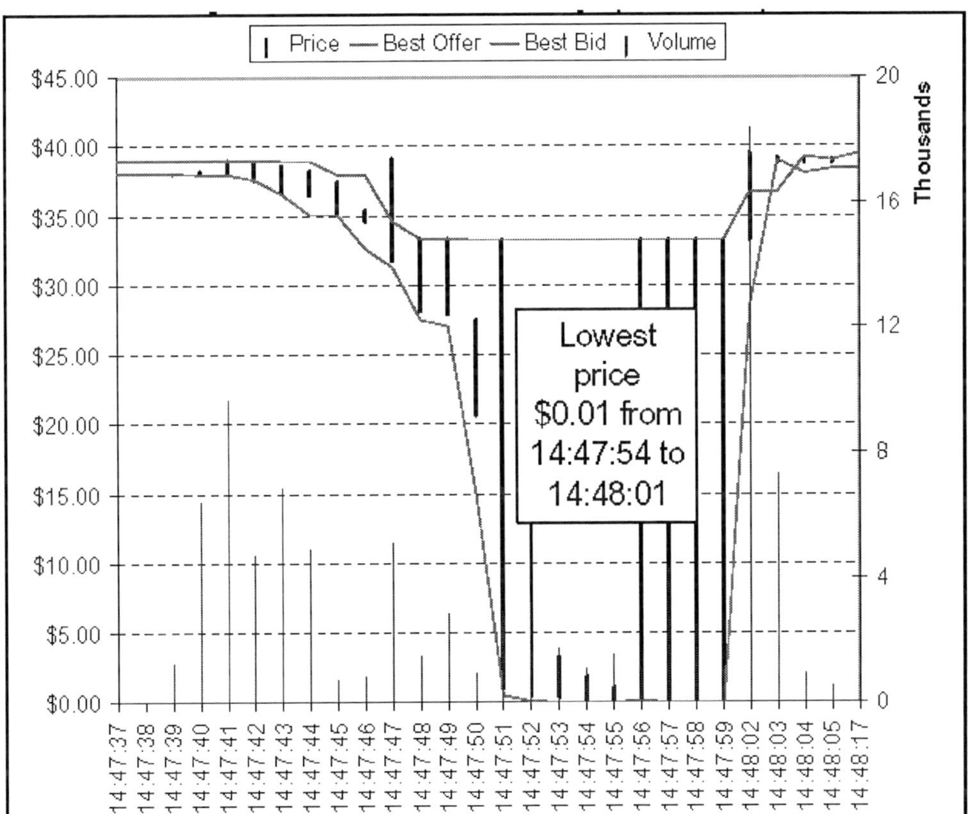


Source: All data from NYSE Trades and Quotes

Figure 14. Price Chart for Accenture plc (Ticker = ACN)[25]

Figure 8 shows that these stub quote executions occurred in more than 200 securities, across large, medium and small capitalization stocks, but with a concentration in small capitalization securities. Although more study is required, the higher level of stub quote executions in smaller capitalization securities is consistent with their tendency to have less liquidity, and thus a greater likelihood that selling interest could overwhelm order books in times of heightened volatility. As noted above, the SEC is reviewing the extent to which the use of stub quotes contributed to the volatility on May 6, and is considering possible policy responses.

One example of a security where there were executions against stub quotes is Accenture (ACN). The data set forth below indicates that share prices of Accenture fell from nearly $40 to a penny and recovered all of their value within a matter of seconds. We are investigating this dramatic spike to determine possible causes and explanations, including its relation to the broader market disruption.

The figure above shows that bids for Accenture plc (ACN) rapidly declined in 7 seconds from about $30 at 2:47:47 p.m., to $0.01 by 2:47:54 p.m.. The black bars show that trades were being made at both the stub quote of $0.01 and the ask price of over $30 within the same second.

**Table 8. Trades Executed at a Loss**

| | Total # trades | Total volume | Total volume ($) |
|---|---|---|---|
| All trades | 1,265,637 | 456,335,890 | 22,381,572,444 |
| Losses | 794,607 | 279,836,213 | 14,135,649,267 |
| | | | |
| 0% to -10% | 761,866 | 269,307,656 | 13,909,304,917 |
| -10% to -20% | 13,607 | 3,988,959 | 145,247,171 |
| -20% to 30% | 3,714 | 1,144,431 | 40,234,001 |
| -30% to -40% | 2,041 | 753,856 | 18,934,582 |
| -40% to -50% | 1,151 | 320,661 | 6,612,612 |
| -50% to -60% | 1,148 | 344,774 | 7,657,548 |
| -60% to -70% | 758 | 314,030 | 4,111,592 |
| -70% to -80% | 505 | 233,617 | 2,021,741 |
| -80% to -90% | 775 | 176,632 | 1,025,499 |
| -90% to -100% | 9,042 | 3,251,597 | 499,604 |

Source: NYSE's Trades and Quotes

ETFs: As previously discussed, the data suggests that ETFs as a class were affected more than any other category of securities. Trades in securities issued by ETFs appear to have accounted for nearly 70% of the securities in which trades were broken on May 6. Figure 15 shows the distribution of ETF daily lows during May 6. A relatively large number of ETFs, approximately 160, experienced lows during the day approximately 100% lower than the May 5 close, represented by the spike on the left hand side of the figure. A significant number of ETFs also experienced less extreme, but still notable lows of between 35% and 100% relative to their corresponding May 5 close.

A larger cluster of ETFs experienced lows approximately 8% below May 5 close. This clustering of daily lows around -8% is consistent with the daily low in the broader market, which was approximately 8.5% for the S&P 500. However, relative to the distribution of losses of all securities, (depicted above in Figure 8), extreme daily lows appear to have been more common in the ETFs (as depicted in Figure 15). Figure 15 does not reveal an obvious relation between ETF market capitalization and daily lows.

Tables 8 and 9 report the total number of trades, the total volume and total dollar volume for ETF trades executed between 2:40 p.m. and 3:00 p.m., for losses and gains, respectively. The tables are based on 838 registered ETFs as derived from Morningstar. The losses/gains are computed as the difference between the trade price and the 2:40 p.m. price, divided by the 2:40 p.m. price, for each stock. The data do not include out-of-sequence trades.

Table 8 indicates that, out of the 280 million ETF shares that traded below the 2:40 p.m. price, approximately 269 million, or 96%, traded at prices above or within 10% of the 2:40 p.m. price. A significant number of shares, approximately 3 million, traded at 90-100% losses. Dollar volume for trades at 90-100% losses is low, at $499,600, but purely as a mechanical consequence of low share prices. Significantly fewer shares of ETFs traded at large gains than traded at large losses. Table 9 indicates that only 712,398 shares traded at gains of 10% to 20%. In the aggregate, approximately 800,000 shares, with a dollar volume of $24.5 million, traded at a more than 10% gain.

**Table 9. Trades Executed at a Gain**

| | Total # trades | Total volume | Total volume ($) |
|---|---|---|---|
| All trades | 1,265,637 | 456,335,890 | 22,381,572,444 |
| Gains | 471,030 | 176,499,677 | 8,245,923,177 |
| 0% to 10% | 468,197 | 175,697,855 | 8,221,468,066 |
| 10% to 20% | 2,392 | 712,398 | 18,350,149 |
| 20% to 30% | 99 | 30,162 | 1,330,565 |
| 30% to 40% | 28 | 6,668 | 240,300 |
| 40% to 50% | 35 | 4,300 | 184,047 |
| 50% to 60% | 12 | 1,600 | 77,897 |
| 60% to 70% | 19 | 5,996 | 266,038 |
| 70% to 80% | 30 | 5,166 | 511,016 |
| 80% to 90% | 41 | 4,500 | 450,227 |
| > 90% | 177 | 31,032 | 3,044,872 |

Source: NYSE Trades and Quotes

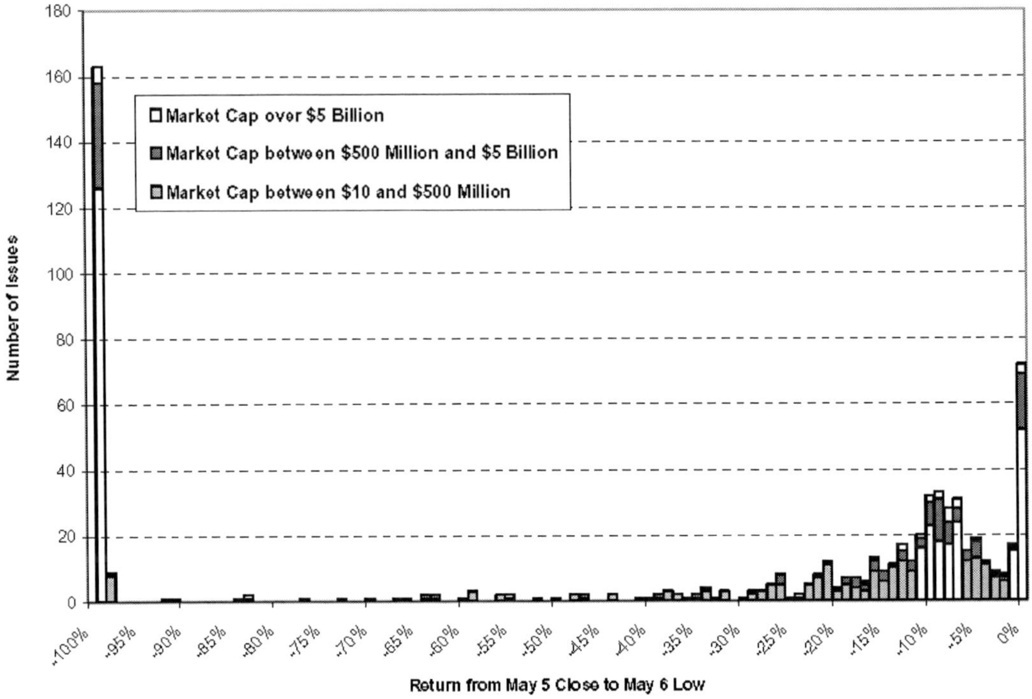


Sources: Thomson Financial Datastream and NYSE Trades and Quotes.

Figure 15. Distribution of May 6 Daily Lows for ETFs[26]

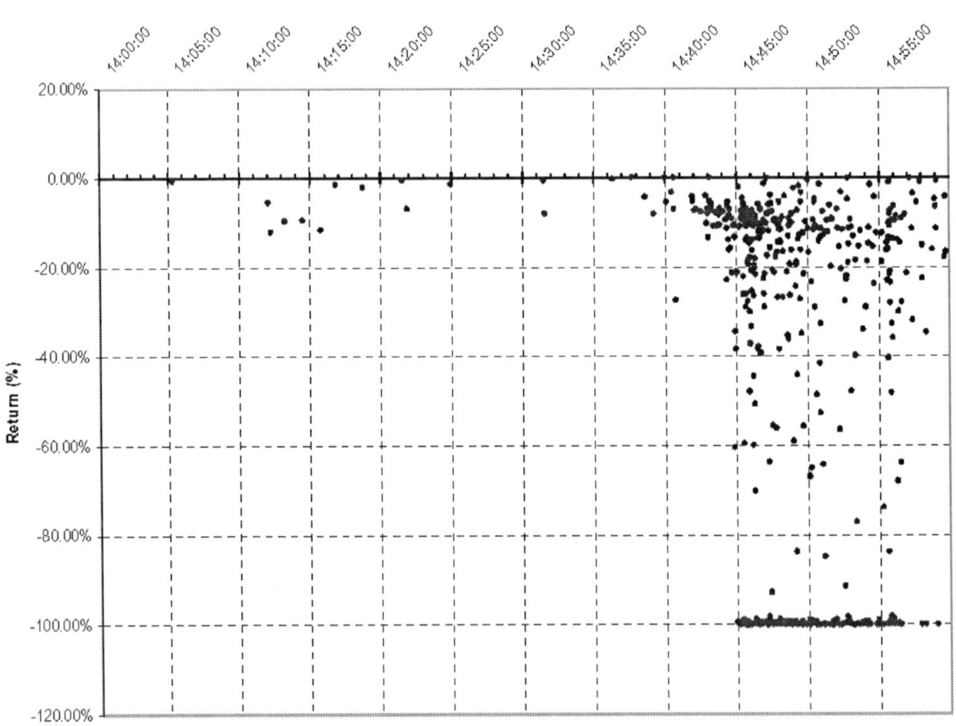


Sources: Thomson Financial Datastream and NYSE Trades and Quotes

Figure 16. Timing of ETF Daily Lows, May 6, 2:00pm to 3:00 pm[27]

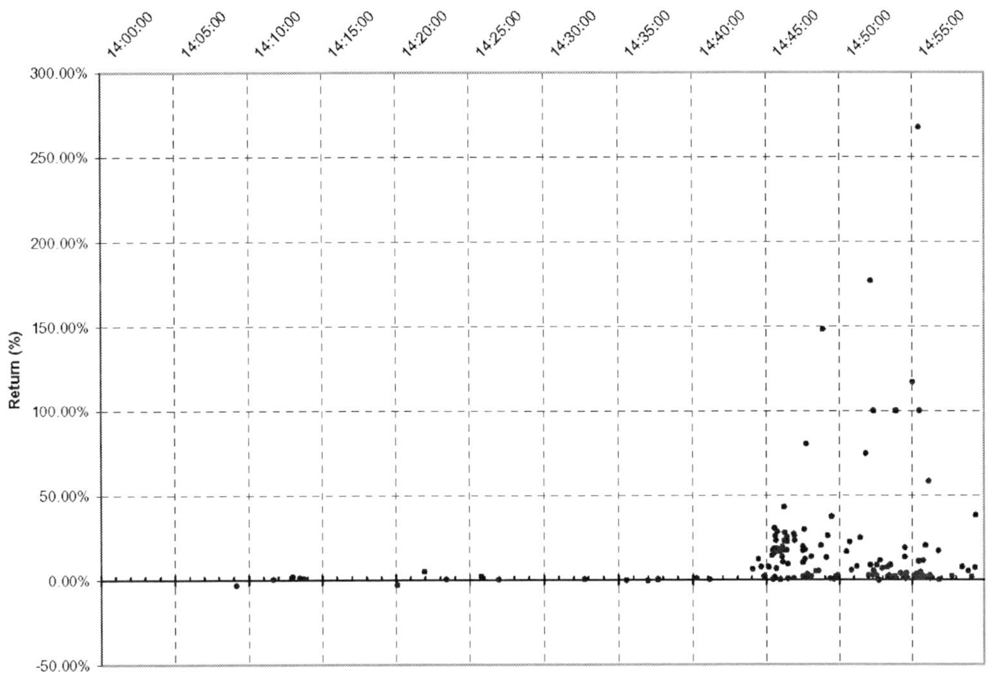


Sources: Thomson Financial Datastream and NYSE Trades and Quotes

Figure 17. Timing of ETF Daily Highs, May 6, 2:00 p.m. to 3:00 p.m[28]

Figure 15 indicates the distribution of ETF daily lows during May 6. A relatively large number of ETFs, approximately 160, experienced lows during the day approximately 100% lower than the May 5 close, represented by the spike on the left-hand side of the figure, and a number of ETFs also experienced less extreme, but still notable, lows between, 35% and 100% below the May 5 close. A larger cluster of ETFs experienced lows approximately 7% below the May 5 close, a concentration that may be a byproduct of the temporary dislocation in the broad market. In some ETFs, daily lows were approximately the same as the May 5 close, represented by the modest spike on the right-hand side of the chart. Relative to the distribution of all securities, depicted above in Figure 8, extreme daily lows appear to have been more common in the ETFs.

Over the one-hour interval between 2:00 p.m. and 3:00 p.m., as shown in Figure 16, many of the daily lows in ETFs occurred after 2:45 p.m. A few ETFs began experiencing relatively modest daily lows of approximately 10% below the May 5 close shortly after 2:10p.m. These lows continued sporadically until around 2:40p.m., when their frequency increased, represented on the graph by the concentration of points on the lower right. Many of these daily lows, beginning near 2:45p.m., were approximately 100% below the May 5 close, represented by the dense line near -100% on the right-hand side of the graph. Comparing this figure with Figure 10, which presents the same analysis for all securities, ETFs appear relatively less likely than other securities to have experienced extreme daily lows during the early part of the hour.

While many ETFs experienced extreme daily lows during the day, as evidenced by the daily lows presented in Figure 16, a significant number of ETFs experienced extreme daily highs. Figure 17 presents these daily highs, plotted against the time at which they occurred.

One ETF experienced a daily high approximately 275% higher than the May 5 close. Consistent with the pattern for extreme daily lows, the extreme daily highs appear to begin near 2:45 p.m. and are notably absent from the early part of the hour.

Figure 18 depicts the number of broken-trade ETFs and the total number of ETFs, broken out by asset category. This behavior is very similar to that previously depicted for individual companies.

Tables10, 11 and Figure 18 present summary statistics on broken trades by fund company, by net assets, and by asset class. Figure 18 illustrates the relation between fund investment objective and the existence of broken trades. It depicts the distribution of total ETFs and ETFs with broken trades by asset category. The broken trades are skewed toward large- and mid-cap equity ETFs, with fewer broken trades occurring in bond, real-estate and ETFs with objectives that do not track the overall market.

Table 10 classifies broken-trade exchange-traded funds by fund family. All but ten of the exchange-traded products with subsequently broken trades were also ETFs, and five of those ten appear to be stock-related ETPs. Table 10 indicates that, on average, 27.1% of all fund companies experienced broken trades. There is, however, considerable cross-sectional variation among fund families. For example, First Trust experienced broken trades in approximately 50% of its ETFs, while PIMCO had no ETFs with broken trades.[29]

One explanation for this variation may be the degree to which families specialize in asset classes that had fewer breaks, such as debt-oriented fund families like PIMCO. It is clear that the breaks occurred in many trades of ETFs in fund families (16 of 26 fund families) and that, conditional on a break occurring within a particular fund family, not all of the ETFs were affected.

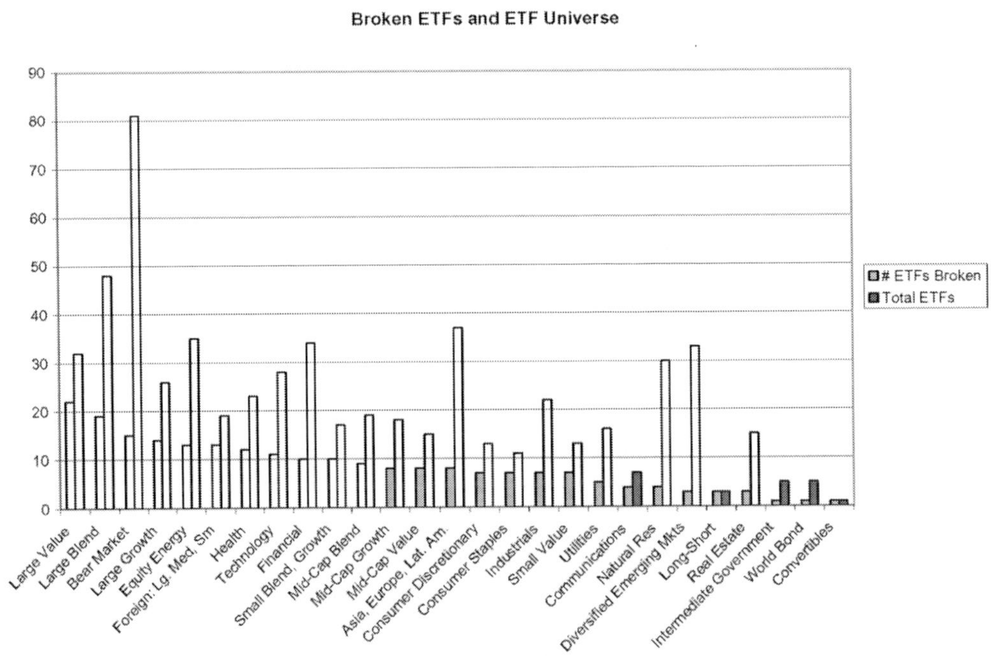


Source: NYSE, NYSE Amex, NYSE Arca, NASDAQ, BATS, CBOE Stock Exchange, ISE, NASDAQ-BX, NSX, Chicago Stock Exchange and FINRA

Figure 18. BrokenTrade ETFs and ETF Universe

**Table 10. Fund Companies**[31]

| ETF Firm Name | Broken | Not Broken | Total |
|---|---|---|---|
| ALPS ETF | 0 | 6 | 6 |
| AdvisorShares | 0 | 1 | 1 |
| Claymore Securities | 9 | 25 | 34 |
| Direxion Funds | 3 | 31 | 34 |
| Emerging Global | 0 | 6 | 6 |
| FaithShares | 1 | 4 | 5 |
| Fidelity Investments | 1 | 0 | 1 |
| First Trust | 21 | 22 | 43 |
| Global X Funds | 0 | 10 | 10 |
| Grail Advisors | 0 | 7 | 7 |
| IndexIQ | 2 | 6 | 8 |
| JETS | 0 | 2 | 2 |
| OOK Advisors | 0 | 2 | 2 |
| Old Mutual | 0 | 4 | 4 |
| PIMCO | 0 | 10 | 10 |
| PowerShares | 43 | 73 | 116 |
| ProShares | 22 | 77 | 99 |
| Rydex/SGI | 17 | 14 | 31 |
| Schwab Funds | 5 | 3 | 8 |
| State Street Global | 14 | 76 | 90 |
| VTL Associates, LLC | 2 | 4 | 6 |
| Van Eck | 2 | 23 | 25 |
| Vanguard | 15 | 31 | 46 |
| WisdomTree | 9 | 33 | 42 |
| XShares | 0 | 5 | 5 |
| iShares | 61 | 136 | 197 |
| **Total** | **227** | **611** | **838** |
| **Percent of Total** | **27.1** | **72.9** | **100.0** |

Source: NYSE, NYSEAmex, NASDAQ, BATS, CBOE Stock Exchange, ISE, NASDAQBX, NSX, Chicago Stock Exchange and FINRA

Table 11 examines the relation between ETF size and broken trades by net asset quartile. The data suggests that the proportion of broken trades in the smallest net asset quartile of ETFs is lower than the others (16.3% versus 30.7%).[30] Table 11 also indicates that while there are differences across quartiles, the relative volume of broken trades to non-broken trades within each quartile did not change very much between May 5 and May 6. For example, the May 5 ratio of daily volume of funds that had broken trades on May 6 to those without broken trades was 63.8% (46,115/(46,115+26,138)). The analogous ratio computed using May 6 volume levels is very similar at 61.7% (28,034/(28,034+17,385)).

The next three charts show the experience of broken trades in three different ETFs.

Figure 19 shows that iShares MSCI EAFE Growth Index Fund (EFG) was thinly traded but within a relatively narrow bid-ask spread. However, a number of trades are executed below the lowest national best bid, and at 2:58:14 p.m. transactions are executed at prices of less than $0.01.

**Table 11. ETFs with Broken Trades**[32]

| | Quartile verage Current Net Assets[33] | Number of ETFs | Average Daily Volume May 6 | Average Daily Volume May 5 | Average Current Net Asset |
|---|---|---|---|---|---|
| Broken | 1 | 34 | 46,115 | 28,034 | $8,321,632 |
| Not Broken | 1 | 175 | 26,138 | 17,385 | $7,690,493 |
| Broken | 2 | 60 | 150,390 | 76,880 | $42,167,498 |
| Not Broken | 2 | 150 | 99,232 | 60,952 | $37,411,891 |
| Broken | 3 | 76 | 265,000 | 192,501 | $188,958,576 |
| Not Broken | 3 | 133 | 1,316,488 | 856,819 | $177,878,106 |
| Broken | 4 | 57 | 5,962,890 | 3,355,924 | $2,586,658,099 |
| Not Broken | 4 | 153 | 20,746,803 | 11,972,562 | $3,463,601,150 |

Sources: Morningstar is the source of current net asset data and Datastream is the source of the average daily volume data

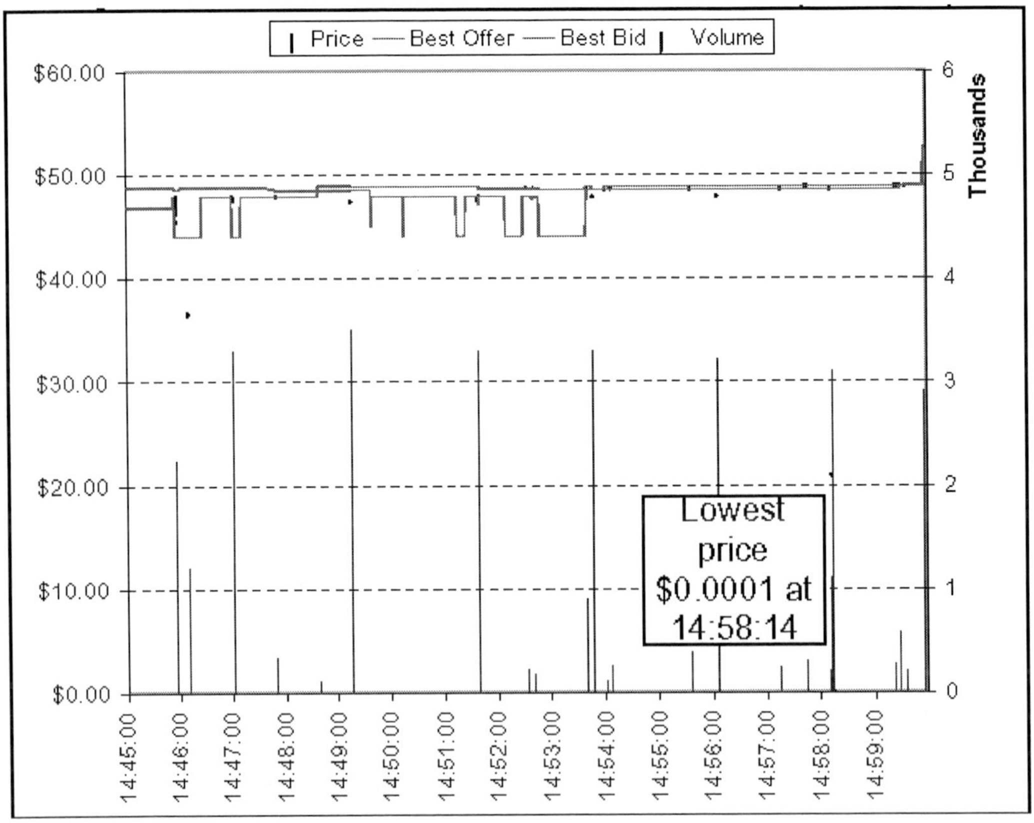


Source: NYSE Trades and Quotes

Figure 19. Price Chart for iShares MSCI EAFE Growth Index Fund (Ticker = EFG)

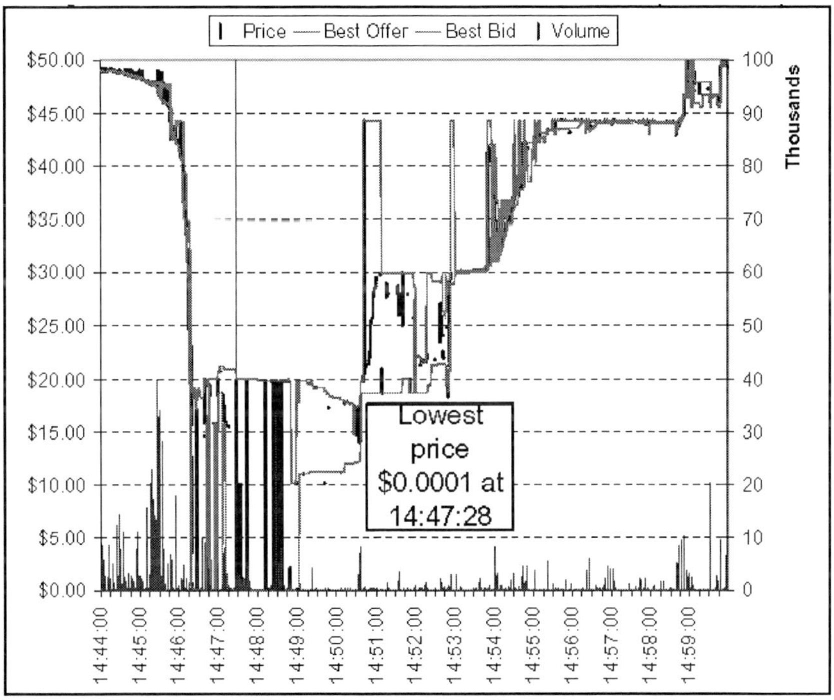


Source: NYSE Trades and Quotes

Figure 20. Price Chart for iShares Russell 1000 Growth Index Fund (Ticker = IWF)

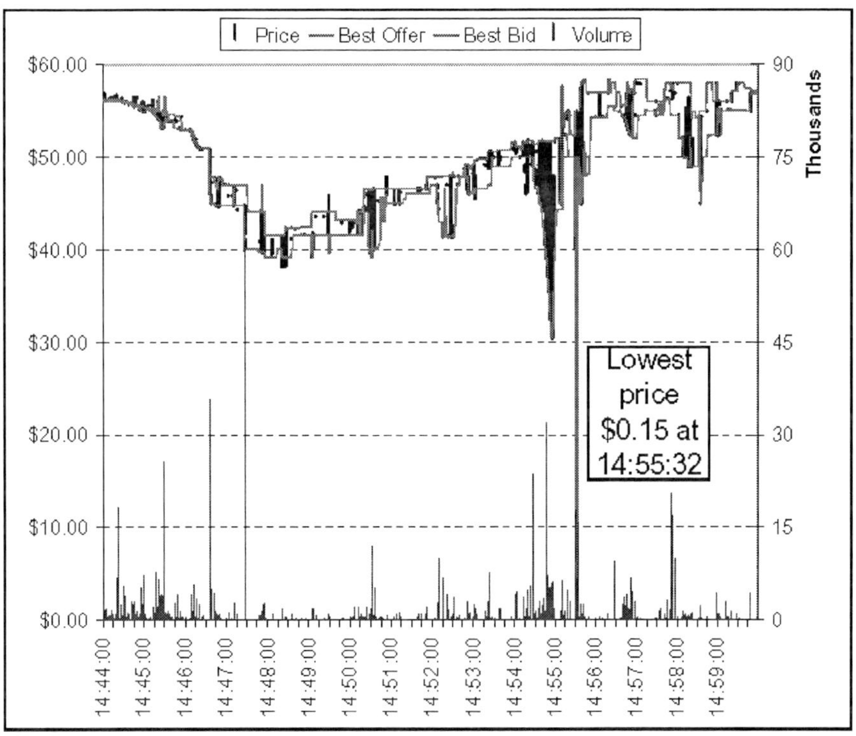


Source: NYSE Trades and Quotes

Figure 21. Price Chart for Vanguard Total Stock Market Fund (Ticker = VTI)

In Figure 20, bids for iShares Russell 1000 Growth Index Fund (IWF) rapidly declined just before 2:46 p.m. A number of trades were executed at stub-quotes of less than $0.01 and at the highest offer-quote of $20.00 within a 3-minute period, which was followed by a two-minute period with almost no trade activity. IWF then slowly recovered with widely varying bid and offer quotes. By 2:56 p.m. the bid-ask spread narrows and the price increased to approximately 90% of its decline.

Figure 21 indicates that Vanguard Total Stock Market Fund (VTI) maintained relatively narrow bid-ask spreads while following the broad market through decline and recovery beginning 2:44 p.m. Just prior to 2:55 p.m., bids suddenly collapsed on increased volume well after the recovery is underway. And at 2:55:32 p.m. bids drop to stub quotes and trades are executed at $0.15 before the price resumes its recovery.

For reference, the tables below rank the top 10 ETFs with broken trade and stocks (by volume, both for the full day and between 2:00 p.m. and 3:00 p.m. on May 6).

**Table 12. Top 10 ETFs with Broken Trades by Trading Volume – Full Day, May 6**

| ETF | Ticker | Volume |
|---|---|---|
| iShares Russell 2000 Index | IWM | 195,387,906 |
| ProShares UltraShort QQQ | QID | 53,291,398 |
| iShares Russell 1000 Growth Index | IWF | 9,002,900 |
| ProShares Ultra Real Estate | URE | 6,983,600 |
| iShares Russell 2000 Value Index | IWN | 6,823,200 |
| iShares Russell 1000 Value Index | IWD | 6,258,200 |
| Vanguard Total Stock Market ETF | VTI | 6,160,500 |
| iShares S&P MidCap 400 Index | IJH | 5,416,800 |
| iShares Russell 1000 Index | IWB | 5,194,400 |
| Rydex S&P Equal Weight | RSP | 4,511,600 |

Sources: NYSE, NSYEAmex, NYSEARCA, NASDAQ, BATS, CBOE Stock Exchange, ISE, NASDAQBX, National Stock Exchange, Chicago Stock Exchange and FINRA.

**Table 13. Top 10 ETFs with Broken Trades by Trading Volume – May 6 from 2 p.m. to 3 p.m.**

| ETF | Ticker | Volume |
|---|---|---|
| iShares Russell 2000 Index | IWM | 58,392,711 |
| ProShares UltraShort QQQ | QID | 21,771,521 |
| iShares Russell 1000 Growth Index | IWF | 3,161,501 |
| iShares Russell 2000 Value Index | IWN | 2,671,281 |
| Vanguard Total Stock Market ETF | VTI | 2,472,422 |
| Rydex S&P Equal Weight | RSP | 2,305,135 |
| ProShares Ultra Real Estate | URE | 2,193,949 |
| iShares Russell 1000 Value Index | IWD | 1,707,294 |
| iShares Russell 1000 Index | IWB | 1,677,658 |
| iShares S&P MidCap 400 Index | IJH | 1,407,322 |

Sources: NYSE, NSYEAmex, NYSEARCA, NASDAQ, BATS, CBOE Stock Exchange, ISE, NASDAQBX, National Stock Exchange, Chicago Stock Exchange and FINRA.

**Table 14. Top 10 Broken Stocks by Trading Volume – Full Day May 6**

| Stock | Ticker | Volume |
|---|---|---|
| Radian Group | RDN | 70,612,297 |
| Apple Inc. | AAPL | 45,923,602 |
| Philip Morris International | PM | 16,460,300 |
| Exelon Corp | EXC | 12,426,400 |
| Amylin Pharmaceuticals | AMLN | 11,626,099 |
| Costco Warehouse | COST | 11,175,900 |
| International Group of Companies | IPG | 11,073,400 |
| Accenture, PLC | ACN | 10,311,600 |
| Amazon | AMZN | 10,195,600 |
| CenterPoint Energy | CNP | 9,322,800 |

Sources: NYSE, NSYEAmex, NYSEARCA, NASDAQ, BATS, CBOE Stock Exchange, ISE, NASDAQBX, National Stock Exchange, Chicago Stock Exchange and FINRA.

**Table 15. Top 10 Broken Stocks by Trading Volume – May 6 from 2 p.m. to 3 p.m.**

| Stock | Ticker | Volume |
|---|---|---|
| Apple Inc. | AAPL | 7,506,380 |
| Radian Group | RDN | 5,298,708 |
| Philip Morris International | PM | 4,140,829 |
| International Group of Companies | IPG | 3,235,083 |
| Provident Energy Trust | PVX | 2,622,676 |
| Exelon Corp | EXC | 2,509,121 |
| CenturyTel, Inc | CTL | 2,248,034 |
| Accenture, PLC | ACN | 2,059,138 |
| Center Point Energy | CNP | 2,018,251 |
| Southwestern Energy Company | SWN | 1,618,107 |

Sources: NYSE, NSYEAmex, NYSEARCA, NASDAQ, BATS, CBOE Stock Exchange, ISE, NASDAQBX, National Stock Exchange, Chicago Stock Exchange and FINRA.

SEC staff also evaluated whether creation and redemption behavior by authorized participants was significantly different on May 5, 6 and 7 between ETFs with broken trades and ETFs without broken trades. The staff was provided creation and redemption data by four ETF advisors. The data contained daily creation and redemption units or shares for all ETFs advised by those firms from approximately April 1 to May 11. Two ETF advisors provided their information in number of shares, while two provided theirs in number of units. Since shares and units are not directly comparable, the two data sets were combined separately in order to run the analysis. Statistical tests were run to determine whether the amount of net creations (creations minus redemptions) differed between ETFs that experienced broken trades and those that did not. The tests were run on creation and redemption data separately for May 5, May 6, and May 7.

The results of the tests do not provide evidence that there was a significant difference in the creation and redemption behavior of authorized participants between ETFs with broken trades and ETFs without broken trades. There are some statistically significant results indicating that ETFs with broken trades had higher creations on May 7 than ETFs without broken trades, although the level of significance is weak. As a robustness check, the same tests were run on all days not including May 5, May 6 and May 7. The results showed that there is no statistical difference in creation and redemption behavior of authorized participants between ETFs with broken trades and ETFs without broken trades during the trading window not including May 5, May 6 or May 7. It is noted that the tests were completed with very small sample size, limiting their power.

The SEC staff continues to investigate precisely why ETFs as a class were affected so dramatically. ETFs are primarily highly transparent pools of securities that seek to track market indices. Thus, unlike other listed securities, the value of an ETF is dependent on the value of the individual securities it owns as well as the transactions in ETF shares by market participants. ETFs are often used by investors and other market participants as an efficient means of gaining (or reducing) exposure to market segments in connection with their implementation of investment or hedging strategies.

As discussed in Appendix A, ETF shares have typically traded at market prices that are closely related to the net asset value of their shares. This pricing discipline principally hinges on the ability of market makers: (a) to effectively hedge their market exposure to ETF shares; and (b) to engage in arbitrage transactions with the ETFs if the market prices of the ETF shares deviate significantly from their net asset values.

As noted above, certain non-ETF securities experienced extreme daily lows earlier than certain ETFs during the one hour interval from 2:00 p.m. to 3:00 p.m. We are currently gathering and reviewing data to ascertain the causes of these collapses and the possible implications for the broader market.

We are also studying the extent to which the use of ETFs may have contributed to the abrupt price declines. For example, institutional investors often utilize index-based ETFs in hedging strategies, which may have prompted unusual liquidity demands during this period of market turmoil. The use of stop loss orders by other investors may have created additional sell pressure on ETF shares in a rapidly declining market.

In addition, we are exploring the impact of "self-help" being invoked by NASDAQ and BATS against NYSE Arca. As NYSE Arca is the primary listing exchange for almost all ETFs, the loss of access to NYSE Arca's liquidity pool may have had a disproportionate impact on market liquidity and trading for ETFs.

**b) Market Activity in Other Selected Securities**

Significant numbers of securities experienced declines in excess of the broad market (meaning, for these purposes, declines of more than 10% from their prices at 2:40 p.m.), but did not cross the 60% broken trade threshold. In addition, a significant number of securities experienced extreme daily highs after approximately 2:44 p.m.[34] In this section, we provide examples of specific selected securities to illustrate how representative securities behaved during the critical minutes of May 6.

For example, some large capitalization securities declined quite substantially. One was Proctor & Gamble (PG), whose price chart for May 6 is set forth in Figure 22.

It can be seen that bids for PG decline rapidly over a one-minute period before rapidly ascending and then recovering. Trades occur in a wide range from the lowest national best bid in a given second to the highest national best offer in that same second.

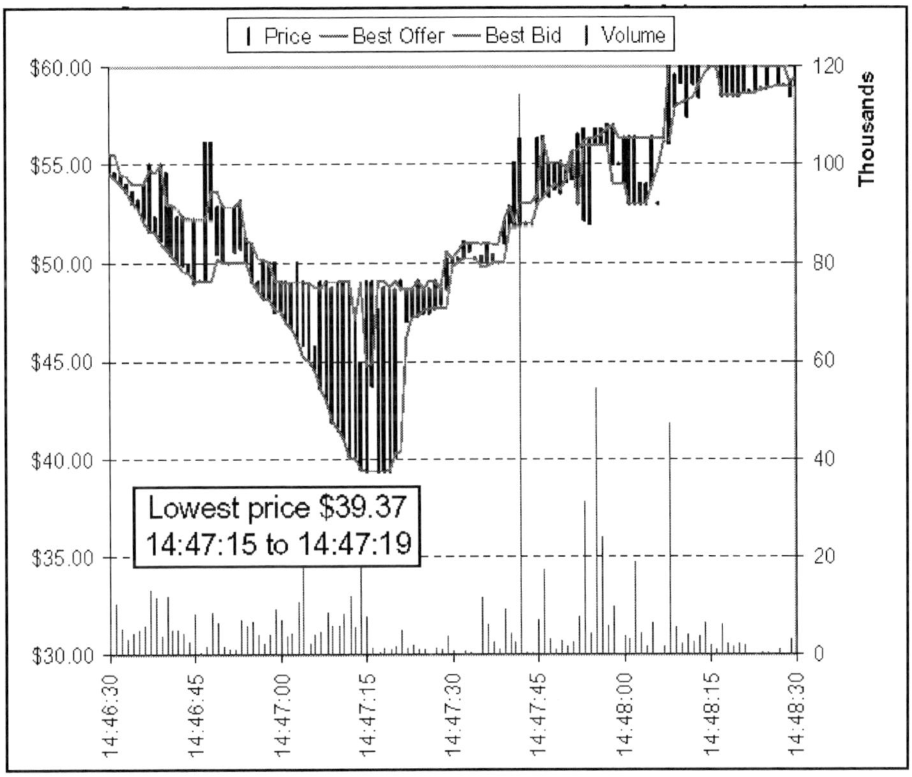


Sources: NYSE Trades and Quotes

Figure 22. Price Chart for The Proctor & Gamble Company (Ticker = PG)

PG declined from more than $60 to a low of $39.37 in approximately 3.5 minutes (a 36.14% decline from the 2:40 p.m. price), then recovered above $60 in approximately one minute. Notably, the decline in PG did not begin until 2:44 p.m., well after the broader market indices, which began their precipitous drop at approximately 2:40 p.m. Accordingly, early reports that an inordinately large trade in PG may have triggered the broad market decline do not appear well founded. Our analysis of the order book data should help shed light on why PG declined and recovered so much more significantly than other large capitalization stocks.

Another large capitalization stock that declined substantially was 3M Co. (MMM), whose price chart is shown in Figure 23.

The bid-ask spread for MMM stays quite narrow, and volume remains significant, even as the price declines from about $82 at 2:44 p.m. to a low of approximately $68 at 2:46 p.m. Prior to reaching this low, the bid-ask spread over any given second dramatically widens and remains erratic before beginning a slow and choppy recovery.

MMM first declines from approximately $82.50 at 2:44 p.m. to approximately $71.00, then slowly begins to recover. Though this 14% decline was substantial, at approximately 2:48 p.m., the price declines sharply for a second time and hits a daily low of $67.98, resulting in a total decline from its 2:40 p.m. price of 18.39%, second only to PG among DJIA stocks. The price then suddenly climbs within a few seconds to approximately $77. As with PG, our analysis of the order book data should shed greater light on why MMM could appear to have recovered from the initial decline, then suffered such a sharp additional decline and rise.

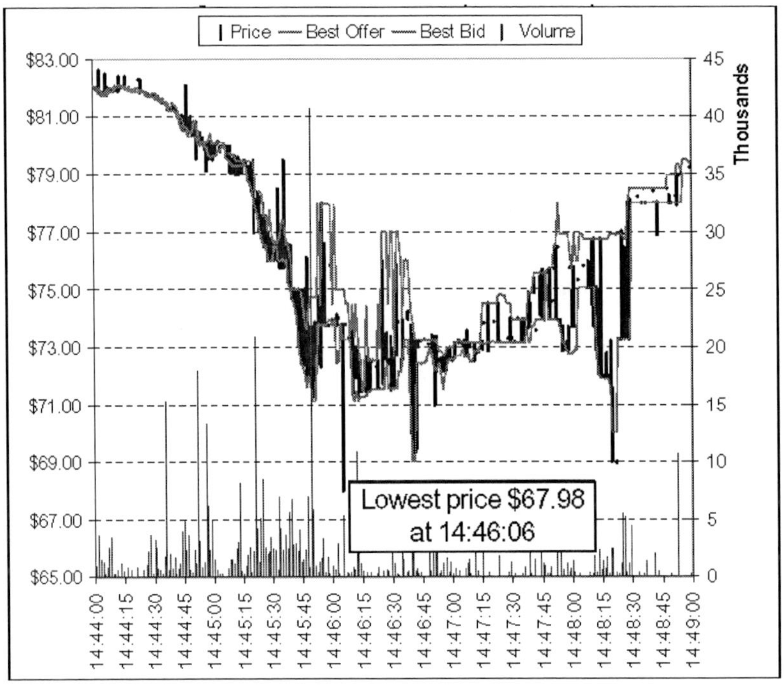


Sources: NYSE Trades and Quotes

Figure 23. Price Chart for 3M Co. (Ticker = MMM)

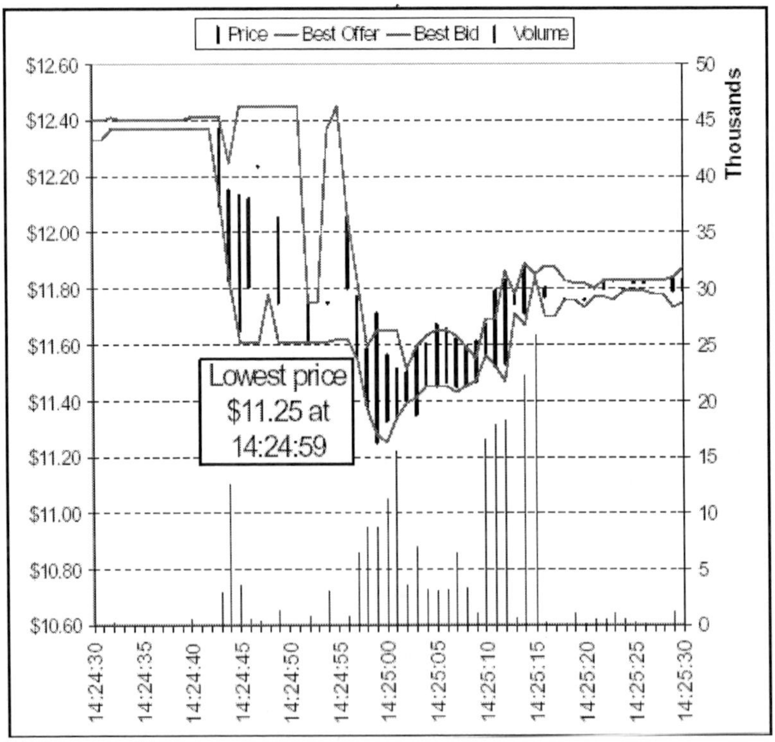


Sources: NYSE Trades and Quotes

Figure 24. Price Chart for Eaton Vance Tax- Managed Buy- Write Opportunities Fund (Ticker = ETV)

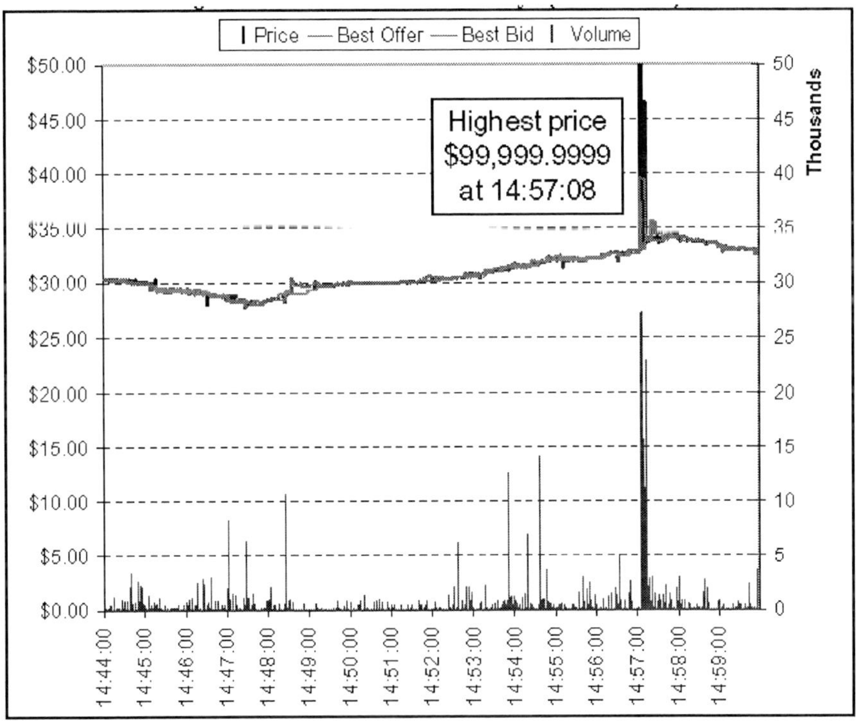


Sources: NYSE Trades and Quotes

Figure 25. Price Chart # 1 for Sotheby's (Ticker = BID)

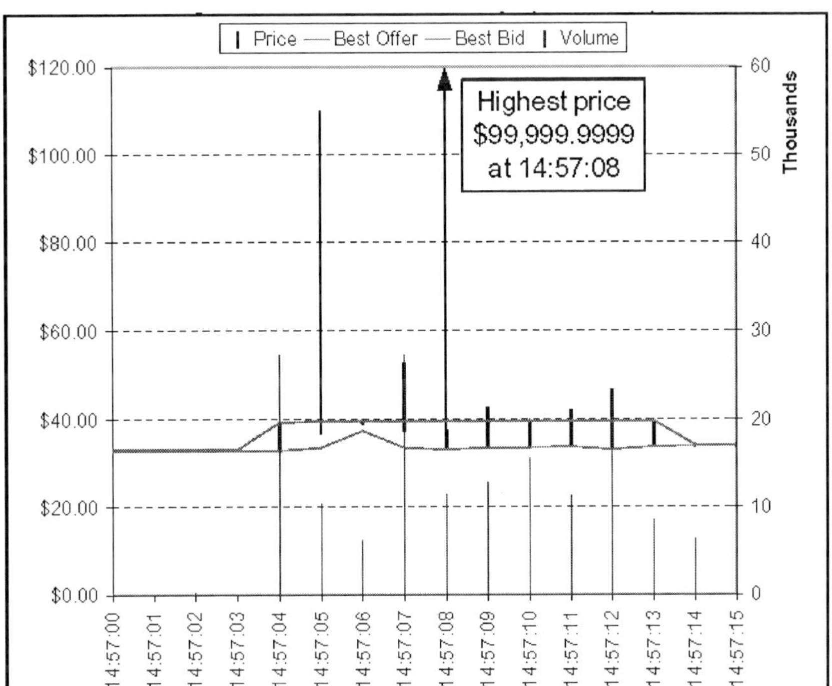


Sources: NYSE Trades and Quotes

Figure 26. Price Chart #2 for Sotheby's (Ticker = BID)

Figure 24 indicates that there is no activity in Eaton Vance Tax-Managed Buy-Write Opportunities Fund (ETV) from 2:24:30 p.m. through 2:24:43 p.m. at which time the bid drops by 6% rather quickly. Activity picks up again at about 2:24:57 p.m. as ETV partially recovers. This event occurred approximately 20 minutes prior to the main drop in broad markets.

In Figure 25, it can be seen that Sotheby's (BID) is actively traded and has a narrow bid-ask spread from 2:44 p.m. through 2:49 p.m. after which volume is low but bid and ask quotes remain stable. However, after about 2:57 p.m. volume spikes dramatically and trades are executed at a high (presumably stub) quote of approximately $100,000. This event is plotted in more detail below.

As Figure 26 shows, BID trades through the national best offer multiple times between 2:57:05 p.m. and 2:57:12 p.m. This includes trades at approximately $100,000 which is presumably a top-end stub quote. In contrast to the process in which bid-quotes for other stocks were shown to rapidly decline (which led to lower execution prices) here the highest offer price remained reasonable during a widening of the bid-ask spread, suggesting that the $100,000 trade occurred deeper into the order book.

In contrast, many other stocks did not experience such substantial declines. Two such examples, IBM and Intel (INTC), are respectively shown below in Figures 27 and 28.

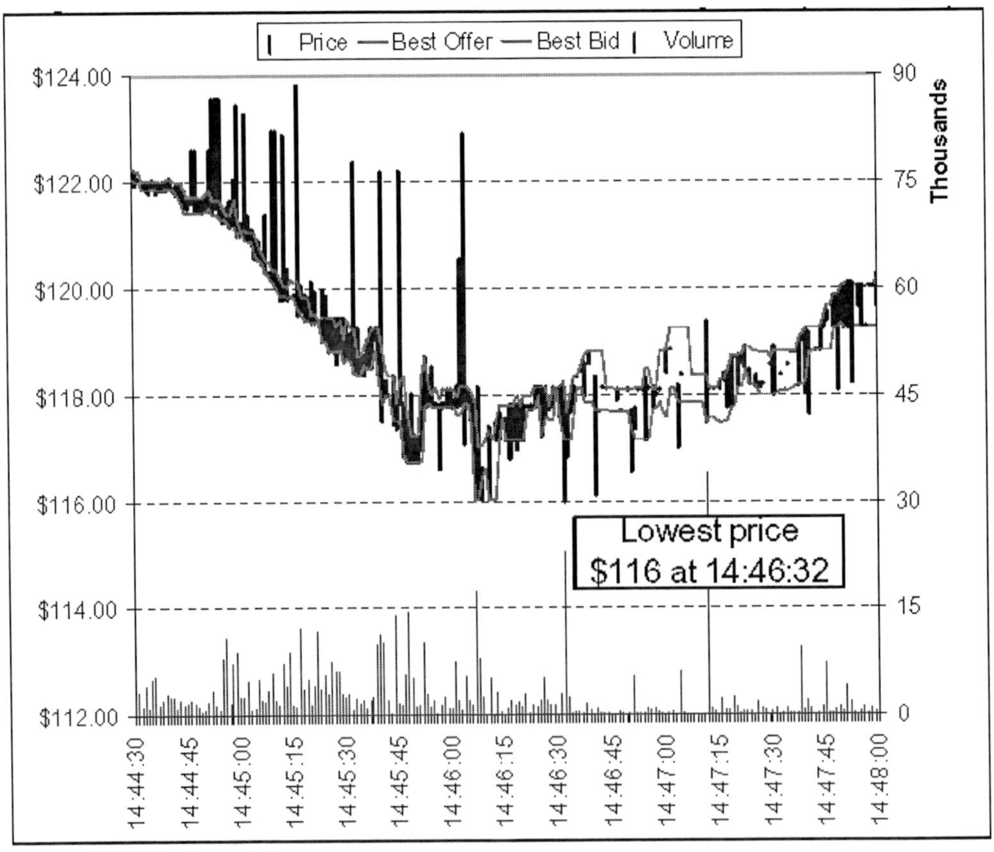


Sources: NYSE Trades and Quotes

Figure 27. Price Chart for International Business Machines Corporation (Ticker = IBM)

It can be seen that IBM trades down from $122 at 2:44:30 p.m. to a low of $116 (an approximate 5% loss) at 2:46:32 p.m. before rebounding to $120 by 2:48:00 p.m. The upward spikes in trade execution represent prices that were above the highest national best offer suggesting that these trades occurred deeper in the order book. Note that activity during the recovery period shows trade prices below the national best bid, but with very low volume.

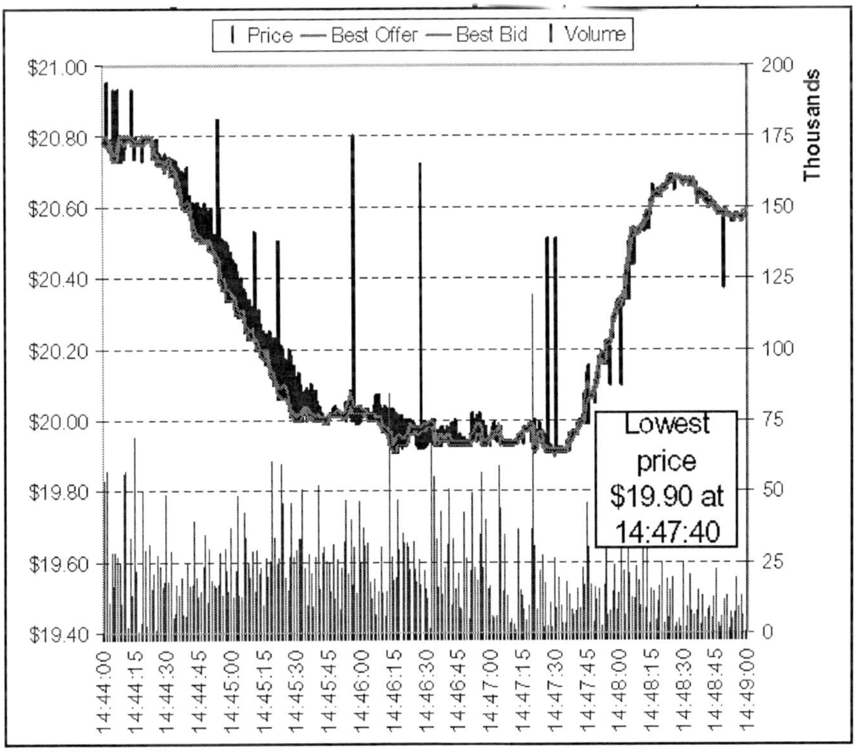


Sources: NYSE Trades and Quotes

Figure 28. Price Chart for Intel Corporation (Ticker = INTC)

**Table 16. Summary Data for SingleSecurity Plots**

| Stock Symbol | Listing Exchange | Event Type | Price ($) | Time | Price at 2:00 p.m. | May 6 Short Sale Ratio | Historical Short Sale Ratio |
|---|---|---|---|---|---|---|---|
| ACN | NYSE | Low | 0.01 | 14:47:54 | 41.78 | 33% | 37% |
| BID | NYSE | High | 100K | 14:57:08 | 32.15 | 51% | 49% |
| EFG | ARCA | Low | < 0.01 | 14:58:14 | 51.10 | 39% | 39% |
| ETV | NYSE | Low | 11.25 | 14:24:59 | 13.68 | 23% | 32% |
| IBM | NYSE | Low | 116.00 | 14:46:32 | 127.00 | 44% | 41% |
| INTC | NASDAQ | Low | 19.90 | 14:47:40 | 21.87 | 45% | 48% |
| IWF | ARCA | Low | < 0.01 | 14:47:28 | 49.65 | 62% | 45% |
| MMM | NYSE | Low | 67.98 | 14:46:06 | 85.64 | 41% | 41% |
| PG | NYSE | Low | 39.37 | 14:47:15 | 62.52 | 45% | 39% |
| VTI | ARCA | Low | 0.15 | 14:55:32 | 56.88 | 43% | 53% |

As indicated above, INTC has constant volume and narrow bid-ask spreads throughout its moderate 4% decline, though the highest offer quote was sometimes breached on the up-side suggesting trades being executed deeper into the order book.

Table 16 presents summary information for each of the securities illustrated in the examples. The Historical Short Sale Ratio represents data from August 3, 2009 through April 23, 2010.35 None of the May 6 Short Sale Ratios are more than 1.5 standard deviations away from their Historical Average.

We continue to evaluate any common drivers that might explain why trading for different securities exhibited different behaviors. Among a variety of factors, we are considering the effects of:

**Stop Loss Market Orders**. As described further below, stop loss orders have stop prices that, for sell orders, are lower than current prices. If prices fall, these orders are intended to prevent losses from exceeding a certain amount (beyond the stop price) by liquidating a long position in the stock. When the stop price is reached, such orders turn into market orders to sell. In fast market conditions, stop loss market orders may cause trades at prices that are much lower than the "stop" price anticipated by an investor, because the market may have moved by a significant amount before the order is executed. They also could potentially, under certain circumstances, trigger a chain reaction of automated selling if they are used in significant numbers for a particular stock. For example, the triggering of one stop loss market order can trigger an automated sell market order that causes a price decline that, in turn, in the absence of liquidity provision, may trigger another stop loss market order at a lower level, and so on.

**NYSE's LRP Mechanism**. Another factor that we will examine closely is the effect of the NYSE's LRP mechanism. As described further below, the NYSE's trading system incorporates LRPs that are intended to dampen volatility in a given stock by temporarily converting from an automated market to a manual auction market when a price movement of a sufficient size is reached. In such a case, trading on the NYSE will "go slow" and pause for a time period to allow an opportunity for additional liquidity to enter the market. During an LRP, the NYSE will display a quotation that is not immediately accessible and can be bypassed, but is not required to be bypassed, by other trading venues and order routers. Some have suggested that LRPs exacerbated price volatility on May 6 by causing a net loss of liquidity as orders were routed to other trading venues. If accurate, this potentially could cause some NYSE securities to decline further than the broad market decline. Others believe that the LRP mechanism served to attract additional liquidity that helped soak up some of the excess selling interest in these securities on May 6. We are analyzing the effect of LRPs closely.

## B. Futures Markets

The CFTC staff has conducted a preliminary review of activity in the futures markets to better understand the events that took place on May 6, 2010. The objective was to collect and analyze preliminary evidence that might be associated with possible causes of the events that occurred in futures markets on May 6, 2010, including, but not limited to erroneous activities (*e.g.*, "fat finger" errors), cyber attacks, and significant system malfunctions. CFTC staff's preliminary review has not, at this time, found evidence of erroneous activities, cyber attacks, or significant system malfunctions.

Preliminary findings suggest that a confluence of economic events, signals from various other markets, and a marked increase in sell orders (in comparison to buy orders) culminated in a significant dislocation of liquidity in the E-mini S&P 500 futures contracts.[36] This liquidity dislocation was also preceded by some reduction in activity of certain liquidity providers.

The analysis focuses on trading and liquidity provision in the June 2010 E-mini S&P 500 futures contract. That single contract month in the E-mini S&P 500 comprised 78.2 percent of the total volume of trading in the 12 most actively traded broad-based stock index futures contracts on May 6, 2010.

### *1. Background*

Consistent with broad market trends on May 6, 2010, trading volume in the E-mini S&P 500 futures was about 2.6 times greater than the average daily trading volume over the prior 30 days. On May 6, trading volume in the E-mini S&P 500 was the fifth highest daily volume over the past five years[37]

Furthermore, the contract experienced a significantly higher level of trading during certain periods of the day. According to Figure 30,on May 6, the intraday-period-by-period trading volumes significantly exceeded the average trading volume for the same intra-day periods observed over the previous 30 days, especially between 2:00 p.m. and 3:30 p.m.

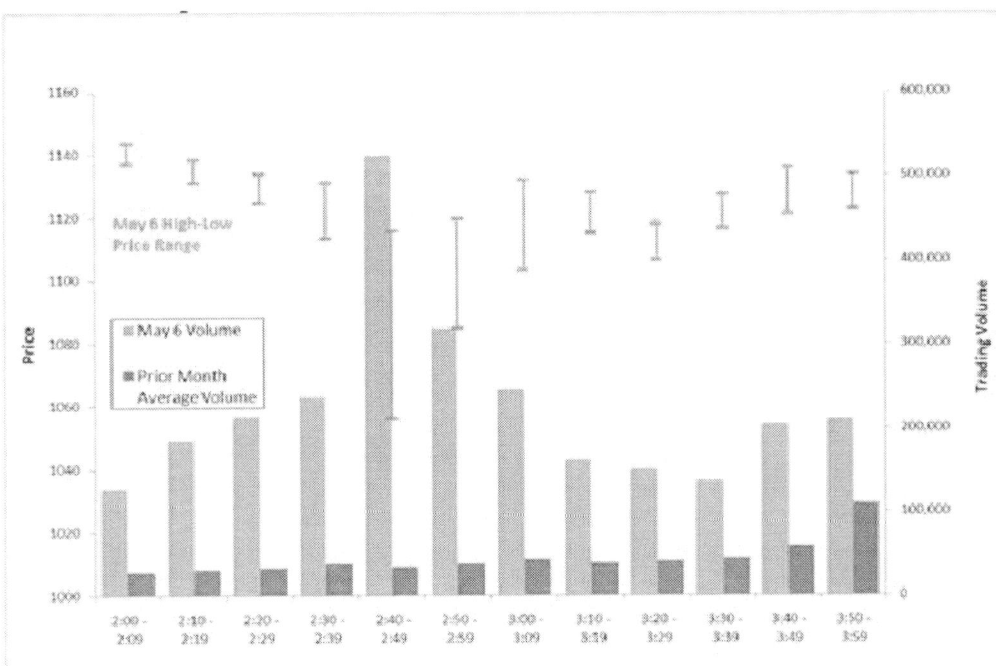


Source: CME Group

Figure 29. CME Emini S&P 500 Futures Trade Price and Volume

The daily trading activity did not result in a significant increase in the number of futures contracts held by market participants at the end of May 6, 2010. This implies many investors participated in the market intraday, but on balance few investors increased their position by the close of trading. Specifically, open interest in the June 2010 E-mini S&P 500 futures contract increased by only 3.74%, to 2,688,328 contracts; at this level, daily open interest on May 6, 2010 did not rank among the highest five days over the previous 5 years.[38] An increase in open interest means there is a cumulative increase in the size of the market participants' positions that remained open at the close of trading.

In line with broad market trends, high trading volume in the June 2010 E-mini S&P 500 contract on May 6, 2010 coincided with significant changes in prices (price volatility). The daily price range in the E-mini S&P 500 was 112.75 points. This represents the second widest daily price range over the past five years. The other four of the top five widest price ranges over the past five years occurred during the financial crisis in the autumn of 2008, including the single largest daily price range of 115.5 points on October 28, 2008. Within the trading day, the widest range between high and low prices (calculated over 10 minute intervals) in the E-mini S&P 500—59.75 points— occurred during the period 2:40 p.m. to 2:49 p.m. (Figure 29).

According to the CME, over 250 Globex executing firms were active in routing E-mini S&P 500 futures contract orders into Globex during the hour beginning at 2 p.m., including the period from 2:40 p.m. to 3:00 p.m. A Globex executing firm is an entity that is directly connected into Globex. Non-Globex executing firms access that trading platform through a Globex executing firm.

Also during the hour of 2 p.m., Globex transactions in the E-mini S & P 500 futures were recorded for 6,939 buy accounts, 6,873 sell accounts, 7,669 buy user IDs, and 7,564 sell user IDs. A buy (sell) account is a unique Globex account that executed one or more buy (sell) orders. A buy (sell) user ID is a unique operator ID (also referred to as a "Tag 50 ID"), identifying the party who entered the order on behalf of the account. A Tag 50 ID may be authorized to enter orders on behalf of multiple accounts. As well, a single account may have multiple authorized Tag 50 IDs.

May 6, 2010 was also the first day in 2010on which the Globex system activated the Stop Logic functionality in any equity index futures market.[39] Under CME rules, this functionality is initiated when the last transaction price would have triggered a series of stop loss orders that, if executed, would have resulted in a cascade in prices outside a predetermined 'no bust' range (6 points in either direction in the case of the E-mini S&P 500 futures contract). The purpose of this functionality is to prevent sudden, cascading declines (or increases) in price caused by order book imbalances.[40]

At 2:40 p.m. the E-mini S&P 500 was trading at 1,113. Five minutes later at 2:45 p.m. the E-mini S&P 500 had fallen another 57 points to 1,056. At 2:45:27 p.m., the E-mini S & P 500 dropped 12.75 points over a period of 500 milliseconds on the sale of 1,100 contracts by multiple market participants. This sequence of trades caused the market to trade down to an intraday low of 1,056. Further, at 2:45:27 p.m., the bid/ ask spread in the E-mini S & P 500 market widened 6.5 points, or 26 ticks. This triggered the Globex 'Stop-Logic,' sending the E-mini S&P 500 into a reserve state at 2:45:28 p.m. The reserve state held execution of any transactions for five seconds. This hold allowed enough orders to flow into the market so that the next executed trade would be within six points of the last trade.[41] At 2:45:33 p.m. the E-mini S&P 500 exited its Stop-Logic reserve state.[42]

**Table 17. CME Equity Index FuYear tures Stop Logic Events by Date: 2007-2010**

| Year | Date | Contract | Contract Name | Time (Central Time) | Total |
|---|---|---|---|---|---|
| **2007** | 9/18/2007 | ESU7 | E MINI S&P 500 | 1:15 PM | 1 |
| | 10/31/2007 | EMDZ7 | E-MINI MID CAP | 1:14 PM | 1 |
| | 12/24/2007 | SPH8 | BIG S&P 500 | 6:52 AM | 1 |
| **2007 Total** | | | | | **3** |
| **2008** | 1/14/2008 | ESH8 | E MINI S&P 500 | 1:01 AM | 1 |
| | 1/21/2008 | SPH8 | BIG S&P 500 | 2:12 AM | 1 |
| | | ESH8 | E MINI S&P 500 | 2:12 AM | 1 |
| | 3/16/2008 | ESH8 | E MINI S&P 500 | 6:14 PM | 1 |
| | | | | 6:17 PM | 1 |
| | | | | 7:06 PM | 1 |
| | 3/17/2008 | ESH8 | E MINI S&P 500 | 2:50 AM | 1 |
| | 7/10/2008 | NQU8 | E MINI NASDAQ 100 | 11:01 PM | 1 |
| | 9/14/2008 | NQZ8 | E MINI NASDAQ 100 | 5:00 PM | 1 |
| | 9/16/2008 | ESU8 | E MINI S&P 500 | 1:14 PM | 1 |
| | 9/25/2008 | SPZ8 | BIG S&P 500 | 10:45 PM | 1 |
| | 10/6/2008 | SPZ8 | BIG S&P 500 | 3:30 PM | 1 |
| | 10/9/2008 | ESZ8 | E MINI S&P 500 | 7:21 PM | 1 |
| | 10/17/2008 | ESZ8 | E MINI S&P 500 | 3:01 AM | 1 |
| | 10/29/2008 | ESZ8 | E MINI S&P 500 | 3:43 PM | 1 |
| | 11/3/2008 | SPZ8 | BIG S&P 500 | 7:22 AM | 1 |
| | 11/13/2008 | ESH9 | E MINI S&P 500 | 11:59 AM | 1 |
| | 11/25/2008 | SPZ8 | BIG S&P 500 | 5:45 AM | 1 |
| **2008 Total** | | | | | **18** |
| 2009 | 1/9/2009 | SPH9 | BIG S&P 500 | 7:30 AM | 1 |
| | 2/27/2009 | SPH9 | BIG S&P 500 | 7:20 AM | 1 |
| | 2/28/2009 | ESZ9 | E MINI S&P 500 | 10:32 AM | 1 |
| | 3/6/2009 | ZDH9 | BIG DOW ($10) | 7:30 AM | 1 |
| | 3/17/2009 | NQM9 | E MINI NASDAQ 100 | 1:17 PM | 1 |
| | 4/23/2009 | YMM9 | E MINI DOW ($5) | 2:53 PM | 1 |
| | 12/17/2009 | NQH0 | E MINI NASDAQ 100 | 8:57 AM | 1 |
| **2009 Total** | | | | | **7** |
| 2010 | 5/6/2010 | ESM0 | E MINI S&P 500 | 1:45 PM | 1 |
| **2010 Total** | | | | | **1** |
| **Total: 2007-2010** | | | | **29** | |

Source: CME Group

Stop Logic functionality was also triggered on May 6 in two currency futures contracts, the Japanese Yen and British Pound contracts. Across all CME Group equity index futures markets, the Stop Logic functionality was activated on seven occasions in 2009, on 18 occasions during 2008 (a year with greater market volatility due to the economic crisis), and on three occasions in 2007. Fourteen of these 29 activations in equity index futures, including the one on May 6, occurred in the E-mini S&P 500 contract. Save for the unusual circumstances of the Fall of 2008, Globex activates Stop Logic an average of five times per year across all equity index futures products, and an average of approximately three times per year in the E-mini contract. All Stop Logic functionality activations in CME equity index futures markets from 2007 through the present are listed in Table 17.

Although the triggering of the Stop Logic functionality in the E-mini S&P 500 futures contract is not unprecedented, the events of May 6 caused significant public concern about the functioning of financial markets. Previous Stop Logic events occurred, including during the financial crisis of 2008, when liquidity concerns played a key role. Consequently, CFTC staff has conducted an analysis of trading activity and liquidity provision in the June 2010 E-mini S&P 500 futures contract during 2:30 p.m. to 3:00 p.m. – the period of the day when trading volume and transaction prices were particularly volatile.

### *2. Role of Liquidity in Markets*

Liquidity reflects the ease with which certain amounts of an asset can be bought or sold without exerting a significant effect on its price. Higher market liquidity can be interpreted as a greater collective willingness to execute orders at given prices.

Market liquidity is not directly observable. In addition, market liquidity has multiple dimensions that are hard to capture by a single indicator. CFTC staff reviewed multiple indicators of liquidity, including, but not limited to, trading volume, bid/offer spread, and depth. High liquidity may manifest itself as high trading volume, narrow bid/offer spreads, and/or high depth of the order book at successive quotes.

As discussed below, preliminary analysis shows that between 2:30 p.m. and 3:00 p.m., trading volume spiked, bid/offer spreads widened, and depth declined. The latter two observations are consistent with a significant decline in liquidity with the bulk of that decline occurring between 2:42 p.m. and 2:45 p.m.

#### a) Trading Volume

CFTC staff has analyzed trading volume and transaction prices for the June 2010 E-mini S&P 500 futures contract during the period 2:30 p.m. to 3:00 p.m. on May 6, 2010.Figure 30 presents transaction prices and trading volume for 10 second intervals from 2:30 p.m. to 3:00 p.m. for the June E-mini S&P 500 contact on May 6, 2010. According to Figure 1, between 2:30 p.m. and approximately 2:45 p.m., volume rose significantly while prices fell. Between 2:45 p.m. and 3:00 p.m. volume fell and prices rose.

During the 30-minute period from 2:30 p.m. to 3:00 p.m., trading volume was about 10 times the average daily trading volume for the same intraday time period calculated over the prior 30 days. High trading volume by itself can be interpreted as an indicator of improved liquidity. However, Figure 30shows that high trading volume was accompanied by significant volatility of trading volume. This suggests a dislocation of market liquidity, with high volume fluctuations at the same time that orders are executed deep into the limit order book.

Consequently, liquidity indicators based on the characteristics of the limit order book may provide additional information about the liquidity dynamics during 2:30 p.m. to 3:00 p.m. on May 6, 2010.

**b) Bid/Offer Spread**

The bid/offer spread is a liquidity indicator based on the characteristics of the limit order book. Specifically, the bid/offer spread is calculated as the difference between the highest quoted price to buy (bid) and the lowest quoted price to sell (offer or ask) one or several contracts or securities. This price difference is a measure of the cost paid by a buyer or a seller who wishes to transact immediately. Similarly, the second, third, fourth, fifth best bid and offer prices represent transaction costs to the buyer and seller willing to buy at increasingly lower prices and sell at increasingly higher prices.

Figure 31presents the bid/offer spreads for the first best and fifth best quotes of the June 2010 E-mini S&P 500 specifically focusing on the period of 2:43 p.m. to 2:48 p.m. along with transaction prices. The spread is measured in ticks—minimum price increments; for the E-mini S&P 500 contract the tick is equal to 0.25 point. The smallest bid/offer spread is one tick (0.25 point) and the smallest spread between the fifth best quotes is 9 ticks (2.25 points).[43] Until approximately 2:45 p.m., both spreads were at their minimums, as is most often observed in this market. At 2:45:28 p.m., the best bid/offer spread widened to 26 ticks (6.5 points). At this time, Globex Stop Logic triggered a 5-second reserve state in the E-mini S&P 500 contract. Following the reserve state, the first and fifth best quote spreads increased to the period maxima of approximately 11 ticks (2.85 points) and 33 ticks (8.25 points), respectively.[44] By 2:50:40 p.m., both spreads declined to about 1 and 9 ticks (0.25 and 2.25 points), respectively.

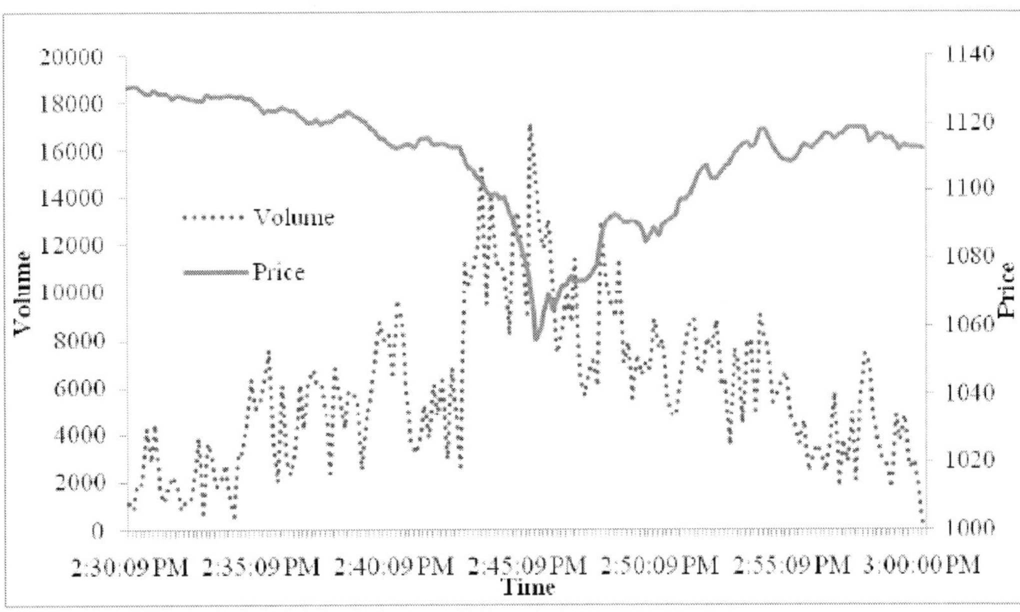


Source: CME Group

Figure 30. Price and Trading Volume in the June 2010 Emini S&P 500 Futures Contract

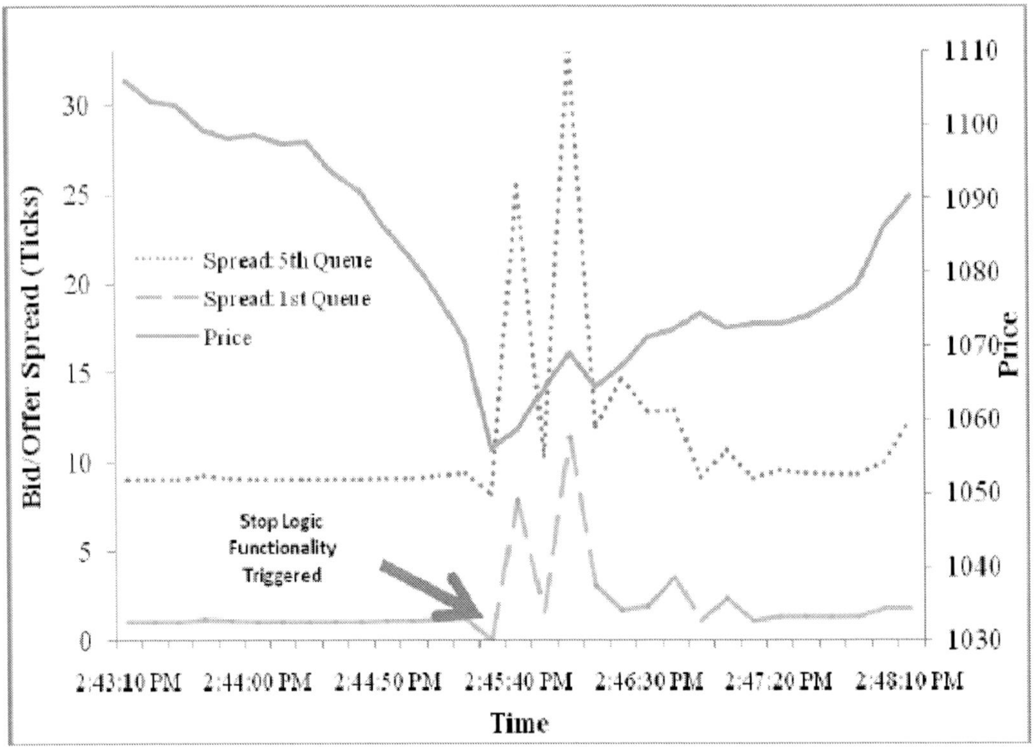


Source: CME Group

Figure 31. Bid/Offer Spread (in Ticks) and Price in the June 2010 Emini S&P 500 Futures Contract

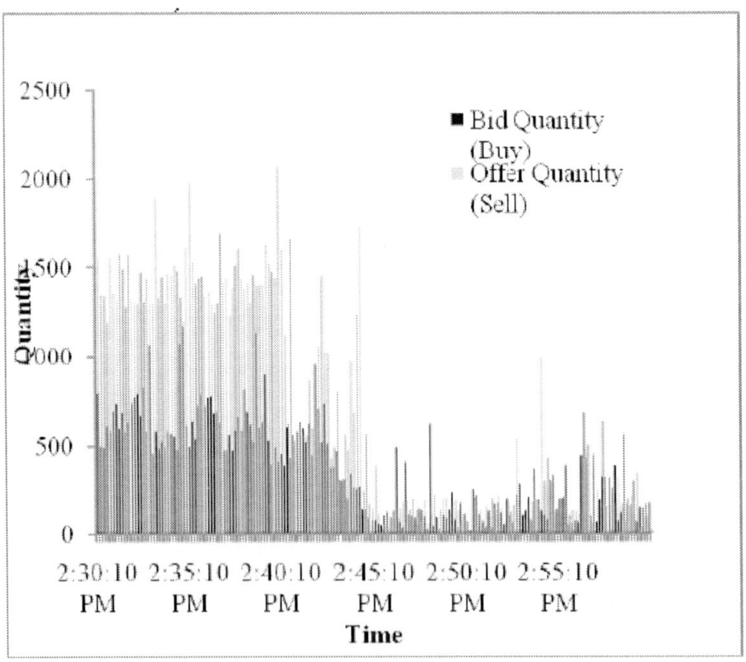


Source: CME Group

Figure 32. Bid/Offer Quantities: 5th Best in the June 2010 Emini S&P 500 Futures Contract

**c) Depth**

Depth is another liquidity indicator based on the size of orders in the limit order book. Depth is calculated as the sum of quantities of the orders resting at a particular price point—e.g., best bid or offer, second, third, fourth or fifth best bid or offer—in the limit order book. High depth (resting orders) on both sides of the limit order book may (but need not) result in higher trading volume (executed orders).

Figure 32 illustrates the depth at the fifth best bid and offer quotes between 2.30 p.m. and 3:00 p.m. According to Figure 32, significant order imbalances existed between orders to buy and orders to sell. In addition, around 2:45 p.m., depth declined dramatically, but the limit order book became approximately balanced (orders to sell became approximately equal to orders to buy), which is its typical state.

### *3. Analysis of Large Traders*

In order to further analyze the liquidity dynamics between 2:30 p.m. and 3:00 p.m., CFTC staff examined the activities of large traders. In the preliminary analysis below, we report (1) the role of liquidity providers (six accounts, as defined below) and (2) activity of the ten largest traders by volume.

First, Figure 33 presents the total transaction sides[45] of two groups of market participants: liquidity providers and liquidity takers.

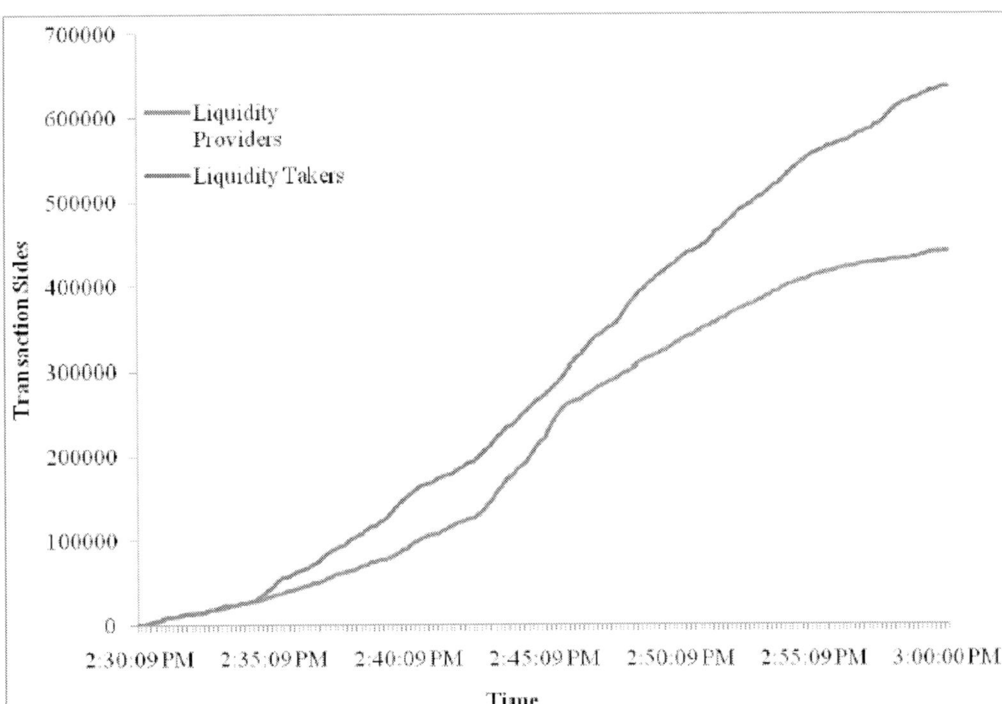


Source: CME Group and CFTC Staff Calculation

Figure 33. Cumulative Number of Transaction Sides of Liquidity Providers and Liquidity Takers in the June 2010 Emini S&P 500 Futures Contract

Liquidity providers are traders that are routinely present in the market to both buy and sell futures contracts, facilitating rapid execution of transactions. In electronic limit order markets such as Globex, where the E-mini S&P 500 futures contract is traded, there are no designated liquidity providers (that is, no trader has an obligation to provide bid and ask quotations on demand). Thus, for the purpose of this preliminary analysis, CFTC staff classified liquidity providers by their activity in the markets.[46]

CFTC staff classified six accounts as liquidity providers. These six accounts participated in about 50 percent of all transaction sides between 2:30 p.m. and 2:34 p.m. The remaining 4,573 accounts (of the total 4,579 accounts transacting between 2:30 p.m. and 3:00 p.m.) are defined as liquidity takers.

CFTC staff examined the behavior of liquidity providers during the time period 2:30 p.m. to 3:00 p.m. and observed that starting at approximately 2:35 p.m. liquidity providers began limiting their trading activity as measured by transaction sides in comparison to liquidity takers (Figure 33).[47] By 2:45:28 p.m., liquidity providers accounted for 46 percent of all transaction sides, lower than their participation percentage between 2:30 p.m. and 2:34 p.m. By 3:00 p.m. the liquidity providers accounted for 41 percent of transaction sides. The decline in the participation of liquidity providers in executed transactions can be interpreted as a partial withdrawal of liquidity by these six providers during a period of significant price movement.

Second, CFTC staff reviewed the activity of the ten largest traders by net volume and by gross volume, in order to ascertain whether there were significant imbalances between large buyers and sellers in the market. For two intraday time periods—2:30 to 2:45 p.m. and 2:46 to 3:00 p.m.—the net volume was computed for each account in the E-mini S&P 500 June 2010 futures contract.[48] During the period from 2:30 to 2:45 p.m., the top 10 net buying accounts bought 51,526 contracts more than they sold. The top 10 net selling accounts sold 72,186 contracts more than they bought. During the period from 2:46 to 3:00 p.m., the top 10 net buying accounts bought 49,180 contracts more than they sold. The top 10 net selling accounts sold 67,544 contracts more than they bought.

In addition, CFTC staff identified the top ten most active accounts by gross volume between 2:00 p.m. and 3:00 p.m. Of those ten, nine trading accounts executed trades on both the long and short side of the market. For these trading accounts, there was a relative balance of activity between the long and short sides of the market.

One out of the top ten trading accounts only entered orders to sell. That trader entered the market at around 2:32 p.m. and finished trading by around 2:51 p.m. The trader's short futures position represented on average, nine percent on the volume traded during that period. The trader sold on the way down and continued to do so even as the price level rose.

We are continuing to analyze trading activity, including conducting interviews with market participants to collect further data.

### *4. Preliminary Findings*

The quantitative evidence presented above suggest that a confluence of economic events, market forces, and trading system functionality led to a significant dislocation of liquidity in the June 2010 E-mini S&P 500 futures contract sometime between 2:30 p.m. and 3:00 p.m. on May 6, 2010.

Prior to that time, a number of economic events and market developments led to a broad-based market desire to lessen risk exposures. This translated into a downward movement in prices across financial markets in conjunction with significant trading volume. At or about 2:30 p.m., the electronic limit order book in the E-mini S&P 500 futures market exhibited a significant imbalance of sell orders and buy orders. In the backdrop of declining prices, this imbalance appears to have contributed to a sudden liquidity dislocation despite increased trading volume. At approximately 2:45 p.m., several sell orders executed deep into the limit order book, which coincided with a significant loss of depth, triggering the Stop Logic functionality. The Stop Logic functionality in the E-mini S&P 500 contract has been triggered a number of times in the past few years, including several times during the financial crisis in the fall of 2008, when market conditions may have resembled those seen on May 6, 2010. Activation of the Stop Logic functionality on May 6, 2010, initiated a five second pause in trading in the E-mini S&P 500 futures contract. After the five second pause, the limit order book became more balanced, which is its typical state, and the price of the E-mini S&P 500 futures contract recovered.

## C. Clearance and Settlement

### *1. Securities Markets*

Securities clearing agencies are self-regulatory organizations that are required to register with the SEC under Section 17A of the Securities Exchange Act. There are two types of securities clearing agencies – clearing corporations and depositories.

Clearing corporations compare member transactions (or report to members the results of exchange comparison operations), clear those trades and prepare instructions for automated settlement of those trades, and often act as intermediaries in making those settlements. Clearing corporations include the National Securities Clearing Corporation ("NSCC"), a subsidiary of the Depository Trust & Clearing Corporation ("DTCC"), and the Options Clearing Corporation ("OCC"). Depositories hold securities in bulk form for their participants and maintain ownership records of the securities on their own books. Currently, the Depository Trust Company, a subsidiary of DTCC, is the primary U.S. securities depository.

There were no significant processing issues at DTCC or OCC as a result of the market events on Thursday, May 6. The clearing agencies' systems operated in an orderly manner both during and subsequent to those market events.

Collection of funds due to the clearing agencies on the morning of Friday, May 7, occurred without incident as all clearing fund participants met their payment obligations on time.

To accommodate the late submission of trade data by exchanges, clearing agencies, where necessary, delayed end-of-day processing on Thursday, May 6. This was particularly the case at the DTCC subsidiary NSCC because of the large number of cancelled trades in the equities markets. Processing was completed at OCC only slightly later than usual.

The market volatility and price decreases on Thursday, May 6, also resulted in substantially higher margin and clearing fund requirements at the clearing agencies on Friday, May 7. The requirements were calculated pursuant to the risk-based margin methodologies in place at the clearing agencies and in accordance with clearing agency rules and procedures. All margin and clearing fund requirements were met by clearing participants Friday morning on time.

### *2. Futures Markets*

The Commodity Exchange Act ("CEA") requires all CFTC regulated designated contract markets ("DCM") to have all contracts that trade on the DCM to be cleared and settled by a CFTC registered derivatives clearing organization ("DCO"). The DCO functions as the central counterparty and guarantor for the positions that result from all contracts traded on the DCM. This means that the DCO is the long to each short position and the short to each long position in all contracts that it clears. DCOs deal exclusively with their clearing participants. Any market participant that is not a clearing member of a particular DCM must have its positions carried by a clearing member. The DCO for CME is the CME Clearing House while the DCO for ICE Futures US is ICE CLEAR US.

One of the critical functions that each CFTC registered DCO performs is the removal of debt obligations among its clearing members at least at the end of the trading session for a given trade date. This is accomplished by independently determining a settlement (or marking) price for each contract that is cleared and marking all open positions to that price. The DCO collects cash from clearing members that have lost money on their positions and pays it to clearing members that have gained money on their positions.

With respect to the trading that took place on May 6 at CME and ICE Futures U.S., the clearing and settlement processes worked effectively and without incident.

The amount that the CME collected and paid to its clearing members as a result of the end-of-day mark-to-market calculation for all contracts cleared by CME was $4,073,195,863. Of this sum, $2,902,837,844 was collected and paid in the customer origin while $1,170,358,019 was collected and paid in the house origin.

The amount collected and paid by ICE CLEAR US to its clearing members as a result of the end-of-day mark-to-market calculation was $749,680,556. Of this sum, $120,701,044 was collected and paid in the customer origin while $628,979,512 was collected and paid in the house origin.

All payments to and from each DCO were met on time.

# V. Next Steps

## A. Areas for Further Analysis

### *1. Securities Markets*

A crucial area for further analysis is how sudden demands for liquidity (particularly by sellers in a rapidly declining market) are transmitted among the various securities, options, and futures markets and products. In today's highly automated and low-latency markets, the links between the various related markets and products are extremely tight.

To conduct this analysis, we are undertaking a detailed market reconstruction, so that cross-market patterns can be detected and the behavior of stocks or traders can be analyzed in detail. Reconstructing the market on May 6 from dozens of different sources and calibrating the time stamps from each source to ensure consistency across all the data is consuming a significant amount of SEC staff resources.[49] The data are voluminous, and include hundreds of millions of records comprising an estimated five to ten terabytes of information. On May 6, there were over 17 million trades between 2:00 p.m. and 3:00 p.m. alone. Overall, the markets processed 10.3 billion shares in NYSE stocks alone that day. By contrast, the key day in the 1987 Market Break Study involved a trading session processing a little over 600 million shares in NYSE stocks.

SEC staff is investigating plausible explanations of events, forming testable hypotheses and using the data available to us to assess them. There are many challenges to completing this analyses. The size and complexity of our markets and those of related markets, the effects of computerized trading, the diversity and opacity of trading strategies and linkages among financial instruments make this a complicated task.

A theory of the May 6 events should attempt to explain a number of the preliminary findings outlined in this chapter, to the extent they are confirmed by a more exhaustive analysis, as well as any other facts uncovered. Among other things, a theory should explain:

- the sudden decline and sudden rebound in stocks generally;
- significant intraday negative returns of certain issues;
- the intraday lows of nearly zero in approximately 200 issues (shown in Figure 8), and the heightened levels of short selling that occurred at or near the intraday low;
- the extreme intraday highs of a significant number of issues, particularly among ETFs; and
- the disproportionate representation of ETFs among extreme returns.

A central component of this research is to understand the basic facts surrounding the event period and examine data from key additional sources. This exploratory work will guide the staff in forming causal hypotheses. For example, we will likely examine in more detail options data, including data on options transactions and quotes to better understand the role that participants in this market may have played.[50] We also will likely examine existing data on institutional and mutual fund holdings, as well as data from broker-dealers that will help attribute trades to specific brokerage accounts. In addition, we will examine trade and order characteristics to determine whether specific order types played a role in the breakdown of the price discovery mechanism.

Another key component of our analysis is to deepen our understanding of the behavior of groups of market participants. We, for example, will continue to examine the role of providers of liquidity, including market participants who have formal obligations under the federal securities laws or SRO rules. To the extent that data is available, we will seek to understand the impact of traders following high-frequency or algorithmic trading strategies. Many proprietary trading firms engage in automated strategies that continually monitor the various markets and products for disparities in prices. When the trading systems for these firms spot such disparities, they can generate in microseconds an enormous volume of orders that are intended to capitalize on these disparities. We would also consider examining the activities of ETF Authorized Participants in order to understand what, if any role, they played, in the markets of May 6. Additionally, our analysis to date has encompassed information about both ETF and non-ETF ETPs, but has not yet ascertained whether or not there are significant differences between the trading experiences of the two.

### *2. Futures Markets*

**a) Additional Analysis of Large Traders and Review of OTC Swaps**

CFTC staff will continue reviewing information from a special call on over 40 large traders for their trading activity in the E-mini S&P 500 and Russell 2000 futures contracts on May 6, 2010. A special call is a CFTC directive to a trader holding a reportable position to furnish any pertinent information concerning the trader's positions, transactions, or activities.[51] A reportable position in the E-mini S&P 500 futures contract is 1,000 contracts.[52] Staff also will continue reviewing information from a special call to swap dealers about their activity in over-the-counter broad-based security index derivatives markets on May 6, 2010. Staff also will continue its detailed review of trader activity on May 6 through a comprehensive examination of trade-register data. To date, staff has received over 25 gigabytes of data in over 307,000 files, with more data expected.

**b) Additional Analysis of May 6 Activity**

CFTC staff will continue to scrutinize a broad range of existing evidence, collect new evidence, and update its analysis of the events of May 6, 2010.

CFTC staff will also continue our analysis of high frequency traders active in the E-mini S&P 500 futures on May 6, 2010.

### *3. Coordinated Analysis*

As reported above, related financial instruments appeared to experience significant volatility, including the sharp decline and recovery in close proximity. This suggests the need to study the linkages between correlated assets in the equities (single stocks, mutual funds and ETFs), options and futures markets. The study could partly focus on examining cross-market linkages by analyzing trading in stock index products such as equity index futures, ETFs, equity index options, and equity index OTC derivatives using, to the extent practicable, market data, special call information, and order book data. The growth, depth, and use of instruments in each of these markets to serve as intra- and cross-market hedges suggest that regulators need to better understand the linkages between these markets.

Given the role that the two agencies play in overseeing key related markets, the staff of the CFTC and SEC should coordinate on a study designed to shed further light on these linkages. Such a study may significantly help design a coordinated system of meaningful and appropriate pauses and halts for these interlinked markets.

## B. Potential Regulatory Responses

The Commissions are considering whether modifications to the existing market-wide circuit breakers are warranted in light of the events of May 6. Any such modifications should be done in a coordinated manner between the securities and futures markets.

An important lesson from the events of May 6 is the need to better understand cross-market linkages between trading venues for exchange-traded funds, equity index futures, and equity index options—instruments used by investors to manage their exposures in the face of broad market movements. A thorough understanding of cross-market linkages will better inform the design of a coordinated system of meaningful and appropriate pauses and halts for these interlinked markets.

In connection with better understanding inter-market mechanisms, it is also important for the agencies to review the various mechanisms used and designed by exchanges to protect orderly markets. As the study of the May 6 events continues, attention should be given to the adequacy of current mechanisms under different stress situations.

### *1. Securities Markets*

As noted above, the SEC is taking a number of steps to identify the cause or causes of the May 6 market disruption as well as factors that may have exacerbated that event, and to develop regulatory initiatives to help prevent a recurrence.

#### a) Implement Stock-by-Stock Circuit Breakers

The SEC staff is working with the stock exchanges and FINRA to promptly develop and implement a cross-market "circuit breaker" mechanism to be applied on a stock-by-stock basis. Although the prices of many stocks on May 6 declined in proportion with the broader market decline that occurred in securities and futures index products, the prices of many other individual stocks declined much more before returning near to the prices at which they were trading prior to the precipitous decline.

A uniform circuit breaker rule, which would briefly pause trading across the securities markets when the price of a security has rapidly declined over a short period of time, should make a recurrence of a severe market disruption, such as the one that occurred on May 6, much less likely.

#### b) Market Orders

As noted above, some of the most disturbing executions on May 6 likely resulted from the use of market orders. Market orders – particularly stop loss orders that convert to market orders – are popular with certain investors, including retail investors, and it is possible such investors may have been on the losing side of a number of these trades.

We are considering ways to address the risks of market orders, and their potential to contribute to sudden price moves. Areas under consideration include: (1) requiring market order "collars," thereby effectively converting market orders into limit orders; (2) prohibiting or limiting the use of market orders; (3) requiring broker-dealers to specifically warn retail customers about the risks of market orders, particularly in volatile markets; and (4) pursuing investor education initiatives as to the risks of market orders.

#### c) Market Making Obligations and Stub Quotes

Liquidity providers to, or "the other side" of, the extraordinarily erroneous trades seen on May 6 appears in many cases to be "stub" quotes (*e.g.*, a $0.01 bid) of market makers that effectively had pulled out of the market. Market makers maintain these nominal quotes to meet exchange requirements that they maintain a two-sided quote throughout the trading day. We are considering steps to deter or prohibit stub quotes, including: (1) requiring all market makers to maintain bona fide quotes that are reasonably related to the market, perhaps using objective parameters that are consistent across markets; or (2) alternatively, relaxing requirements that market makers maintain a two-sided quote throughout the day, and thereby obviate the need for market makers to post stub quotes that could be executed against in severe market conditions.

**d) Revise Procedures for Breaking Clearly Erroneous Trades**

The SEC expects the exchanges and FINRA to improve the process for breaking "clearly erroneous" trades. Of course, the primary objective should be a market structure that minimizes the need to correct erroneous trades, and the initiatives described above should do that. To the extent any erroneous trades continue to occur, however, they should be resolved promptly and consistently across markets through a transparent process with objective standards. The SROs are considering a specified percentage threshold away from the market price at which erroneous trades uniformly would be broken. This should provide market participants clarity and certainty as to whether their trades will stand in the event the market becomes particularly volatile.

**e) Current Initiatives to Strengthen Market Integrity**

The SEC had already undertaken a number of broader initiatives to strengthen the integrity our markets, even before the events of May 6.

In January, the SEC published a concept release on equity market structure ("Market Structure Concept Release")[53] that highlighted many aspects of today's highly automated markets and requested public comment on a wide variety of issues. The Market Structure Concept Release was designed to further the SEC's broad review of market structure to assess whether its rules have kept pace with, among other things, changes in trading technology and practices.

The events of May 6 implicate a number of issues raised in the Market Structure Concept Release. For example, the Release asked whether the current market structure appropriately minimizes the short-term volatility that can be harmful to long-term investors. It asked whether the relatively good performance of the market structure in 2008 indicated that systemic risk was appropriately minimized in the current market structure and, if not, what further steps the SEC should take to address systemic risk. Finally, it noted the dominant role of high-frequency trading firms in today's market structure and observed that they had largely replaced the role of specialists and market makers with affirmative and negative obligations for market liquidity and market quality. More specifically, the Market Structure Concept Release asked whether there is any evidence that proprietary firms increase or reduce the amount of liquidity provided to the market during times of stress. It also asked whether co-location conveyed any unfair advantage and discussed various types of short-term trading strategies, including "directional" strategies, such as "momentum ignition," that could present serious problems in today's market structure by exacerbating short-term volatility.

We are also considering whether initiatives are warranted to address destabilizing short-term trading strategies, to the extent they contributed to the May 6 market disruption. For example, a variety of directional strategies that might be employed by proprietary trading firms are discussed in the Market Structure Concept Release. It is too early to know whether short-term professional trading strategies played any role in the events of May 6. If they contributed significantly to the precipitous decline, however, we must consider whether additional regulatory requirements are necessary to prevent such strategies from threatening the fairness and integrity of the markets.

In February, moreover, the SEC adopted a short sale circuit breaker. That rule is designed to limit short selling where an individual stock is under stress and has experienced a decline of 10 percent from the previous day's close. At that point, the restrictions of the rule provide assurances to investors that short sellers are not taking the stock down. In so doing, we believe that the rule will promote investor confidence.

In addition, the SEC has published a series of concrete market structure proposals that are designed to strengthen the U.S. securities markets and to protect investors. These include the proposal to prohibit flash orders and the proposal to increase the transparency of "dark" pools of liquidity, as well as the market access proposal to strengthen broker-dealer risk management controls and the large trader reporting proposal to enhance the SEC's surveillance and enforcement capabilities. These proposals are described in greater detail below.

**(1) Market Access Proposal**

In January, the SEC proposed a rule that would require effective risk management controls for broker-dealers with access to markets, including those providing customers sponsored access to the markets. Our proposal would effectively prohibit the growing practice by some broker-dealers of providing "unfiltered" sponsored access, where a customer is permitted to directly access the markets using the broker-dealer's market participant identifier but without the imposition of effective pre-trade risk management controls. All broker-dealers accessing the markets should implement controls to effectively manage the risks associated with this activity, and our proposal would unequivocally require them to do so. These risks include the potential breach of a credit or capital limit, the submission of erroneous orders as a result of computer malfunction or human error, and the failure to comply with regulatory requirements. Effective risk management controls for market access arrangements are necessary to protect the broker-dealer, the markets, the financial system, and ultimately investors. Such controls would help prevent trading activity that could trigger a severe market disruption.

**(2) Large Trader Reporting Proposal**

Last month, the SEC proposed to create a large trader reporting system that would enhance our ability to identify large market participants, collect information on their trades, and analyze their trading activity. To keep pace with rapid technological advances that have impacted trading strategies and the ways in which some market participants trade, the SEC must be able to readily identify large traders operating in the U.S. securities markets, and obtain basic identifying information on each large trader, its accounts, and its affiliates. In addition, to support its regulatory and enforcement activities, the SEC must have a mechanism to track efficiently and obtain promptly trading records on large trader activity.

The current system for collecting transaction data from registered broker-dealers is generally utilized in more narrowly-focused investigations involving trading in particular securities, and is not generally conducive to larger-scale market reconstructions and analyses involving numerous stocks during periods of peak trading volume. In addition, existing tools often require weeks or longer to compile trading data to identify potentially large traders. The SEC needs to develop the tools necessary to readily identify large traders and be able to evaluate their trading activity is heightened by the fact that large traders, including certain high-frequency traders, are playing an increasingly prominent role in the securities markets.

The proposed rule would enhance the SEC's ability to identify those "large trader" market participants that conduct a substantial amount of trading activity in U.S. securities, as measured by volume or market value. In addition, the proposal would facilitate the SEC's ability to obtain from broker-dealers records of large trader activity. By providing the SEC with prompt access to information about large traders and their trading activity, the proposed rule is intended to facilitate the SEC's efforts in reconstructing market activity and performing analyses of trading data, as well as assist in investigations of manipulative, abusive, and other illegal trading activity.

**(3) Consideration of Consolidated Audit Trail Proposal**

As noted above, SEC staff have been working, in consultation with SROs and others, on a rule proposal that would require the SROs to jointly develop, implement and maintain a consolidated order tracking system, or consolidated audit trail. If adopted, this rule proposal should result in a continuous reporting mechanism for market participants that would capture the data needed for effective cross-market surveillance. The proposed changes would significantly improve the SEC's ability to conduct timely and accurate trading analyses for market reconstructions and complex investigations, as well as inspections and examinations. For example, the proposed consolidated audit trail would enable the SEC to access in real time the majority of the data needed to reconstruct the type of market disruption that occurred on May 6, with remaining information available within a matter of days rather than weeks.

## *2. Futures Markets*

### a) Review of Electronic Trading and Market Access

CFTC staff will also continue our analysis, already begun by our Office of Chief Economist, of liquidity provision in futures markets, with a particular focus on electronic trading. The subjects to be reviewed here include high frequency and algorithmic trading, automatic execution innovations on trading platforms, market access issues, and co-location.

### b) Review of Co-Location

CFTC staff is considering a proposed rulemaking with respect to exchange co-location and proximity hosting services. The purpose of the proposed rule would be to ensure that all otherwise qualified and eligible market participants that seek co-location or proximity hosting services offered by futures exchanges have equal access to such services without barriers that exclude access, or that bar otherwise qualified third-party vendors from providing co-location and/or proximity hosting services. Another purpose of the proposal would be to ensure that futures exchanges that offer co-location or proximity hosting services disclose publically the latencies for each available connectivity option, so that participants can make informed decisions.

### c) Additional Analysis of Large Traders and Review of OTC Swaps

The CFTC will continue reviewing information from a special call on major swap traders for their trading activity on May 6, 2010. A special call is a CFTC directive to a trader holding a reportable position to furnish any pertinent information concerning the trader's positions, transactions, or activities.[54] A reportable position in the E-mini S&P 500 futures contract is 1,000 contracts.[55] There will also be a review of special call information about the activity of swap dealers in over-the-counter broad-based security index derivatives markets on May 6, 2010. Staff also will continue its detailed review of trader activity on May 6 through a comprehensive examination of trade-register data.

**d) Automation of Account Identification**

CFTC staff will also be considering possible rules to enhance the CFTC's surveillance capabilities. These measures include automation of the statement of reporting traders in the large trader reporting system and obtaining account ownership and control information in the exchange trade registers.[56] These initiatives would increase the timeliness and efficiency of account identification, an essential step in data analysis.

# APPENDIX A. OVERVIEW OF THE SECURITIES MARKET STRUCTURE

## A. The National Market System and Regulation NMS

In Section 11A of the Securities Exchange Act of 1934 (added to the Exchange Act in 1975), Congress directed the SEC to facilitate the establishment of a national market system for securities in accordance with specified findings and objectives. Congress recognized that the securities markets are an important national asset that must be preserved and strengthened, and that new data processing and communications techniques create the opportunity for more efficient and effective market operations. It mandated a national market system composed of multiple competing markets that are linked through technology. A national market system should be contrasted with a structure in which trading is confined to a single trading venue, such as one particular exchange. Congress determined that promoting competition among trading venues and giving as many market makers as possible an opportunity to provide liquidity in stocks would promote greater liquidity and price continuity than a single dominant trading venue.

Over the years, the SEC has sought to keep market structure rules up-to-date with continually changing economic conditions and technology advances. The most recent major updating of the national market system rules occurred in 2005, when the SEC adopted Regulation NMS.[57] Regulation NMS addresses four areas: (1) a "trade-through" rule that prevents the execution of trades at prices that are inferior to a displayed and immediately accessible quotation on another trading venue; (2) an "access" rule that, among other things, promotes private linkages among market participants and trading venues; (3) a "sub-penny" rule that prohibits the display, ranking, or accepting of orders with sub-penny prices; and (4) amendments to the joint-industry plans for collecting and distributing consolidated market data to the public.

The trade-through rule[58] is probably the most well-known aspect of Regulation NMS and arguably has affected the equities markets most significantly since it was adopted in 2005. The Regulation NMS trade-through rule eliminated a prior rule that benefited dominant exchanges with trading floors by protecting their manual quotations (that is, orders were required to be routed to the exchange in an attempt to access a manual quotation that could take as long as 10-20 seconds, rather than to another venue with an immediately accessible quotation at an inferior price).

To compete under the new regulatory structure, all exchanges developed electronic systems that are capable of providing immediate responses to incoming orders and updating their quotations immediately. These systems enable the exchanges to display quotations that are protected against trade-throughs. Trade-through protection was designed to promote best execution and price stability by preventing one trading venue from ignoring the immediately accessible quotations of another trading venue in a downturn (as well as upturn). However, the trade-through rule does not protect a trading venue's quotation if it is not immediately accessible.

## B. The Nature of Trading in the Current Equities Market Structure

### *1. Trading Centers*

At least partly as a result of Regulation NMS, trading in U.S-listed stocks has changed dramatically in recent years. Trading volume now is dispersed among many different trading venues. For example, the share of the New York Stock Exchange in the trading in NYSE-listed stocks declined from 79.1 percent in 2005 to 25.1 percent in 2009. National securities exchanges and another type of trading venue, electronic communications networks ("ECNs"), both display quotations in the consolidated quotation data that is widely distributed to the public. In addition, two other types of trading centers exist –dark pools and broker-dealers that execute trades internally – neither of which display quotations in the consolidated quotation data. Nevertheless, more than 70 percent of volume continues to be executed by public trading venues that display quotations across a wide range of U.S-listed stocks. Figure 1 below sets forth the major types of trading venues, along with estimates of their trading volume in September 2009:[59]

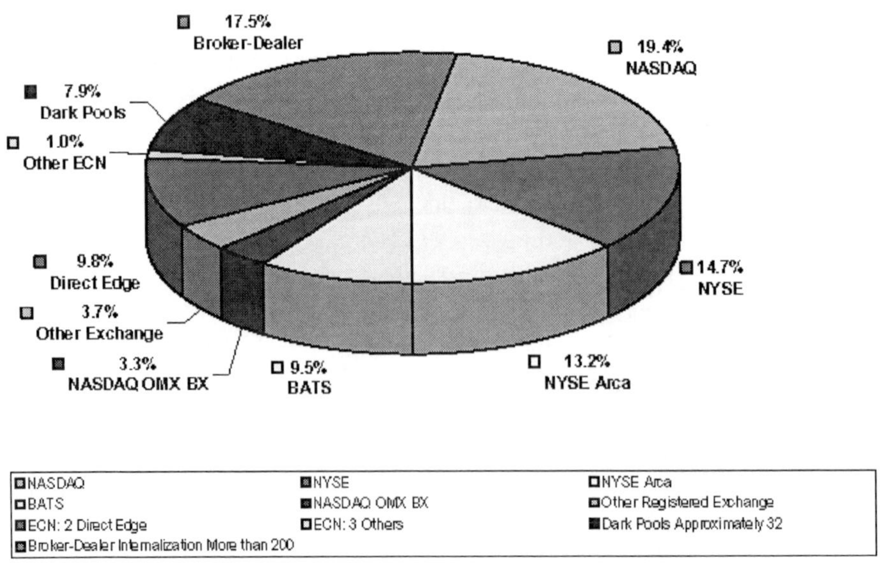


Figure 1. Trading Centers and Estimated Percentage of Share Volume in NMS Stocks

**a) Registered Exchanges**

Registered exchanges (such as NASDAQ, NYSE, NYSE Arca and BATS, among others) must undertake self-regulatory responsibility for their members and file their proposed rule changes for approval with the SEC. These proposed rule changes publicly disclose, among other things, the trading services and fees of exchanges.

The registered exchanges all have adopted highly automated trading systems that can offer extremely high-speed, or "low-latency," order responses and executions. The average response times at some exchanges, for example, have been reduced to less than 1 millisecond.[60] Many exchanges also offer individual data feeds that deliver information concerning their orders and trades directly to customers. To further increase speed in transmitting market data and order messages, many exchanges also offer co-location services that enable exchange customers to place their servers in close proximity to the exchange's matching engine.

Registered exchanges typically offer a wide range of order types for trading on their automated systems. Some of their order types are displayable in full if they are not executed immediately. Others are undisplayed, in full or in part. For example, a reserve order type will display part of the size of an order at a particular price, while holding the balance of the order in reserve and refreshing the displayed size as needed. In general, displayed orders are given execution priority at any given price over fully undisplayed orders and the undisplayed size of reserve orders.[61]

In addition, many exchanges have adopted a "maker-taker" pricing model in an effort to attract liquidity providers. Under this model, non-marketable, resting orders that offer (make) liquidity at a particular price receive a liquidity rebate if they are executed, while incoming orders that execute against (take) the liquidity of resting orders are charged an access fee. Rule 610(c) of Regulation NMS caps the amount of the access fee for executions against the best displayed prices of an exchange at 0.3 cents per share. Exchanges typically charge a somewhat higher access fee than the amount of their liquidity rebates, and retain the difference as compensation. Sometimes, however, exchanges have offered "inverted" pricing and pay a liquidity rebate that exceeds the access fee.

**b) ECNs**

ECNs, as well as dark pools (discussed below) are regulated as alternative trading systems ("ATSs"). The key characteristic of an ECN is that it provides its best-priced orders for inclusion in the consolidated quotation data, whether voluntarily or as required by Rule 301(b)(3) of Regulation ATS. In general, ECNs offer trading services (such as displayed and undisplayed order types, maker-taker pricing, and data feeds) that are analogous to those of registered exchanges.

**c) Dark Pools**

Dark pools are ATSs that, in contrast to ECNs, do not provide their best-priced orders for inclusion in the consolidated quotation data. In general, dark pools offer trading services to institutional investors and others that seek to execute large trading interest in a manner that will minimize the movement of prices against the trading interest and thereby reduce trading costs. There are approximately 32 dark pools that actively trade NMS stocks.[62] ATSs (both dark pools and ECNs) fall within the statutory definition of an exchange, but are exempted if they comply with Regulation ATS. Regulation ATS requires ATSs to be registered as broker-dealers with the SEC, which entails becoming a member of the Financial Industry Regulatory Authority ("FINRA") and fully complying with the broker-dealer regulatory regime. Unlike a registered exchange, an ATS is not required to file proposed rule changes with the SEC or otherwise publicly disclose its trading services and fees. ATSs also do not have any self-regulatory responsibilities, such as market surveillance.

Dark pools can vary quite widely in the services they offer their customers. For example, some dark pools, such as block crossing networks, offer specialized size discovery mechanisms that attempt to bring large buyers and sellers in the same NMS stock together anonymously and to facilitate a trade between them. The average trade size of these block crossing networks can be as high as 50,000 shares.[63] Most dark pools, though they may handle large orders, primarily execute trades with small sizes that are more comparable to the average size of trades in the public markets, which was less than 300 shares in July 2009.[64] These dark pools that primarily match smaller orders (though the matched orders may be "child" orders of much larger "parent" orders) execute more than 90% of dark pool trading volume.[65] The majority of this volume is executed by dark pools that are sponsored by multi-service broker-dealers. These broker-dealers also offer order routing services, trade as principal in the sponsored ATS, or both.

### d) Broker-Dealer Internalization

The other type of undisplayed trading center is a non-ATS broker-dealer that internally executes trades, whether as agent or principal. Notably, many broker-dealers may submit orders to exchanges or ECNs, which then are included in the consolidated quotation data. The internalized executions of broker-dealers, however, primarily reflect liquidity that is not included in the consolidated quotation data. There are a large number of broker-dealers that execute trades internally in NMS stocks.[66]

Broker-dealers that internalize executions generally fall into two categories – OTC market makers[67] and block positioners.[68] Broker-dealers that act as OTC market makers and block positioners conduct their business primarily by directly negotiating with customers or with other broker-dealers representing customer orders. OTC market makers, for example, appear to handle a very large percentage of marketable (immediately executable) order flow of individual investors that is routed by retail brokerage firms.[69]

### e) Market Linkages

In adopting Regulations NMS, the SEC also included an "access" rule that, among other things, promotes private linkages among market participants and trading venues. In contrast to some markets where trading is concentrated on a single exchange or market, because liquidity on the equity markets is dispersed across a large number of trading centers of different types, linking the various trading venues is critical to the successful operation of the national market system.

Rule 611 of Regulation NMS provides protection against trade-throughs.[70] A trade-through is the execution of a trade at a price inferior to a protected quotation for an NMS stock. A protected quotation must be displayed by an automated trading center, must be disseminated in the consolidated quotation data, and must be an automated quotation that is the best bid or best offer of a national securities exchange or FINRA.[71] Importantly, Rule 611 applies to all trading centers, not just those that display protected quotations. Trading center is defined broadly in Rule 600(b)(78) to include, among others, all exchanges, all ATSs (including ECNs and dark pools), all OTC market makers, and any other broker-dealer that executes orders internally, whether as agent or principal. In practice, the national best bid and national best offer ("NBBO")[72] is the best bid and best offer from among the protected quotations, i.e., the best bid and best offer of all the stock exchanges and FINRA's ADF.[73]

Protection against trade-throughs is an important linkage among trading centers because it provides a baseline assurance that: (1) marketable orders will receive at least the best displayed price, regardless of the particular trading center that executes the order or where the best price is displayed in the national market system; and (2) quotations that are displayed at one trading center will not be bypassed by trades with inferior prices at any trading center in the national market system.

Rule 611 also helps promote linkages among trading centers by encouraging them, when they do not have available trading interest at the best price, to route marketable orders to a trading center that is displaying the best price. Although Rule 611 does not directly require such routing services (a trading center can, for example, cancel and return an order when it does not have the best price), competitive factors have led many trading centers to offer routing services to their customers. With Regulation NMS, the SEC adopted a "private linkages" approach that relies exclusively on brokers to provide routing services, both among exchanges and between customers and exchanges.[74] Under this approach, market participants obtain access to the various trading centers through broker-dealers that are members or subscribers of the particular trading center.[75]Rule 610(a) of Regulation NMS, for example, prohibits an SRO trading facility from imposing unfairly discriminatory terms that would prevent or inhibit any person from obtaining efficient access through an SRO member to the displayed quotations of the SRO trading facility.[76]

In a dispersed and complex market structure with many different trading centers offering a wide spectrum of services, brokers play a significant role in linking trading centers together into a unified national market system. Brokers compete to offer the sophisticated technology tools that are needed to monitor liquidity at many different venues and to implement order routing strategies. To perform this function, brokers may monitor the execution of orders at both displayed and undisplayed trading centers to assess the availability of undisplayed trading interest. Brokers may, for example, construct real-time "heat maps" in an effort to discern and access both displayed and undisplayed liquidity at trading centers throughout the national market system.

Using their knowledge of available liquidity, many brokers offer smart order routing technology to access such liquidity. Many brokers also offer sophisticated algorithms that will take the large orders of institutional investors and others, divide a large "parent" order into many smaller "child" orders, and route the child orders over time to different trading centers in accordance with the particular trading strategy chosen by the customer. Such algorithms may be "aggressive," for example, and seek to take liquidity quickly at many different trading centers, or they may be "passive," and submit resting orders at one or more trading centers and await executions at favorable prices. To the extent they help customers cope with the dispersal of liquidity among a large number of trading centers of different types and achieve the best execution of their customers' orders, the routing services of brokers can contribute to the broader policy goal of promoting efficient markets.

The linkage function of brokers also is supported by a broker's legal duty of best execution. This duty requires a broker to obtain the most favorable terms reasonably available when executing a customer order.[77] Of course, this legal duty is not the only pressure on brokers to obtain best execution. The existence of strong competitive pressure to attract and retain customers encourages brokers to provide high quality routing services to their customers.[78]

**f) Professional Liquidity Providers on Exchanges and ECNs**

Liquidity on equities exchanges and ECNs is derived from orders to buy or sell securities as well as quotations submitted by members of an exchange that are registered as market makers. Professional liquidity providers are proprietary traders in the business of providing liquidity to the market, often through the submission of limit orders that rest on the electronic order books of exchanges and ECNs.[79] They include registered entities, such as exchange specialists and market makers, as well as unregistered proprietary trading firms that engage in passive market making and other types of trading strategies. As discussed below, some types of professional liquidity providers have certain obligations, such as to provide liquidity whether the market is up or down and maintain fair and orderly markets. Other professional liquidity providers do not have such responsibilities, including some of the high frequency proprietary trading firms that also are discussed below.

(1) Market Makers

In general, the rules of national securities exchanges allow a member, on a voluntary basis, to register as a market maker on a security-by-security basis and subject to certain obligations. While the rules of a national securities exchange may contain provisions that provide for market makers, these rules do not require any member to register as a market maker.[80] Accordingly, an exchange may not have registered market makers even though its rulebook provides for them. In addition, the rules of many exchanges permit multiple members to register as market makers for the same security.

Pursuant to exchange rules, registered market makers are required to engage in a course of dealings for their own account to assist in the maintenance, insofar as reasonably practicable, of fair and orderly markets. These exchange rules generally require a market maker to maintain a continuous two-sided quotation in the security or securities for which the member is registered as a market maker. Such rules, however, do not generally dictate the prices at which a market maker must quote. For example, when a market maker's liquidity has been exhausted, or if it is unwilling to provide liquidity, it may at that time submit what is called a stub quote – for example, an offer to buy a given stock at a penny – to comply with its obligation to maintain a continuous two-sided quotation.[81] Previously, market makers' quotations were required to be "reasonably related to the prevailing market." In requesting the deletion of this requirement, exchanges argued that the market structure had changed since the requirement was originally introduced in 1987 and that the requirement was no longer a meaningful means of ensuring market execution quality because of the highly competitive and increasingly automated environment of equities trading, and also because markets were required to abide by the trade-through protections of Regulation NMS.[82] In addition, it was believed that the duty of best execution would ensure that market makers with the most competitive quotations receive executions and thereby provide incentives for them to quote at or near the NBBO, and that the quality of a market maker's executions could also be reviewed by looking at market execution quality reports.[83]

Certain exchanges have a single market maker for each security traded on that exchange. In the past, NYSE maintained a "specialist"-based market structure, with the specialist serving as the market professional that managed trading in the specific securities he was assigned.[84] The NYSE specialist was responsible for the execution of all orders coming into the Exchange, for conducting auctions on the NYSE floor, and for maintaining an orderly market in assigned securities. Specialists' dealer activities were governed, in part, by negative and affirmative trading obligations. Rule 11b-1 under the Exchange Act [85] requires exchanges that permit members to register as specialists to have rules governing specialists' dealer transactions so that their proprietary trades conform to the negative and affirmative obligations. The negative obligation as set forth in Rule 11b-1 under the Act requires that a specialist's dealings be restricted, so far as practicable, to those reasonably necessary to permit the specialist to maintain a fair and orderly market.[86] The affirmative obligation as set forth in Rule 11b-1 under the Act requires a specialist to engage in a course of dealings for its own account to assist in the maintenance, so far as practicable, of a fair and orderly market.[87]

In 2008, in order to adapt to the more electronic marketplace and increased competition from other trading venues, NYSE replaced its specialist system with a system of "Designated Market Makers" ("DMMs"). DMMs are similar to specialists in many ways, including in that there is only a single DMM on NYSE for each stock. Some obligations, such as the negative obligations specialists were subject to, no longer apply to DMMs. In addition, DMMs now have the ability to trade on parity with other market participants, as well as functionality reserved solely for DMMs that permits them to transmit a schedule setting forth additional liquidity that DMMs commit to provide in their assigned securities at specific price points. At the same time, DMMs are subject to other responsibilities, some the same as those previously imposed on specialists and others new. For example, DMMs are subject to quoting depth guidelines and are obligated to maintain a bid or an offer at the NBBO for a certain percentage of the trading day.

(2) High Frequency Traders

Highly automated trading systems have helped enable a business model for a new type of professional liquidity provider that is distinct from the more traditional exchange specialist and over-the-counter ("OTC") market maker. In particular, proprietary traders now use high speed systems by submitting large numbers of orders that can result in more than 1 million trades per day by a single firm. These proprietary traders often are labeled as engaging in high-frequency trading ("HFT"), though the term does not have a settled definition and may encompass a variety of strategies in addition to passive market making.

HFT traders can be organized in a variety of ways, including as a proprietary trading firm (which may or may not be a registered broker-dealer and member of FINRA), as the proprietary trading desk of a multi-service broker-dealer, or as a hedge fund (all of which are referred to hereinafter collectively as a "proprietary firm"). Other characteristics often attributed to proprietary firms engaged in HFT are: (1) the use of extraordinarily high-speed and sophisticated computer programs for generating, routing, and executing orders; (2) use of co-location services and individual data feeds offered by exchanges and others to minimize network and other types of latencies; (3) very short time-frames for establishing and liquidating positions; (4) the submission of numerous orders that are cancelled shortly after submission; and (5) ending the trading day in as close to a flat position as possible (that is, not carrying significant, unhedged positions over-night). Given the competitive pressures to maximize their speed of trading, HFT firms typically will attempt to streamline the code for their trading algorithms. However, every check and filter in that code reduces its speed, creating a tension.

HFT is one of the most significant market structure developments in recent years. Estimates of HFT volume in the equity markets vary widely, though they often are 50 percent of total volume or higher.[88] By any measure, HFT is a dominant component of the current market structure and is likely to affect nearly all aspects of its performance. In addition, though the term HFT implies a large volume of trades, some of the concerns that have been raised about particular strategies used by proprietary firms do not necessarily involve a large number of trades. Indeed, any particular proprietary firm may simultaneously be employing many different strategies, some of which generate a large number of trades and some that do not. Conceivably, some of these strategies – for example, if they dampen short-term volatility or promote efficient pricing by narrowing spreads – may benefit market quality and long-term investors and others could be harmful.

### g) Relevant Equity Market Structure Features

A number of features relating to the equity markets are relevant to the events of May 6, 2010 and are discussed below:

#### (1) Order Types

*Market Orders:* In certain cases, and particularly for illiquid securities, a large order or influx of orders can soak up available liquidity across the market, resulting in an order, particularly if it is a market order, breaking through many price levels in an effort to obtain an execution at any price. A market order is an order to buy or sell a stock at the best available market price. Market orders do not require an execution at a specific price or price range. With market orders, the order submitted is generally assured an execution; however, there is no limit on what the execution price can be. This contrasts with limit orders, which are submitted with a specified limit price. Limit orders guard against executions at prices at which the order submitter is not willing to trade, though the trade-off is that the order may not be executed if the market suddenly moves away from the specified limit price.

Stop loss market orders are orders that turn into market orders when the stop price of the order is reached. When an investor places a stop loss market order to sell, the investor is instructing the broker to sell a stock at the market if it falls to a certain price. In a normal market, where liquidity exists as the stock price goes up or down, this strategy can protect an investor from taking a major loss if the stock drops significantly by selling at a predetermined price to minimize the loss. However, during times of extreme market volatility, the use of market orders when stop loss levels are triggered could result in executions at aberrant prices if all other liquidity has already been exhausted.

The rules of some exchanges provide a "collar" for market orders. For example, on BATS, any portion of a market order that would otherwise execute at a price more than $0.50 or 5 percent worse than the NBBO at the time the order initially reaches the exchange, whichever is greater, will be cancelled.[89] BATS's market order thresholds are intended to help avoid executions on BATS of market orders at prices that are significantly worse than the initial NBBO, particularly in thinly-traded securities. BATS market participants that intend to trade against liquidity at price points beyond the market order thresholds can specify that intent by instead submitting a marketable limit order.[90]

Similarly, on NASDAQ, subject to certain exceptions,[91] market orders (called "Unpriced Orders" on NASDAQ) are "Collared Orders" that, for any portion of a Collared Order that would execute at a price more than $0.25 or 5 percent worse than the NBBO at the time when the order reaches NASDAQ, whichever is greater, will be cancelled. In proposing to adopt its collar for market orders, NASDAQ stated that it was intended to reduce the risk that unpriced orders might execute at prices significantly worse than the NBBO. Nasdaq noted that market participants generally expect that their orders will be executed in full at a price reasonably related to the prevailing market, but that participants might not be aware if there is insufficient liquidity at or near the NBBO to fill the entire order, particularly for thinly-traded securities.[92]

*Intermarket Sweep Orders:* Regulation NMS also introduced the use of intermarket sweep orders. An intermarket sweep order is a limit order that meets the following requirements: (1) when routed to a trading center, the limit order is identified as an intermarket sweep order; and (2) simultaneously with the routing of the limit order identified as an intermarket sweep order, one or more additional limit orders, as necessary, are routed to execute against the full displayed size of all protected quotations with a superior price.[93] These additional limit orders must be marked as intermarket sweep orders to allow the receiving market center to execute the order immediately without regard to better-priced quotations displayed at other trading centers (by definition, each of the additional limit orders would meet the requirements for an intermarket sweep order).

A trading center may immediately execute any order identified as an intermarket sweep order.[94] It therefore need not delay its execution for the updating of the better-priced quotations at other trading centers to which orders were routed simultaneously with the intermarket sweep order. A trading center itself may also route out intermarket sweep orders and thereby clear the way for immediate internal executions at the trading center.[95]

(2) Temporary Unavailability of Market-Specific Liquidity

*Liquidity Replenishment Points:* NYSE utilizes a hybrid floor/electronic trading model, unlike most other markets today which are fully electronic. In attempting to meld the traditional open-outcry floor-based auction model with today's technology, NYSE's trading system utilizes what are known as "liquidity replenishment points" ("LRPs").[96] LRPs are best thought of as a "speed bump" and are intended to dampen volatility in a given stock by temporarily converting from an automated market to a manual auction market when a price movement of sufficient size is reached. In such a case, trading on NYSE in that stock will "go slow" and pause for a time period to allow the Designated Market Maker to solicit additional liquidity before returning to an automated market. This "speed bump" occurs even when there may be additional interest on NYSE's book beyond the LRP price point.

LRPs are calculated by NYSE automatically throughout the trading day. Specifically, the LRP is calculated upon the opening trade of the day in the security or, if there is no opening trade, on the opening quote, and is recalculated (i) every 30 seconds thereafter based on the last sale; (ii) after a manual trade by the DMM; (iii) when automatic executions resume after an LRP is reached; and (iv) upon the first sale or quote after automatic executions resume following an LRP. The precise LRP value varies according to the security's share price and average daily volume within specified ranges. LRPs are calculated by adding or subtracting the LRP value to the last sale price or quote as appropriate on the exchange in the relevant security.[97]

When an incoming order on the NYSE would result in an execution [at or] outside an LRP or the stock is quoted outside an LRP, automatic executions in the security are suspended on that side of the market. In addition, NYSE will suspend automated quotations in the security, and will identify its quote on the consolidated tape with a "non-firm" indicator. This is referred to as a "slow market" or "going slow" in the security. NYSE will resume automated quotations and automatic executions as soon as possible after an LRP is reached, once the DMM manually determines the reopening price. In many cases, this occurs in a fraction of a second, but when the market is particularly volatile, it can take a minute or more. Upon resumption of automatic executions, a new LRP is calculated for the security. On days of major market volatility, stocks with significant and continual declines may cause NYSE trading to remain in the "go slow" mode for extended periods or to intermittently return to automated execution status before quickly again hitting another LRP and thereby "going slow" again.

*Self-Help:* An exchange may exclude the quotations of another exchange from its determination of whether the other exchange has a better "protected" price to which it must route orders for execution under Regulation NMS if that other exchange is experiencing a failure, material delay, or malfunction in its systems or equipment.[98] This is known as invoking "self-help" against the other exchange.[99] This mechanism gives trading centers a remedy if another trading center repeatedly fails to provide an immediate response (within one second) to incoming orders attempting to access its quotes.

(3) Stub Quotes

As noted above, in order to comply with their obligation to maintain continuous two-sided quotations, market makers are permitted under the rules of certain exchanges to utilize stub quotes. When a market order is submitted to an exchange, the order immediately will seek the best available liquidity, including the protected quotes of other markets, regardless of price. In times of market stress, if the only liquidity available is, for example, a one-cent stub quote, the market order, by its terms, will execute against the stub quote.

(4) Clearly Erroneous Executions Rules

Erroneous trades can result from a variety of causes, including human error or computer malfunction. Because the markets today are increasingly fast, automated, and interconnected, an erroneous trade on one market can very rapidly trigger a wave of similarly erroneous trades on other markets.[100]

The equities exchanges have each adopted "clearly erroneous execution rules" that are designed to permit them to break trades that are clearly erroneous. Under these rules, which were last revised in late 2009 to make them more consistent across the various exchanges, an exchange member may request that an exchange officer review a potentially erroneous execution and declare it null and void. Alternatively, an equities exchange may review potentially erroneous executions on its own motion.

The clearly erroneous execution rules recognize that, in most circumstances, trades that are executed between parties should be honored. On rare occasions, however, the price of the executed trade indicates a "clearly erroneous error" may exist, suggesting that it is unrealistic to expect that the parties to the trade had come to a meeting of the minds regarding the terms of the transaction and that the trade should be broken.

In determining whether to break trades, the rules permit equities exchanges to consider breaking a trade only if the price exceeds the consolidated last sale price by more than a specified percentage amount: 10% for stocks priced under $25; 5% for stocks priced between $25 and $50; and 3% for stocks priced over $50. These percentage thresholds may be (i) doubled for executions occurring between 9:30 a.m. and 10:00 a.m., when the S & P 500 Futures are up or down between 3% and 5% at 9:15 a.m. or (ii) tripled when the S & P 500 Futures are up or down 5% or greater at 9:15 a.m.

The equities exchanges also may consider additional factors to determine whether an execution is clearly erroneous, including but not limited to, system malfunctions or disruptions, volume and volatility for the security, news released for the security, whether trading in the security was recently halted/resumed, whether the security was subject to a corporate action, overall market conditions, consideration of primary market indications, and executions inconsistent with the trading pattern in the stock.

When an event involves erroneous trades that occur in multiple markets, the rules provide that the equities exchanges may use a higher percentage threshold in an effort to coordinate a result across markets. Although not required by the rules, the markets generally convene conference calls to discuss coordinated action when such events occur. Each exchange, however, retains the right to make its own determination on whether to nullify trades.

Pursuant to exchange rules, a clearly erroneous determination may generally be appealed, unless a determination is made that the number of the affected transactions is such that immediate finality is necessary to maintain a fair and orderly market and to protect investors and the public interest. In addition, the equities markets generally do not allow appeals of clearly erroneous rulings that are made in conjunction with other market centers.

This was the clearly erroneous execution framework in existence on May 6, 2010.

(5) Short Sales

Short selling is defined by Rule 200 of Regulation SHO as "any sale of a security which the seller does not own or any sale which is consummated by the delivery of a security borrowed by, or for the account of, the seller."[101] Short selling often can play an important role in the market for a variety of reasons, including contributing to efficient price discovery, mitigating market bubbles, increasing market liquidity, promoting capital formation, facilitating hedging and other risk management activities, and limiting upward market manipulations. There are, however, circumstances in which short selling can be used as a tool to manipulate the market.[102]

Due to its concerns regarding persistent fails to deliver[103] and potentially abusive "naked" short selling, the SEC adopted Regulation SHO, which became effective in early 2005.[104] As adopted in 2005, this Regulation imposed three general requirements with respect to short sales: a marking requirement, a locate requirement and a close-out requirement. Since 2005, the SEC has adopted several amendments to Regulation SHO. Two of the most recent amendments included further tightening the Regulation's close-out requirement and adding a short sale price test restriction.

In connection with further tightening the Regulation's close-out requirement, in the fall of 2008, the SEC adopted temporary Rule 204T of Regulation SHO, with an expiration date of July 31, 2009.[105] Temporary Rule 204T strengthened the close-out requirements of Regulation SHO for fails to deliver resulting from sales of any equity security. Prior to the adoption of temporary Rule 204T, Regulation SHO's close-out requirement had applied only to those securities with a persistent and substantial level of fails to deliver (known as "threshold securities"). Due to the positive impact that temporary Rule 204T, as well as other recent SEC actions, had on reducing fails to deliver in equity securities, the SEC made the requirements of temporary Rule 204T permanent, with some limited modifications.[106]

With respect to adding a short sale price test restriction, in February 2010, the SEC approved Rule 201 of Regulation SHO, which restricts short selling in NMS stocks to a price above the national best bid after a stock's price has declined by 10% or more from the prior day's closing price.[107] The Rule became effective on May 10, 2010 and has a six month implementation period. Thus, compliance with the Rule was not required on May 6, 2010.

Rule 201 requires a trading center to establish, maintain, and enforce written policies and procedures that are reasonably designed to prevent the execution or display of a short sale order of an NMS stock at a price that is less than or equal to the current national best bid once the circuit breaker has been triggered. The price test restriction, once in effect, will apply to all short sales in that stock for the remainder of the day and the following day, unless an exception applies. Under the Rule, the listing market for the NMS stock must determine whether the stock's price has decreased by 10% or more from its prior day's closing price. The listing market must then immediately notify the single plan processor responsible for consolidating information for the NMS stock that the circuit breaker has been triggered. The single plan processor is then required to disseminate the information to the markets.

### *2. Overview of Listed Options Markets*

A listed option is any option traded on a registered national securities exchange or automated facility of a national securities association. To date, all orders in listed options are executed only on registered national securities exchanges. The Options Clearing Corporation ("OCC"), a clearing agency registered with the SEC, is considered the issuer and guarantor of each listed options contract, and all listed options transactions are centrally cleared through OCC.

Listed options are currently traded on eight national securities exchanges, owned by six entities. These eight exchanges are BATS, BOX (a facility of BX), CBOE, ISE, NASDAQ OMX Phlx, NOM (a facility of Nasdaq), NYSE Amex, and NYSE Arca. Based on market share data for April 2010 obtained from the OCC,[108] the exchange with the highest market share of option volume was CBOE, with 33.88%. The two exchanges owned by The NASDAQ OMX Group, Inc. together had a market share of 23.91% (NASDAQ OMX Phlx had 21.51% and NOM had 2.40%). The two exchanges owned by NYSE Euronext together had a market share of 23.63% (NYSE Arca had 12.98% and NYSE Amex had 10.65%). ISE had a market share of 19.17% and BOX had a market share of 2.21%.

Similar to NMS stocks, most listed options are traded on multiple exchanges. In contrast to some markets where trading is concentrated on a single exchange or market, because liquidity on the options markets is dispersed across eight exchanges, linking the various exchanges is critical to the successful operation of the national market system for listed options. The options exchanges have implemented a joint industry plan to enhance the linking of the trading of listed options across the multiple exchanges. Most recently, in August 2009, the options exchanges implemented a new plan (the "Options Plan"), approved by the SEC,[109] which includes a "trade-through" rule that prevents the execution of trades on one options exchange at prices lower than a Protected Bid or higher than a Protected Offer.[110] Each exchange adopted rules to implement the Options Plan that prohibit its members from effecting trade-throughs, subject to certain enumerated exceptions. The approach to trade-throughs under the Options Plan is similar to that taken by the SEC under Rule 611 of Regulation NMS.[111]

As with NMS stocks, linkage among options exchange is an important protection against trade-throughs because it provides a baseline assurance that: (1) marketable orders will receive at least the best displayed price, regardless of the particular exchange that executes the order or where the best price is displayed in the national market system; and (2) quotations that are displayed at one exchange will not be bypassed by trades with inferior prices at any other options exchange in the national market system.

The trade-through prohibition for listed options also helps promote linkages among exchanges by encouraging them, when they do not have available trading interest at the best price, to route marketable orders to an exchange that is displaying the best price. Although the options exchanges are not required to route orders to better prices (an exchange can, for example, cancel and return an order when it does not have the best price), competitive factors have led options exchanges to offer routing services to their customers. Pursuant to the Options Plan, the options exchanges effectively adopted a "private linkage" approach that relies exclusively on brokers to provide routing services among exchanges.[112]

Just like registered exchanges that trade NMS stocks, registered exchanges that trade listed options must undertake self-regulatory responsibility for their members and file their proposed rule changes for approval with the SEC. These proposed rule changes publicly disclose, among other things, the trading services and fees of exchanges.

The registered exchanges that trade listed options have various market structures. Some are fully electronic (such as ISE, BATS, and NOM), while others have hybrid models that combine electronic trading with floor trading (such as CBOE, NYSE Amex, and NASDAQ OMX Phlx). In addition, some of the options exchanges have in the past few years adopted the "maker-taker" pricing model that is prevalent in the markets trading NMS stocks. The introduction of the marker-taker model followed the reduction of the quoting increment in certain options in 2007.[113] Under this model, non-marketable, resting orders that offer (make) liquidity at a particular price receive a liquidity rebate if they are executed, while incoming orders that execute against (take) the liquidity of resting orders are charged an access fee. The SEC recently published for comment a proposal that would cap the amount of fees an options exchange could charge for executions against the best displayed prices of the exchange at $0.30 per contract.[114] Exchanges typically charge a somewhat higher access fee than the amount of their liquidity rebates, and retain the difference as compensation.

Some other options exchanges use a "broker payment" model. These exchanges generally charge no or low fees for the execution of customers' orders,[115] but often charge other types of fees on a per-transaction basis. For example, most options exchanges charge a surcharge or "royalty" fee for executions in certain index option classes. Many exchanges also charge a payment for order flow or "marketing" fee to market makers that trade with customer orders on the exchange. The exchange then makes the proceeds from such "marketing" fees available to collectively fund payment for order flow to brokers directing order flow to the exchange.

The registered options exchanges typically offer a wide range of order types for trading on their markets. Examples of order types include market orders,[116] limit orders, and intermarket sweep orders.[117] Some of the order types are displayable in full if they are not executed immediately. Others are un-displayed, in full or in part. For example, a reserve order type will display part of the size of an order at a particular price, while holding the balance of the order in reserve and refreshing the displayed size as needed.[118] In general, displayed orders are given execution priority at any given price over fully un-displayed orders and the un-displayed size of reserve orders.[119]

Unlike with NMS stocks, all listed option orders are executed on registered national securities exchanges. Thus, broker-dealers cannot internally execute trades in listed options in the over-the-counter market. Instead, all such trades must be sent to a registered exchange for execution pursuant to the exchange priority rules. In addition, there is one registered ATS that conducts a listed options business. Any orders matched by this ATS, however, must be sent to a registered exchange for execution pursuant to the exchange's priority rules.

As with NMS stocks, in a dispersed and complex market structure with many different options exchanges offering a wide spectrum of services, brokers play a significant role in linking exchanges together into a unified national market system. Brokers compete to offer the sophisticated technology tools that are needed to monitor liquidity at many different venues and to implement order routing strategies. To perform this function, brokers may monitor the execution of orders at the various exchanges to assess the available liquidity. Using their knowledge of available liquidity, brokers can offer smart order routing technology to access such liquidity. Many brokers also offer sophisticated algorithms that will take the large orders of institutional investors and others, divide a large "parent" order into many smaller "child" orders, and route the child orders over time to different exchanges in accordance with the particular trading strategy chosen by the customer.

As with NMS stocks, the linkage function of brokers also is supported by a broker's duty of best execution. This duty requires a broker to obtain the most favorable terms reasonably available when executing a customer order.[120] Of course, this duty is not the only pressure on brokers to obtain best execution. The existence of strong competitive pressure to attract and retain customers encourages brokers to provide high quality routing services to their customers.[121]

As with the trading of NMS stocks, liquidity on options exchanges is derived from orders to buy or sell particular options series as well as quotations submitted by members of an exchange that are registered as market makers. Generally, however, investors in listed options depend upon the liquidity supplied by professional liquidity providers, such as market makers, to a greater extent than in the market for NMS stocks. This is due in part to the greater dispersion of trading interest across the thousands of series of listed options.[122] Professional liquidity providers are proprietary traders in the business of providing liquidity to the market, often through the submission of quotations, as well as limit orders that rest on the electronic order books of exchanges. They include registered entities, such as exchange specialists and market makers, as well as unregistered proprietary trading firms that engage in passive market making and other types of trading strategies. Some types of professional liquidity providers have certain obligations, such as to provide liquidity whether the market is up or down and maintain fair and orderly markets. Other professional liquidity providers do not have such responsibilities.

In general, the rules of the options exchanges allow a member, on a voluntary basis, to register as a market maker, either on a class-by-class or series-by-series basis. Members registered as market makers have certain obligations. Pursuant to the options exchanges' rules, the transactions of a market maker in its market making capacity generally must constitute a course of dealings reasonably calculated to contribute to the maintenance of a fair and orderly market. These exchange rules also generally require a market maker to maintain a continuous two-sided quotation in the options for which the member is registered for a specified percentage of the time, or in a specified number of series or classes. For example, the NOM rules require that its market makers maintain a two-sided market on a continuous basis in at least 75% of the options series in which they are registered. On some options exchanges such rules also limit how wide a market maker can quote.[123] Other options exchanges, such as NOM, do not have any limitations on the price at which market makers can quote.

While the options exchanges' rules may contain provisions that provide for market makers, these rules do not require any particular member to register as a market maker.[124] Some exchanges do not trade options on their market unless there is at least one market maker registered in the class. At least one options exchange does allow options to trade without any market maker registered in the option.[125] Accordingly, an exchange may not have registered market makers even though its rulebook provides for them. In addition, the rules of the options exchanges permit multiple members to register as market makers for the same option. Some of the exchanges may have a "lead" or "primary" market maker assigned in a given option, while others do not.

Each options exchange has adopted an "obvious error rule" that is designed to permit the exchange to adjust or nullify options transactions that are obviously erroneous. An obvious error will be deemed to have occurred when the execution price of a transaction differs from the theoretical price[126] for the option by an amount equal to at least the specified minimum amount indicated in the rule. On some exchanges, an obvious error also will be deemed to occur if there are erroneous prints or quotes in the underlying, or if there are verifiable systems disruptions or malfunctions. If the options exchange determines to adjust the transaction price, the transaction price would be adjusted to the theoretical price plus or minus an adjustment penalty that is set forth in the rule. A member of an options exchange may request that its options transaction be reviewed. Several of the options exchanges also have the discretion to review options transactions on their own motion.

### *3. Overview of ETFs*

As a general matter, exchange-traded products ("ETPs") are issuers of exchange-traded securities that give investors exposure to an investment benchmark or strategy. ETPs exist in a variety of legal forms, including exchange-traded funds ("ETFs") registered as investment companies under the Investment Company Act of 1940 ("1940 Act"), exchange-traded notes ("ETNs"), trust-issued receipts, commodity and currency trusts, and commodity pools. All ETPs register offers and sales of shares under the Securities Act of 1933 ("Securities Act"), and a national securities exchange lists the securities issued by the ETPs for trading on a secondary market.

An ETF is registered under the 1940 Act as an open-end investment company or a unit investment trust ("UIT"). Unlike typical open-end investment companies ("mutual funds") or UITs, ETFs issue and redeem shares only in large aggregations or blocks (such as 50,000 ETF shares) commonly called "Creation Units." Purchase and redemption orders for Creation Units are placed by or through participants in the Depository Trust Company that have executed a "Participation Agreement" with the distributor of the ETF ("Authorized Participants"). Authorized Participants may purchase a Creation Unit with a "Portfolio Deposit" equal in value to the aggregate net asset value ("NAV") of the ETF shares in the Creation Unit. The Portfolio Deposit generally consists of a basket of securities announced by the ETF's investment adviser or sponsor at the beginning of each business day and usually mirrors the composition of the ETF's portfolio. Under certain circumstances, the Portfolio Deposit may also consist of cash or of cash in lieu of certain securities. The value of a Creation Unit could range from hundreds of thousands of dollars to several million dollars. After purchasing a Creation Unit, an Authorized Participant may hold the ETF shares, or sell ETF shares to other investors. ETF shares are not redeemable from the ETF except when aggregated into Creation Units, and then only by or through Authorized Participants. Authorized Participants thus act as the intermediary between investors and the ETF.

Like operating companies or closed-end funds, ETFs register offers and sales of shares under the Securities Act, and a national securities exchange lists the ETF shares for trading. As with any listed security, investors also may trade ETF shares in off-exchange transactions. In either case, ETF shares trade at negotiated prices. The development of the secondary market in ETF shares depends upon the activities of market makers and upon the willingness of Authorized Participants to engage in purchase and sale transactions in ETF shares in the secondary market.

If an Authorized Participant presents a Creation Unit to the ETF for redemption, it generally receives a "Redemption Basket" that consists of securities identified by the ETF investment adviser or sponsor at the beginning of the day and that usually matches the Portfolio Deposit. In some circumstances, the Redemption Basket could also consist of cash or of cash in lieu of certain securities. As with purchases from the ETF, redemptions from the ETF are priced at NAV. An investor holding fewer ETF shares than the amount needed to constitute a Creation Unit may dispose of those ETF shares only by selling them in the secondary market at market price, which may be higher or lower than the NAV of the ETF shares. The investor also pays customary brokerage commissions on sales in the secondary market.

In the past, ETF shares have not typically traded in the secondary market at a significant premium or discount in relation to NAV because of the arbitrage opportunities inherent in the ETF structure. Under normal circumstances, if ETF shares begin to trade at a discount (i.e., a price less than NAV), arbitrageurs may purchase ETF shares in the secondary market and, after accumulating enough shares to equal a Creation Unit, redeem them directly from the ETF at NAV if an Authorized Participant, or indirectly through that person, thereby acquiring the more valuable securities in the Redemption Basket. In purchasing the ETF shares for this purpose, arbitrageurs create greater market demand for the shares, which may raise the market price to a level closer to NAV. In contrast, if ETF shares trade at a premium (i.e., a price greater than NAV), arbitrageurs may purchase the securities in the Portfolio Deposit, use them to obtain the more valuable Creation Units from the ETF, and then sell the individual ETF shares in the secondary market to realize a profit. As the supply of individual

ETF shares available in the secondary market increases, the price of the ETF shares may fall to levels closer to NAV. Market makers have also been able to maintain efficient markets in ETF shares even in the absence of an actual arbitrage transaction by hedging their exposures.

The 1940 Act does not provide for the ETF structure. Accordingly, ETFs that are registered as investment companies under the 1940 Act first must apply to the SEC to obtain exemptive relief from certain provisions of the 1940 Act to permit their unique operations. The SEC issued the first order to an ETF organized as a UIT in 1992, and began issuing orders to ETFs organized as open-end funds in 1996.[127] The SEC now has issued more than 88 orders to permit ETF operations. As of May 11, 2010, there were 843 ETFs operating in reliance on these orders with a combined total of approximately $740 billion in net assets.

Unlike ETFs, ETNs are senior, unsecured, unsubordinated debt securities issued by banks. ETNs are similar to ETFs in that they offer exchange-traded securities that provide investment exposure to certain market benchmarks or strategies. However, ETNs do not hold portfolios of securities and are not registered as investment companies under the 1940 Act. An investor in an ETN is therefore exposed to the credit risk of the issuer. ETNs can be redeemed from the issuer in large blocks of securities such as 50,000, typically on a weekly basis. There are approximately 90 ETNs.

Other types of ETPs include trust-issued receipts. Trust-issued receipts represent interests in a fixed trust of specified securities. Unlike other types of ETPs, owners of trust-issued receipts have the same rights and privileges as if they owned the underlying securities beneficially outside of the trust structure, and can receive the reports and communications that the issuers of the underlying securities send to their respective beneficial owners. ETPs also include commodities and currency trusts, as well as commodity pools. While these ETPs trade like ETFs, their portfolios consist of physical commodities, currency, or futures, rather than securities, and they are not registered as investment companies under the 1940 Act.

## APPENDIX B.OVERVIEW OF THE FUTURES MARKET STRUCTURE

A futures contract is an agreement to purchase or sell a commodity for delivery in the future at a price that is determined when the contract is bought or sold. Each party is obligated to fulfill the terms of the contract at the specified price. Futures contracts are used to assume or shift price risk, and most positions are satisfied by offset or cash settlement, rather than delivery of the underlying commodity or financial instrument.

### 1. Designated Contract Markets

U.S. futures exchanges (designated by the CFTC as contract markets, as described below) are a critical component of the U.S. and world economies, providing significant benefits to the public at large as well as market participants.[128] Futures markets offer individuals and firms in a myriad of industries important vehicles for hedging economic risks,[129] resulting in more efficient production, lower costs, and other benefits. They also provide vital forums for discovering prices.[130] For these reasons, futures exchanges are affected with a significant national public interest. Further, as self-regulatory organizations, futures exchanges must exercise their regulatory authority effectively, impartially, and in the public interest. As essential forums for the execution of futures transactions and for price discovery, exchanges must ensure fair and financially secure trading facilities.[131] They must also fulfill self-regulatory responsibilities through programs and policies that help ensure market integrity, financial integrity, and the strict protection of market participants and the public.[132]

Futures contracts must be traded on CFTC-regulated exchanges, called Designated Contract Markets (DCMs) pursuant to Section 5 of the Commodity Exchange Act (CEA).[133] DCMs may allow access to their facilities to all types of traders, including retail customers. DCMs may list for trading futures or options contracts based on any underlying commodity, index, or instrument. To obtain and maintain a designation, a DCM must comply with the designation criteria and 18 core principles set forth in Sections 5(b) and 5(d) of the CEA and Part 38 of the CFTC's regulations.[134]

The CFTC monitors the discharge of each DCM's self-regulatory responsibilities and ongoing compliance with the CEA and CFTC regulations, including the core principles applicable to DCMs, through its program of regular rule enforcement reviews. Periodic rule enforcement reviews examine, among other things, a DCM's audit trail, trade practice, disciplinary, and dispute resolution programs. Accurate audit trails are essential to reconstruction of trading such as that which occurred on May 6.

DCMs may implement new rules or rule amendments or list new products by filing with the CFTC a certification that the rule or rule amendment complies with the CEA and CFTC regulations and policies, or by requesting approval from the CFTC.[135]

Currently, there are 14 DCMs designated by the CFTC that are actively trading. The total trading volume on all of these exchanges combined in 2009 was approximately 2.7 billion contracts.

## 2. Futures Market Structure

The market structure of U.S. futures markets differs from the market structure of U.S. equities markets. In the cash equity markets, the same security may be traded on multiple venues that are linked. Under current practice, a given futures contract trades on only one exchange. For example, the E-mini S&P 500 futures contract and the S&P 500 futures contract trade exclusively on the Chicago Mercantile Exchange (CME), and the Russell 2000 futures contract trades exclusively on ICE Futures U.S. Futures exchanges are not linked in the way securities trading venues are linked. Futures contracts are not "issued" by a public company for registration and listing on an exchange. Rather, futures exchanges design and list them for trading.

The equities and futures markets also differ with respect to clearing. Equities are cleared through the National Securities Clearing Corporation. Options on equities are cleared through the Options Clearing Corporation. In the futures markets, individual exchanges are responsible for maintaining the financial integrity of trading in their listed contracts. To fulfill this obligation, exchanges select the clearinghouse(s) that will clear and settle their contracts, a clearing model which is also known as "exchange-directed clearing."

The CEA requires that all CFTC-regulated DCMs have all DCM-traded contracts cleared and settled by a CFTC registered derivatives clearing organization (DCO).[136] One of the critical functions that each DCO performs is the removal of debt obligations among clearing members. At a minimum, this is done at the end of the trading session for a given trade date.[137] This process is accomplished by independently determining a settlement (or marking) price for each contract that is cleared and marking all open positions to that price. The DCO collects cash from clearing members that have lost money on their positions and pays it to clearing members that have gained money on their positions.

Exchange-directed clearing has been the standard in the futures industry since the industry's inception. The clearinghouse associated with a futures exchange can be either vertically integrated into the exchange company itself, or serve as a third-party clearing services provider. Historically, most clearinghouses have been integrated into particular futures exchanges. The CEA mirrors the exchange-directed clearing model by placing upon exchanges the statutory obligation to ensure the financial integrity of their listed contracts.[138]

## 3. Equity Futures Products

### *a. Broad-Based Index Futures*[139]

Stock index futures are financial instruments whereby traders buy or sell a standardized value of a stock index for settlement on a future date at a specified price. The fundamental economic purpose of stock index futures is to provide a risk management tool for financial institutions and other market participants active in the stock market. They are widely used by mutual funds, pension funds, endowments, foundations and other entities holding securities, as an effective way to protect against adverse price movements associated with holding stock portfolios by selling futures or as a way to efficiently manage the purchase and sale of stocks as portfolios are balanced or adjusted.

Stock index futures are cash settled and do not provide for delivery of the shares underlying the indices. For most stock index futures contracts, contract expiration is on the third Friday of the contract month. All open contracts are then settled in cash, based on the Special Opening Quotation price for the relevant index on the expiration day.[140] Each futures exchange establishes a contract size by specifying a multiplier. For example, with respect to the CME E-mini S&P 500 contract, the contract size is set at $50 times the S&P 500 Index value, equal to a notional value of $55,000 per contract when the index is at 1,100. Stock index futures are subject to price limits and circuit breaker trading halts that are coordinated with trading in the underlying securities markets (circuit breakers are discussed in more detail below). Trading and open interest in stock index futures is concentrated in the nearby month, which typically accounts for over 90 percent of total activity in all months combined.

Two DCMs, CME and ICE Futures U.S., trade broad-based equity index futures, the CME and ICE Futures U.S. The combined total trading volume of all equity index products traded at CME and ICE in 2009 was approximately 766 million contracts.

Stock index futures contracts were introduced in the early 1980's, beginning with the Kansas City Board of Trade's Value Line Average futures contract and the CME's S&P 500 index futures contract. The CME and other futures markets have listed for trading futures on various broad market sector indices. These include the CME Nasdaq 100, S&P MidCap 400, and S&P Small Cap 600 index futures, the Chicago Board of Trade ("CBOT") Dow Jones Industrial Average Index future and the ICE Futures US Russell 2,000 index future. In addition, the CME and other exchanges list options on certain stock index futures contracts, including the CME E-mini S&P 500.

As noted, the CME first launched an S&P 500 futures contract in the early 1980s; that contract continues to trade today. That contract, however, has a larger contract size, $250 times the level of the S&P 500, compared to the $50 multiplier for the E-mini S&P 500 contract. The original S&P 500 contract is traded via open outcry during the day trading session and on CME Globex during overnight electronic trading hours, while the E-mini S&P 500 contract is traded exclusively on Globex. From Monday through Thursday, the E-mini S&P 500 contract trades from 4:30 to 5:30 p.m. and from 6:00 p.m. to 4:15 p.m. the following day. (It therefore trades until 4:15 p.m. on Friday.) It also trades from 6:00 p.m. Sunday through 4:15 p.m. Monday. Open outcry trading in the original S&P 500 contract, which takes place from 9:30 a.m. through 4:15 p.m. Monday through Friday, overlaps with electronic trading in the E-mini S&P 500 during those hours. Electronic trading in the original S&P 500 contract (which as noted above takes place only outside of its open outcry trading hours) also overlaps with the E-mini S&P 500 contract during overnight hours.

The E-mini S&P 500 contract was launched in 1997, as a smaller contract size version of the original S&P 500 futures contract. Since that time, trading volume and open interest in the E-mini version has grown dramatically such that, today, the E-mini S&P 500 contract is the most actively traded domestic stock index futures contract.[141]

Both the E-mini S&P 500 and the pit-traded S&P 500 futures contracts exhibit substantial trading volume and open interest. In April 2010, trading in the E-mini S&P 500 and the pit-traded S&P 500 futures contracts accounted for about 78 percent of the total trading volume and about 80 percent of total open interest of all domestic stock index futures contracts. For this same period, the E-mini S&P 500 contract alone accounted for about 77 percent of total US stock index futures and options activity. In this regard, in April 2010, the average daily trading volume in the E-mini S&P 500 contract was about 2.1 million contracts, compared to about 17,000 contracts for the S&P 500 contract. As of the close on May 5, total open interest in the E-mini S&P 500 contract was about 2.6 million contracts (representing a notional value of about $152.4 billion), compared to about 328,000 contracts for the S&P 500 contract. The $152.4 billion notional value of the E-mini S&P 500 contract, however, represents only about one percent of the $14.1 trillion notional value of the entire U.S. stock market, as represented by the Russell 3000 index.

The Russell 2000 Index Mini futures contract trades on ICE Futures U.S. It was originally listed in October 2001 on the CME but moved to ICE Futures U.S. in September 2008. April 2010 average daily volume for the contract was 150,885. Open interest as of May 5, 2010 was 392,394 representing 10% of total U.S. stock index futures open interest.

***b. Security Futures***

The term "security futures product" (SFP) encompasses security futures and options on security futures. Security futures includes both futures on a single security (called single stock futures) and futures on narrow-based security indices.

The Commodity Futures Modernization Act of 2000 (CFMA) lifted the ban on trading of futures contracts based on single stocks. A security future is a contract for the sale or future delivery of a single security or of a narrow-based security index.142 Previously, these products were prohibited from being offered in the United States. With the passage of the CFMA, broad-based security index futures, which are not considered security futures products, continue to trade under the sole jurisdiction of the CFTC, while security futures products are subject to the joint jurisdiction of the CFTC and the SEC.[143]

Contract markets that have been designated by the CFTC may trade security futures products if they notice register with the SEC and comply with certain requirements of the Securities Exchange Act of 1934.[144] Likewise, national securities exchanges and national securities associations registered with the SEC may trade security futures products if they notice register with the CFTC and comply with certain requirements of the CEA.[145]

Only one DCM trades single stock and narrow based index futures contracts, OneChicago, which was designated as a contract market by the CFTC in 2002. At expiration of a single stock futures contract, the contract is settled by delivery of shares of the underlying stock. OneChicago lists 1,936 futures products, of which 233 are futures on Exchange Traded Funds. The total trading volume on OneChicago in 2009 was approximately 3 million contracts.

## 4. Electronic Trading

### *a. History of Electronic Futures Trading*

Electronic futures trading began at both CME and CBOT in 1992. Over the almost two decades since then, electronic trading has come to be the prevalent form of trading in U.S. futures markets. Electronic trading volume surpassed open outcry trading volume at CBOT in 2004, at CME in 2005, and at the New York Mercantile Exchange (NYMEX) in 2007. As of the end of April 2010, electronic trading accounted for approximately 88 percent of the combined volume of all CME Group exchanges[146]— which collectively account for approximately 97 percent of all U.S. futures and options volume—while open outcry trading had declined to approximately 12 percent of the combined volume of those exchanges.[147] For example, in 2009, total trading volume for the S&P 500 futures contract was approximately 10.4 million contracts as compared to approximately 556 million contracts for the E-mini S&P 500 contract.

The IntercontinentalExchange, Inc. was launched as a fully electronic trading venue in 2000. It acquired the former New York Board of Trade, now ICE Futures U.S., whose markets traded only by open outcry, in 2006. ICE launched electronic trading at ICE Futures U.S. in 2007, and by the end of 2007 all futures contracts there were exclusively traded electronically, with only options on futures still traded by open outcry.

### *b. Electronic Trading Platforms*

Equity index futures on U.S. futures exchanges are traded on two electronic trading systems, CME Group's Globex system and the IntercontinentalExchange, Inc.'s ICE Trading System.

CME Globex supports electronic trading at all CME Group exchanges. The CME Globex system also supports the electronic trading of partner exchanges including the Kansas City Board of Trade, Minneapolis Grain Exchange, Dubai Mercantile Exchange, BM&F Bovespa, and Korea Exchange. Launched in 1992, CME Globex is now accessed by customers in more than 85 countries and foreign territories, and is available for trading nearly 24 hours a day from Sunday evening to Friday afternoon. In the first quarter of 2010, CME Globex processed an average daily volume of approximately 9.5 million contracts for CME, CBOT, NYMEX and COMEX products.

The IntercontinentalExchange, Inc.'s ICE Trading System supports electronic trading at all ICE futures exchanges, including ICE Futures U.S. (regulated by the CFTC), ICE Europe (regulated by the United Kingdom's Financial Services Authority), and ICE Canada (regulated by Canada's Manitoba Securities Commission). It also supports electronic trading for ICE's OTC swaps markets in oil, electricity, and natural gas. It is accessed by customers in 50 countries and is available for trading for about 23 hours a day from Sunday evening through Friday afternoon. During April 2010, the ICE Trading System processed an average daily volume of about 428,000 contracts for ICE Futures U.S., and an overall combined average daily volume of almost 1.4 million contracts for all trading on the system.

## 5. Order Display and System Speed

CME's Globex system displays bid and offer prices and volume 10-deep in the order book for the E-mini S&P 500 contract, and the ICE Trading System displays the full depth of all bids and offers in the order book for all futures contracts traded on ICE Futures U.S. At both exchanges, traders can use front-end systems as an interface to enter their orders into the respective electronic trading system.[148] CME and ICE offer a range of different connectivity options to market participants. Market participants' decisions related to application design, network infrastructure, hardware and configuration affect how a participant accesses the market.

Once an order message is received by the Globex matching engine, the system affixes a time stamp to the order message and transmits it back to the end-user acknowledging the time of receipt at the matching engine. In the E-mini S&P 500 market on May 6, the average latency at the matching engine level during the period from 2:30 p.m. -3:00 p.m. was 3 milliseconds. The average latency during this period for market data updates to the last best price and 10-deep book was 1.5 milliseconds. Similarly, once an order message is received by the ICE Trading System's matching engine, the system affixes a time stamp to the order message and transmits it back to the end-user acknowledging the time of receipt at the matching engine. In the Russell 2000 market on May 6, the average latency at the matching engine level during the period from 2:30 p.m. -3:00 p.m. was 250 microseconds. The average latency during this period for market data updates to the last best price and full order book depth was 250 microseconds.

During the period from 2:30 p.m. to 3:00 p.m. on May 6 in the June E-mini S&P 500 index futures contract, the average number of trades per second was approximately 106 trades, and the average volume per second was approximately 600 contracts. The peak number of trades per second occurred at 1:43:21 p.m. with 889 trades. The peak volume in one second occurred at 2:46:51 p.m., with 4,456 contracts traded. In comparison, on May 13, the Thursday following May 6, the peak message volume in the E-mini S&P 500 occurred between 9:30 a.m. - 10:00 a.m. The average volume per second was 133 contracts and the peak volume per second was 2,806 contracts. The average number of trades per second was 39 and the peak number of trades per second was 891 trades.

During the period from 2:30 to 3:00 p.m. on May 6 in the Russell 2000 index futures contract, the average number of trades per second was 32 trades, and the average volume per second was 44 contracts. The peak number of trades per second occurred at 2:41:41 p.m. with 320 trades. The peak volume in one second occurred at 2:41:44 p.m. with 431 contracts traded. For comparison, during the period of 2:30 p.m. -3:00 p.m. on May 13, the average volume per second was 11 contracts and the peak volume per second was 194 contracts. The average number of trades per second was 7.7 trades and the peak number of trades per second was 126 trades.

## 6. Co-location

A driving force behind the growth of electronic trading in the futures industry has been the continuing evolution of technologies for generating and executing orders. These technologies have improved the speed, capacity, and sophistication of trading functions that are available to market participants.

Many trading firms have trading strategies that are highly dependent upon speed in a number of areas: speed of market data delivery from exchange servers to the firms' servers; speed of processing of firms' trading engines; speed of access to exchange servers by firms' servers; and, speed of order execution and response by exchanges. For some trading firms, speed is now measured in microseconds, and any latency or delay in order arrival or execution can adversely affect their trading strategy. These trading firms are typically referred to as "high frequency" and/or "algorithmic" traders. High frequency traders are professional traders that use computer systems to engage in strategies that generate a large number of trades on a daily basis. Competition among high frequency traders has led to extensive use of co-location and/or proximity hosting services.[149]

Co-location and proximity services refer to trading market and/or certain third-party facility space that is made available to market participants for the purpose of locating their network and computing hardware closer to the trading market's matching engine. Along with space, co-location and proximity hosting services usually involve providing various levels of power, telecommunications, and other ancillary products and services necessary to maintain the trading firms' trading systems.

## 7. Futures Market Participants

As shown in the CFTC's Commitments of Traders (COT) reports, almost all of the participants in equity index futures markets are reportable traders on whom the CFTC regularly collects substantial information.[150] The vast majority of these traders are classified as "commercial traders"[151] For example, in the E-mini S&P 500 futures market, approximately 90 percent of all traders are reportable, and 70 percent are classified as commercial traders. The commercial category includes institutional investors such as pension funds, endowments, corporations, insurance companies, broker-dealers, large U.S. and non-U.S. commercial banks, and swaps dealers.

The remaining traders include hedge funds and other managed funds, as well as day traders. Day traders typically are in and out of the market rapidly, and usually do not maintain significant open interest from one trading day to the next, or even one hour to the next, although they may represent a significant portion of daily volume. A new type of futures market day trader, high frequency traders (described above), employ computer trading algorithms to spot market trends that signal when to enter and exit a market, and to execute their trading strategies. High frequency traders typically place large numbers of orders for small-quantities of contracts, either within a single market or across many different markets.

## 8. Order Entry

Participants in equity index futures markets place orders in a variety of ways. Some use the traditional method of telephoning an order to an exchange member firm, which takes the order and transmits it either to an electronic trading system or to an exchange floor.[152] The majority of participants, however, transmit their orders electronically themselves. Many of these orders are first transmitted to the exchange clearing member firm that guarantees that participant's trades, and then to the trading system. Some participants who have been approved by their clearing members and the exchange can transmit their orders directly to the trading system.

In 2008, CME implemented "Globex Credit Controls," a risk management system that enables intermediaries to set credit limits for each customer placing orders directly to Globex. While these risk limits are set by the intermediary firm, they are applied on an automated basis by the electronic trading system as a backstop to the firm's own risk management architecture. In April 2010, CME promulgated its Rule 949 and Advisory 10-153, which specifically require members to make use of these controls. Starting at the beginning of 2011, CME will be reviewing member firms' use of these controls (e.g., the reasonableness of the size of the limits) in light of the firms' financial resources.

ICE has an integrated pre-trade risk management system within the ICE Trading System to allow futures commission merchants to set credit limits for each customer placing orders into the system. Once set by the FCM, the limits are automatically applied to the user by the ICE Trading System. Modifications to the credit limits take effect in real-time in the trading system and can be made via the ICE website 24 hours a day, 7 days a week. These credit settings can be used as the primary risk management tool for firms or as a backstop to the firm's own risk management architecture. All participants who trade ICE U.S. Futures' contracts must utilize these controls to trade on the ICE trading system.

## 9. Market Making in Futures Markets

Futures exchanges are not required to have market makers. However, a futures exchange may enter into agreements with an exchange member calling for the member to act as a market maker on a specific product or products, in order to provide liquidity for new product or in low volume contracts.[153] Market maker agreements provide the market maker with certain incentives if the market maker, trading for its own account, complies with the particular obligations. These market maker agreements generally specify volume requirements and impose an affirmative duty on the market maker to make a continuous, two-sided market within some specified bid-ask spread in order to receive the incentives.[154] The requirement that the market maker provide its quotes in a particular bid-ask spread means that any quotes the market maker provides to qualify for the market maker program must be within a certain range of the then current market price.

Market maker programs must comply with applicable core principles and designation criteria set out in the CEA,[155] and prior to its implementation, a program's criteria must be submitted to the CFTC, either by self-certification or for approval.[156] In reviewing market maker programs, the CFTC considers, among other things, whether market maker incentives would encourage wash or fictitious trading or other trading abuses. The CFTC also examines whether the exchange has adequate regulatory compliance mechanisms in place to detect trade practice abuses by market maker program participants.

## 10. Existing Mechanisms to Promote Orderly Markets and Customer Protection

Both CME Globex and the ICE Trading System have automatic safety features— termed "pre-trade risk management functionality"—to protect against errors in the entry of orders (such as "fat finger" errors), extreme price swings, and erroneous prices. As discussed below, these features help ensure fair and orderly markets.

First, CME Globex and the ICE Trading System both automatically reject orders priced outside a range of reasonability, also known as a "price band."[157] For instance, on the E-mini S&P 500 futures contract, the price band is 12 points (approximately one percent) above and 12 points below the last executed trade.[158] This prevents clearly erroneous orders from entering the trading system and helps to prevent "fat finger" errors.

Second, both CME and ICE have maximum order size limitations that prevent entry into the trading system of an order that exceeds a maximum quantity established by the exchange. In the E-mini contract, for example, the maximum quantity is 2,000 contracts. This protection also helps to prevent "fat finger" errors. With the S&P 500 Index at 1,100 points as it was on May 6, two thousand E-mini contracts would have a notional value of $110 million. The average transaction size in the E-mini contract, however, tends to be six contracts, or $330,000.

Third, both CME Globex and the ICE Trading System have protections with regard to "stop loss" orders.[159] Such orders are triggered if the market declines to a level pre-selected by the person entering the order. CME and ICE rules provide that when the market declines to the trader's pre-selected stop level for such an order, the order becomes a limit order executable only down to a price within the range of reasonability permitted by the system, instead of becoming a market order.[160] Requiring that stop orders have a limit avoids the possibility that such stop orders could be executed no matter how low the market goes. This requirement for all stop orders to convert to limit orders prevents, for example, any stop orders from being posted or executed at a price unreasonably below the market.

Fourth, CME Globex has "Stop Logic" functionality that protects against cascading stop orders—the domino effect of one stop order triggering others.[161] Globex's Stop Logic functionality pauses trading—the pause is termed "the Stop Logic reserve period"—when the trading engine recognizes that it has a series of resting stop orders that could lead to a cascade and move the market up or down beyond a specified amount. The length of the Stop Logic reserve period varies by product and time of day. For the E-mini S&P 500, the period is 5 seconds from 9:30 a.m. to 4:15 p.m. and 10 seconds during the balance of the trading session. The pause allows new orders to enter the system to restore liquidity and balance to the order book.[162]

## 11. Trade Cancellation

Trade cancellation policies balance the adverse effects on market integrity of executing trades and publishing trade information inconsistent with prevailing market conditions. The intent is to preserve legitimate expectations that executed transactions will not be cancelled.

At CME, a "no-bust range" is established for each product traded electronically on CME Globex. Trade prices within the no-bust range—six points above or below the market price in the case of the E-mini S&P 500 contract—will not generally be busted or adjusted. The only exception to this rule is if the Globex Control Center (GCC) determines that not busting or adjusting a trade within the no-bust range will have a material, adverse effect on the market.[163] Exchange rules state that the GCC can adjust trade prices or bust trades when such action is necessary to mitigate market disrupting events caused by the improper or erroneous use of the electronic trading system or by system defects. The GCC may review a trade based on its analysis of market conditions or on a request for review by a Globex user. A request for review must be made as soon as possible, but will generally not be considered if more than eight minutes have passed since the trade occurred. On May 6, CME received no requests to cancel any trades in the E-mini S&P 500 futures market, and CME did not cancel any trades.

ICE Futures U.S. has established a "No Cancellation Range" ("NCR") for each ICE Futures U.S. product traded on its electronic platform. The NCR for the Russell 2000 Index Mini futures contract is 400 index points above or below the current anchor price (the anchor price is generally the last traded price). Trades within the NCR are not, under most circumstances, cancelled, whether as the result of error or otherwise. Traders generally have 5 minutes from the time of executing a trade in which to notify ICE Futures U.S. of an alleged error trade. ICE generally decides whether an alleged error trade will stand or be cancelled within 15 minutes after the time the alleged error trade occurred. On May 6, ICE received no requests to cancel any trades in the Russell 2000 contract, and did not cancel any trades.

## 12. Internalization of Orders by Futures Commission Merchants

In futures markets, FCMs can match orders in two limited ways. Such orders can be matched as a block trade or as an exchange of physicals for related positions transaction ("EFRP"), with the permission of customers.[164] However, all such transactions must be reported to the exchange promptly, and are included in the exchange's audit trail and in market data the exchange subsequently transmits to market participants. If a block trade or EFRP is not executed, the FCM can match orders only if it follows strict exchange rules governing cross-trades, which require that, before the FCM can match such orders, they must be exposed to the market for a certain period of time during which they are visible to and available for matching by any market participant. Both the orders and any resulting permissible cross-trade are included in the exchange's market data transmitted to market participants, as well as in the exchange's audit trail. This differs from the situation in equities markets, where orders internalized by broker-dealers may not be included in consolidated quotation data visible to the entire market.

## 13. Sources of Regulatory Data

The CFTC's primary mission is fostering markets that accurately reflect the forces of supply and demand for the underlying commodity and are free of abusive trading practices. In this capacity, the CFTC conducts oversight of trade execution facilities through its market surveillance and market compliance programs.

The surveillance program identifies situations that could pose a threat of manipulation and to initiate appropriate preventive actions. Each day, for all active futures and option contract markets, CFTC staff monitors the daily activities of large traders, key price relationships, and relevant supply and demand factors in a continuous review for potential market problems. Surveillance is not conducted exclusively at the CFTC, surveillance issues are usually handled jointly by the CFTC and the appropriate futures exchange. Relevant surveillance information is shared and corrective actions are taken, when appropriate. Potential problem situations are jointly monitored and, if necessary, verbal contacts are made with the participants in question. These contacts may be for the purpose of understanding their trading, confirming reported positions, alerting the brokers or traders as to the regulatory concern for the situation, or warning them to trade responsibly. If an exchange fails to take actions that the CFTC deems appropriate, the CFTC has broad emergency powers under which it can order the exchange to take actions specified by the CFTC.

The CFTC's surveillance program uses many sources of market information to accomplish its objectives. Some of this information is publicly available, including data on the overall supply, demand, and marketing of the underlying commodity; futures, option, and cash prices; and trading volume and open interest data. Other information is highly confidential under statutory requirements, including data which identifies the activity or positions of individual traders.

Exchanges report the daily positions and transactions of each clearing member to the CFTC. The data are transmitted electronically during the morning after the "as of" date. They show, separately for proprietary and customer accounts, the aggregate position and trading volume of each clearing member in each futures and option contract. The data are used to identify the clearing firms that clear the largest buy or sell volumes or hold the biggest positions in a particular market.

The clearing member data do not identify the beneficial owners of the positions. Information on beneficial owners, however, is provided through the CFTC's large trader reporting system ("LTRS"). Under the CFTC's LTRS, clearing members, FCMs, and foreign brokers (collectively called reporting firms) file daily reports with the CFTC pursuant to Part 17 of the CFTC's regulations, 17 CFR Part 17. As is the case with clearing member data, the data are transmitted electronically during the morning after the "as of" date. The reports show futures and option positions of traders with positions at or above specific reporting levels as set by the CFTC. Current reporting levels are found in CFTC Regulation 15.03(b), 17 CFR 15.03(b).[165]

If, at the daily market close, a reporting firm has a trader with a position at or above the CFTC's reporting level in any single futures or option expiration month, the firm reports that trader's entire position in all futures and options expiration months in that commodity, regardless of size. The CFTC uses addition information obtained from the reporting firms—i.e., CFTC Form 102: Identification of "Special Accounts"—and traders themselves— i.e., Form 40 "Statement of Reporting Trader"—to aggregate positions of a trader that may exist across multiple accounts or firms.

The CFTC also collects trade data on a daily, transaction date + 1 ("T+1"), basis from all U.S. futures exchanges through "Trade Capture Reports." Trade Capture Reports contain trade and related order information for every matched trade facilitated by an exchange, whether executed via open outcry or electronically, or non-competitively (e.g., block trades, exchange for physical, etc.). Among the data included in the Trade Capture Report are trade date, product, contract month, trade execution time, price, quantity, trade type (e.g., open outcry outright future, electronic outright option, give-up, spread, block, etc.), trader ID, order entry operator ID, clearing member, opposite broker and opposite clearing member, order entry date, order entry time, order number, customer type indicator, trading account numbers, and numerous other data points. Additional information is also required for options on futures, including put/call indicators and strike price, as well as for give-ups, spreads, and other special trade types.

All transactional data is received overnight, loaded in the CFTC's databases, and processed by specialized software applications that detect patterns of potentially abusive trades or otherwise raise concern. Alerts are available to staff the following morning for more detailed and individualized analysis using additional tools and resources for data mining, research, and investigation.

Time and sales quotes for pit and electronic transactions are also received from the exchanges daily. CFTC staff is able to access the market quotes to validate alerts as well as reconstruct markets for the time periods in question. Currently, staff is working with exchanges to receive all order book information in addition to the executed order information already provided in the Trade Capture Report. This project is expected to be completed within the next year; at present such data remains available to staff through "special calls" (described below) requesting exchange data.

In addition to information received daily, the CFTC may also obtain information through what is referred to as a Special Call. Under CFTC Regulation 18.05, every trader who holds or controls a reportable futures or option position is required to keep books and records showing details concerning all positions and transactions in the commodity, as well as details concerning all positions and transactions in the cash commodity, and all commercial activity that the trader hedges in the futures or option contract in which the trader is reportable.[166] Such information must be made available to the CFTC upon request. A current use of the special call provision is in the capture of relevant information of index activity in commodity markets. To obtain the necessary data on OTC swap agreements, CFTC staff issued a special call to financial firms to receive data about the index activity of a variety of investors.

# APPENDIX C. CROSS-MARKET CIRCUIT BREAKERS

Circuit breakers are coordinated, cross-market trading halts that were designed to operate during significant market declines and to substitute orderly, pre-planned halts for the *ad hoc* trading halts which can occur when market liquidity is exhausted. Circuit breakers also provide opportunities for markets and market participants to assess market conditions and potential systemic stress during a historic market decline. The U.S. securities and futures markets adopted circuit breaker procedures in October 1988 in response to their experiences during the historic market declines of October 1987 and to recommendations contained in studies of the pricing and liquidity problems that arose during the sharp price swings and volume surges on October 20, 1987, that came close to shutting down the markets.

In addition, futures exchanges have "price limits" for stock index futures contracts.[167] These price limits were also adopted in response to the historic market declines in October 1987. A price limit, in itself, does not halt trading in the futures, but prohibits trading at prices below (and sometimes above) the pre-set limit based on the previous session's settlement price. Intra-day price limits are removed at pre-set times during the trading session, such as 10-minutes after the futures are determined to be "locked limit" down (up).[168] Daily price limits remain in effect for the entire trading session. Specific price limits are set for each stock index futures contract.

## 1. Cross-Market Circuit Breaker Halts

### *a. The October 1987 Market Break and the Adoption of Circuit Breakers in 1988*

In October 1987, the U.S. securities markets experienced an extraordinary surge in price volatility and trading volumes ("October 1987 Market Break"). On Monday, October 19, the DJIA declined 508 points, representing a record one-day decline of almost 23%. On October 20, the DJIA again declined sharply before share prices stabilized. The combination of historic price swings and unprecedented trading volumes overwhelmed the operational capacities and liquidity of the securities and futures markets. By mid-day on October 20, heavy selling pressure had produced large order imbalances and numerous *ad hoc* trading halts in individual stocks. Liquidity and pricing difficulties also resulted in uncoordinated mid-day trading suspensions on major options exchanges and several large stock index futures exchanges. While the subsequent rally in market prices in the afternoon averted more widespread financial problems, the near shutdown of the markets on October 20 became a central focus of several studies of the October 1987 Market Break and resulted in the adoption of circuit breaker procedures in 1988.

Immediately following the October 1987 Market Break, the Presidential Task Force on Market Mechanisms was established with Nicholas F. Brady as Chairman. The report issued by the Task Force on January 8, 1988 ("Brady Report") recommended a number of initiatives to address future periods of extreme market volatility, including the implementation of circuit breaker mechanisms coordinated across the markets for stocks, options, and stock index futures. The Brady Report noted that the market disorders of October 1987 "became, in effect, *ad hoc* circuit breakers, reflecting the natural limits to market liquidity." Accordingly, the Brady Report maintained that the October 1987 Market Break "demonstrates that it is far better to design and implement coherent, coordinated circuit breaker mechanisms in advance, than to be left at the mercy of the unavoidable circuit breakers of chaos and system failure."[169]

After the issuance of the Brady Report, the President's Working Group on Financial Markets ("Working Group") was formed with the mandate to determine the extent to which coordinated regulatory action was necessary to strengthen the nation's financial markets.[170] The May 1988 Interim Report ("Interim Report") of the Working Group recommended a number of initiatives to assist the markets in coping with future periods of extraordinary price swings and volume surges, including the adoption of circuit breakers that would provide coordinated trading halts and reopenings for large, rapid market declines that threaten to create panic conditions.[171] The Working Group recommended that all U.S. markets for stocks, options, and futures halt trading for one hour if the DJIA declined 250 points from its previous day's closing level and halt trading for two hours if the DJIA declined 400 points from its previous day's closing level.[172] In addition, the Working Group anticipated quarterly reviews of the circuit breaker thresholds to determine whether changes in index levels necessitated changes to the triggers so that they continue to reflect percentage declines approximately equivalent to 12% and 20%.[173]

Partly in response to the October 1987 Market Break and the recommendations of the Brady Report and the Working Group, the securities and stock index futures markets submitted proposals to the SEC and CFTC in 1988 to implement circuit breakers that would impose temporary trading halts following significant market declines. The circuit breaker rules for the securities and stock index futures markets were implemented in October 1988.[174]

The circuit breakers approved in 1988 provided for a one-hour trading halt in all securities markets if the DJIA declined 250 points from its previous day's closing level and for a subsequent two-hour trading halt if the DJIA declined 400 points from its previous day's close. In approving the original circuit breakers, the SEC and CFTC noted that the circuit breakers were not an attempt to prevent markets from reaching new price levels, but an effort by the securities and futures markets to arrive at a coordinated means to address potentially destabilizing market volatility along the lines of the historic decline of the October 1987 Market Break.[175] The SEC and CFTC also believed that circuit breakers would help promote stability in the equity and equity-related markets by providing for increased information flows and enhanced opportunity to assess information during times of extreme market movements. The SEC and CFTC believed that circuit breakers could provide market participants with an opportunity to re-establish an equilibrium between buying and selling interest and ensure that market participants had a reasonable opportunity to become aware of and respond to a dramatic market decline.[176]

### *a) Modifications to the Circuit Breakers from 1996 to 1998*

The SEC and CFTC approved several modifications to the markets' circuit breaker rules starting in 1996. In July 1996, the agencies approved rule modifications to reduce the length of the trading halts by half. In addition, when the SEC and CFTC approved a six-month extension of the circuit breakers in October 1996,[177] the agencies urged the markets to reach a consensus on the size of increases in the trigger levels required to ensure that cross-market trading halts would be imposed only during market declines of historic proportions.[178] In response to the agencies' recommendations, the markets submitted proposals to increase the circuit breaker triggers to levels of 350 and 550 points in the DJIA.[179] In approving the

350/550 trigger levels through January 31, 1998, the agencies stated that the new trigger levels represented a substantial improvement over the existing 250/400 trigger levels. Nevertheless, the agencies noted that trigger levels should be amended to reflect an extraordinary decline under prevailing market conditions and that the SEC and CFTC would work with the markets to develop procedures for reevaluating the circuit breaker triggers on at least an annual basis.[180]

On October 27, 1997, the nation's securities markets fell by a then-record absolute amount, with the DJIA declining 554.26 points (7.18 percent) to close at 7161.15. This was first and only day that the cross-market trading halt circuit breaker procedures were implemented. At 2:36 p.m., the DJIA had declined 350 points, thereby triggering a 30-minute halt on the stock, options, and index futures markets. After trading resumed at 3:06 p.m., prices fell rapidly to reach the 550-point circuit breaker level at 3:30 p.m., thereby ending the trading session 30 minutes prior to the normal stock market close.

Immediately following the events of October 27, the markets and regulators began considering further revisions to the circuit breaker procedures. There was general consensus that the 7 percent decline in the DJIA on October 27 did not justify the early closure of the markets on that day. Accordingly, an agreement was reached by the markets and the agencies that trigger points for circuit breaker halts should be increased substantially and measures should be taken to permit normal market closings if circuit breaker thresholds were reached late in a trading session.

Accordingly, the SEC and the CFTC approved revised circuit breaker rules for the markets in April 1998.[181] The revised rules established trading halts following one-day declines in the DJIA of 10 percent, 20 percent, and 30 percent. The NYSE would calculate the trigger levels at the beginning of each calendar quarter, using the average closing value of the DJIA for the previous month to establish specific point values for the quarter. Trading would halt for one hour if the DJIA declined 10 percent prior to 2:00 p.m., and for one-half hour if the DJIA declined 10 percent between 2:00 p.m. and 2:30 p.m. If the DJIA declined by 10 percent at or after 2:30 p.m., trading would not halt at the 10 percent level. If the DJIA declined 20 percent prior to 1:00 p.m., trading would halt for two hours; trading would halt for one hour if the DJIA declined 20 percent between 1:00 p.m. and 2:00 p.m., and trading would halt for the remainder of the day if a 20 percent decline occurred at or after 2:00 p.m. If the DJIA declined 30 percent at any time, trading would halt for the remainder of the day.

These were the circuit breaker levels in place on May 6, 2010.[182]

## 2. CME Price Limit "Speed Bumps"

In response to the historic market volatility in October 1987, the CME adopted downside intra-day price limits for index futures even before the cross-market circuit breaker trading halts were established. The CME's 1988 price limits were set at 5 percent, 10 percent, and 15 percent, as well as a daily limit at 20 percent. These were not coordinated with the circuit breakers or any stock exchange rules and were based on the price of the index futures contract from the previous day's settlement price. For each of the intra-day price limits, trading would be subject to the price limit for 10 minutes after a "locked limit" finding by exchange officials. If the futures contract were limit offered at the end of that 10-minute period, then trading would halt for two minutes, after which the next price limit would be in effect. The daily price limit of 20 percent would remain in effect for the remainder of the trading session.

The futures price limits also have changed since their adoption in 1988. The CME eliminated the 5 percent and 15 percent intra-day price limits effective on January 1, 2008 in order to harmonize rules across CME and CBOT contracts. The CME and ICE 10 percent and 20 percent intra-day price limits act as "speed bumps" - once a stock index futures contract is determined to be locked limit, the limit remains in effect and/or halts for a period of time determined by the exchange, after which, the next price limit becomes effective. The daily price limit of 20% was replaced by a new limit of 30%.

The CME also currently maintains a 5% price limit above or below the regular trading hour closing level applicable to overnight electronic trading only. No trading may occur at a price more than 5% above or below the regular trading hours closing level. If the price limit is bid or offered at the limit within five minutes prior to the opening of regular trading hours, then trading will be halted for the remainder of electronic trading hours until the commencement of regular trading hours at 9:30 a.m. During the trading halt, the CME will provide an indicative opening price for the re-opening of regular trading hours.

These were the index futures price limits in place on May 6, 2010.

A review of the history of price limit declarations shows that the 5 percent price limit was hit for the S&P 500 and E-mini S&P 500 futures contracts only 5 times since 1988.[183] At no time during that period were any higher level price limits hit. However, over the period 1998 through 2007, when the 5 percent price limit was in effect, there was a total of six days when the E-mini S&P 500 futures contract fell by 5% or more during the trading day. This discrepancy could be explained by method used to calculate the 5 percent price limit, which is reset each calendar quarter based on the average settlement price over the prior calendar month. After the CME eliminated the 5 percent limit, the E-mini S&P 500 fell by more than 5% on 21 days.

## Appendix D. Futures Market Information

A. Most Active U.S. Stock Index Futures

B. List of Active Designated Contract Markets

C. Detailed Trading Statistics for the E-mini S&P 500 June 2010 futures on May 6, 2010. Volume, Price, Account, User Summary by hour, minute and second

## A. Most active u.s. Stock index futures

| | Name | Multiplier | Index Close 5/6/10 | Notional Value at close | Open Interest as of close on 5/6/10 | Notional Futures on Close on 5/5/10 | Market Share of US Stock Index futures (Notional futures) | Volume on 5/6/10 (30-day avg. vol.) |
|---|---|---|---|---|---|---|---|---|
| 1 | CME E-MINI S&P 500 | $50 x Index | 1,128 | $56,400 | 2,719,296 | $152,482,722,429 | 48.97% | 5,682,565 (2,482,578) |
| 2 | CME S&P 500 STOCK INDEX | $250 x Index | 1,128 | $281,250 | 333,153 | $95,546,157,913 | 30.69% | 54,701 (72,622) |
| 3 | ICE US RUSSELL 2000 MINI INDEX FUTURE | $100 x Index | 672 | $67,200 | 399,159 | $27,419,678,895 | 8.81% | 392,565 (171,686) |
| 4 | CME NASDAQ-100 STOCK INDEX (MINI) | $20 x Index | 1,893 | $37,860 | 381,569 | $15,439,860,428 | 4.96% | 736,784 (320,934) |
| 5 | CME NASDAQ-100 STOCK INDEX | $100 x Index | 1,893 | $189,300 | 26,667 | $4,882,124,351 | 1.57% | 4,302 (1,823) |
| 6 | CME E-MINI S&P 400 STOCK INDEX | $100 x Index | 776 | $77,600 | 97,062 | $7,841,925,535 | 2.52% | 56,629 (29,161) |
| 7 | CME S&P 400 MIDCAP STOCK IDX | $500 x Index | 776 | $388,000 | 1,788 | $720,427,400 | 0.23% | 115 (61) |
| 8 | CBT DOW JONES INDUSTRIAL AVG- x $5 | $5 x Index | 10,520 | $52,600 | 84,706 | $4,557,248,441 | 1.46% | 326, 704 (145,245) |
| 9 | CBT DOW JONES INDUSTRIAL AVG x $10 | $10 x Index | 10,520 | $105,200 | 11,045 | $1,190,212,740 | 0.38% | 894 (720) |

**Table. (Continued)**

| | Name | Multiplier | Index Close 5/6/10 | Notional Value at close | Open Interest as of close on 5/6/10 | Notional Futures on Close on 5/5/10 | Market Share of US Stock Index futures (Notional futures) | Volume on 5/6/10 (30-day avg. vol.) |
|---|---|---|---|---|---|---|---|---|
| 10 | CBT DOW JONES INDUSTRIAL AVG x $25 | $25 x Index | 10,520 | $263,000 | 28 | $7,311,500 | 0.00% | 10 (5) |
| 11 | ICUS RUSSEL 1000 MINI INDEX FUTURE | $100 x Index | 621 | $62,100 | 19,589 | $1,250,936,760 | 0.40% | 1842 (918) |
| 12 | CME E-MINI S&P SMALLCAP 600 INDEX | $100 x Index | 360 | $36,000 | 689 | $23,348,990 | 0.01% | 392 (141) |

## B. Dcms with Contracts ThZat Actively Trade

1. ***CBOE Futures Exchange***. An electronic exchange operating in Chicago, IL; CBOE Futures lists contracts on various volatility measures; CBOE Futures is a subsidiary of the Chicago Board of Options Exchange (designated on August 7, 2003).
2. ***CBOT***. CBOT (Board of Trade of the City of Chicago, Inc.) is located in Chicago, IL; Trading takes place both electronically on CME Globex and on trading floors; CBOT listed contracts include agricultural, indexes, interest rates, and treasuries; originally organized as a grain cash market in 1848, and became a subsidiary of the CME Group, Inc. in 2007.
3. ***CCFE***. An electronic exchange located in Chicago, IL; CCFE (Chicago Climate Futures Exchange, LLC) is a wholly owned subsidiary of the Chicago Climate Exchange Inc. (CCX); CCFE listed contracts include emissions contracts (designated November 9, 2004).
4. ***CME***. CME (Chicago Mercantile Exchange Inc.) is located in Chicago, IL; trading takes place both electronically on CME Globex and on trading floors; CME listed contracts include agricultural, weather, FX, indexes, and real estate; began operation in 1898; the parent of CME (CME Group, Inc.) purchased CBOT in 2007.
5. ***COMEX***. COMEX (The Commodity Exchange, Inc) is located in New York, NY; trading take place electronically on CME Globex and on trading floors in New York; COMEX lists contracts on precious metals; COMEX became a subsidiary of the New York Mercantile Exchange in 1994.
6. ***ELX***. An electronic exchange located in New York, NY; ELX (ELX Futures, L.P.) was founded by a consortium of dealers, trading firms, and technology providers, including a number of large commercial and investment banks; ELX currently lists only treasury contracts. (designated May 22, 2009).
7. ***ICE US***. ICE U.S. (ICE Futures US, Inc) is located in New York, NY; trading takes place both electronically on the ICE Trading system and on trading floors in New York; ICE US listed contracts include currencies, iron ore, agricultural products, and the Russell 1000 stock index. NYBOT was created by the merger of the Coffee, Sugar and Cocoa Exchange and the New York Cotton Exchange in 2004; NYBOT changed its name to ICE Futures US, Inc. after it became a wholly-owned subsidiary of the IntercontinentalExchange in 2007.
8. ***KCBT***. KCBT (Kansas City Board of Trade) is located in Kansas City, KS; trading takes place both electronically on CME Globex and on trading floors in Kansas City; listed contracts include wheat and a broad-based stock index; KCBT futures trading in grains began in 1876.
9. ***MGEX***. MGEX (Minneapolis Grain Exchange) is located in Minneapolis, MN; trading takes place both electronically on CME Globex and on trading floors; listed contracts include wheat and agricultural indexes; MGEX was started in 1881 and renamed MGEX in 1947.
10. ***NFX***. NFX (NASDAQ OMX Futures Exchange) is an electronic exchange in New York, NY; primarily lists currency and currency-related contracts. NFX was started as Philadelphia Board of Trade; its parent (then PHLX) was bought by NASDAQ OMX in 2008.

11. ***NYMEX***. NYMEX (New York Mercantile Exchange) is located in New York, NY; trading takes place both electronically on CME Globex and on trading floors in New York; listed contracts include energy-related and, emissions. NYMEX was originally founded in 1872 as the Butter and Cheese Exchange of New York (which became NYMEX in 1882) and became a wholly-owned subsidiary of CME Group Inc. in 2008.
12. ***NADEX***. NADEX (North American Derivatives Exchange, Inc.) is a Chicago-based, electronic exchange offering retail-oriented, binary and variable payout options on stock indices, foreign exchange rates, economic events, metals, and certain agricultural commodities (designated February 18, 2004).
13. ***NYSE Liffe***. NYSE Liffe (NYSE Liffe U.S. LLC) is an electronic exchange located in New York, NY; listed contracts include precious metals and equity indexes; NYSE Liffe was launched in 2008 as a subsidiary of NYSE Euronext (designated August 21, 2008).
14. ***OneChicago***. OneChicago (OneChicago LLC Futures Exchange; also called OCX) is an electronic exchange located in Chicago, IL; listed contracts include individual stocks, narrow-based indexes, and exchange traded funds. OneChicago is owned by a consortium that includes Interactive Brokers Group, LLC, the CME Group, Inc., and the CBOE (designated June 11, 2002).

## C. Detailed Trading Statistics for the e-Mini S&P 500 June 2010 futures

This section contains detailed trading data for the CME e-mini S&P 500 June 2010 futures contract covering the following three time periods (all times Eastern Daylight Time):

- Activity by hour from May 5 4:00 PM through May 6 5:00 PM
- Activity by minute from May 6 1:00 PM through May 6 4:15 PM
- Activity by second from May 6 2:41:00 PM through May 6 2:50:00 PM

For each time slice, the following information is displayed:

- The number of trades (Trades)
- The number of individual contracts traded (Volume)
- The price of the first trade (First)
- The highest trade price (High)
- The lowest trade price (Low)
- The price of the last trade (Last)
- The difference between the last price and the first price (Last – First Range)
- The difference between the highest price and the lowest price (High/Low Range)
- The volume weighted average price (VWAP)
- The number of unique Globex accounts executing buys (Buy Accts)
- The number of unique Globex accounts executing sells (Sell Accts)
- The number of unique parties executing buys (Buy User IDs)[184]
- The number of unique parties executing sells (Sell User IDs)

- A graphical display of the volume (Volume Graph)

As can be seen in the tables, the number of User IDs is normally greater than the number of Accounts. This can be due to the use of a single account by multiple User IDs. For example, there is not a specific limit to the number of automated trading systems (ATS) that an individual can use to trade his personal account. Each ATS would be given a unique User ID.

The numbers for Buy Accts and Sell Accts provide a rough idea of the breadth of participation from an account owner/controller standpoint. The numbers for Buy User IDs and Sell User IDs provide a rough idea of the breadth of participation from the standpoint of users directly interfacing with the Globex system. Many participants were both buyers and sellers and they would be included in both the Buy and Sell columns.

Source of data: CME Group as of May 13, 2010

**CME EMini SP Futures June 2010 Contract Summarized Activity By Hour (Eastern Daylight Time) Trade Date May 6, 2010**

| Row | Date | Time (EDT) | Trades | Volume | First | High | Low | Last | Last - First Range | High/Low Range | VWAP | Buy Accts | Sell Accts | Buy User IDs | Sell User IDs | Volume Graph |
|---|---|---|---|---|---|---|---|---|---|---|---|---|---|---|---|---|
| 1 | 5/5/2010 | 4 PM | 732 | 5,817 | 1163.75 | 1164.25 | 1163.50 | 1163.75 | 0.00 | 0.75 | 1163.890 | 181 | 157 | 196 | 162 | 5,817 |
| 2 | | 5 PM | 749 | 4,808 | 1163.50 | 1165.00 | 1163.00 | 1164.50 | 1.00 | 2.00 | 1163.867 | 143 | 166 | 151 | 171 | 4,808 |
| 3 | | 6 PM | 1,117 | 5,053 | 1164.75 | 1166.25 | 1164.50 | 1166.25 | 1.50 | 1.75 | 1165.403 | 209 | 264 | 223 | 281 | 5,053 |
| 4 | | 7 PM | 1,453 | 5,368 | 1166.25 | 1167.00 | 1165.00 | 1166.50 | 0.25 | 2.00 | 1166.108 | 203 | 228 | 218 | 253 | 5,368 |
| 5 | | 8 PM | 2,988 | 9,572 | 1166.50 | 1167.00 | 1164.50 | 1166.25 | -0.25 | 2.50 | 1165.952 | 254 | 266 | 301 | 295 | 9,572 |
| 6 | | 9 PM | 1,513 | 4,312 | 1166.50 | 1167.00 | 1165.75 | 1166.75 | 0.25 | 1.25 | 1166.451 | 172 | 184 | 183 | 206 | 4,312 |
| 7 | | 10 PM | 1,690 | 5,196 | 1167.00 | 1167.25 | 1165.50 | 1166.75 | -0.25 | 1.75 | 1166.492 | 218 | 209 | 238 | 228 | 5,196 |
| 8 | | 11 PM | 1,370 | 3,430 | 1167.00 | 1167.00 | 1165.50 | 1165.75 | -1.25 | 1.50 | 1166.247 | 161 | 128 | 179 | 141 | 3,430 |
| 9 | | 12 AM | 1,813 | 6,008 | 1165.75 | 1166.00 | 1164.00 | 1164.75 | -1.00 | 2.00 | 1164.717 | 266 | 199 | 315 | 223 | 6,008 |
| 10 | 5/6/2010 | 1 AM | 1,221 | 4,890 | 1164.75 | 1165.00 | 1164.00 | 1164.25 | -0.50 | 1.00 | 1164.328 | 151 | 154 | 166 | 160 | 4,890 |
| 11 | | 2 AM | 7,204 | 34,675 | 1164.25 | 1165.25 | 1159.25 | 1159.50 | -4.75 | 6.00 | 1162.248 | 591 | 583 | 656 | 655 | 34,675 |
| 12 | | 3 AM | 24,652 | 71,899 | 1159.75 | 1166.50 | 1158.00 | 1165.25 | 5.50 | 8.50 | 1161.506 | 785 | 769 | 937 | 913 | 71,899 |
| 13 | | 4 AM | 14,339 | 43,310 | 1165.25 | 1167.75 | 1163.00 | 1167.50 | 2.25 | 4.75 | 1165.649 | 593 | 594 | 700 | 691 | 43,310 |
| 14 | | 5 AM | 9,014 | 30,262 | 1167.25 | 1168.00 | 1164.75 | 1166.50 | -0.75 | 3.25 | 1166.422 | 433 | 467 | 507 | 554 | 30,262 |
| 15 | | 6 AM | 7,953 | 30,743 | 1166.75 | 1168.75 | 1166.75 | 1168.50 | 1.75 | 2.00 | 1168.051 | 433 | 559 | 498 | 636 | 30,743 |
| 16 | | 7 AM | 19,841 | 64,871 | 1168.25 | 1168.75 | 1162.25 | 1163.00 | -5.25 | 6.50 | 1165.817 | 855 | 785 | 1,009 | 940 | 64,871 |
| 17 | | 8 AM | 34,226 | 152,841 | 1163.00 | 1165.00 | 1155.50 | 1156.00 | -7.00 | 9.50 | 1160.594 | 2,086 | 1,728 | 2,415 | 1,971 | 152,841 |
| 18 | | 9 AM | 93,015 | 398,117 | 1156.25 | 1164.50 | 1155.25 | 1161.75 | 5.50 | 9.25 | 1159.933 | 4,325 | 4,200 | 4,953 | 4,755 | 398,117 |
| 19 | | 10 AM | 113,467 | 524,215 | 1161.50 | 1165.00 | 1153.25 | 1155.50 | -6.00 | 11.75 | 1158.877 | 4,949 | 4,843 | 5,661 | 5,524 | 524,215 |
| 20 | | 11 AM | 122,268 | 618,337 | 1155.50 | 1155.50 | 1147.25 | 1151.75 | -3.75 | 8.25 | 1151.039 | 5,540 | 4,804 | 6,252 | 5,377 | 618,337 |
| 21 | | 12 PM | 73,439 | 347,471 | 1152.00 | 1157.25 | 1148.50 | 1152.00 | 0.00 | 8.75 | 1153.052 | 3,495 | 3,681 | 3,888 | 4,124 | 347,471 |
| 22 | | 1 PM | 83,577 | 414,013 | 1152.25 | 1153.50 | 1140.75 | 1142.25 | -10.00 | 12.75 | 1145.918 | 4,368 | 3,866 | 4,850 | 4,271 | 414,013 |
| 23 | | 2 PM | 290,556 | 1,600,843 | 1142.25 | 1143.75 | 1056.00 | 1112.75 | -29.50 | 87.75 | 1113.142 | 6,939 | 6,873 | 7,609 | 7,564 | 1,600,843 |
| 24 | | 3 PM | 247,380 | 1,109,014 | 1112.75 | 1136.00 | 1103.25 | 1123.00 | 10.25 | 32.75 | 1122.277 | 4,735 | 5,215 | 5,214 | 5,698 | 1,109,014 |
| 25 | | 4 PM | 30,105 | 177,523 | 1123.50 | 1125.00 | 1119.50 | 1122.75 | -0.75 | 5.50 | 1122.310 | 1,609 | 1,330 | 1,727 | 1,429 | 177,523 |

**CME EMini SP Futures June 2010 Contract Summarized Activity By Minute 1:00 PM3:15 PM (Eastern Daylight Time) Trade Date May 6, 2010**

| Row | Time (EDT) | Trades | Volume | First | High | Low | Last | Last - First Range | High /Low Range | VWAP | Buy Accts | Sell Accts | Buy User IDs | Sell User IDs | Volume Graph |
|---|---|---|---|---|---|---|---|---|---|---|---|---|---|---|---|
| 1 | 1:00 PM | 2,211 | 9,653 | 1152.25 | 1153.50 | 1151.75 | 1153.00 | 0.75 | 1.75 | 1152.724 | 253 | 405 | 284 | 452 | 9,653 |
| 2 | 1:01 PM | 724 | 3,089 | 1153.00 | 1153.25 | 1152.25 | 1152.25 | -0.75 | 1.00 | 1152.812 | 134 | 138 | 151 | 166 | 3,089 |
| 3 | 1:02 PM | 1,140 | 5,034 | 1152.25 | 1152.75 | 1151.25 | 1152.00 | -0.25 | 1.50 | 1151.966 | 201 | 183 | 232 | 209 | 5,034 |
| 4 | 1:03 PM | 544 | 1,885 | 1152.25 | 1152.25 | 1151.25 | 1151.25 | -1.00 | 1.00 | 1151.579 | 121 | 79 | 139 | 97 | 1,885 |
| 5 | 1:04 PM | 629 | 2,732 | 1151.25 | 1152.50 | 1151.25 | 1152.25 | 1.00 | 1.25 | 1152.094 | 76 | 135 | 95 | 160 | 2,732 |
| 6 | 1:05 PM | 879 | 3,112 | 1152.25 | 1152.75 | 1151.75 | 1152.50 | 0.25 | 1.00 | 1152.367 | 125 | 162 | 149 | 183 | 3,112 |
| 7 | 1:06 PM | 854 | 3,334 | 1152.25 | 1152.75 | 1151.50 | 1151.75 | -0.50 | 1.25 | 1151.850 | 118 | 111 | 150 | 132 | 3,334 |
| 8 | 1:07 PM | 1,484 | 4,860 | 1151.75 | 1151.75 | 1150.25 | 1150.50 | -1.25 | 1.50 | 1150.864 | 204 | 202 | 242 | 243 | 4,860 |
| 9 | 1:08 PM | 1,234 | 4,996 | 1150.25 | 1151.00 | 1150.00 | 1150.50 | 0.25 | 1.00 | 1150.424 | 181 | 164 | 220 | 191 | 4,996 |
| 10 | 1:09 PM | 520 | 2,237 | 1150.75 | 1151.50 | 1150.50 | 1151.25 | 0.50 | 1.00 | 1150.867 | 84 | 118 | 97 | 138 | 2,237 |
| 11 | 1:10 PM | 581 | 2,516 | 1151.25 | 1151.75 | 1150.50 | 1151.00 | -0.25 | 1.25 | 1151.250 | 109 | 120 | 135 | 138 | 2,516 |
| 12 | 1:11 PM | 2,143 | 9,643 | 1151.00 | 1151.00 | 1148.75 | 1149.25 | -1.75 | 2.25 | 1149.609 | 313 | 236 | 371 | 273 | 9,643 |
| 13 | 1:12 PM | 1,418 | 8,563 | 1149.25 | 1149.25 | 1148.25 | 1148.50 | -0.75 | 1.00 | 1148.767 | 246 | 192 | 297 | 226 | 8,563 |
| 14 | 1:13 PM | 1,720 | 8,078 | 1148.25 | 1149.00 | 1147.75 | 1148.50 | 0.25 | 1.25 | 1148.308 | 322 | 226 | 369 | 265 | 8,078 |
| 15 | 1:14 PM | 1,696 | 8,144 | 1148.50 | 1149.00 | 1147.25 | 1147.50 | -1.00 | 1.75 | 1148.174 | 381 | 198 | 426 | 231 | 8,144 |
| 16 | 1:15 PM | 1,963 | 9,130 | 1147.50 | 1148.50 | 1147.25 | 1147.50 | 0.00 | 1.25 | 1148.000 | 259 | 209 | 307 | 254 | 9,130 |
| 17 | 1:16 PM | 2,625 | 13,845 | 1147.75 | 1148.50 | 1146.75 | 1147.25 | -0.50 | 1.75 | 1147.400 | 410 | 355 | 483 | 399 | 13,845 |
| 18 | 1:17 PM | 3,259 | 18,800 | 1147.25 | 1147.50 | 1145.50 | 1146.50 | -0.75 | 2.00 | 1146.316 | 600 | 454 | 694 | 510 | 18,800 |
| 19 | 1:18 PM | 1,494 | 8,070 | 1146.50 | 1147.25 | 1146.25 | 1146.50 | 0.00 | 1.00 | 1146.730 | 270 | 195 | 311 | 230 | 8,070 |
| 20 | 1:19 PM | 1,253 | 5,010 | 1146.50 | 1147.50 | 1146.50 | 1147.00 | 0.50 | 1.00 | 1147.051 | 185 | 211 | 212 | 238 | 5,010 |
| 21 | 1:20 PM | 1,877 | 8,456 | 1147.25 | 1147.50 | 1146.25 | 1146.25 | -1.00 | 1.25 | 1147.037 | 258 | 193 | 301 | 221 | 8,456 |
| 22 | 1:21 PM | 1,197 | 5,020 | 1146.25 | 1147.25 | 1146.00 | 1146.50 | 0.25 | 1.25 | 1146.604 | 185 | 156 | 219 | 189 | 5,020 |
| 23 | 1:22 PM | 504 | 2,009 | 1146.75 | 1146.75 | 1146.00 | 1146.25 | -0.50 | 0.75 | 1146.411 | 116 | 90 | 131 | 104 | 2,009 |
| 24 | 1:23 PM | 1,913 | 12,084 | 1146.25 | 1146.50 | 1145.25 | 1145.25 | -1.00 | 1.25 | 1145.789 | 337 | 243 | 407 | 280 | 12,084 |
| 25 | 1:24 PM | 3,181 | 18,284 | 1145.25 | 1145.50 | 1144.50 | 1145.00 | -0.25 | 1.00 | 1145.001 | 598 | 411 | 691 | 472 | 18,284 |
| 26 | 1:25 PM | 2,087 | 9,681 | 1144.75 | 1145.75 | 1144.25 | 1145.50 | 0.75 | 1.50 | 1144.870 | 406 | 269 | 477 | 293 | 9,681 |
| 27 | 1:26 PM | 2,007 | 9,837 | 1145.75 | 1146.25 | 1145.25 | 1146.25 | 0.50 | 1.00 | 1145.776 | 266 | 250 | 323 | 305 | 9,837 |
| 28 | 1:27 PM | 1,033 | 6,052 | 1146.25 | 1146.50 | 1145.75 | 1146.25 | 0.00 | 0.75 | 1146.204 | 173 | 182 | 193 | 216 | 6,052 |
| 29 | 1:28 PM | 1,530 | 5,544 | 1146.00 | 1146.50 | 1145.50 | 1146.25 | 0.25 | 1.00 | 1145.986 | 153 | 191 | 188 | 227 | 5,544 |
| 30 | 1:29 PM | 1,095 | 4,838 | 1146.25 | 1147.50 | 1146.25 | 1147.50 | 1.25 | 1.25 | 1146.895 | 203 | 280 | 227 | 316 | 4,838 |
| 31 | 1:30 PM | 817 | 3,254 | 1147.25 | 1147.50 | 1146.75 | 1146.75 | -0.50 | 0.75 | 1147.219 | 182 | 192 | 192 | 226 | 3,254 |
| 32 | 1:31 PM | 735 | 2,374 | 1147.00 | 1147.00 | 1146.50 | 1147.00 | 0.00 | 0.50 | 1146.812 | 139 | 142 | 164 | 160 | 2,374 |
| 33 | 1:32 PM | 744 | 3,221 | 1147.00 | 1147.25 | 1146.50 | 1146.75 | -0.25 | 0.75 | 1146.994 | 127 | 129 | 149 | 153 | 3,221 |
| 34 | 1:33 PM | 1,061 | 3,608 | 1146.75 | 1146.75 | 1145.75 | 1146.00 | -0.75 | 1.00 | 1146.203 | 185 | 171 | 215 | 202 | 3,608 |
| 35 | 1:34 PM | 773 | 2,427 | 1146.00 | 1146.50 | 1145.50 | 1146.25 | 0.25 | 1.00 | 1145.975 | 128 | 142 | 149 | 158 | 2,427 |
| 36 | 1:35 PM | 664 | 2,514 | 1146.25 | 1146.50 | 1145.75 | 1146.25 | 0.00 | 0.75 | 1146.095 | 138 | 91 | 158 | 108 | 2,514 |
| 37 | 1:36 PM | 1,564 | 9,536 | 1146.25 | 1146.50 | 1144.75 | 1144.75 | -1.50 | 1.75 | 1145.268 | 305 | 236 | 349 | 271 | 9,536 |
| 38 | 1:37 PM | 1,768 | 7,963 | 1144.75 | 1145.75 | 1144.25 | 1145.00 | 0.25 | 1.50 | 1144.912 | 297 | 212 | 355 | 242 | 7,963 |
| 39 | 1:38 PM | 1,847 | 10,833 | 1145.00 | 1145.00 | 1143.75 | 1144.00 | -1.00 | 1.25 | 1144.256 | 366 | 329 | 418 | 375 | 10,833 |
| 40 | 1:39 PM | 1,217 | 6,900 | 1144.00 | 1145.00 | 1143.75 | 1144.25 | 0.25 | 1.25 | 1144.605 | 236 | 194 | 273 | 232 | 6,900 |
| 41 | 1:40 PM | 3,003 | 19,136 | 1144.50 | 1144.50 | 1142.75 | 1143.00 | -1.50 | 1.75 | 1143.368 | 577 | 430 | 650 | 477 | 19,136 |
| 42 | 1:41 PM | 2,357 | 13,605 | 1143.00 | 1144.00 | 1142.50 | 1143.75 | 0.75 | 1.50 | 1143.173 | 351 | 342 | 398 | 393 | 13,605 |
| 43 | 1:42 PM | 963 | 4,703 | 1143.75 | 1144.00 | 1143.50 | 1143.75 | 0.00 | 0.50 | 1143.834 | 178 | 161 | 201 | 181 | 4,703 |
| 44 | 1:43 PM | 859 | 4,315 | 1144.00 | 1144.50 | 1143.75 | 1144.00 | 0.00 | 0.75 | 1144.211 | 188 | 185 | 208 | 211 | 4,315 |
| 45 | 1:44 PM | 1,184 | 5,763 | 1144.25 | 1144.75 | 1144.00 | 1144.50 | 0.25 | 0.75 | 1144.386 | 203 | 150 | 233 | 185 | 5,763 |
| 46 | 1:45 PM | 863 | 5,790 | 1144.50 | 1145.00 | 1144.25 | 1145.00 | 0.50 | 0.75 | 1144.828 | 205 | 186 | 229 | 207 | 5,790 |
| 47 | 1:46 PM | 1,116 | 7,157 | 1145.00 | 1145.25 | 1144.25 | 1145.00 | 0.00 | 1.00 | 1144.827 | 221 | 184 | 252 | 220 | 7,157 |
| 48 | 1:47 PM | 874 | 4,457 | 1145.00 | 1145.50 | 1144.50 | 1145.25 | 0.25 | 1.00 | 1144.979 | 142 | 208 | 169 | 232 | 4,457 |
| 49 | 1:48 PM | 919 | 3,922 | 1145.50 | 1145.75 | 1144.25 | 1144.50 | -1.00 | 1.50 | 1145.047 | 204 | 196 | 229 | 220 | 3,922 |
| 50 | 1:49 PM | 955 | 4,795 | 1144.25 | 1145.00 | 1144.00 | 1144.25 | 0.00 | 1.00 | 1144.502 | 138 | 159 | 157 | 186 | 4,795 |

## (Continued)

| Row | Time (EDT) | Trades | Volume | First | High | Low | Last | Last - First Range | High /Low Range | VWAP | Buy Accts | Sell Accts | Buy User IDs | Sell User IDs | Volume Graph |
|---|---|---|---|---|---|---|---|---|---|---|---|---|---|---|---|
| 51 | 1:50 PM | 859 | 3,530 | 1144.50 | 1144.50 | 1143.75 | 1144.25 | -0.25 | 0.75 | 1144.146 | 152 | 178 | 188 | 199 | 3,530 |
| 52 | 1:51 PM | 535 | 1,991 | 1144.25 | 1144.75 | 1144.00 | 1144.75 | 0.50 | 0.75 | 1144.488 | 121 | 106 | 142 | 124 | 1,991 |
| 53 | 1:52 PM | 559 | 2,437 | 1144.50 | 1144.75 | 1144.25 | 1144.25 | -0.25 | 0.50 | 1144.449 | 147 | 85 | 159 | 95 | 2,437 |
| 54 | 1:53 PM | 1,262 | 5,103 | 1144.25 | 1145.00 | 1144.00 | 1144.50 | 0.25 | 1.00 | 1144.484 | 196 | 151 | 230 | 170 | 5,103 |
| 55 | 1:54 PM | 1,273 | 5,363 | 1144.25 | 1144.75 | 1143.50 | 1143.75 | -0.50 | 0.75 | 1143.856 | 276 | 275 | 266 | 263 | 5,363 |
| 56 | 1:55 PM | 1,286 | 6,229 | 1143.75 | 1144.00 | 1142.75 | 1143.00 | -0.75 | 1.25 | 1143.290 | 243 | 246 | 278 | 283 | 6,229 |
| 57 | 1:56 PM | 3,607 | 22,058 | 1143.00 | 1143.25 | 1140.75 | 1141.25 | -1.75 | 2.50 | 1141.613 | 713 | 521 | 817 | 572 | 22,058 |
| 58 | 1:57 PM | 2,329 | 11,814 | 1141.00 | 1143.00 | 1141.00 | 1143.00 | 2.00 | 2.00 | 1142.141 | 289 | 333 | 329 | 376 | 11,814 |
| 59 | 1:58 PM | 1,639 | 8,610 | 1142.75 | 1143.75 | 1142.50 | 1142.75 | 0.00 | 1.25 | 1143.179 | 271 | 279 | 302 | 327 | 8,610 |
| 60 | 1:59 PM | 1,150 | 6,069 | 1142.75 | 1142.75 | 1141.75 | 1142.25 | -0.50 | 1.00 | 1142.221 | 231 | 186 | 270 | 214 | 6,069 |
| 61 | 2:00 PM | 1,522 | 8,523 | 1142.25 | 1143.50 | 1142.00 | 1143.25 | 1.00 | 1.50 | 1142.869 | 207 | 260 | 254 | 292 | 8,523 |
| 62 | 2:01 PM | 1,173 | 6,806 | 1143.25 | 1143.75 | 1142.50 | 1143.25 | 0.00 | 1.25 | 1143.237 | 168 | 212 | 194 | 240 | 6,806 |
| 63 | 2:02 PM | 1,314 | 6,373 | 1143.25 | 1143.50 | 1142.25 | 1142.50 | -0.75 | 1.25 | 1142.872 | 164 | 184 | 198 | 224 | 6,373 |
| 64 | 2:03 PM | 1,467 | 6,691 | 1142.75 | 1142.75 | 1141.50 | 1142.00 | -0.75 | 1.25 | 1142.066 | 245 | 240 | 289 | 275 | 6,691 |
| 65 | 2:04 PM | 2,844 | 13,478 | 1141.75 | 1142.25 | 1140.25 | 1141.00 | -0.75 | 2.00 | 1141.183 | 418 | 339 | 479 | 388 | 13,478 |
| 66 | 2:05 PM | 1,899 | 9,946 | 1141.00 | 1141.75 | 1140.75 | 1141.00 | 0.00 | 1.00 | 1141.048 | 323 | 202 | 373 | 232 | 9,946 |
| 67 | 2:06 PM | 3,230 | 23,234 | 1141.00 | 1141.25 | 1139.00 | 1139.25 | -1.75 | 2.25 | 1139.953 | 679 | 452 | 758 | 502 | 23,234 |
| 68 | 2:07 PM | 2,458 | 14,820 | 1139.00 | 1140.50 | 1138.75 | 1140.50 | 1.50 | 1.75 | 1139.477 | 398 | 385 | 456 | 429 | 14,820 |
| 69 | 2:08 PM | 2,550 | 15,361 | 1140.25 | 1140.50 | 1138.25 | 1138.25 | -2.00 | 2.25 | 1139.106 | 435 | 304 | 500 | 351 | 15,361 |
| 70 | 2:09 PM | 3,751 | 21,942 | 1138.25 | 1138.50 | 1137.25 | 1137.75 | -0.50 | 1.25 | 1137.833 | 662 | 489 | 763 | 546 | 21,942 |
| 71 | 2:10 PM | 3,369 | 22,577 | 1137.50 | 1138.25 | 1136.00 | 1136.25 | -1.25 | 2.25 | 1137.251 | 583 | 437 | 651 | 486 | 22,577 |
| 72 | 2:11 PM | 7,309 | 37,762 | 1136.25 | 1137.25 | 1133.50 | 1134.00 | -2.25 | 3.75 | 1135.314 | 807 | 654 | 930 | 726 | 37,762 |
| 73 | 2:12 PM | 4,419 | 22,212 | 1134.00 | 1136.75 | 1134.00 | 1136.50 | 2.50 | 2.75 | 1135.512 | 500 | 439 | 557 | 498 | 22,212 |
| 74 | 2:13 PM | 3,181 | 15,895 | 1136.50 | 1138.00 | 1136.00 | 1137.50 | 1.00 | 2.00 | 1137.258 | 362 | 475 | 406 | 534 | 15,895 |
| 75 | 2:14 PM | 1,929 | 8,471 | 1137.50 | 1137.75 | 1136.50 | 1137.00 | -0.50 | 1.25 | 1137.171 | 214 | 274 | 244 | 307 | 8,471 |
| 76 | 2:15 PM | 2,227 | 11,221 | 1137.00 | 1138.00 | 1136.75 | 1137.00 | 0.00 | 1.25 | 1137.493 | 312 | 276 | 352 | 319 | 11,221 |
| 77 | 2:16 PM | 1,989 | 9,677 | 1137.25 | 1137.50 | 1135.50 | 1135.50 | -1.75 | 2.00 | 1136.732 | 271 | 242 | 315 | 279 | 9,677 |
| 78 | 2:17 PM | 3,466 | 15,947 | 1135.50 | 1135.75 | 1133.25 | 1133.50 | -2.00 | 2.50 | 1134.739 | 481 | 383 | 561 | 442 | 15,947 |
| 79 | 2:18 PM | 5,353 | 27,127 | 1133.50 | 1133.75 | 1131.00 | 1133.75 | 0.25 | 2.75 | 1132.452 | 665 | 628 | 768 | 693 | 27,127 |
| 80 | 2:19 PM | 2,289 | 13,431 | 1133.75 | 1134.25 | 1131.50 | 1131.75 | -2.00 | 2.75 | 1132.789 | 378 | 305 | 424 | 362 | 13,431 |
| 81 | 2:20 PM | 6,930 | 37,893 | 1131.75 | 1132.00 | 1128.25 | 1128.50 | -3.25 | 3.75 | 1130.122 | 753 | 715 | 863 | 792 | 37,893 |
| 82 | 2:21 PM | 6,519 | 30,954 | 1128.25 | 1129.50 | 1125.75 | 1125.75 | -2.50 | 3.75 | 1127.951 | 776 | 639 | 880 | 749 | 30,954 |
| 83 | 2:22 PM | 5,868 | 29,438 | 1126.00 | 1129.00 | 1124.75 | 1129.00 | 3.00 | 4.25 | 1127.144 | 578 | 545 | 673 | 633 | 29,438 |
| 84 | 2:23 PM | 3,064 | 13,631 | 1128.75 | 1130.00 | 1128.25 | 1129.50 | 0.75 | 1.75 | 1129.132 | 348 | 422 | 385 | 476 | 13,631 |
| 85 | 2:24 PM | 4,590 | 27,243 | 1129.50 | 1132.50 | 1129.25 | 1132.25 | 2.75 | 3.25 | 1130.730 | 439 | 512 | 493 | 585 | 27,243 |
| 86 | 2:25 PM | 2,716 | 12,503 | 1132.25 | 1132.75 | 1131.00 | 1132.75 | 0.50 | 1.75 | 1131.976 | 351 | 431 | 380 | 485 | 12,503 |
| 87 | 2:26 PM | 3,341 | 18,074 | 1132.50 | 1133.75 | 1132.25 | 1133.25 | 0.75 | 1.50 | 1133.216 | 402 | 481 | 462 | 527 | 18,074 |
| 88 | 2:27 PM | 3,109 | 16,079 | 1133.25 | 1133.50 | 1131.25 | 1132.25 | -1.00 | 2.25 | 1132.473 | 301 | 353 | 340 | 413 | 16,079 |
| 89 | 2:28 PM | 3,012 | 14,046 | 1132.25 | 1132.50 | 1130.00 | 1130.25 | -2.00 | 2.50 | 1131.005 | 356 | 358 | 409 | 410 | 14,046 |
| 90 | 2:29 PM | 2,684 | 12,150 | 1130.25 | 1131.25 | 1129.50 | 1130.25 | 0.00 | 1.75 | 1130.230 | 336 | 292 | 383 | 345 | 12,150 |
| 91 | 2:30 PM | 2,768 | 12,878 | 1130.25 | 1131.00 | 1128.00 | 1128.75 | -1.50 | 3.00 | 1129.476 | 391 | 329 | 449 | 381 | 12,878 |
| 92 | 2:31 PM | 2,931 | 13,014 | 1128.75 | 1130.00 | 1127.25 | 1127.75 | -1.00 | 2.75 | 1128.652 | 370 | 319 | 424 | 357 | 13,014 |
| 93 | 2:32 PM | 2,233 | 10,135 | 1127.50 | 1128.00 | 1126.25 | 1126.50 | -1.00 | 1.75 | 1127.072 | 391 | 279 | 445 | 303 | 10,135 |
| 94 | 2:33 PM | 3,081 | 14,914 | 1126.75 | 1128.50 | 1126.25 | 1127.75 | 1.00 | 2.25 | 1127.612 | 380 | 262 | 435 | 304 | 14,914 |
| 95 | 2:34 PM | 3,418 | 22,939 | 1127.50 | 1128.00 | 1125.75 | 1126.00 | -1.50 | 2.25 | 1127.055 | 378 | 301 | 434 | 348 | 22,939 |
| 96 | 2:35 PM | 6,431 | 31,297 | 1126.00 | 1126.00 | 1122.50 | 1124.50 | -1.50 | 3.50 | 1124.045 | 788 | 631 | 898 | 717 | 31,297 |
| 97 | 2:36 PM | 5,149 | 25,391 | 1124.50 | 1124.50 | 1120.00 | 1120.00 | -4.50 | 4.50 | 1122.544 | 659 | 539 | 729 | 606 | 25,391 |
| 98 | 2:37 PM | 5,923 | 32,938 | 1120.00 | 1121.50 | 1119.50 | 1121.25 | 1.25 | 2.00 | 1120.354 | 720 | 536 | 814 | 607 | 32,938 |
| 99 | 2:38 PM | 6,094 | 29,242 | 1121.25 | 1123.50 | 1121.00 | 1121.00 | -0.25 | 2.50 | 1122.423 | 562 | 510 | 644 | 589 | 29,242 |
| 100 | 2:39 PM | 8,441 | 42,855 | 1121.25 | 1121.25 | 1113.50 | 1114.00 | -7.25 | 7.75 | 1116.926 | 836 | 839 | 953 | 958 | 42,855 |

**(Continued)**

| Row | Time (EDT) | Trades | Volume | First | High | Low | Last | Last - First Range | High /Low Range | VWAP | Buy Accts | Sell Accts | Buy User IDs | Sell User IDs | Volume Graph |
|---|---|---|---|---|---|---|---|---|---|---|---|---|---|---|---|
| 101 | 2:40 PM | 7,100 | 37,916 | 1114.00 | 1114.25 | 1111.25 | 1113.00 | -1.00 | 3.00 | 1113.050 | 783 | 590 | 899 | 659 | 37,916 |
| 102 | 2:41 PM | 5,644 | 30,279 | 1113.25 | 1115.75 | 1113.00 | 1114.00 | 0.75 | 2.75 | 1114.355 | 630 | 540 | 719 | 624 | 30,279 |
| 103 | 2:42 PM | 7,497 | 38,943 | 1114.00 | 1114.25 | 1106.50 | 1107.00 | -7.00 | 7.75 | 1111.189 | 690 | 739 | 789 | 831 | 38,943 |
| 104 | 2:43 PM | 13,983 | 73,083 | 1107.00 | 1107.25 | 1098.00 | 1098.75 | -8.25 | 9.25 | 1101.973 | 974 | 914 | 1104 | 1032 | 73,083 |
| 105 | 2:44 PM | 14,388 | 67,432 | 1098.50 | 1098.75 | 1080.50 | 1082.00 | -16.50 | 18.25 | 1092.413 | 838 | 992 | 959 | 1131 | 67,432 |
| 106 | 2:45 PM | 14,645 | 78,412 | 1081.50 | 1082.00 | 1056.00 | 1069.00 | -12.50 | 26.00 | 1069.028 | 986 | 922 | 1115 | 1010 | 78,412 |
| 107 | 2:46 PM | 7,800 | 55,833 | 1068.75 | 1077.75 | 1061.00 | 1072.50 | 3.75 | 16.75 | 1070.273 | 756 | 595 | 823 | 651 | 55,833 |
| 108 | 2:47 PM | 5,939 | 44,721 | 1072.75 | 1088.25 | 1070.75 | 1086.00 | 13.25 | 17.50 | 1076.332 | 646 | 573 | 712 | 621 | 44,721 |
| 109 | 2:48 PM | 7,818 | 54,995 | 1085.75 | 1097.00 | 1082.00 | 1090.50 | 4.75 | 15.00 | 1091.335 | 737 | 745 | 800 | 851 | 54,995 |
| 110 | 2:49 PM | 5,494 | 42,133 | 1090.50 | 1093.25 | 1083.25 | 1088.75 | -1.75 | 10.00 | 1088.248 | 538 | 514 | 591 | 565 | 42,133 |
| 111 | 2:50 PM | 4,787 | 37,168 | 1089.00 | 1097.75 | 1084.75 | 1097.00 | 8.00 | 13.00 | 1090.106 | 541 | 524 | 596 | 569 | 37,168 |
| 112 | 2:51 PM | 7,964 | 47,024 | 1097.00 | 1109.75 | 1094.25 | 1107.50 | 10.50 | 15.50 | 1101.499 | 744 | 767 | 836 | 865 | 47,024 |
| 113 | 2:52 PM | 5,695 | 39,953 | 1107.25 | 1111.50 | 1102.25 | 1111.25 | 4.00 | 9.25 | 1105.792 | 579 | 740 | 650 | 825 | 39,953 |
| 114 | 2:53 PM | 6,750 | 41,315 | 1111.50 | 1118.00 | 1109.50 | 1117.75 | 6.25 | 8.50 | 1113.585 | 614 | 810 | 685 | 909 | 41,315 |
| 115 | 2:54 PM | 6,689 | 39,728 | 1118.00 | 1119.00 | 1107.50 | 1109.25 | -8.75 | 11.50 | 1113.659 | 592 | 907 | 664 | 1006 | 39,728 |
| 116 | 2:55 PM | 4,429 | 22,460 | 1109.25 | 1114.25 | 1107.75 | 1112.50 | 3.25 | 6.50 | 1110.954 | 521 | 453 | 579 | 496 | 22,460 |
| 117 | 2:56 PM | 4,541 | 20,325 | 1112.50 | 1117.50 | 1112.50 | 1116.50 | 4.00 | 5.00 | 1115.534 | 421 | 506 | 472 | 568 | 20,325 |
| 118 | 2:57 PM | 3,536 | 26,535 | 1116.50 | 1119.50 | 1115.75 | 1118.75 | 2.25 | 3.75 | 1118.314 | 458 | 567 | 513 | 603 | 26,535 |
| 119 | 2:58 PM | 5,173 | 22,715 | 1118.75 | 1118.75 | 1113.75 | 1115.75 | -3.00 | 5.00 | 1115.829 | 421 | 604 | 461 | 666 | 22,715 |
| 120 | 2:59 PM | 4,643 | 20,765 | 1115.75 | 1116.00 | 1110.75 | 1112.75 | -3.00 | 5.25 | 1113.017 | 397 | 488 | 459 | 544 | 20,765 |
| 121 | 3:00 PM | 5,975 | 30,079 | 1112.75 | 1112.75 | 1103.25 | 1105.50 | -7.25 | 9.50 | 1107.815 | 494 | 661 | 564 | 737 | 30,079 |
| 122 | 3:01 PM | 4,811 | 20,309 | 1105.75 | 1115.25 | 1105.75 | 1113.00 | 7.25 | 9.50 | 1110.935 | 628 | 532 | 716 | 590 | 20,309 |
| 123 | 3:02 PM | 4,111 | 20,445 | 1112.75 | 1116.50 | 1110.50 | 1116.50 | 3.75 | 6.00 | 1113.190 | 405 | 444 | 445 | 494 | 20,445 |
| 124 | 3:03 PM | 5,457 | 23,106 | 1116.25 | 1121.00 | 1115.75 | 1120.00 | 3.75 | 5.25 | 1118.382 | 557 | 661 | 630 | 723 | 23,106 |
| 125 | 3:04 PM | 4,856 | 22,346 | 1120.00 | 1121.25 | 1117.75 | 1119.00 | -1.00 | 3.50 | 1119.233 | 426 | 515 | 484 | 581 | 22,346 |
| 126 | 3:05 PM | 5,715 | 27,322 | 1118.75 | 1123.50 | 1116.75 | 1123.50 | 4.75 | 6.75 | 1119.836 | 496 | 578 | 560 | 631 | 27,322 |
| 127 | 3:06 PM | 5,147 | 22,114 | 1123.75 | 1124.00 | 1120.25 | 1121.75 | -2.00 | 3.75 | 1122.412 | 461 | 555 | 525 | 636 | 22,114 |
| 128 | 3:07 PM | 4,109 | 24,415 | 1121.75 | 1126.50 | 1121.00 | 1126.00 | 4.25 | 5.50 | 1123.137 | 463 | 520 | 515 | 584 | 24,415 |
| 129 | 3:08 PM | 6,410 | 27,632 | 1126.25 | 1131.25 | 1125.50 | 1131.00 | 4.75 | 5.75 | 1127.955 | 633 | 798 | 710 | 881 | 27,632 |
| 130 | 3:09 PM | 6,749 | 28,343 | 1131.25 | 1131.75 | 1125.00 | 1126.25 | -5.00 | 6.75 | 1128.235 | 569 | 762 | 628 | 861 | 28,343 |
| 131 | 3:10 PM | 3,751 | 18,702 | 1126.50 | 1128.00 | 1125.75 | 1127.75 | 1.25 | 2.25 | 1126.762 | 382 | 374 | 423 | 422 | 18,702 |
| 132 | 3:11 PM | 6,450 | 25,509 | 1128.00 | 1128.00 | 1117.50 | 1118.25 | -9.75 | 10.50 | 1122.901 | 565 | 590 | 631 | 669 | 25,509 |
| 133 | 3:12 PM | 4,867 | 16,313 | 1118.25 | 1122.25 | 1117.75 | 1120.25 | 2.00 | 4.50 | 1120.268 | 490 | 443 | 578 | 505 | 16,313 |
| 134 | 3:13 PM | 3,372 | 11,372 | 1120.25 | 1122.50 | 1119.00 | 1121.25 | 1.00 | 3.50 | 1120.292 | 352 | 351 | 396 | 410 | 11,372 |
| 135 | 3:14 PM | 2,170 | 8,121 | 1121.25 | 1121.75 | 1119.25 | 1119.75 | -1.50 | 2.50 | 1120.707 | 229 | 267 | 260 | 297 | 8,121 |
| 136 | 3:15 PM | 3,620 | 15,347 | 1119.75 | 1121.25 | 1118.00 | 1120.25 | 0.50 | 3.25 | 1119.750 | 363 | 388 | 417 | 437 | 15,347 |
| 137 | 3:16 PM | 3,674 | 12,236 | 1120.25 | 1122.75 | 1120.25 | 1122.00 | 1.75 | 2.50 | 1121.620 | 333 | 304 | 386 | 347 | 12,236 |
| 138 | 3:17 PM | 3,139 | 12,052 | 1121.75 | 1125.50 | 1121.00 | 1125.00 | 3.25 | 4.50 | 1123.507 | 386 | 344 | 438 | 393 | 12,052 |
| 139 | 3:18 PM | 5,900 | 21,477 | 1125.00 | 1125.75 | 1118.50 | 1119.00 | -6.00 | 7.25 | 1121.851 | 436 | 490 | 504 | 568 | 21,477 |
| 140 | 3:19 PM | 4,962 | 20,821 | 1119.00 | 1119.00 | 1115.25 | 1115.75 | -3.25 | 3.75 | 1117.026 | 482 | 482 | 547 | 552 | 20,821 |
| 141 | 3:20 PM | 5,739 | 20,310 | 1115.75 | 1116.00 | 1111.75 | 1112.25 | -3.50 | 4.25 | 1113.553 | 614 | 551 | 706 | 633 | 20,310 |
| 142 | 3:21 PM | 6,334 | 23,136 | 1112.00 | 1113.50 | 1108.00 | 1113.25 | 1.25 | 5.50 | 1110.479 | 657 | 573 | 751 | 650 | 23,136 |
| 143 | 3:22 PM | 3,632 | 13,831 | 1113.25 | 1116.75 | 1112.50 | 1114.75 | 1.50 | 4.25 | 1114.068 | 516 | 432 | 588 | 496 | 13,831 |
| 144 | 3:23 PM | 3,861 | 14,472 | 1114.75 | 1115.50 | 1111.50 | 1112.50 | -2.25 | 4.00 | 1113.478 | 381 | 397 | 444 | 451 | 14,472 |
| 145 | 3:24 PM | 2,230 | 7,490 | 1112.50 | 1113.50 | 1111.75 | 1112.25 | -0.25 | 1.75 | 1112.577 | 231 | 202 | 262 | 237 | 7,490 |
| 146 | 3:25 PM | 3,979 | 14,881 | 1112.25 | 1112.25 | 1108.25 | 1108.50 | -3.75 | 4.00 | 1110.268 | 436 | 425 | 485 | 486 | 14,881 |
| 147 | 3:26 PM | 5,071 | 19,247 | 1108.25 | 1112.00 | 1106.50 | 1107.25 | -1.00 | 5.50 | 1108.335 | 552 | 469 | 633 | 539 | 19,247 |
| 148 | 3:27 PM | 3,514 | 11,622 | 1107.25 | 1111.25 | 1106.50 | 1110.00 | 2.75 | 4.75 | 1108.517 | 476 | 348 | 545 | 400 | 11,622 |
| 149 | 3:28 PM | 2,230 | 8,758 | 1110.00 | 1111.00 | 1109.00 | 1110.50 | 0.50 | 2.00 | 1110.079 | 261 | 239 | 289 | 276 | 8,758 |
| 150 | 3:29 PM | 4,647 | 16,857 | 1110.50 | 1118.00 | 1110.00 | 1117.50 | 7.00 | 8.00 | 1115.133 | 543 | 510 | 617 | 561 | 16,857 |

**(Continued)**

| Row | Time (EDT) | Trades | Volume | First | High | Low | Last | Last - First Range | High /Low Range | VWAP | Buy Accts | Sell Accts | Buy User IDs | Sell User IDs | Volume Graph |
|---|---|---|---|---|---|---|---|---|---|---|---|---|---|---|---|
| 151 | 3:30 PM | 4,700 | 17,153 | 1117.75 | 1122.00 | 1116.50 | 1121.50 | 3.75 | 5.50 | 1118.999 | 469 | 638 | 519 | 663 | 17,153 |
| 152 | 3:31 PM | 4,288 | 15,811 | 1121.50 | 1122.25 | 1118.25 | 1121.00 | -0.50 | 4.00 | 1120.193 | 410 | 566 | 463 | 632 | 15,811 |
| 153 | 3:32 PM | 2,877 | 11,096 | 1121.00 | 1121.25 | 1117.00 | 1119.25 | -1.75 | 4.25 | 1119.014 | 329 | 363 | 367 | 421 | 11,096 |
| 154 | 3:33 PM | 2,789 | 11,402 | 1119.50 | 1120.25 | 1118.00 | 1119.00 | -0.50 | 2.25 | 1119.245 | 259 | 252 | 289 | 289 | 11,402 |
| 155 | 3:34 PM | 2,523 | 10,495 | 1119.00 | 1122.50 | 1118.75 | 1122.00 | 3.00 | 3.75 | 1120.688 | 337 | 295 | 380 | 331 | 10,495 |
| 156 | 3:35 PM | 4,281 | 16,895 | 1122.25 | 1126.25 | 1120.00 | 1125.50 | 3.25 | 6.25 | 1123.863 | 497 | 542 | 553 | 600 | 16,895 |
| 157 | 3:36 PM | 4,664 | 15,980 | 1125.50 | 1127.25 | 1123.75 | 1124.50 | -1.00 | 3.50 | 1125.700 | 411 | 585 | 461 | 659 | 15,980 |
| 158 | 3:37 PM | 3,541 | 13,798 | 1124.50 | 1124.50 | 1121.50 | 1121.75 | -2.75 | 3.00 | 1122.571 | 393 | 398 | 445 | 444 | 13,798 |
| 159 | 3:38 PM | 3,152 | 14,019 | 1121.75 | 1123.25 | 1120.25 | 1122.75 | 1.00 | 3.00 | 1121.699 | 345 | 298 | 390 | 336 | 14,019 |
| 160 | 3:39 PM | 2,239 | 9,543 | 1122.75 | 1124.50 | 1122.00 | 1122.00 | -0.75 | 2.50 | 1123.195 | 291 | 288 | 328 | 328 | 9,543 |
| 161 | 3:40 PM | 3,132 | 14,200 | 1122.00 | 1123.25 | 1121.25 | 1122.00 | 0.00 | 2.00 | 1122.173 | 264 | 314 | 301 | 350 | 14,200 |
| 162 | 3:41 PM | 2,781 | 14,018 | 1122.00 | 1125.00 | 1121.50 | 1124.75 | 2.75 | 3.50 | 1122.843 | 325 | 276 | 369 | 308 | 14,018 |
| 163 | 3:42 PM | 4,129 | 20,843 | 1124.50 | 1126.50 | 1123.25 | 1125.50 | 1.00 | 3.25 | 1125.139 | 384 | 411 | 438 | 460 | 20,843 |
| 164 | 3:43 PM | 2,613 | 14,759 | 1125.75 | 1127.25 | 1125.00 | 1127.00 | 1.25 | 2.25 | 1126.243 | 302 | 362 | 331 | 401 | 14,759 |
| 165 | 3:44 PM | 2,373 | 9,782 | 1127.25 | 1127.25 | 1125.50 | 1125.75 | -1.50 | 1.75 | 1126.335 | 258 | 318 | 287 | 354 | 9,782 |
| 166 | 3:45 PM | 3,477 | 18,902 | 1125.50 | 1128.00 | 1124.50 | 1127.75 | 2.25 | 3.50 | 1125.709 | 435 | 469 | 492 | 514 | 18,902 |
| 167 | 3:46 PM | 3,378 | 16,747 | 1128.00 | 1128.00 | 1125.75 | 1126.75 | -1.25 | 2.25 | 1127.037 | 394 | 332 | 429 | 384 | 16,747 |
| 168 | 3:47 PM | 3,295 | 18,379 | 1126.75 | 1130.00 | 1126.50 | 1129.75 | 3.00 | 3.50 | 1128.657 | 410 | 433 | 445 | 484 | 18,379 |
| 169 | 3:48 PM | 7,560 | 41,942 | 1129.75 | 1136.00 | 1129.50 | 1134.75 | 5.00 | 6.50 | 1133.156 | 705 | 861 | 775 | 948 | 41,942 |
| 170 | 3:49 PM | 6,756 | 34,999 | 1134.75 | 1135.75 | 1132.25 | 1133.50 | -1.25 | 3.50 | 1133.945 | 508 | 653 | 559 | 725 | 34,999 |
| 171 | 3:50 PM | 4,380 | 24,016 | 1133.75 | 1134.00 | 1130.00 | 1131.00 | -2.75 | 4.00 | 1131.096 | 478 | 455 | 531 | 509 | 24,016 |
| 172 | 3:51 PM | 3,147 | 14,376 | 1131.25 | 1131.75 | 1129.50 | 1129.50 | -1.75 | 2.25 | 1130.569 | 341 | 320 | 381 | 357 | 14,376 |
| 173 | 3:52 PM | 3,086 | 12,720 | 1129.50 | 1131.50 | 1129.50 | 1131.00 | 1.50 | 2.00 | 1130.219 | 347 | 268 | 381 | 299 | 12,720 |
| 174 | 3:53 PM | 2,489 | 12,039 | 1131.00 | 1133.75 | 1130.75 | 1132.00 | 1.00 | 3.00 | 1132.266 | 387 | 297 | 424 | 331 | 12,039 |
| 175 | 3:54 PM | 3,126 | 12,940 | 1132.00 | 1132.75 | 1130.75 | 1131.75 | -0.25 | 2.00 | 1131.791 | 274 | 360 | 289 | 390 | 12,940 |
| 176 | 3:55 PM | 2,630 | 13,383 | 1132.00 | 1132.00 | 1129.75 | 1130.25 | -1.75 | 2.25 | 1130.613 | 262 | 312 | 278 | 349 | 13,383 |
| 177 | 3:56 PM | 4,949 | 27,735 | 1130.25 | 1130.50 | 1126.00 | 1126.25 | -4.00 | 4.50 | 1127.954 | 467 | 476 | 501 | 527 | 27,735 |
| 178 | 3:57 PM | 4,019 | 25,401 | 1126.00 | 1127.25 | 1125.50 | 1125.75 | -0.25 | 1.75 | 1126.170 | 458 | 294 | 494 | 324 | 25,401 |
| 179 | 3:58 PM | 2,944 | 17,147 | 1125.75 | 1126.50 | 1125.25 | 1126.00 | 0.25 | 1.25 | 1125.925 | 311 | 257 | 321 | 277 | 17,147 |
| 180 | 3:59 PM | 5,580 | 49,829 | 1126.00 | 1126.25 | 1123.00 | 1123.00 | -3.00 | 3.25 | 1125.008 | 495 | 399 | 529 | 432 | 49,829 |
| 181 | 4:00 PM | 7,144 | 41,540 | 1123.50 | 1125.00 | 1122.25 | 1123.00 | -0.50 | 2.75 | 1123.565 | 637 | 444 | 656 | 466 | 41,540 |
| 182 | 4:01 PM | 4,153 | 25,393 | 1123.00 | 1123.50 | 1119.50 | 1121.75 | -1.25 | 4.00 | 1121.074 | 498 | 427 | 539 | 462 | 25,393 |
| 183 | 4:02 PM | 2,727 | 17,112 | 1122.00 | 1124.00 | 1120.25 | 1123.75 | 1.75 | 3.75 | 1121.772 | 356 | 294 | 381 | 323 | 17,112 |
| 184 | 4:03 PM | 1,962 | 13,194 | 1123.75 | 1124.50 | 1122.00 | 1124.25 | 0.50 | 2.50 | 1123.326 | 245 | 257 | 265 | 280 | 13,194 |
| 185 | 4:04 PM | 1,641 | 10,631 | 1124.25 | 1124.50 | 1122.50 | 1124.00 | -0.25 | 2.00 | 1123.807 | 182 | 213 | 192 | 235 | 10,631 |
| 186 | 4:05 PM | 1,174 | 5,859 | 1124.00 | 1124.50 | 1123.00 | 1123.00 | -1.00 | 1.50 | 1123.596 | 181 | 141 | 186 | 158 | 5,859 |
| 187 | 4:06 PM | 1,502 | 6,522 | 1123.00 | 1123.75 | 1122.25 | 1123.25 | 0.25 | 1.50 | 1122.888 | 150 | 168 | 164 | 184 | 6,522 |
| 188 | 4:07 PM | 1,453 | 7,492 | 1123.25 | 1123.50 | 1121.50 | 1122.00 | -1.25 | 2.00 | 1122.639 | 185 | 134 | 196 | 143 | 7,492 |
| 189 | 4:08 PM | 1,245 | 7,770 | 1122.00 | 1122.25 | 1121.00 | 1121.50 | -0.50 | 1.25 | 1121.641 | 168 | 139 | 178 | 161 | 7,770 |
| 190 | 4:09 PM | 1,022 | 5,105 | 1121.75 | 1122.00 | 1121.00 | 1121.25 | -0.50 | 1.00 | 1121.492 | 154 | 105 | 160 | 118 | 5,105 |
| 191 | 4:10 PM | 1,575 | 9,974 | 1121.25 | 1122.00 | 1119.50 | 1120.50 | -0.75 | 2.50 | 1120.303 | 275 | 185 | 292 | 199 | 9,974 |
| 192 | 4:11 PM | 1,027 | 5,020 | 1120.25 | 1121.00 | 1119.75 | 1120.00 | -0.25 | 1.25 | 1120.392 | 163 | 157 | 169 | 165 | 5,020 |
| 193 | 4:12 PM | 612 | 3,237 | 1120.00 | 1120.75 | 1120.00 | 1120.50 | 0.50 | 0.75 | 1120.315 | 131 | 105 | 137 | 112 | 3,237 |
| 194 | 4:13 PM | 1,414 | 6,391 | 1120.50 | 1121.75 | 1120.50 | 1121.75 | 1.25 | 1.25 | 1121.069 | 161 | 181 | 167 | 186 | 6,391 |
| 195 | 4:14 PM | 1,454 | 12,283 | 1121.50 | 1122.75 | 1121.25 | 1122.75 | 1.25 | 1.50 | 1122.219 | 256 | 268 | 255 | 270 | 12,283 |

**CME Emini SP Futures June 2010 Contract Summarized Activity By Second 2:41 PM2:50 PM (Eastern Daylight Time) Trade Date May 6, 2010**

| Row | Time (EDT) | Trades | Volume | First | High | Low | Last | Last - First Range | High /Low Range | VWAP | Buy Accts | Sell Accts | Buy User IDs | Sell User IDs | Volume Graph |
|---|---|---|---|---|---|---|---|---|---|---|---|---|---|---|---|
| 1 | 2:41:00 PM | 40 | 185 | 1113.25 | 1113.25 | 1113.00 | 1113.25 | 0.00 | 0.25 | 1113.230 | 13 | 22 | 13 | 22 | 185 |
| 2 | 2:41:01 PM | 74 | 524 | 1113.25 | 1113.50 | 1113.00 | 1113.00 | -0.25 | 0.50 | 1113.229 | 27 | 19 | 29 | 22 | 524 |
| 3 | 2:41:02 PM | 26 | 195 | 1113.25 | 1113.50 | 1113.25 | 1113.25 | 0.00 | 0.25 | 1113.382 | 14 | 9 | 14 | 9 | 195 |
| 4 | 2:41:03 PM | 6 | 29 | 1113.50 | 1113.50 | 1113.50 | 1113.50 | 0.00 | 0.00 | 1113.500 | 5 | 1 | 5 | 1 | 29 |
| 5 | 2:41:04 PM | 15 | 72 | 1113.50 | 1113.50 | 1113.25 | 1113.25 | -0.25 | 0.25 | 1113.483 | 11 | 4 | 11 | 4 | 72 |
| 6 | 2:41:05 PM | 159 | 1,089 | 1113.50 | 1114.00 | 1113.50 | 1114.00 | 0.50 | 0.50 | 1113.581 | 21 | 57 | 26 | 60 | 1,089 |
| 7 | 2:41:06 PM | 31 | 295 | 1113.75 | 1114.00 | 1113.75 | 1114.00 | 0.25 | 0.25 | 1113.968 | 17 | 7 | 17 | 6 | 295 |
| 8 | 2:41:07 PM | 140 | 503 | 1114.00 | 1114.25 | 1113.75 | 1114.25 | 0.25 | 0.50 | 1113.996 | 46 | 43 | 52 | 45 | 503 |
| 9 | 2:41:08 PM | 123 | 352 | 1114.50 | 1114.75 | 1114.25 | 1114.75 | 0.25 | 0.50 | 1114.548 | 43 | 47 | 45 | 53 | 352 |
| 10 | 2:41:09 PM | 129 | 644 | 1114.75 | 1115.00 | 1114.50 | 1115.00 | 0.25 | 0.50 | 1114.903 | 52 | 46 | 57 | 51 | 644 |
| 11 | 2:41:10 PM | 142 | 654 | 1115.00 | 1115.25 | 1114.75 | 1115.00 | 0.00 | 0.50 | 1115.088 | 34 | 57 | 39 | 66 | 654 |
| 12 | 2:41:11 PM | 122 | 449 | 1115.25 | 1115.25 | 1115.00 | 1115.25 | 0.00 | 0.25 | 1115.223 | 34 | 47 | 36 | 55 | 449 |
| 13 | 2:41:12 PM | 102 | 537 | 1115.25 | 1115.25 | 1114.75 | 1115.00 | -0.25 | 0.50 | 1115.091 | 37 | 21 | 39 | 22 | 537 |
| 14 | 2:41:13 PM | 46 | 175 | 1115.00 | 1115.00 | 1114.75 | 1115.00 | 0.00 | 0.25 | 1114.823 | 25 | 8 | 26 | 8 | 175 |
| 15 | 2:41:14 PM | 153 | 1,099 | 1115.00 | 1115.00 | 1114.75 | 1114.75 | -0.25 | 0.25 | 1114.807 | 38 | 33 | 40 | 47 | 1,099 |
| 16 | 2:41:15 PM | 99 | 439 | 1114.75 | 1115.00 | 1114.50 | 1114.75 | 0.00 | 0.50 | 1114.739 | 25 | 31 | 27 | 36 | 439 |
| 17 | 2:41:16 PM | 131 | 603 | 1114.75 | 1115.00 | 1114.50 | 1114.50 | -0.25 | 0.50 | 1114.707 | 36 | 31 | 37 | 35 | 603 |
| 18 | 2:41:17 PM | 45 | 248 | 1114.75 | 1115.00 | 1114.50 | 1115.00 | 0.25 | 0.50 | 1114.787 | 15 | 15 | 16 | 15 | 248 |
| 19 | 2:41:18 PM | 91 | 803 | 1115.00 | 1115.00 | 1114.75 | 1115.00 | 0.00 | 0.25 | 1114.994 | 23 | 41 | 24 | 46 | 803 |
| 20 | 2:41:19 PM | 75 | 299 | 1115.25 | 1115.50 | 1115.00 | 1115.50 | 0.25 | 0.50 | 1115.254 | 21 | 24 | 25 | 25 | 299 |
| 21 | 2:41:20 PM | 85 | 515 | 1115.25 | 1115.50 | 1115.00 | 1115.25 | 0.00 | 0.50 | 1115.264 | 33 | 14 | 35 | 19 | 515 |
| 22 | 2:41:21 PM | 90 | 392 | 1115.00 | 1115.50 | 1115.00 | 1115.25 | 0.25 | 0.50 | 1115.306 | 19 | 49 | 22 | 50 | 392 |
| 23 | 2:41:22 PM | 60 | 267 | 1115.25 | 1115.25 | 1114.75 | 1114.75 | -0.50 | 0.50 | 1114.991 | 28 | 10 | 32 | 10 | 267 |
| 24 | 2:41:23 PM | 175 | 984 | 1114.75 | 1115.00 | 1114.50 | 1115.00 | 0.25 | 0.50 | 1114.858 | 45 | 51 | 49 | 57 | 984 |
| 25 | 2:41:24 PM | 69 | 321 | 1115.00 | 1115.50 | 1115.00 | 1115.25 | 0.25 | 0.50 | 1115.240 | 9 | 36 | 10 | 40 | 321 |
| 26 | 2:41:25 PM | 32 | 111 | 1115.25 | 1115.50 | 1115.25 | 1115.25 | 0.00 | 0.25 | 1115.430 | 9 | 20 | 9 | 22 | 111 |
| 27 | 2:41:26 PM | 20 | 79 | 1115.25 | 1115.50 | 1115.25 | 1115.50 | 0.25 | 0.25 | 1115.459 | 12 | 9 | 12 | 9 | 79 |
| 28 | 2:41:27 PM | 28 | 105 | 1115.25 | 1115.50 | 1115.25 | 1115.50 | 0.25 | 0.25 | 1115.452 | 10 | 15 | 11 | 15 | 105 |
| 29 | 2:41:28 PM | 145 | 688 | 1115.25 | 1115.50 | 1115.25 | 1115.25 | 0.00 | 0.25 | 1115.299 | 36 | 29 | 38 | 28 | 688 |
| 30 | 2:41:29 PM | 90 | 370 | 1115.50 | 1115.75 | 1115.50 | 1115.75 | 0.25 | 0.25 | 1115.567 | 18 | 40 | 19 | 46 | 370 |
| 31 | 2:41:30 PM | 123 | 575 | 1115.50 | 1115.50 | 1115.00 | 1115.50 | 0.00 | 0.50 | 1115.407 | 39 | 18 | 39 | 21 | 575 |
| 32 | 2:41:31 PM | 35 | 132 | 1115.50 | 1115.75 | 1115.50 | 1115.50 | 0.00 | 0.25 | 1115.572 | 12 | 17 | 12 | 17 | 132 |
| 33 | 2:41:32 PM | 179 | 873 | 1115.50 | 1115.75 | 1114.75 | 1115.00 | -0.50 | 1.00 | 1115.243 | 60 | 14 | 70 | 16 | 873 |
| 34 | 2:41:33 PM | 58 | 308 | 1114.75 | 1115.00 | 1114.75 | 1115.00 | 0.25 | 0.25 | 1114.892 | 17 | 22 | 18 | 27 | 308 |
| 35 | 2:41:34 PM | 66 | 271 | 1115.00 | 1115.25 | 1114.75 | 1115.00 | 0.00 | 0.50 | 1115.030 | 18 | 23 | 20 | 23 | 271 |
| 36 | 2:41:35 PM | 306 | 1,557 | 1115.00 | 1115.00 | 1114.00 | 1114.25 | -0.75 | 1.00 | 1114.466 | 70 | 20 | 91 | 23 | 1,557 |
| 37 | 2:41:36 PM | 174 | 840 | 1114.25 | 1114.50 | 1113.75 | 1113.75 | -0.50 | 0.75 | 1114.094 | 43 | 34 | 51 | 36 | 840 |
| 38 | 2:41:37 PM | 124 | 654 | 1113.75 | 1114.25 | 1113.75 | 1114.00 | 0.25 | 0.50 | 1114.021 | 25 | 36 | 29 | 41 | 654 |
| 39 | 2:41:38 PM | 93 | 714 | 1113.75 | 1114.00 | 1113.75 | 1114.00 | 0.25 | 0.25 | 1113.788 | 37 | 18 | 39 | 18 | 714 |
| 40 | 2:41:39 PM | 65 | 232 | 1113.75 | 1114.00 | 1113.50 | 1113.75 | 0.00 | 0.50 | 1113.748 | 11 | 29 | 12 | 31 | 232 |
| 41 | 2:41:40 PM | 37 | 208 | 1113.75 | 1114.00 | 1113.50 | 1113.50 | -0.25 | 0.50 | 1113.807 | 20 | 11 | 21 | 11 | 208 |
| 42 | 2:41:41 PM | 107 | 442 | 1113.75 | 1114.00 | 1113.50 | 1113.50 | -0.25 | 0.50 | 1113.852 | 18 | 43 | 23 | 43 | 442 |
| 43 | 2:41:42 PM | 39 | 265 | 1113.50 | 1113.75 | 1113.50 | 1113.75 | 0.25 | 0.25 | 1113.593 | 23 | 17 | 24 | 16 | 265 |
| 44 | 2:41:43 PM | 200 | 1,154 | 1113.75 | 1114.25 | 1113.50 | 1114.00 | 0.25 | 0.75 | 1113.876 | 27 | 41 | 33 | 55 | 1,154 |
| 45 | 2:41:44 PM | 151 | 646 | 1114.00 | 1114.50 | 1113.75 | 1114.00 | 0.00 | 0.75 | 1114.038 | 27 | 30 | 33 | 37 | 646 |
| 46 | 2:41:45 PM | 11 | 81 | 1114.00 | 1114.25 | 1114.00 | 1114.25 | 0.25 | 0.25 | 1114.164 | 6 | 6 | 6 | 7 | 81 |
| 47 | 2:41:46 PM | 52 | 325 | 1114.00 | 1114.50 | 1114.00 | 1114.50 | 0.50 | 0.50 | 1114.317 | 15 | 24 | 15 | 27 | 325 |
| 48 | 2:41:47 PM | 112 | 1,160 | 1114.50 | 1114.50 | 1113.75 | 1114.00 | -0.50 | 0.75 | 1114.221 | 44 | 15 | 47 | 20 | 1,160 |
| 49 | 2:41:48 PM | 32 | 117 | 1114.00 | 1114.00 | 1113.75 | 1113.75 | -0.25 | 0.25 | 1113.951 | 7 | 16 | 8 | 16 | 117 |
| 50 | 2:41:49 PM | 59 | 365 | 1113.75 | 1114.00 | 1113.75 | 1113.75 | 0.00 | 0.25 | 1113.977 | 13 | 17 | 15 | 23 | 365 |
| 51 | 2:41:50 PM | 58 | 438 | 1114.00 | 1114.00 | 1113.75 | 1114.00 | 0.00 | 0.25 | 1113.792 | 22 | 11 | 21 | 13 | 438 |
| 52 | 2:41:51 PM | 90 | 638 | 1114.00 | 1114.00 | 1113.50 | 1113.50 | -0.50 | 0.50 | 1113.641 | 23 | 19 | 27 | 20 | 638 |
| 53 | 2:41:52 PM | 52 | 181 | 1113.50 | 1113.50 | 1113.25 | 1113.25 | -0.25 | 0.25 | 1113.385 | 21 | 15 | 23 | 15 | 181 |
| 54 | 2:41:53 PM | 235 | 1,710 | 1113.50 | 1114.00 | 1113.25 | 1114.00 | 0.50 | 0.75 | 1113.809 | 23 | 58 | 30 | 67 | 1,710 |
| 55 | 2:41:54 PM | 65 | 319 | 1113.75 | 1113.75 | 1113.50 | 1113.50 | -0.25 | 0.25 | 1113.741 | 21 | 12 | 21 | 11 | 319 |
| 56 | 2:41:55 PM | 80 | 463 | 1113.50 | 1113.75 | 1113.50 | 1113.75 | 0.25 | 0.25 | 1113.545 | 26 | 14 | 27 | 17 | 463 |
| 57 | 2:41:56 PM | 22 | 180 | 1113.50 | 1113.75 | 1113.50 | 1113.50 | 0.00 | 0.25 | 1113.560 | 18 | 9 | 18 | 9 | 180 |
| 58 | 2:41:57 PM | 77 | 330 | 1113.50 | 1113.50 | 1113.25 | 1113.25 | -0.25 | 0.25 | 1113.314 | 29 | 20 | 29 | 21 | 330 |
| 59 | 2:41:58 PM | 56 | 247 | 1113.25 | 1113.50 | 1113.25 | 1113.25 | 0.00 | 0.25 | 1113.463 | 11 | 20 | 11 | 18 | 247 |
| 60 | 2:41:59 PM | 343 | 1,828 | 1113.25 | 1114.25 | 1113.25 | 1114.00 | 0.75 | 1.00 | 1113.888 | 24 | 77 | 25 | 90 | 1,828 |

**(Continued)**

| Row | Time (EDT) | Trades | Volume | First | High | Low | Last | Last - First Range | High /Low Range | VWAP | Buy Accts | Sell Accts | Buy User IDs | Sell User IDs | Volume Graph |
|---|---|---|---|---|---|---|---|---|---|---|---|---|---|---|---|
| 61 | 2:42:00 PM | 37 | 97 | 1114.00 | 1114.25 | 1114.00 | 1114.25 | 0.25 | 0.25 | 1114.052 | 17 | 11 | 18 | 13 | 97 |
| 62 | 2:42:01 PM | 57 | 320 | 1114.25 | 1114.25 | 1113.75 | 1114.00 | -0.25 | 0.50 | 1113.997 | 31 | 8 | 30 | 8 | 320 |
| 63 | 2:42:02 PM | 22 | 309 | 1114.00 | 1114.25 | 1114.00 | 1114.00 | 0.00 | 0.25 | 1114.014 | 8 | 11 | 8 | 11 | 309 |
| 64 | 2:42:03 PM | 40 | 712 | 1114.25 | 1114.25 | 1114.00 | 1114.25 | 0.00 | 0.25 | 1114.188 | 19 | 12 | 21 | 13 | 712 |
| 65 | 2:42:04 PM | 56 | 335 | 1114.00 | 1114.00 | 1113.50 | 1113.75 | -0.25 | 0.50 | 1113.798 | 30 | 8 | 32 | 10 | 335 |
| 66 | 2:42:05 PM | 5 | 15 | 1113.75 | 1113.75 | 1113.50 | 1113.50 | -0.25 | 0.25 | 1113.700 | 3 | 4 | 3 | 4 | 15 |
| 67 | 2:42:06 PM | 65 | 353 | 1113.50 | 1113.50 | 1113.25 | 1113.25 | -0.25 | 0.25 | 1113.460 | 33 | 14 | 33 | 19 | 353 |
| 68 | 2:42:07 PM | 63 | 260 | 1113.25 | 1113.50 | 1113.25 | 1113.25 | 0.00 | 0.25 | 1113.253 | 20 | 12 | 20 | 12 | 260 |
| 69 | 2:42:08 PM | 60 | 221 | 1113.50 | 1113.50 | 1113.25 | 1113.50 | 0.00 | 0.25 | 1113.441 | 17 | 23 | 19 | 21 | 221 |
| 70 | 2:42:09 PM | 65 | 296 | 1113.50 | 1113.75 | 1113.25 | 1113.50 | 0.00 | 0.50 | 1113.593 | 15 | 27 | 17 | 26 | 296 |
| 71 | 2:42:10 PM | 67 | 466 | 1113.50 | 1113.50 | 1113.25 | 1113.25 | -0.25 | 0.25 | 1113.430 | 22 | 14 | 25 | 16 | 466 |
| 72 | 2:42:11 PM | 75 | 345 | 1113.25 | 1113.50 | 1113.25 | 1113.50 | 0.25 | 0.25 | 1113.260 | 22 | 10 | 23 | 10 | 345 |
| 73 | 2:42:12 PM | 118 | 468 | 1113.50 | 1113.50 | 1113.00 | 1113.00 | -0.50 | 0.50 | 1113.213 | 32 | 20 | 32 | 21 | 468 |
| 74 | 2:42:13 PM | 282 | 1,813 | 1113.00 | 1113.25 | 1112.50 | 1112.50 | -0.50 | 0.75 | 1112.878 | 67 | 52 | 78 | 70 | 1,813 |
| 75 | 2:42:14 PM | 58 | 182 | 1112.50 | 1112.75 | 1112.50 | 1112.50 | 0.00 | 0.25 | 1112.589 | 9 | 38 | 9 | 38 | 182 |
| 76 | 2:42:15 PM | 265 | 1,646 | 1112.50 | 1113.00 | 1112.50 | 1112.75 | 0.25 | 0.50 | 1112.874 | 28 | 60 | 40 | 76 | 1,646 |
| 77 | 2:42:16 PM | 27 | 327 | 1112.75 | 1113.00 | 1112.75 | 1112.75 | 0.00 | 0.25 | 1112.924 | 11 | 14 | 12 | 15 | 327 |
| 78 | 2:42:17 PM | 47 | 509 | 1112.75 | 1113.00 | 1112.75 | 1112.75 | 0.00 | 0.25 | 1112.800 | 15 | 15 | 19 | 20 | 509 |
| 79 | 2:42:18 PM | 78 | 706 | 1113.00 | 1113.00 | 1112.75 | 1113.00 | 0.00 | 0.25 | 1112.899 | 15 | 26 | 15 | 30 | 706 |
| 80 | 2:42:19 PM | 60 | 381 | 1112.75 | 1113.00 | 1112.75 | 1112.75 | 0.00 | 0.25 | 1112.754 | 19 | 10 | 22 | 10 | 381 |
| 81 | 2:42:20 PM | 55 | 342 | 1112.75 | 1113.00 | 1112.75 | 1113.00 | 0.25 | 0.25 | 1112.990 | 3 | 24 | 3 | 26 | 342 |
| 82 | 2:42:21 PM | 220 | 1,925 | 1113.25 | 1113.75 | 1113.00 | 1113.50 | 0.25 | 0.75 | 1113.312 | 46 | 49 | 55 | 59 | 1,925 |
| 83 | 2:42:22 PM | 119 | 677 | 1113.50 | 1113.50 | 1113.00 | 1113.00 | -0.50 | 0.50 | 1113.116 | 35 | 13 | 46 | 16 | 677 |
| 84 | 2:42:23 PM | 149 | 616 | 1113.00 | 1113.50 | 1112.75 | 1113.50 | 0.50 | 0.75 | 1113.168 | 20 | 41 | 29 | 56 | 616 |
| 85 | 2:42:24 PM | 18 | 44 | 1113.50 | 1113.50 | 1113.25 | 1113.25 | -0.25 | 0.25 | 1113.278 | 7 | 8 | 8 | 7 | 44 |
| 86 | 2:42:25 PM | 22 | 97 | 1113.50 | 1113.50 | 1113.25 | 1113.25 | -0.25 | 0.25 | 1113.356 | 8 | 12 | 8 | 12 | 97 |
| 87 | 2:42:26 PM | 126 | 969 | 1113.25 | 1113.50 | 1113.00 | 1113.00 | -0.25 | 0.50 | 1113.229 | 32 | 27 | 39 | 30 | 969 |
| 88 | 2:42:27 PM | 36 | 169 | 1113.00 | 1113.00 | 1112.75 | 1113.00 | 0.00 | 0.25 | 1112.999 | 9 | 16 | 9 | 15 | 169 |
| 89 | 2:42:28 PM | 29 | 224 | 1113.00 | 1113.25 | 1113.00 | 1113.00 | 0.00 | 0.25 | 1113.032 | 11 | 14 | 11 | 14 | 224 |
| 90 | 2:42:29 PM | 8 | 20 | 1113.00 | 1113.25 | 1113.00 | 1113.00 | 0.00 | 0.25 | 1113.075 | 3 | 7 | 3 | 7 | 20 |
| 91 | 2:42:30 PM | 28 | 114 | 1113.00 | 1113.00 | 1113.00 | 1113.00 | 0.00 | 0.00 | 1113.000 | 16 | 4 | 18 | 4 | 114 |
| 92 | 2:42:31 PM | 18 | 47 | 1113.00 | 1113.00 | 1112.75 | 1113.00 | 0.00 | 0.25 | 1112.952 | 14 | 3 | 15 | 3 | 47 |
| 93 | 2:42:32 PM | 42 | 137 | 1112.75 | 1113.00 | 1112.75 | 1113.00 | 0.25 | 0.25 | 1112.796 | 21 | 6 | 21 | 6 | 137 |
| 94 | 2:42:33 PM | 47 | 197 | 1113.00 | 1113.00 | 1112.75 | 1112.75 | -0.25 | 0.25 | 1112.924 | 9 | 24 | 9 | 22 | 197 |
| 95 | 2:42:34 PM | 170 | 671 | 1112.75 | 1113.00 | 1112.50 | 1112.75 | 0.00 | 0.50 | 1112.582 | 54 | 17 | 72 | 19 | 671 |
| 96 | 2:42:35 PM | 100 | 550 | 1112.50 | 1112.50 | 1112.25 | 1112.50 | 0.00 | 0.25 | 1112.420 | 25 | 31 | 27 | 35 | 550 |
| 97 | 2:42:36 PM | 39 | 152 | 1112.50 | 1112.50 | 1112.25 | 1112.25 | -0.25 | 0.25 | 1112.355 | 16 | 11 | 16 | 11 | 152 |
| 98 | 2:42:37 PM | 66 | 317 | 1112.50 | 1112.75 | 1112.25 | 1112.50 | 0.00 | 0.50 | 1112.446 | 21 | 26 | 23 | 27 | 317 |
| 99 | 2:42:38 PM | 45 | 219 | 1112.50 | 1113.00 | 1112.50 | 1112.75 | 0.25 | 0.50 | 1112.753 | 7 | 24 | 7 | 27 | 219 |
| 100 | 2:42:39 PM | 21 | 209 | 1112.75 | 1113.00 | 1112.75 | 1112.75 | 0.00 | 0.25 | 1112.841 | 7 | 11 | 8 | 11 | 209 |
| 101 | 2:42:40 PM | 24 | 120 | 1112.75 | 1112.75 | 1112.75 | 1112.75 | 0.00 | 0.00 | 1112.750 | 14 | 6 | 16 | 6 | 120 |
| 102 | 2:42:41 PM | 111 | 606 | 1112.75 | 1112.75 | 1112.25 | 1112.50 | -0.25 | 0.50 | 1112.498 | 36 | 20 | 42 | 20 | 606 |
| 103 | 2:42:42 PM | 55 | 237 | 1112.50 | 1112.75 | 1112.50 | 1112.75 | 0.25 | 0.25 | 1112.714 | 7 | 24 | 7 | 19 | 237 |
| 104 | 2:42:43 PM | 86 | 293 | 1112.50 | 1112.50 | 1112.25 | 1112.50 | 0.00 | 0.25 | 1112.365 | 32 | 16 | 37 | 17 | 293 |
| 105 | 2:42:44 PM | 680 | 3,154 | 1112.50 | 1112.50 | 1111.00 | 1111.00 | -1.50 | 1.50 | 1111.583 | 133 | 82 | 165 | 97 | 3,154 |
| 106 | 2:42:45 PM | 289 | 1,123 | 1111.25 | 1111.25 | 1110.50 | 1110.75 | -0.50 | 0.75 | 1110.792 | 69 | 67 | 81 | 69 | 1,123 |
| 107 | 2:42:46 PM | 176 | 646 | 1110.75 | 1111.25 | 1110.50 | 1110.75 | 0.00 | 0.75 | 1110.822 | 25 | 59 | 29 | 64 | 646 |
| 108 | 2:42:47 PM | 275 | 1,113 | 1110.75 | 1111.25 | 1110.25 | 1110.25 | -0.50 | 1.00 | 1110.657 | 51 | 41 | 71 | 46 | 1,113 |
| 109 | 2:42:48 PM | 608 | 2,764 | 1110.50 | 1110.50 | 1109.25 | 1109.50 | -1.00 | 1.25 | 1109.672 | 127 | 78 | 146 | 93 | 2,764 |
| 110 | 2:42:49 PM | 267 | 1,141 | 1109.50 | 1109.75 | 1109.00 | 1109.50 | 0.00 | 0.75 | 1109.304 | 58 | 55 | 66 | 59 | 1,141 |
| 111 | 2:42:50 PM | 376 | 1,714 | 1109.50 | 1109.50 | 1108.50 | 1108.75 | -0.75 | 1.00 | 1108.867 | 78 | 51 | 95 | 56 | 1,714 |
| 112 | 2:42:51 PM | 106 | 878 | 1108.75 | 1109.00 | 1108.75 | 1109.00 | 0.25 | 0.25 | 1108.792 | 22 | 41 | 23 | 44 | 878 |
| 113 | 2:42:52 PM | 215 | 970 | 1108.75 | 1109.25 | 1108.50 | 1109.00 | 0.25 | 0.75 | 1108.858 | 51 | 47 | 58 | 50 | 970 |
| 114 | 2:42:53 PM | 85 | 603 | 1108.75 | 1109.25 | 1108.75 | 1109.25 | 0.50 | 0.50 | 1108.961 | 21 | 39 | 26 | 41 | 603 |
| 115 | 2:42:54 PM | 288 | 1,605 | 1109.00 | 1109.50 | 1108.75 | 1109.00 | 0.00 | 0.75 | 1109.128 | 57 | 45 | 68 | 53 | 1,605 |
| 116 | 2:42:55 PM | 170 | 717 | 1108.75 | 1109.00 | 1108.25 | 1108.25 | -0.50 | 0.75 | 1108.705 | 45 | 36 | 47 | 35 | 717 |
| 117 | 2:42:56 PM | 164 | 1,044 | 1108.50 | 1108.50 | 1107.75 | 1108.00 | -0.50 | 0.75 | 1108.119 | 61 | 41 | 64 | 47 | 1,044 |
| 118 | 2:42:57 PM | 246 | 960 | 1108.00 | 1108.00 | 1107.25 | 1107.25 | -0.75 | 0.75 | 1107.570 | 71 | 42 | 86 | 48 | 960 |
| 119 | 2:42:58 PM | 215 | 1,181 | 1107.25 | 1107.50 | 1106.75 | 1106.75 | -0.50 | 0.75 | 1107.057 | 56 | 54 | 60 | 60 | 1,181 |
| 120 | 2:42:59 PM | 156 | 617 | 1107.00 | 1107.25 | 1106.50 | 1107.00 | 0.00 | 0.75 | 1106.964 | 36 | 51 | 39 | 52 | 617 |

**(Continued)**

| Row | Time (EDT) | Trades | Volume | First | High | Low | Last | Last - First Range | High /Low Range | VWAP | Buy Accts | Sell Accts | Buy User IDs | Sell User IDs | Volume Graph |
|---|---|---|---|---|---|---|---|---|---|---|---|---|---|---|---|
| 121 | 2:43:00 PM | 392 | 1,913 | 1107.00 | 1107.25 | 1106.25 | 1106.25 | -0.75 | 1.00 | 1106.766 | 68 | 47 | 91 | 61 | 1,913 |
| 122 | 2:43:01 PM | 235 | 1,002 | 1106.25 | 1106.50 | 1105.75 | 1106.00 | -0.25 | 0.75 | 1106.125 | 57 | 42 | 66 | 52 | 1,002 |
| 123 | 2:43:02 PM | 202 | 718 | 1106.00 | 1106.00 | 1105.25 | 1105.50 | -0.50 | 0.75 | 1105.593 | 56 | 40 | 57 | 43 | 718 |
| 124 | 2:43:03 PM | 244 | 908 | 1105.50 | 1105.50 | 1104.75 | 1105.00 | -0.50 | 0.75 | 1105.107 | 61 | 52 | 70 | 59 | 908 |
| 125 | 2:43:04 PM | 100 | 352 | 1105.00 | 1105.25 | 1104.75 | 1105.00 | 0.00 | 0.50 | 1105.002 | 28 | 31 | 29 | 34 | 352 |
| 126 | 2:43:05 PM | 87 | 388 | 1105.00 | 1105.25 | 1104.75 | 1104.75 | -0.25 | 0.50 | 1105.012 | 44 | 18 | 48 | 20 | 388 |
| 127 | 2:43:06 PM | 206 | 972 | 1104.75 | 1105.50 | 1104.50 | 1105.25 | 0.50 | 1.00 | 1105.046 | 38 | 62 | 43 | 72 | 972 |
| 128 | 2:43:07 PM | 394 | 1,911 | 1105.50 | 1106.00 | 1105.25 | 1105.50 | 0.00 | 0.75 | 1105.482 | 83 | 68 | 99 | 82 | 1,911 |
| 129 | 2:43:08 PM | 340 | 1,748 | 1105.75 | 1106.50 | 1105.25 | 1106.00 | 0.25 | 1.25 | 1105.935 | 69 | 58 | 83 | 74 | 1,748 |
| 130 | 2:43:09 PM | 188 | 949 | 1106.25 | 1106.50 | 1106.00 | 1106.00 | -0.25 | 0.50 | 1106.161 | 53 | 44 | 58 | 51 | 949 |
| 131 | 2:43:10 PM | 243 | 1,590 | 1106.00 | 1106.00 | 1105.50 | 1105.75 | -0.25 | 0.50 | 1105.795 | 72 | 37 | 81 | 42 | 1,590 |
| 132 | 2:43:11 PM | 485 | 2,276 | 1105.50 | 1105.75 | 1104.50 | 1104.50 | -1.00 | 1.25 | 1104.934 | 104 | 49 | 123 | 60 | 2,276 |
| 133 | 2:43:12 PM | 548 | 2,201 | 1104.50 | 1104.50 | 1103.50 | 1103.50 | -1.00 | 1.00 | 1103.915 | 80 | 71 | 103 | 80 | 2,201 |
| 134 | 2:43:13 PM | 215 | 877 | 1103.50 | 1103.50 | 1102.75 | 1103.00 | -0.50 | 0.75 | 1103.174 | 69 | 39 | 72 | 47 | 877 |
| 135 | 2:43:14 PM | 137 | 725 | 1103.00 | 1103.50 | 1103.00 | 1103.00 | 0.00 | 0.50 | 1103.151 | 42 | 49 | 45 | 51 | 725 |
| 136 | 2:43:15 PM | 115 | 306 | 1103.00 | 1103.25 | 1102.75 | 1103.25 | 0.25 | 0.50 | 1103.068 | 37 | 36 | 41 | 38 | 306 |
| 137 | 2:43:16 PM | 127 | 842 | 1103.25 | 1103.50 | 1103.00 | 1103.50 | 0.25 | 0.50 | 1103.319 | 34 | 47 | 37 | 50 | 842 |
| 138 | 2:43:17 PM | 124 | 929 | 1103.50 | 1103.75 | 1103.25 | 1103.75 | 0.25 | 0.50 | 1103.549 | 47 | 33 | 53 | 35 | 929 |
| 139 | 2:43:18 PM | 252 | 939 | 1103.50 | 1104.00 | 1103.25 | 1103.75 | 0.25 | 0.75 | 1103.567 | 55 | 44 | 65 | 51 | 939 |
| 140 | 2:43:19 PM | 254 | 1,379 | 1103.75 | 1104.00 | 1103.25 | 1103.25 | -0.50 | 0.75 | 1103.494 | 54 | 39 | 69 | 48 | 1,379 |
| 141 | 2:43:20 PM | 272 | 1,137 | 1103.25 | 1103.50 | 1102.75 | 1103.50 | 0.25 | 0.75 | 1103.171 | 53 | 60 | 63 | 77 | 1,137 |
| 142 | 2:43:21 PM | 889 | 4,316 | 1103.50 | 1104.00 | 1101.50 | 1101.50 | -2.00 | 2.50 | 1102.844 | 112 | 93 | 142 | 115 | 4,316 |
| 143 | 2:43:22 PM | 327 | 1,428 | 1101.50 | 1102.75 | 1101.50 | 1102.25 | 0.75 | 1.25 | 1102.358 | 50 | 55 | 66 | 77 | 1,428 |
| 144 | 2:43:23 PM | 177 | 1,137 | 1102.50 | 1103.25 | 1102.25 | 1103.00 | 0.50 | 1.00 | 1102.771 | 29 | 54 | 39 | 57 | 1,137 |
| 145 | 2:43:24 PM | 202 | 1,530 | 1103.00 | 1103.25 | 1102.75 | 1103.00 | 0.00 | 0.50 | 1103.068 | 46 | 42 | 53 | 47 | 1,530 |
| 146 | 2:43:25 PM | 83 | 761 | 1102.75 | 1103.00 | 1102.50 | 1102.75 | 0.00 | 0.50 | 1102.719 | 35 | 23 | 37 | 26 | 761 |
| 147 | 2:43:26 PM | 156 | 1,103 | 1102.75 | 1103.50 | 1102.50 | 1103.25 | 0.50 | 1.00 | 1102.987 | 29 | 51 | 33 | 58 | 1,103 |
| 148 | 2:43:27 PM | 61 | 472 | 1103.25 | 1103.25 | 1103.00 | 1103.25 | 0.00 | 0.25 | 1103.228 | 22 | 22 | 22 | 26 | 472 |
| 149 | 2:43:28 PM | 255 | 1,781 | 1103.00 | 1103.75 | 1102.75 | 1103.75 | 0.75 | 1.00 | 1103.170 | 58 | 56 | 68 | 64 | 1,781 |
| 150 | 2:43:29 PM | 264 | 1,728 | 1103.50 | 1103.75 | 1102.50 | 1102.75 | -0.75 | 1.25 | 1103.108 | 65 | 43 | 78 | 48 | 1,728 |
| 151 | 2:43:30 PM | 172 | 512 | 1102.50 | 1102.75 | 1101.50 | 1101.75 | -0.75 | 1.25 | 1102.132 | 57 | 28 | 62 | 30 | 512 |
| 152 | 2:43:31 PM | 232 | 737 | 1101.75 | 1102.00 | 1100.75 | 1100.75 | -1.00 | 1.25 | 1101.274 | 82 | 43 | 91 | 46 | 737 |
| 153 | 2:43:32 PM | 342 | 1,652 | 1101.00 | 1101.25 | 1100.50 | 1101.00 | 0.00 | 0.75 | 1100.939 | 67 | 56 | 80 | 60 | 1,652 |
| 154 | 2:43:33 PM | 127 | 483 | 1100.75 | 1101.00 | 1100.50 | 1100.50 | -0.25 | 0.50 | 1100.764 | 41 | 30 | 43 | 32 | 483 |
| 155 | 2:43:34 PM | 131 | 788 | 1100.75 | 1101.00 | 1100.50 | 1100.50 | -0.25 | 0.50 | 1100.798 | 44 | 39 | 43 | 41 | 788 |
| 156 | 2:43:35 PM | 192 | 1,193 | 1100.75 | 1101.00 | 1100.25 | 1100.50 | -0.25 | 0.75 | 1100.660 | 51 | 27 | 58 | 31 | 1,193 |
| 157 | 2:43:36 PM | 156 | 1,086 | 1100.50 | 1100.75 | 1100.25 | 1100.75 | 0.25 | 0.50 | 1100.492 | 32 | 50 | 38 | 56 | 1,086 |
| 158 | 2:43:37 PM | 202 | 913 | 1100.25 | 1100.75 | 1100.00 | 1100.50 | 0.25 | 0.75 | 1100.372 | 55 | 56 | 59 | 66 | 913 |
| 159 | 2:43:38 PM | 152 | 1,181 | 1100.50 | 1100.75 | 1100.00 | 1100.50 | 0.00 | 0.75 | 1100.341 | 40 | 38 | 45 | 45 | 1,181 |
| 160 | 2:43:39 PM | 190 | 882 | 1100.25 | 1100.50 | 1099.50 | 1099.50 | -0.75 | 1.00 | 1099.910 | 82 | 27 | 92 | 29 | 882 |
| 161 | 2:43:40 PM | 429 | 1,742 | 1099.50 | 1100.50 | 1099.00 | 1100.00 | 0.50 | 1.50 | 1099.832 | 64 | 82 | 77 | 95 | 1,742 |
| 162 | 2:43:41 PM | 403 | 2,012 | 1100.25 | 1100.25 | 1099.00 | 1100.00 | -0.25 | 1.25 | 1099.659 | 56 | 50 | 71 | 65 | 2,012 |
| 163 | 2:43:42 PM | 130 | 718 | 1100.00 | 1100.50 | 1099.75 | 1100.00 | 0.00 | 0.75 | 1100.128 | 34 | 40 | 39 | 46 | 718 |
| 164 | 2:43:43 PM | 609 | 3,573 | 1100.00 | 1100.50 | 1098.75 | 1099.75 | -0.25 | 1.75 | 1099.347 | 93 | 54 | 112 | 69 | 3,573 |
| 165 | 2:43:44 PM | 246 | 1,278 | 1099.75 | 1100.00 | 1098.75 | 1098.75 | -1.00 | 1.25 | 1099.249 | 53 | 41 | 64 | 52 | 1,278 |
| 166 | 2:43:45 PM | 333 | 1,284 | 1098.50 | 1100.00 | 1098.50 | 1099.75 | 1.25 | 1.50 | 1099.473 | 35 | 73 | 43 | 85 | 1,284 |
| 167 | 2:43:46 PM | 194 | 1,135 | 1099.75 | 1100.00 | 1099.00 | 1099.25 | -0.50 | 1.00 | 1099.637 | 45 | 40 | 53 | 46 | 1,135 |
| 168 | 2:43:47 PM | 156 | 846 | 1099.25 | 1099.50 | 1098.25 | 1098.50 | -0.75 | 1.25 | 1098.792 | 58 | 26 | 62 | 28 | 846 |
| 169 | 2:43:48 PM | 133 | 707 | 1098.50 | 1098.75 | 1098.25 | 1098.75 | 0.25 | 0.50 | 1098.571 | 34 | 38 | 41 | 42 | 707 |
| 170 | 2:43:49 PM | 189 | 846 | 1098.75 | 1099.00 | 1098.00 | 1098.25 | -0.50 | 1.00 | 1098.369 | 47 | 43 | 54 | 46 | 846 |
| 171 | 2:43:50 PM | 224 | 1,012 | 1098.25 | 1099.25 | 1098.00 | 1099.25 | 1.00 | 1.25 | 1098.693 | 39 | 57 | 42 | 64 | 1,012 |
| 172 | 2:43:51 PM | 211 | 1,171 | 1099.25 | 1099.25 | 1098.25 | 1099.00 | -0.25 | 1.00 | 1098.635 | 44 | 40 | 53 | 53 | 1,171 |
| 173 | 2:43:52 PM | 214 | 1,397 | 1099.00 | 1099.25 | 1098.50 | 1099.25 | 0.25 | 0.75 | 1098.835 | 39 | 54 | 44 | 63 | 1,397 |
| 174 | 2:43:53 PM | 229 | 1,392 | 1099.25 | 1099.50 | 1098.75 | 1099.50 | 0.25 | 0.75 | 1099.228 | 40 | 55 | 52 | 62 | 1,392 |
| 175 | 2:43:54 PM | 53 | 371 | 1099.50 | 1099.50 | 1099.00 | 1099.00 | -0.50 | 0.50 | 1099.162 | 20 | 14 | 23 | 15 | 371 |
| 176 | 2:43:55 PM | 147 | 1,128 | 1099.25 | 1099.75 | 1099.25 | 1099.50 | 0.25 | 0.50 | 1099.447 | 41 | 43 | 47 | 52 | 1,128 |
| 177 | 2:43:56 PM | 149 | 1,221 | 1099.50 | 1099.50 | 1099.00 | 1099.25 | -0.25 | 0.50 | 1099.245 | 46 | 20 | 57 | 22 | 1,221 |
| 178 | 2:43:57 PM | 189 | 1,105 | 1099.25 | 1099.25 | 1098.50 | 1099.25 | 0.00 | 0.75 | 1098.967 | 56 | 34 | 65 | 45 | 1,105 |
| 179 | 2:43:58 PM | 164 | 954 | 1099.00 | 1099.50 | 1098.75 | 1098.75 | -0.25 | 0.75 | 1099.132 | 40 | 35 | 43 | 39 | 954 |
| 180 | 2:43:59 PM | 111 | 1,446 | 1099.00 | 1099.00 | 1098.50 | 1098.75 | -0.25 | 0.50 | 1098.867 | 41 | 18 | 49 | 20 | 1,446 |

**(Continued)**

| Row | Time (EDT) | Trades | Volume | First | High | Low | Last | Last - First Range | High /Low Range | VWAP | Buy Accts | Sell Accts | Buy User IDs | Sell User IDs | Volume Graph |
|---|---|---|---|---|---|---|---|---|---|---|---|---|---|---|---|
| 181 | 2:44:00 PM | 170 | 1,049 | 1098.50 | 1098.50 | 1098.00 | 1098.00 | -0.50 | 0.50 | 1098.256 | 56 | 29 | 60 | 37 | 1,049 |
| 182 | 2:44:01 PM | 77 | 700 | 1098.25 | 1098.50 | 1098.00 | 1098.50 | 0.25 | 0.50 | 1098.240 | 24 | 36 | 26 | 37 | 700 |
| 183 | 2:44:02 PM | 319 | 2,314 | 1098.50 | 1098.75 | 1097.50 | 1098.00 | -0.50 | 1.25 | 1098.048 | 86 | 41 | 98 | 52 | 2,314 |
| 184 | 2:44:03 PM | 203 | 1,422 | 1098.00 | 1098.00 | 1096.75 | 1097.50 | -0.50 | 1.25 | 1097.484 | 65 | 52 | 81 | 53 | 1,422 |
| 185 | 2:44:04 PM | 510 | 1,267 | 1096.75 | 1097.25 | 1096.50 | 1097.00 | 0.25 | 0.75 | 1096.948 | 55 | 66 | 61 | 79 | 1,267 |
| 186 | 2:44:05 PM | 204 | 691 | 1097.25 | 1097.25 | 1096.75 | 1097.00 | -0.25 | 0.50 | 1096.920 | 45 | 41 | 52 | 44 | 691 |
| 187 | 2:44:06 PM | 369 | 1,519 | 1096.75 | 1097.50 | 1096.25 | 1097.25 | 0.50 | 1.25 | 1097.011 | 42 | 60 | 52 | 71 | 1,519 |
| 188 | 2:44:07 PM | 180 | 1,036 | 1097.25 | 1097.75 | 1097.00 | 1097.50 | 0.25 | 0.75 | 1097.487 | 33 | 46 | 41 | 53 | 1,036 |
| 189 | 2:44:08 PM | 138 | 936 | 1097.75 | 1098.00 | 1097.50 | 1097.75 | 0.00 | 0.50 | 1097.829 | 42 | 41 | 51 | 48 | 936 |
| 190 | 2:44:09 PM | 59 | 315 | 1097.75 | 1097.75 | 1097.50 | 1097.50 | -0.25 | 0.25 | 1097.643 | 18 | 27 | 19 | 27 | 315 |
| 191 | 2:44:10 PM | 121 | 862 | 1097.50 | 1098.00 | 1097.25 | 1097.75 | 0.25 | 0.75 | 1097.605 | 39 | 31 | 39 | 35 | 862 |
| 192 | 2:44:11 PM | 195 | 1,479 | 1097.75 | 1098.50 | 1097.75 | 1098.25 | 0.50 | 0.75 | 1098.054 | 44 | 56 | 50 | 62 | 1,479 |
| 193 | 2:44:12 PM | 184 | 2,095 | 1098.00 | 1098.75 | 1098.00 | 1098.50 | 0.50 | 0.75 | 1098.364 | 50 | 66 | 52 | 64 | 2,095 |
| 194 | 2:44:13 PM | 110 | 569 | 1098.75 | 1098.75 | 1098.50 | 1098.50 | -0.25 | 0.25 | 1098.616 | 53 | 22 | 56 | 22 | 569 |
| 195 | 2:44:14 PM | 160 | 1,822 | 1098.75 | 1098.75 | 1098.25 | 1098.75 | 0.00 | 0.50 | 1098.419 | 52 | 35 | 59 | 42 | 1,822 |
| 196 | 2:44:15 PM | 96 | 912 | 1098.50 | 1098.75 | 1098.25 | 1098.50 | 0.00 | 0.50 | 1098.451 | 35 | 28 | 38 | 32 | 912 |
| 197 | 2:44:16 PM | 57 | 499 | 1098.25 | 1098.50 | 1098.25 | 1098.25 | 0.00 | 0.25 | 1098.289 | 24 | 20 | 25 | 19 | 499 |
| 198 | 2:44:17 PM | 187 | 768 | 1098.25 | 1098.50 | 1098.00 | 1098.50 | 0.25 | 0.50 | 1098.348 | 34 | 54 | 36 | 55 | 768 |
| 199 | 2:44:18 PM | 156 | 971 | 1098.25 | 1098.50 | 1097.75 | 1098.00 | -0.25 | 0.75 | 1098.004 | 48 | 31 | 57 | 33 | 971 |
| 200 | 2:44:19 PM | 119 | 674 | 1098.25 | 1098.25 | 1097.50 | 1097.75 | -0.50 | 0.75 | 1097.898 | 34 | 27 | 41 | 29 | 674 |
| 201 | 2:44:20 PM | 189 | 983 | 1097.50 | 1098.25 | 1097.50 | 1097.75 | 0.25 | 0.75 | 1098.063 | 28 | 59 | 34 | 65 | 983 |
| 202 | 2:44:21 PM | 74 | 263 | 1097.75 | 1098.00 | 1097.50 | 1097.50 | -0.25 | 0.50 | 1097.858 | 24 | 18 | 26 | 15 | 263 |
| 203 | 2:44:22 PM | 196 | 935 | 1097.50 | 1097.75 | 1097.25 | 1097.50 | 0.00 | 0.50 | 1097.474 | 52 | 39 | 57 | 43 | 935 |
| 204 | 2:44:23 PM | 80 | 209 | 1097.50 | 1097.75 | 1097.00 | 1097.25 | -0.25 | 0.75 | 1097.188 | 27 | 20 | 29 | 20 | 209 |
| 205 | 2:44:24 PM | 119 | 388 | 1097.00 | 1097.25 | 1096.25 | 1096.50 | -0.50 | 1.00 | 1096.671 | 46 | 32 | 55 | 33 | 388 |
| 206 | 2:44:25 PM | 98 | 406 | 1096.50 | 1096.50 | 1096.00 | 1096.00 | -0.50 | 0.50 | 1096.169 | 34 | 40 | 36 | 42 | 406 |
| 207 | 2:44:26 PM | 181 | 700 | 1096.00 | 1096.25 | 1095.25 | 1095.50 | -0.50 | 1.00 | 1095.696 | 44 | 55 | 48 | 57 | 700 |
| 208 | 2:44:27 PM | 477 | 1,807 | 1095.50 | 1095.75 | 1093.25 | 1094.75 | -0.75 | 2.50 | 1094.812 | 94 | 76 | 108 | 80 | 1,807 |
| 209 | 2:44:28 PM | 516 | 1,909 | 1094.75 | 1095.75 | 1093.25 | 1094.25 | -0.50 | 2.50 | 1094.848 | 55 | 63 | 73 | 77 | 1,909 |
| 210 | 2:44:29 PM | 162 | 627 | 1094.25 | 1094.25 | 1093.50 | 1093.50 | -0.75 | 0.75 | 1094.028 | 45 | 29 | 48 | 35 | 627 |
| 211 | 2:44:30 PM | 449 | 2,681 | 1093.50 | 1095.00 | 1093.50 | 1094.75 | 1.25 | 1.50 | 1094.437 | 40 | 67 | 48 | 76 | 2,681 |
| 212 | 2:44:31 PM | 146 | 1,132 | 1094.50 | 1095.00 | 1094.25 | 1094.75 | 0.25 | 0.75 | 1094.655 | 34 | 35 | 40 | 37 | 1,132 |
| 213 | 2:44:32 PM | 203 | 818 | 1094.75 | 1094.75 | 1093.25 | 1093.75 | -1.00 | 1.50 | 1093.823 | 53 | 26 | 59 | 32 | 818 |
| 214 | 2:44:33 PM | 136 | 833 | 1093.50 | 1094.25 | 1093.50 | 1093.75 | 0.25 | 0.75 | 1093.877 | 32 | 43 | 34 | 47 | 833 |
| 215 | 2:44:34 PM | 234 | 1,132 | 1093.50 | 1093.75 | 1092.50 | 1092.50 | -1.00 | 1.25 | 1093.135 | 55 | 32 | 61 | 37 | 1,132 |
| 216 | 2:44:35 PM | 349 | 1,040 | 1092.75 | 1093.25 | 1092.25 | 1093.25 | 0.50 | 1.00 | 1092.624 | 52 | 57 | 62 | 59 | 1,040 |
| 217 | 2:44:36 PM | 314 | 1,368 | 1093.00 | 1093.25 | 1091.50 | 1091.50 | -1.50 | 1.75 | 1092.449 | 64 | 50 | 74 | 53 | 1,368 |
| 218 | 2:44:37 PM | 442 | 1,730 | 1091.75 | 1092.25 | 1090.50 | 1091.25 | -0.50 | 1.75 | 1091.246 | 68 | 50 | 84 | 56 | 1,730 |
| 219 | 2:44:38 PM | 176 | 698 | 1091.00 | 1091.25 | 1090.50 | 1091.00 | 0.00 | 0.75 | 1090.883 | 36 | 38 | 38 | 42 | 698 |
| 220 | 2:44:39 PM | 284 | 1,078 | 1090.75 | 1091.25 | 1089.75 | 1091.25 | 0.50 | 1.50 | 1090.284 | 67 | 64 | 77 | 71 | 1,078 |
| 221 | 2:44:40 PM | 271 | 1,896 | 1091.00 | 1091.75 | 1090.75 | 1091.00 | 0.00 | 1.00 | 1091.289 | 54 | 60 | 69 | 72 | 1,896 |
| 222 | 2:44:41 PM | 263 | 1,059 | 1090.75 | 1091.25 | 1089.75 | 1089.75 | -1.00 | 1.50 | 1090.576 | 65 | 51 | 71 | 61 | 1,059 |
| 223 | 2:44:42 PM | 193 | 850 | 1090.00 | 1090.00 | 1088.50 | 1089.00 | -1.00 | 1.50 | 1089.348 | 67 | 25 | 75 | 28 | 850 |
| 224 | 2:44:43 PM | 320 | 1,197 | 1089.00 | 1089.25 | 1088.25 | 1088.75 | -0.25 | 1.00 | 1088.776 | 44 | 63 | 47 | 68 | 1,197 |
| 225 | 2:44:44 PM | 328 | 1,182 | 1088.50 | 1088.75 | 1086.75 | 1087.00 | -1.50 | 2.00 | 1087.544 | 70 | 45 | 88 | 47 | 1,182 |
| 226 | 2:44:45 PM | 260 | 891 | 1086.75 | 1088.25 | 1086.50 | 1088.00 | 1.25 | 1.75 | 1087.372 | 47 | 60 | 50 | 63 | 891 |
| 227 | 2:44:46 PM | 354 | 1,815 | 1088.00 | 1088.50 | 1086.50 | 1086.50 | -1.50 | 2.00 | 1087.713 | 63 | 46 | 72 | 47 | 1,815 |
| 228 | 2:44:47 PM | 439 | 1,613 | 1086.50 | 1087.75 | 1086.25 | 1086.75 | 0.25 | 1.50 | 1086.996 | 63 | 49 | 82 | 66 | 1,613 |
| 229 | 2:44:48 PM | 502 | 1,718 | 1086.50 | 1086.50 | 1084.75 | 1085.00 | -1.50 | 1.75 | 1085.604 | 65 | 67 | 85 | 75 | 1,718 |
| 230 | 2:44:49 PM | 325 | 1,158 | 1085.00 | 1086.25 | 1084.25 | 1086.00 | 1.00 | 2.00 | 1085.184 | 38 | 64 | 51 | 72 | 1,158 |
| 231 | 2:44:50 PM | 236 | 1,451 | 1086.00 | 1086.25 | 1085.25 | 1085.75 | -0.25 | 1.00 | 1085.644 | 51 | 55 | 59 | 59 | 1,451 |
| 232 | 2:44:51 PM | 220 | 1,889 | 1085.75 | 1086.75 | 1085.75 | 1086.00 | 0.25 | 1.00 | 1086.251 | 43 | 54 | 53 | 59 | 1,889 |
| 233 | 2:44:52 PM | 348 | 1,667 | 1086.00 | 1086.25 | 1084.50 | 1085.25 | -0.75 | 1.75 | 1085.410 | 80 | 48 | 92 | 53 | 1,667 |
| 234 | 2:44:53 PM | 126 | 549 | 1085.25 | 1085.25 | 1084.00 | 1084.50 | -0.75 | 1.25 | 1084.611 | 40 | 31 | 44 | 33 | 549 |
| 235 | 2:44:54 PM | 250 | 775 | 1084.25 | 1084.75 | 1083.75 | 1084.75 | 0.50 | 1.00 | 1084.251 | 41 | 47 | 49 | 52 | 775 |
| 236 | 2:44:55 PM | 370 | 1,543 | 1084.50 | 1084.50 | 1082.00 | 1082.25 | -2.25 | 2.50 | 1083.358 | 76 | 46 | 85 | 50 | 1,543 |
| 237 | 2:44:56 PM | 317 | 921 | 1082.00 | 1082.25 | 1081.00 | 1081.50 | -0.50 | 1.25 | 1081.574 | 48 | 61 | 60 | 72 | 921 |
| 238 | 2:44:57 PM | 301 | 858 | 1081.50 | 1082.75 | 1081.00 | 1081.25 | -0.25 | 1.75 | 1081.875 | 50 | 58 | 59 | 64 | 858 |
| 239 | 2:44:58 PM | 197 | 579 | 1081.50 | 1082.00 | 1080.50 | 1081.50 | 0.00 | 1.50 | 1081.292 | 39 | 38 | 44 | 43 | 579 |
| 240 | 2:44:59 PM | 249 | 1,184 | 1081.25 | 1082.50 | 1080.75 | 1082.00 | 0.75 | 1.75 | 1081.787 | 46 | 57 | 52 | 66 | 1,184 |

**(Continued)**

| Row | Time (EDT) | Trades | Volume | First | High | Low | Last | Last - First Range | High /Low Range | VWAP | Buy Accts | Sell Accts | Buy User IDs | Sell User IDs | Volume Graph |
|---|---|---|---|---|---|---|---|---|---|---|---|---|---|---|---|
| 241 | 2:45:00 PM | 179 | 1,136 | 1081.50 | 1082.00 | 1081.00 | 1081.25 | -0.25 | 1.00 | 1081.537 | 42 | 38 | 45 | 42 | 1,136 |
| 242 | 2:45:01 PM | 163 | 633 | 1081.00 | 1081.50 | 1080.50 | 1080.75 | -0.25 | 1.00 | 1081.084 | 49 | 47 | 53 | 49 | 633 |
| 243 | 2:45:02 PM | 168 | 797 | 1081.00 | 1081.25 | 1080.25 | 1081.00 | 0.00 | 1.00 | 1080.854 | 40 | 39 | 47 | 45 | 797 |
| 244 | 2:45:03 PM | 438 | 1,678 | 1081.25 | 1081.25 | 1078.25 | 1078.75 | -2.50 | 3.00 | 1079.915 | 87 | 51 | 108 | 58 | 1,678 |
| 245 | 2:45:04 PM | 147 | 647 | 1079.00 | 1079.50 | 1078.75 | 1079.25 | 0.25 | 0.75 | 1079.194 | 39 | 45 | 43 | 51 | 647 |
| 246 | 2:45:05 PM | 107 | 388 | 1079.25 | 1079.75 | 1079.00 | 1079.75 | 0.50 | 0.75 | 1079.368 | 30 | 38 | 32 | 39 | 388 |
| 247 | 2:45:06 PM | 312 | 1,136 | 1079.50 | 1079.50 | 1077.75 | 1078.25 | -1.25 | 1.75 | 1078.809 | 54 | 43 | 59 | 49 | 1,136 |
| 248 | 2:45:07 PM | 215 | 688 | 1078.25 | 1078.50 | 1077.25 | 1077.25 | -1.00 | 1.25 | 1077.902 | 39 | 40 | 42 | 45 | 688 |
| 249 | 2:45:08 PM | 412 | 1,320 | 1077.50 | 1077.75 | 1076.00 | 1076.75 | -0.75 | 1.75 | 1076.956 | 64 | 55 | 73 | 62 | 1,320 |
| 250 | 2:45:09 PM | 234 | 659 | 1076.75 | 1077.00 | 1075.50 | 1076.75 | 0.00 | 1.50 | 1076.412 | 38 | 45 | 39 | 51 | 659 |
| 251 | 2:45:10 PM | 390 | 1,396 | 1077.00 | 1077.00 | 1074.75 | 1074.75 | -2.25 | 2.25 | 1076.140 | 50 | 51 | 59 | 56 | 1,396 |
| 252 | 2:45:11 PM | 436 | 1,348 | 1075.25 | 1077.00 | 1074.50 | 1076.00 | 0.75 | 2.50 | 1075.844 | 49 | 66 | 55 | 75 | 1,348 |
| 253 | 2:45:12 PM | 627 | 1,543 | 1076.25 | 1076.50 | 1071.75 | 1074.00 | -2.25 | 4.75 | 1074.310 | 68 | 50 | 76 | 57 | 1,543 |
| 254 | 2:45:13 PM | 387 | 1,400 | 1074.00 | 1075.75 | 1071.25 | 1071.75 | -2.25 | 4.50 | 1074.146 | 58 | 48 | 65 | 54 | 1,400 |
| 255 | 2:45:14 PM | 323 | 1,703 | 1071.75 | 1075.50 | 1071.50 | 1074.50 | 2.75 | 4.00 | 1074.399 | 41 | 51 | 48 | 60 | 1,703 |
| 256 | 2:45:15 PM | 279 | 2,549 | 1075.00 | 1075.00 | 1072.75 | 1073.25 | -1.75 | 2.25 | 1073.559 | 55 | 40 | 64 | 46 | 2,549 |
| 257 | 2:45:16 PM | 235 | 1,186 | 1073.50 | 1074.50 | 1072.75 | 1074.25 | 0.75 | 1.75 | 1073.567 | 40 | 45 | 42 | 58 | 1,186 |
| 258 | 2:45:17 PM | 358 | 2,157 | 1074.25 | 1075.25 | 1072.50 | 1072.50 | -1.75 | 2.75 | 1074.149 | 60 | 50 | 72 | 57 | 2,157 |
| 259 | 2:45:18 PM | 523 | 2,663 | 1072.75 | 1072.75 | 1066.50 | 1072.50 | -0.25 | 6.25 | 1071.324 | 103 | 60 | 118 | 67 | 2,663 |
| 260 | 2:45:19 PM | 273 | 1,223 | 1072.25 | 1072.50 | 1070.00 | 1070.75 | -1.50 | 2.50 | 1071.532 | 51 | 49 | 58 | 54 | 1,223 |
| 261 | 2:45:20 PM | 249 | 1,467 | 1070.75 | 1073.25 | 1070.75 | 1071.75 | 1.00 | 2.50 | 1072.383 | 40 | 62 | 45 | 68 | 1,467 |
| 262 | 2:45:21 PM | 361 | 1,601 | 1071.75 | 1071.75 | 1066.75 | 1069.00 | -2.75 | 5.00 | 1069.051 | 71 | 37 | 81 | 37 | 1,601 |
| 263 | 2:45:22 PM | 337 | 1,692 | 1069.00 | 1071.25 | 1066.50 | 1071.25 | 2.25 | 4.75 | 1069.555 | 58 | 52 | 66 | 61 | 1,692 |
| 264 | 2:45:23 PM | 171 | 831 | 1071.00 | 1071.25 | 1068.75 | 1069.25 | -1.75 | 2.50 | 1069.925 | 42 | 33 | 47 | 37 | 831 |
| 265 | 2:45:24 PM | 185 | 1,081 | 1068.75 | 1070.75 | 1068.75 | 1070.75 | 2.00 | 2.00 | 1069.970 | 33 | 42 | 34 | 46 | 1,081 |
| 266 | 2:45:25 PM | 247 | 2,430 | 1070.50 | 1070.75 | 1068.75 | 1069.25 | -1.25 | 2.00 | 1069.838 | 44 | 31 | 51 | 36 | 2,430 |
| 267 | 2:45:26 PM | 572 | 3,594 | 1069.25 | 1071.00 | 1062.75 | 1064.50 | -4.75 | 8.25 | 1068.156 | 95 | 62 | 109 | 75 | 3,594 |
| 268 | 2:45:27 PM | 390 | 1,527 | 1064.50 | 1069.50 | 1063.00 | 1063.00 | -1.50 | 6.50 | 1067.946 | 55 | 55 | 62 | 63 | 1,527 |
| 269 | 2:45:28 PM | 133 | 705 | 1063.00 | 1063.00 | 1056.00 | 1056.00 | -7.00 | 7.00 | 1060.909 | 28 | 13 | 27 | 13 | 705 |
| 270 | 2:45:29 PM | 0 | 0 | | | | | **Stop Logic Halt** | | | | | | | |
| 271 | 2:45:30 PM | 0 | 0 | | | | | **Stop Logic Halt** | | | | | | | |
| 272 | 2:45:31 PM | 0 | 0 | | | | | **Stop Logic Halt** | | | | | | | |
| 273 | 2:45:32 PM | 0 | 0 | | | | | **Stop Logic Halt** | | | | | | | |
| 274 | 2:45:33 PM | 688 | 2,990 | 1056.75 | 1061.00 | 1056.50 | 1061.00 | 4.25 | 4.50 | 1057.120 | 110 | 94 | 123 | 104 | 2,990 |
| 275 | 2:45:34 PM | 201 | 1,637 | 1060.50 | 1064.75 | 1060.25 | 1064.75 | 4.25 | 4.50 | 1063.772 | 38 | 33 | 44 | 39 | 1,637 |
| 276 | 2:45:35 PM | 305 | 2,488 | 1064.50 | 1064.75 | 1060.75 | 1061.50 | -3.00 | 4.00 | 1063.174 | 65 | 34 | 73 | 39 | 2,488 |
| 277 | 2:45:36 PM | 183 | 930 | 1061.50 | 1062.75 | 1059.75 | 1062.75 | 1.25 | 3.00 | 1061.439 | 51 | 37 | 56 | 40 | 930 |
| 278 | 2:45:37 PM | 186 | 1,342 | 1062.75 | 1066.75 | 1062.75 | 1065.00 | 2.25 | 4.00 | 1064.701 | 33 | 44 | 39 | 53 | 1,342 |
| 279 | 2:45:38 PM | 80 | 430 | 1065.00 | 1066.00 | 1064.50 | 1065.00 | 0.00 | 1.50 | 1065.455 | 31 | 31 | 33 | 33 | 430 |
| 280 | 2:45:39 PM | 299 | 2,521 | 1065.00 | 1066.00 | 1058.50 | 1058.75 | -6.25 | 7.50 | 1062.613 | 81 | 31 | 90 | 37 | 2,521 |
| 281 | 2:45:40 PM | 267 | 2,242 | 1058.75 | 1065.75 | 1058.25 | 1059.50 | 0.75 | 7.50 | 1062.432 | 46 | 45 | 50 | 52 | 2,242 |
| 282 | 2:45:41 PM | 159 | 1,225 | 1062.25 | 1062.75 | 1057.50 | 1058.50 | -3.75 | 5.25 | 1060.095 | 51 | 33 | 57 | 41 | 1,225 |
| 283 | 2:45:42 PM | 263 | 1,605 | 1059.00 | 1066.75 | 1057.50 | 1059.25 | 0.25 | 9.25 | 1061.802 | 41 | 63 | 48 | 65 | 1,605 |
| 284 | 2:45:43 PM | 106 | 711 | 1058.50 | 1061.25 | 1057.25 | 1061.00 | 2.50 | 4.00 | 1058.831 | 41 | 30 | 46 | 36 | 711 |
| 285 | 2:45:44 PM | 160 | 1,077 | 1061.00 | 1062.50 | 1058.00 | 1061.25 | 0.25 | 4.50 | 1060.375 | 38 | 42 | 43 | 48 | 1,077 |
| 286 | 2:45:45 PM | 146 | 1,109 | 1062.50 | 1062.50 | 1058.25 | 1059.00 | -3.50 | 4.25 | 1060.047 | 53 | 26 | 61 | 33 | 1,109 |
| 287 | 2:45:46 PM | 157 | 1,145 | 1061.25 | 1062.25 | 1058.50 | 1062.00 | 0.75 | 3.75 | 1060.145 | 43 | 49 | 49 | 54 | 1,145 |
| 288 | 2:45:47 PM | 203 | 1,237 | 1061.75 | 1063.50 | 1059.75 | 1062.25 | 0.50 | 3.75 | 1061.904 | 37 | 37 | 44 | 48 | 1,237 |
| 289 | 2:45:48 PM | 154 | 938 | 1062.25 | 1063.25 | 1062.00 | 1062.50 | 0.25 | 1.25 | 1062.393 | 37 | 33 | 40 | 36 | 938 |
| 290 | 2:45:49 PM | 133 | 571 | 1062.50 | 1064.25 | 1062.25 | 1064.25 | 1.75 | 2.00 | 1063.649 | 28 | 38 | 32 | 40 | 571 |
| 291 | 2:45:50 PM | 126 | 532 | 1064.25 | 1065.25 | 1063.50 | 1065.25 | 1.00 | 1.75 | 1064.420 | 35 | 36 | 40 | 42 | 532 |
| 292 | 2:45:51 PM | 177 | 871 | 1065.25 | 1068.25 | 1065.00 | 1068.25 | 3.00 | 3.25 | 1065.790 | 30 | 53 | 33 | 54 | 871 |
| 293 | 2:45:52 PM | 121 | 666 | 1065.75 | 1068.50 | 1065.25 | 1068.00 | 2.25 | 3.25 | 1067.091 | 34 | 30 | 37 | 30 | 666 |
| 294 | 2:45:53 PM | 180 | 1,609 | 1067.75 | 1070.00 | 1067.00 | 1069.50 | 1.75 | 3.00 | 1068.991 | 42 | 50 | 45 | 53 | 1,609 |
| 295 | 2:45:54 PM | 289 | 1,675 | 1069.75 | 1073.50 | 1069.50 | 1073.50 | 3.75 | 4.00 | 1071.237 | 59 | 65 | 62 | 69 | 1,675 |
| 296 | 2:45:55 PM | 412 | 2,235 | 1073.25 | 1075.00 | 1070.25 | 1070.75 | -2.50 | 4.75 | 1072.412 | 65 | 54 | 77 | 54 | 2,235 |
| 297 | 2:45:56 PM | 168 | 956 | 1070.25 | 1071.25 | 1069.75 | 1069.75 | -0.50 | 1.50 | 1070.486 | 52 | 31 | 55 | 36 | 956 |
| 298 | 2:45:57 PM | 114 | 760 | 1069.75 | 1071.75 | 1069.50 | 1071.75 | 2.00 | 2.25 | 1070.562 | 36 | 34 | 39 | 35 | 760 |
| 299 | 2:45:58 PM | 233 | 1,790 | 1071.25 | 1074.25 | 1068.50 | 1070.25 | -1.00 | 5.75 | 1071.076 | 70 | 36 | 72 | 42 | 1,790 |
| 300 | 2:45:59 PM | 284 | 1,942 | 1070.00 | 1072.50 | 1065.00 | 1069.00 | -1.00 | 7.50 | 1068.054 | 71 | 42 | 78 | 45 | 1,942 |

**(Continued)**

| Row | Time (EDT) | Trades | Volume | First | High | Low | Last | Last - First Range | High /Low Range | VWAP | Buy Accts | Sell Accts | Buy User IDs | Sell User IDs | Volume Graph |
|---|---|---|---|---|---|---|---|---|---|---|---|---|---|---|---|
| 301 | 2:46:00 PM | 297 | 3,110 | 1068.75 | 1072.00 | 1061.00 | 1072.00 | 3.25 | 11.00 | 1064.924 | 76 | 52 | 80 | 58 | 3,110 |
| 302 | 2:46:01 PM | 167 | 480 | 1071.00 | 1071.75 | 1063.25 | 1066.00 | -5.00 | 8.50 | 1067.491 | 32 | 29 | 36 | 32 | 480 |
| 303 | 2:46:02 PM | 110 | 856 | 1067.50 | 1069.25 | 1063.75 | 1064.50 | -3.00 | 5.50 | 1066.697 | 32 | 25 | 32 | 30 | 856 |
| 304 | 2:46:03 PM | 148 | 741 | 1063.75 | 1070.00 | 1063.75 | 1066.75 | 3.00 | 6.25 | 1067.304 | 36 | 33 | 42 | 34 | 741 |
| 305 | 2:46:04 PM | 108 | 638 | 1066.75 | 1067.25 | 1063.75 | 1066.75 | -1.00 | 3.50 | 1066.247 | 38 | 27 | 40 | 29 | 638 |
| 306 | 2:46:05 PM | 112 | 339 | 1065.75 | 1067.00 | 1064.25 | 1064.25 | -1.50 | 2.75 | 1065.759 | 31 | 30 | 33 | 27 | 339 |
| 307 | 2:46:06 PM | 121 | 987 | 1065.75 | 1067.50 | 1063.50 | 1066.00 | 0.25 | 4.00 | 1064.643 | 38 | 24 | 40 | 29 | 987 |
| 308 | 2:46:07 PM | 244 | 1,484 | 1064.50 | 1067.50 | 1062.75 | 1067.25 | 2.75 | 4.75 | 1064.520 | 48 | 40 | 55 | 46 | 1,484 |
| 309 | 2:46:08 PM | 127 | 981 | 1063.75 | 1067.50 | 1063.00 | 1065.25 | 1.50 | 4.50 | 1065.028 | 35 | 31 | 38 | 35 | 981 |
| 310 | 2:46:09 PM | 134 | 353 | 1065.50 | 1065.75 | 1063.00 | 1064.50 | -1.00 | 2.75 | 1064.688 | 33 | 24 | 33 | 25 | 353 |
| 311 | 2:46:10 PM | 113 | 482 | 1064.50 | 1064.75 | 1063.00 | 1063.50 | -1.00 | 1.75 | 1063.830 | 39 | 29 | 41 | 31 | 482 |
| 312 | 2:46:11 PM | 115 | 1,075 | 1063.50 | 1065.00 | 1062.25 | 1062.75 | -0.75 | 2.75 | 1064.064 | 43 | 33 | 45 | 37 | 1,075 |
| 313 | 2:46:12 PM | 137 | 612 | 1062.75 | 1065.50 | 1062.25 | 1065.50 | 2.75 | 3.25 | 1064.184 | 23 | 35 | 25 | 38 | 612 |
| 314 | 2:46:13 PM | 75 | 269 | 1065.75 | 1065.75 | 1063.00 | 1065.75 | 0.00 | 2.75 | 1065.117 | 27 | 26 | 28 | 30 | 269 |
| 315 | 2:46:14 PM | 106 | 658 | 1065.50 | 1065.75 | 1064.25 | 1064.75 | -0.75 | 1.50 | 1065.089 | 40 | 26 | 44 | 28 | 658 |
| 316 | 2:46:15 PM | 104 | 539 | 1065.00 | 1065.75 | 1063.50 | 1064.75 | -0.25 | 2.25 | 1064.384 | 33 | 27 | 39 | 33 | 539 |
| 317 | 2:46:16 PM | 130 | 1,275 | 1064.75 | 1068.25 | 1063.75 | 1065.50 | 0.75 | 4.50 | 1066.139 | 33 | 64 | 35 | 68 | 1,275 |
| 318 | 2:46:17 PM | 125 | 884 | 1066.25 | 1066.75 | 1064.00 | 1065.75 | -0.50 | 2.75 | 1064.845 | 38 | 31 | 41 | 34 | 884 |
| 319 | 2:46:18 PM | 92 | 1,104 | 1065.75 | 1066.75 | 1065.50 | 1066.75 | 1.00 | 1.25 | 1066.047 | 22 | 27 | 25 | 31 | 1,104 |
| 320 | 2:46:19 PM | 97 | 563 | 1066.75 | 1068.00 | 1066.25 | 1067.25 | 0.50 | 1.75 | 1066.886 | 35 | 25 | 37 | 28 | 563 |
| 321 | 2:46:20 PM | 115 | 608 | 1067.25 | 1069.75 | 1066.50 | 1068.00 | 0.75 | 3.25 | 1067.811 | 29 | 41 | 31 | 49 | 608 |
| 322 | 2:46:21 PM | 118 | 519 | 1068.00 | 1069.75 | 1067.75 | 1068.75 | 0.75 | 2.00 | 1068.663 | 33 | 24 | 35 | 27 | 519 |
| 323 | 2:46:22 PM | 78 | 303 | 1069.50 | 1069.75 | 1068.75 | 1069.75 | 0.25 | 1.00 | 1069.229 | 22 | 22 | 24 | 24 | 303 |
| 324 | 2:46:23 PM | 89 | 606 | 1069.75 | 1071.00 | 1069.25 | 1071.00 | 1.25 | 1.75 | 1070.003 | 27 | 40 | 31 | 42 | 606 |
| 325 | 2:46:24 PM | 206 | 701 | 1071.00 | 1072.75 | 1070.00 | 1070.50 | -0.50 | 2.75 | 1071.316 | 38 | 49 | 40 | 57 | 701 |
| 326 | 2:46:25 PM | 203 | 1,558 | 1070.25 | 1072.75 | 1069.50 | 1072.25 | 2.00 | 3.25 | 1070.929 | 48 | 36 | 50 | 43 | 1,558 |
| 327 | 2:46:26 PM | 127 | 1,835 | 1072.25 | 1072.25 | 1068.75 | 1070.25 | -2.00 | 3.50 | 1069.976 | 43 | 26 | 48 | 28 | 1,835 |
| 328 | 2:46:27 PM | 138 | 927 | 1070.75 | 1071.00 | 1068.25 | 1069.00 | -1.75 | 2.75 | 1069.257 | 38 | 37 | 39 | 41 | 927 |
| 329 | 2:46:28 PM | 124 | 873 | 1070.00 | 1072.75 | 1067.75 | 1072.25 | 2.25 | 5.00 | 1070.933 | 33 | 46 | 35 | 49 | 873 |
| 330 | 2:46:29 PM | 104 | 427 | 1071.25 | 1072.25 | 1070.75 | 1071.25 | 0.00 | 1.50 | 1071.412 | 23 | 26 | 25 | 26 | 427 |
| 331 | 2:46:30 PM | 180 | 1,083 | 1071.25 | 1074.75 | 1071.00 | 1074.75 | 3.50 | 3.75 | 1073.468 | 32 | 43 | 34 | 49 | 1,083 |
| 332 | 2:46:31 PM | 118 | 739 | 1073.50 | 1074.75 | 1072.75 | 1073.00 | -0.50 | 2.00 | 1073.595 | 28 | 31 | 32 | 31 | 739 |
| 333 | 2:46:32 PM | 58 | 336 | 1073.50 | 1073.50 | 1072.75 | 1073.25 | -0.25 | 0.75 | 1073.056 | 23 | 17 | 26 | 18 | 336 |
| 334 | 2:46:33 PM | 282 | 1,950 | 1073.50 | 1077.75 | 1073.00 | 1074.75 | 1.25 | 4.75 | 1075.677 | 43 | 66 | 40 | 76 | 1,950 |
| 335 | 2:46:34 PM | 127 | 673 | 1074.75 | 1075.75 | 1072.75 | 1073.00 | -1.75 | 3.00 | 1074.145 | 33 | 23 | 37 | 27 | 673 |
| 336 | 2:46:35 PM | 100 | 1,086 | 1073.00 | 1074.75 | 1072.75 | 1074.00 | 1.00 | 2.00 | 1074.185 | 29 | 31 | 33 | 36 | 1,086 |
| 337 | 2:46:36 PM | 76 | 1,448 | 1073.75 | 1074.00 | 1072.50 | 1072.75 | -1.00 | 1.50 | 1073.508 | 40 | 19 | 42 | 22 | 1,448 |
| 338 | 2:46:37 PM | 88 | 926 | 1072.75 | 1073.00 | 1072.25 | 1072.50 | -0.25 | 0.75 | 1072.617 | 26 | 32 | 26 | 38 | 926 |
| 339 | 2:46:38 PM | 184 | 1,038 | 1072.50 | 1073.00 | 1071.00 | 1071.50 | -1.00 | 2.00 | 1071.864 | 38 | 31 | 41 | 32 | 1,038 |
| 340 | 2:46:39 PM | 320 | 665 | 1072.00 | 1072.50 | 1071.00 | 1072.25 | 0.25 | 1.50 | 1071.604 | 25 | 43 | 28 | 43 | 665 |
| 341 | 2:46:40 PM | 288 | 1,786 | 1071.50 | 1073.75 | 1071.00 | 1071.50 | 0.00 | 2.75 | 1072.478 | 28 | 42 | 32 | 51 | 1,786 |
| 342 | 2:46:41 PM | 142 | 1,271 | 1072.00 | 1073.75 | 1071.25 | 1072.75 | 0.75 | 2.50 | 1072.059 | 27 | 33 | 33 | 37 | 1,271 |
| 343 | 2:46:42 PM | 70 | 424 | 1072.75 | 1073.75 | 1072.25 | 1073.25 | 0.50 | 1.50 | 1073.153 | 19 | 27 | 19 | 31 | 424 |
| 344 | 2:46:43 PM | 72 | 466 | 1073.50 | 1073.75 | 1073.25 | 1073.50 | 0.00 | 0.50 | 1073.351 | 22 | 24 | 23 | 28 | 466 |
| 345 | 2:46:44 PM | 125 | 958 | 1073.50 | 1074.25 | 1073.25 | 1074.00 | 0.50 | 1.00 | 1073.653 | 28 | 31 | 31 | 36 | 958 |
| 346 | 2:46:45 PM | 57 | 590 | 1074.00 | 1074.50 | 1073.75 | 1074.50 | 0.50 | 0.75 | 1074.123 | 16 | 28 | 22 | 27 | 590 |
| 347 | 2:46:46 PM | 76 | 683 | 1074.50 | 1074.50 | 1073.50 | 1074.00 | -0.50 | 1.00 | 1073.991 | 26 | 22 | 30 | 24 | 683 |
| 348 | 2:46:47 PM | 75 | 862 | 1073.75 | 1075.25 | 1073.50 | 1074.25 | 0.50 | 1.75 | 1074.077 | 26 | 34 | 26 | 40 | 862 |
| 349 | 2:46:48 PM | 75 | 738 | 1074.50 | 1075.00 | 1074.00 | 1075.00 | 0.50 | 1.00 | 1074.519 | 27 | 20 | 29 | 23 | 738 |
| 350 | 2:46:49 PM | 116 | 920 | 1074.50 | 1075.25 | 1073.50 | 1074.50 | 0.00 | 1.75 | 1074.220 | 41 | 24 | 45 | 28 | 920 |
| 351 | 2:46:50 PM | 183 | 1,888 | 1074.25 | 1076.25 | 1074.25 | 1075.75 | 1.50 | 2.00 | 1075.027 | 29 | 41 | 35 | 49 | 1,888 |
| 352 | 2:46:51 PM | 251 | 4,456 | 1075.50 | 1075.50 | 1069.50 | 1070.25 | -5.25 | 6.00 | 1072.623 | 92 | 32 | 97 | 37 | 4,456 |
| 353 | 2:46:52 PM | 126 | 512 | 1071.00 | 1072.50 | 1069.75 | 1071.50 | 0.50 | 2.75 | 1070.887 | 25 | 20 | 27 | 23 | 512 |
| 354 | 2:46:53 PM | 72 | 368 | 1070.75 | 1071.00 | 1070.00 | 1070.50 | -0.25 | 1.00 | 1070.584 | 20 | 24 | 22 | 27 | 368 |
| 355 | 2:46:54 PM | 137 | 867 | 1070.00 | 1072.75 | 1069.50 | 1069.75 | -0.25 | 3.25 | 1071.144 | 25 | 35 | 26 | 42 | 867 |
| 356 | 2:46:55 PM | 162 | 854 | 1069.75 | 1071.75 | 1069.50 | 1071.75 | 2.00 | 2.25 | 1070.456 | 33 | 29 | 36 | 33 | 854 |
| 357 | 2:46:56 PM | 143 | 1,256 | 1071.75 | 1074.50 | 1071.50 | 1072.50 | 0.75 | 3.00 | 1072.984 | 29 | 46 | 30 | 49 | 1,256 |
| 358 | 2:46:57 PM | 41 | 367 | 1073.25 | 1074.00 | 1073.00 | 1073.50 | 0.25 | 1.00 | 1073.480 | 13 | 19 | 13 | 23 | 367 |
| 359 | 2:46:58 PM | 51 | 393 | 1073.25 | 1073.75 | 1072.50 | 1072.75 | -0.50 | 1.25 | 1073.223 | 11 | 18 | 14 | 22 | 393 |
| 360 | 2:46:59 PM | 41 | 443 | 1072.50 | 1073.00 | 1072.50 | 1072.50 | 0.00 | 0.50 | 1072.621 | 10 | 16 | 11 | 20 | 443 |

**(Continued)**

| Row | Time (EDT) | Trades | Volume | First | High | Low | Last | Last - First Range | High /Low Range | VWAP | Buy Accts | Sell Accts | Buy User IDs | Sell User IDs | Volume Graph |
|---|---|---|---|---|---|---|---|---|---|---|---|---|---|---|---|
| 361 | 2:47:00 PM | 154 | 1,207 | 1072.75 | 1073.50 | 1071.75 | 1072.75 | 0.00 | 1.75 | 1072.326 | 29 | 24 | 34 | 29 | 1,207 |
| 362 | 2:47:01 PM | 54 | 198 | 1072.75 | 1073.00 | 1071.25 | 1073.00 | 0.25 | 1.75 | 1072.188 | 21 | 19 | 23 | 22 | 198 |
| 363 | 2:47:02 PM | 46 | 570 | 1072.25 | 1073.00 | 1072.25 | 1072.50 | 0.25 | 0.75 | 1072.652 | 15 | 19 | 19 | 19 | 570 |
| 364 | 2:47:03 PM | 41 | 215 | 1072.50 | 1072.50 | 1071.75 | 1072.00 | -0.50 | 0.75 | 1072.286 | 19 | 18 | 20 | 19 | 215 |
| 365 | 2:47:04 PM | 72 | 535 | 1072.25 | 1073.00 | 1072.00 | 1072.50 | 0.25 | 1.00 | 1072.526 | 16 | 30 | 19 | 34 | 535 |
| 366 | 2:47:05 PM | 43 | 267 | 1072.50 | 1072.50 | 1072.00 | 1072.50 | 0.00 | 0.50 | 1072.279 | 18 | 14 | 19 | 16 | 267 |
| 367 | 2:47:06 PM | 57 | 695 | 1072.50 | 1072.50 | 1072.00 | 1072.25 | -0.25 | 0.50 | 1072.227 | 21 | 13 | 26 | 19 | 695 |
| 368 | 2:47:07 PM | 157 | 1,197 | 1072.25 | 1072.75 | 1070.75 | 1072.25 | 0.00 | 2.00 | 1071.912 | 41 | 31 | 43 | 33 | 1,197 |
| 369 | 2:47:08 PM | 57 | 1,073 | 1072.25 | 1072.50 | 1071.75 | 1072.50 | 0.25 | 0.75 | 1072.130 | 34 | 24 | 17 | 28 | 1,073 |
| 370 | 2:47:09 PM | 73 | 529 | 1072.50 | 1073.00 | 1072.25 | 1073.00 | 0.50 | 0.75 | 1072.648 | 13 | 30 | 18 | 32 | 529 |
| 371 | 2:47:10 PM | 49 | 537 | 1073.00 | 1073.50 | 1073.00 | 1073.50 | 0.50 | 0.50 | 1073.426 | 17 | 28 | 18 | 30 | 537 |
| 372 | 2:47:11 PM | 66 | 701 | 1073.50 | 1074.00 | 1073.25 | 1073.75 | 0.25 | 0.75 | 1073.529 | 23 | 26 | 23 | 28 | 701 |
| 373 | 2:47:12 PM | 57 | 478 | 1073.75 | 1074.00 | 1073.00 | 1073.75 | 0.00 | 1.00 | 1073.742 | 17 | 26 | 21 | 27 | 478 |
| 374 | 2:47:13 PM | 42 | 309 | 1073.75 | 1074.00 | 1073.25 | 1073.75 | 0.00 | 0.75 | 1073.733 | 19 | 19 | 20 | 19 | 309 |
| 375 | 2:47:14 PM | 31 | 304 | 1073.75 | 1074.00 | 1073.25 | 1073.75 | 0.00 | 0.75 | 1073.688 | 12 | 15 | 15 | 15 | 304 |
| 376 | 2:47:15 PM | 83 | 1,061 | 1073.75 | 1074.50 | 1073.00 | 1073.25 | -0.50 | 1.50 | 1073.792 | 38 | 18 | 42 | 18 | 1,061 |
| 377 | 2:47:16 PM | 24 | 205 | 1073.25 | 1074.00 | 1073.00 | 1073.25 | 0.00 | 1.00 | 1073.082 | 13 | 13 | 13 | 13 | 205 |
| 378 | 2:47:17 PM | 47 | 599 | 1073.00 | 1073.75 | 1073.00 | 1073.75 | 0.75 | 0.75 | 1073.377 | 13 | 19 | 13 | 21 | 599 |
| 379 | 2:47:18 PM | 82 | 1,180 | 1073.50 | 1073.75 | 1072.75 | 1072.75 | -0.75 | 1.00 | 1073.313 | 26 | 23 | 29 | 23 | 1,180 |
| 380 | 2:47:19 PM | 30 | 270 | 1073.00 | 1073.25 | 1072.50 | 1073.00 | 0.00 | 0.75 | 1072.931 | 19 | 9 | 21 | 9 | 270 |
| 381 | 2:47:20 PM | 54 | 303 | 1073.25 | 1073.75 | 1073.00 | 1073.50 | 0.25 | 0.75 | 1073.301 | 17 | 30 | 18 | 30 | 303 |
| 382 | 2:47:21 PM | 50 | 444 | 1073.50 | 1073.50 | 1073.00 | 1073.25 | -0.25 | 0.50 | 1073.319 | 17 | 17 | 17 | 18 | 444 |
| 383 | 2:47:22 PM | 101 | 1,407 | 1073.25 | 1074.00 | 1073.00 | 1074.00 | 0.75 | 1.00 | 1073.769 | 23 | 40 | 25 | 36 | 1,407 |
| 384 | 2:47:23 PM | 76 | 744 | 1073.75 | 1074.00 | 1073.25 | 1074.00 | 0.25 | 0.75 | 1073.616 | 21 | 20 | 21 | 19 | 744 |
| 385 | 2:47:24 PM | 123 | 680 | 1073.75 | 1073.75 | 1072.50 | 1073.50 | -0.25 | 1.25 | 1073.358 | 33 | 25 | 36 | 27 | 680 |
| 386 | 2:47:25 PM | 64 | 870 | 1073.75 | 1074.00 | 1072.50 | 1073.25 | -0.50 | 1.50 | 1073.107 | 22 | 24 | 21 | 27 | 870 |
| 387 | 2:47:26 PM | 47 | 718 | 1073.50 | 1073.75 | 1073.25 | 1073.75 | 0.25 | 0.50 | 1073.456 | 14 | 19 | 18 | 20 | 718 |
| 388 | 2:47:27 PM | 71 | 722 | 1074.00 | 1074.50 | 1073.75 | 1074.25 | 0.25 | 0.75 | 1074.087 | 24 | 27 | 24 | 31 | 722 |
| 389 | 2:47:28 PM | 34 | 186 | 1074.50 | 1074.50 | 1074.25 | 1074.25 | -0.25 | 0.25 | 1074.356 | 15 | 17 | 16 | 17 | 186 |
| 390 | 2:47:29 PM | 64 | 397 | 1074.50 | 1074.50 | 1073.75 | 1074.00 | -0.50 | 0.75 | 1074.132 | 32 | 21 | 40 | 23 | 397 |
| 391 | 2:47:30 PM | 158 | 1,969 | 1074.00 | 1074.75 | 1073.00 | 1074.50 | 0.50 | 1.75 | 1073.887 | 40 | 39 | 48 | 41 | 1,969 |
| 392 | 2:47:31 PM | 137 | 402 | 1074.50 | 1074.75 | 1073.00 | 1073.00 | -1.50 | 1.75 | 1073.905 | 34 | 17 | 39 | 19 | 402 |
| 393 | 2:47:32 PM | 84 | 632 | 1073.75 | 1074.00 | 1072.75 | 1074.00 | 0.25 | 1.25 | 1073.703 | 29 | 19 | 31 | 21 | 632 |
| 394 | 2:47:33 PM | 109 | 641 | 1074.00 | 1074.50 | 1073.50 | 1074.00 | 0.00 | 1.00 | 1073.968 | 28 | 28 | 34 | 30 | 641 |
| 395 | 2:47:34 PM | 129 | 788 | 1074.25 | 1074.75 | 1073.00 | 1074.50 | 0.25 | 1.75 | 1073.839 | 34 | 26 | 40 | 28 | 788 |
| 396 | 2:47:35 PM | 34 | 276 | 1074.00 | 1074.25 | 1073.25 | 1073.25 | -0.75 | 1.00 | 1073.349 | 13 | 17 | 14 | 19 | 276 |
| 397 | 2:47:36 PM | 221 | 1,396 | 1073.50 | 1075.00 | 1073.00 | 1074.25 | 0.75 | 2.00 | 1074.262 | 33 | 61 | 39 | 68 | 1,396 |
| 398 | 2:47:37 PM | 56 | 364 | 1074.25 | 1075.00 | 1073.50 | 1075.00 | 0.75 | 1.50 | 1074.471 | 19 | 21 | 19 | 23 | 364 |
| 399 | 2:47:38 PM | 45 | 243 | 1074.75 | 1075.25 | 1074.50 | 1075.25 | 0.50 | 0.75 | 1075.089 | 20 | 19 | 22 | 20 | 243 |
| 400 | 2:47:39 PM | 108 | 422 | 1075.00 | 1075.75 | 1074.50 | 1075.75 | 0.75 | 1.25 | 1075.117 | 30 | 37 | 33 | 39 | 422 |
| 401 | 2:47:40 PM | 57 | 414 | 1075.50 | 1076.00 | 1075.25 | 1075.75 | 0.25 | 0.75 | 1075.506 | 30 | 23 | 34 | 25 | 414 |
| 402 | 2:47:41 PM | 77 | 463 | 1075.25 | 1076.00 | 1075.25 | 1075.75 | 0.50 | 0.75 | 1075.389 | 22 | 26 | 28 | 30 | 463 |
| 403 | 2:47:42 PM | 107 | 544 | 1075.75 | 1076.75 | 1075.50 | 1075.75 | 0.00 | 1.25 | 1076.127 | 26 | 37 | 29 | 41 | 544 |
| 404 | 2:47:43 PM | 75 | 337 | 1076.00 | 1077.00 | 1076.00 | 1077.00 | 1.00 | 1.00 | 1076.596 | 21 | 30 | 22 | 31 | 337 |
| 405 | 2:47:44 PM | 128 | 433 | 1076.75 | 1077.50 | 1076.00 | 1076.50 | -0.25 | 1.50 | 1076.780 | 53 | 23 | 56 | 24 | 433 |
| 406 | 2:47:45 PM | 256 | 1,716 | 1076.50 | 1079.50 | 1076.25 | 1077.50 | 1.00 | 3.25 | 1077.623 | 50 | 79 | 54 | 83 | 1,716 |
| 407 | 2:47:46 PM | 105 | 556 | 1077.50 | 1078.50 | 1076.25 | 1077.75 | 0.25 | 2.25 | 1077.003 | 36 | 34 | 40 | 37 | 556 |
| 408 | 2:47:47 PM | 82 | 663 | 1077.75 | 1078.50 | 1077.50 | 1078.00 | 0.25 | 1.00 | 1078.012 | 26 | 27 | 32 | 30 | 663 |
| 409 | 2:47:48 PM | 98 | 592 | 1078.00 | 1079.00 | 1077.50 | 1077.50 | -0.50 | 1.50 | 1078.138 | 36 | 28 | 39 | 28 | 592 |
| 410 | 2:47:49 PM | 74 | 316 | 1078.50 | 1078.50 | 1077.50 | 1078.25 | -0.25 | 1.00 | 1078.078 | 33 | 21 | 35 | 23 | 316 |
| 411 | 2:47:50 PM | 124 | 795 | 1078.00 | 1078.75 | 1077.50 | 1077.75 | -0.25 | 1.25 | 1077.991 | 40 | 28 | 51 | 30 | 795 |
| 412 | 2:47:51 PM | 169 | 1,011 | 1077.75 | 1079.50 | 1077.50 | 1079.25 | 1.50 | 2.00 | 1078.846 | 28 | 45 | 30 | 48 | 1,011 |
| 413 | 2:47:52 PM | 98 | 1,203 | 1079.25 | 1080.25 | 1079.00 | 1080.25 | 1.00 | 1.25 | 1079.812 | 37 | 46 | 39 | 50 | 1,203 |
| 414 | 2:47:53 PM | 130 | 770 | 1080.25 | 1081.25 | 1080.00 | 1081.25 | 1.00 | 1.25 | 1080.604 | 29 | 46 | 32 | 48 | 770 |
| 415 | 2:47:54 PM | 305 | 1,486 | 1081.25 | 1083.25 | 1080.00 | 1081.00 | -0.25 | 3.25 | 1081.832 | 60 | 68 | 69 | 75 | 1,486 |
| 416 | 2:47:55 PM | 136 | 1,655 | 1081.00 | 1081.75 | 1078.00 | 1081.75 | 0.75 | 3.75 | 1079.775 | 60 | 44 | 63 | 47 | 1,655 |
| 417 | 2:47:56 PM | 327 | 2,364 | 1081.75 | 1084.75 | 1077.75 | 1084.00 | 2.25 | 7.00 | 1081.643 | 52 | 81 | 59 | 85 | 2,364 |
| 418 | 2:47:57 PM | 153 | 1,017 | 1084.00 | 1085.25 | 1083.25 | 1085.00 | 1.00 | 2.00 | 1084.748 | 37 | 44 | 44 | 46 | 1,017 |
| 419 | 2:47:58 PM | 234 | 1,743 | 1085.00 | 1088.25 | 1084.50 | 1088.25 | 3.25 | 3.75 | 1085.611 | 46 | 70 | 46 | 71 | 1,743 |
| 420 | 2:47:59 PM | 174 | 909 | 1086.50 | 1088.25 | 1085.00 | 1086.00 | -0.50 | 3.25 | 1086.133 | 40 | 34 | 41 | 35 | 909 |

## (Continued)

| Row | Time (EDT) | Trades | Volume | First | High | Low | Last | Last - First Range | High /Low Range | VWAP | Buy Accts | Sell Accts | Buy User IDs | Sell User IDs | Volume Graph |
|---|---|---|---|---|---|---|---|---|---|---|---|---|---|---|---|
| 421 | 2:48:00 PM | 183 | 1,555 | 1085.75 | 1086.75 | 1082.00 | 1082.00 | -3.75 | 4.75 | 1085.323 | 43 | 40 | 45 | 43 | 1,555 |
| 422 | 2:48:01 PM | 366 | 2,584 | 1086.00 | 1090.75 | 1082.00 | 1089.50 | 3.50 | 8.75 | 1087.360 | 46 | 99 | 53 | 102 | 2,584 |
| 423 | 2:48:02 PM | 88 | 643 | 1089.50 | 1090.75 | 1089.50 | 1090.25 | 0.75 | 1.25 | 1090.117 | 29 | 33 | 32 | 36 | 643 |
| 424 | 2:48:03 PM | 95 | 415 | 1090.50 | 1091.75 | 1090.25 | 1091.50 | 1.00 | 1.50 | 1091.066 | 42 | 34 | 46 | 34 | 415 |
| 425 | 2:48:04 PM | 108 | 811 | 1091.50 | 1092.00 | 1090.75 | 1092.00 | 0.50 | 1.25 | 1091.507 | 40 | 33 | 41 | 37 | 811 |
| 426 | 2:48:05 PM | 177 | 1,091 | 1092.00 | 1094.25 | 1090.25 | 1092.50 | 0.50 | 4.00 | 1092.034 | 47 | 69 | 51 | 77 | 1,091 |
| 427 | 2:48:06 PM | 109 | 641 | 1092.25 | 1094.50 | 1090.25 | 1092.00 | -0.25 | 4.25 | 1092.878 | 44 | 46 | 48 | 46 | 641 |
| 428 | 2:48:07 PM | 85 | 449 | 1092.25 | 1093.25 | 1090.25 | 1091.25 | -1.00 | 3.00 | 1091.146 | 37 | 35 | 38 | 36 | 449 |
| 429 | 2:48:08 PM | 84 | 915 | 1091.00 | 1091.75 | 1090.50 | 1091.00 | 0.00 | 1.25 | 1091.121 | 39 | 35 | 44 | 36 | 915 |
| 430 | 2:48:09 PM | 111 | 1,362 | 1090.50 | 1092.00 | 1090.25 | 1090.50 | 0.00 | 1.75 | 1091.432 | 31 | 47 | 33 | 50 | 1,362 |
| 431 | 2:48:10 PM | 110 | 864 | 1090.50 | 1092.25 | 1090.25 | 1090.50 | 0.00 | 2.00 | 1091.324 | 33 | 40 | 37 | 44 | 864 |
| 432 | 2:48:11 PM | 143 | 1,553 | 1090.25 | 1093.25 | 1090.00 | 1090.75 | 0.50 | 3.25 | 1091.522 | 38 | 70 | 40 | 75 | 1,553 |
| 433 | 2:48:12 PM | 85 | 1,095 | 1090.75 | 1093.50 | 1090.25 | 1092.00 | 1.25 | 3.25 | 1092.289 | 23 | 37 | 28 | 39 | 1,095 |
| 434 | 2:48:13 PM | 109 | 1,325 | 1093.00 | 1094.00 | 1092.00 | 1093.50 | 0.50 | 2.00 | 1093.301 | 30 | 49 | 33 | 64 | 1,325 |
| 435 | 2:48:14 PM | 153 | 1,556 | 1093.50 | 1095.25 | 1093.00 | 1095.00 | 1.50 | 2.25 | 1094.181 | 34 | 73 | 38 | 84 | 1,556 |
| 436 | 2:48:15 PM | 86 | 884 | 1095.25 | 1095.25 | 1093.00 | 1094.50 | -0.75 | 2.25 | 1094.093 | 35 | 28 | 43 | 34 | 884 |
| 437 | 2:48:16 PM | 83 | 533 | 1093.25 | 1094.50 | 1093.00 | 1093.00 | -0.25 | 1.50 | 1093.348 | 26 | 37 | 29 | 41 | 533 |
| 438 | 2:48:17 PM | 173 | 794 | 1092.75 | 1094.50 | 1090.25 | 1091.75 | -1.00 | 4.25 | 1092.369 | 59 | 56 | 65 | 61 | 794 |
| 439 | 2:48:18 PM | 72 | 404 | 1091.75 | 1093.25 | 1091.00 | 1091.50 | -0.25 | 2.25 | 1091.443 | 32 | 27 | 33 | 29 | 404 |
| 440 | 2:48:19 PM | 81 | 529 | 1091.25 | 1093.00 | 1091.00 | 1091.75 | 0.50 | 2.00 | 1091.586 | 29 | 38 | 32 | 40 | 529 |
| 441 | 2:48:20 PM | 102 | 562 | 1092.25 | 1094.00 | 1091.25 | 1092.50 | 0.25 | 2.75 | 1092.306 | 36 | 45 | 38 | 49 | 562 |
| 442 | 2:48:21 PM | 79 | 384 | 1092.50 | 1092.75 | 1090.75 | 1092.00 | -0.50 | 2.00 | 1092.105 | 22 | 30 | 23 | 32 | 384 |
| 443 | 2:48:22 PM | 168 | 798 | 1092.25 | 1093.25 | 1091.25 | 1092.00 | -0.25 | 2.00 | 1092.374 | 33 | 32 | 35 | 35 | 798 |
| 444 | 2:48:23 PM | 100 | 1,137 | 1091.50 | 1092.00 | 1090.75 | 1091.25 | -0.25 | 1.25 | 1091.332 | 26 | 26 | 31 | 27 | 1,137 |
| 445 | 2:48:24 PM | 115 | 539 | 1091.25 | 1091.75 | 1090.50 | 1091.25 | 0.00 | 1.25 | 1091.305 | 31 | 27 | 36 | 30 | 539 |
| 446 | 2:48:25 PM | 133 | 979 | 1091.75 | 1092.00 | 1090.75 | 1091.75 | 0.00 | 1.25 | 1091.466 | 25 | 44 | 27 | 51 | 979 |
| 447 | 2:48:26 PM | 81 | 658 | 1092.00 | 1092.00 | 1090.50 | 1091.75 | -0.25 | 1.50 | 1091.196 | 32 | 29 | 34 | 34 | 658 |
| 448 | 2:48:27 PM | 539 | 2,614 | 1091.75 | 1093.75 | 1090.75 | 1091.75 | 0.00 | 3.00 | 1092.525 | 26 | 68 | 30 | 74 | 2,614 |
| 449 | 2:48:28 PM | 94 | 744 | 1091.50 | 1093.75 | 1091.25 | 1093.00 | 1.50 | 2.50 | 1092.921 | 31 | 27 | 34 | 29 | 744 |
| 450 | 2:48:29 PM | 81 | 485 | 1092.75 | 1093.25 | 1092.00 | 1093.00 | 0.25 | 1.25 | 1092.771 | 30 | 25 | 32 | 24 | 485 |
| 451 | 2:48:30 PM | 134 | 1,722 | 1093.00 | 1094.00 | 1092.50 | 1093.50 | 0.50 | 1.50 | 1093.524 | 45 | 51 | 49 | 55 | 1,722 |
| 452 | 2:48:31 PM | 84 | 413 | 1092.75 | 1093.50 | 1092.25 | 1092.75 | 0.00 | 1.25 | 1092.647 | 23 | 30 | 28 | 32 | 413 |
| 453 | 2:48:32 PM | 213 | 1,303 | 1092.75 | 1094.75 | 1092.75 | 1094.00 | 1.25 | 2.00 | 1093.620 | 30 | 59 | 36 | 63 | 1,303 |
| 454 | 2:48:33 PM | 174 | 861 | 1094.00 | 1095.00 | 1093.25 | 1094.00 | 0.00 | 1.75 | 1094.190 | 29 | 38 | 35 | 42 | 861 |
| 455 | 2:48:34 PM | 229 | 2,060 | 1094.00 | 1097.00 | 1093.50 | 1095.25 | 1.25 | 3.50 | 1095.259 | 37 | 91 | 42 | 97 | 2,060 |
| 456 | 2:48:35 PM | 246 | 1,051 | 1095.75 | 1096.75 | 1093.00 | 1094.25 | -1.50 | 3.75 | 1095.086 | 58 | 33 | 62 | 41 | 1,051 |
| 457 | 2:48:36 PM | 114 | 515 | 1094.75 | 1095.00 | 1092.75 | 1093.25 | -1.50 | 2.25 | 1093.586 | 30 | 19 | 33 | 21 | 515 |
| 458 | 2:48:37 PM | 128 | 721 | 1093.25 | 1093.75 | 1092.25 | 1093.25 | 0.00 | 1.50 | 1092.962 | 34 | 32 | 36 | 37 | 721 |
| 459 | 2:48:38 PM | 126 | 1,432 | 1093.00 | 1094.25 | 1091.75 | 1091.75 | -1.25 | 2.50 | 1092.906 | 41 | 35 | 41 | 37 | 1,432 |
| 460 | 2:48:39 PM | 106 | 1,081 | 1091.75 | 1092.75 | 1091.25 | 1092.00 | 0.25 | 1.50 | 1091.885 | 36 | 32 | 40 | 36 | 1,081 |
| 461 | 2:48:40 PM | 100 | 552 | 1092.50 | 1092.75 | 1091.25 | 1091.50 | -1.00 | 1.50 | 1091.727 | 30 | 26 | 33 | 27 | 552 |
| 462 | 2:48:41 PM | 241 | 1,407 | 1091.50 | 1093.25 | 1089.25 | 1089.25 | -2.25 | 4.00 | 1091.496 | 65 | 44 | 69 | 48 | 1,407 |
| 463 | 2:48:42 PM | 97 | 560 | 1090.75 | 1090.75 | 1089.25 | 1089.50 | -1.25 | 1.50 | 1089.841 | 29 | 26 | 30 | 29 | 560 |
| 464 | 2:48:43 PM | 110 | 701 | 1089.50 | 1089.75 | 1087.00 | 1087.50 | -2.00 | 2.75 | 1088.796 | 41 | 34 | 45 | 36 | 701 |
| 465 | 2:48:44 PM | 137 | 620 | 1087.50 | 1088.25 | 1085.25 | 1086.00 | -1.50 | 3.00 | 1086.752 | 42 | 31 | 44 | 33 | 620 |
| 466 | 2:48:45 PM | 463 | 789 | 1086.00 | 1087.50 | 1083.25 | 1085.00 | -1.00 | 4.25 | 1084.997 | 58 | 29 | 61 | 30 | 789 |
| 467 | 2:48:46 PM | 98 | 273 | 1085.00 | 1086.25 | 1083.75 | 1086.25 | 1.25 | 2.50 | 1084.992 | 22 | 31 | 26 | 31 | 273 |
| 468 | 2:48:47 PM | 80 | 308 | 1086.25 | 1086.50 | 1085.25 | 1086.50 | 0.25 | 1.25 | 1085.821 | 32 | 29 | 38 | 30 | 308 |
| 469 | 2:48:48 PM | 124 | 1,314 | 1086.00 | 1090.00 | 1086.00 | 1089.50 | 3.50 | 4.00 | 1088.815 | 20 | 50 | 20 | 56 | 1,314 |
| 470 | 2:48:49 PM | 89 | 504 | 1089.75 | 1091.25 | 1089.50 | 1090.50 | 0.75 | 1.75 | 1090.189 | 27 | 35 | 29 | 38 | 504 |
| 471 | 2:48:50 PM | 113 | 717 | 1090.75 | 1091.50 | 1089.50 | 1091.50 | 0.75 | 2.00 | 1090.793 | 35 | 39 | 37 | 39 | 717 |
| 472 | 2:48:51 PM | 66 | 961 | 1091.25 | 1091.50 | 1090.50 | 1091.25 | 0.00 | 1.00 | 1090.951 | 20 | 27 | 23 | 30 | 961 |
| 473 | 2:48:52 PM | 101 | 1,085 | 1091.00 | 1092.25 | 1090.00 | 1090.00 | -1.00 | 2.25 | 1090.940 | 37 | 31 | 38 | 32 | 1,085 |
| 474 | 2:48:53 PM | 62 | 476 | 1091.25 | 1091.25 | 1089.75 | 1090.50 | -0.75 | 1.50 | 1090.365 | 25 | 20 | 30 | 21 | 476 |
| 475 | 2:48:54 PM | 51 | 395 | 1090.50 | 1090.50 | 1089.50 | 1089.75 | -0.75 | 1.00 | 1089.948 | 22 | 22 | 24 | 25 | 395 |
| 476 | 2:48:55 PM | 58 | 576 | 1089.75 | 1090.25 | 1089.25 | 1089.25 | -0.50 | 1.00 | 1089.534 | 26 | 25 | 29 | 27 | 576 |
| 477 | 2:48:56 PM | 96 | 1,289 | 1089.25 | 1089.75 | 1087.75 | 1089.00 | -0.25 | 2.00 | 1089.218 | 26 | 28 | 30 | 31 | 1,289 |
| 478 | 2:48:57 PM | 36 | 306 | 1088.00 | 1089.75 | 1088.00 | 1089.00 | 1.00 | 1.75 | 1089.141 | 19 | 25 | 19 | 26 | 306 |
| 479 | 2:48:58 PM | 102 | 1,351 | 1088.75 | 1090.50 | 1088.50 | 1090.50 | 1.75 | 2.00 | 1089.785 | 33 | 52 | 36 | 53 | 1,351 |
| 480 | 2:48:59 PM | 47 | 749 | 1090.50 | 1090.50 | 1088.75 | 1090.50 | 0.00 | 1.75 | 1089.115 | 26 | 18 | 32 | 18 | 749 |

**(Continued)**

| Row | Time (EDT) | Trades | Volume | First | High | Low | Last | Last - First Range | High /Low Range | VWAP | Buy Accts | Sell Accts | Buy User IDs | Sell User IDs | Volume Graph |
|---|---|---|---|---|---|---|---|---|---|---|---|---|---|---|---|
| 481 | 2:49:00 PM | 97 | 391 | 1090.50 | 1090.75 | 1088.75 | 1090.00 | -0.50 | 2.00 | 1089.750 | 32 | 25 | 38 | 26 | 391 |
| 482 | 2:49:01 PM | 67 | 463 | 1089.75 | 1091.00 | 1089.00 | 1090.50 | 0.75 | 2.00 | 1090.273 | 22 | 31 | 23 | 33 | 463 |
| 483 | 2:49:02 PM | 89 | 440 | 1090.50 | 1091.50 | 1089.50 | 1091.25 | 0.75 | 2.00 | 1090.819 | 32 | 32 | 35 | 32 | 440 |
| 484 | 2:49:03 PM | 81 | 574 | 1091.00 | 1091.50 | 1089.00 | 1090.75 | -0.25 | 2.50 | 1090.407 | 36 | 18 | 39 | 22 | 574 |
| 485 | 2:49:04 PM | 29 | 179 | 1090.75 | 1090.75 | 1089.75 | 1090.00 | -0.75 | 1.00 | 1090.306 | 15 | 10 | 16 | 13 | 179 |
| 486 | 2:49:05 PM | 92 | 731 | 1089.75 | 1091.00 | 1089.50 | 1089.75 | 0.00 | 1.50 | 1090.053 | 25 | 31 | 29 | 34 | 731 |
| 487 | 2:49:06 PM | 50 | 412 | 1090.25 | 1090.50 | 1089.75 | 1089.75 | -0.50 | 0.75 | 1090.026 | 20 | 14 | 21 | 18 | 412 |
| 488 | 2:49:07 PM | 82 | 718 | 1090.25 | 1091.50 | 1089.75 | 1090.50 | 0.25 | 1.75 | 1090.989 | 24 | 35 | 24 | 38 | 718 |
| 489 | 2:49:08 PM | 123 | 657 | 1090.50 | 1091.25 | 1090.00 | 1091.00 | 0.50 | 1.25 | 1090.683 | 27 | 30 | 31 | 32 | 657 |
| 490 | 2:49:09 PM | 158 | 985 | 1091.25 | 1091.50 | 1090.00 | 1090.75 | -0.50 | 1.50 | 1091.002 | 36 | 34 | 37 | 38 | 985 |
| 491 | 2:49:10 PM | 56 | 399 | 1090.50 | 1091.25 | 1090.50 | 1090.75 | 0.25 | 0.75 | 1090.882 | 16 | 19 | 20 | 22 | 399 |
| 492 | 2:49:11 PM | 51 | 449 | 1090.75 | 1091.25 | 1090.50 | 1091.00 | 0.25 | 0.75 | 1090.863 | 22 | 16 | 23 | 19 | 449 |
| 493 | 2:49:12 PM | 61 | 439 | 1090.75 | 1091.50 | 1090.50 | 1091.25 | 0.50 | 1.00 | 1091.016 | 21 | 21 | 24 | 22 | 439 |
| 494 | 2:49:13 PM | 81 | 469 | 1091.25 | 1091.50 | 1090.75 | 1091.25 | 0.00 | 0.75 | 1091.212 | 23 | 22 | 26 | 23 | 469 |
| 495 | 2:49:14 PM | 188 | 1,780 | 1091.25 | 1093.25 | 1091.25 | 1092.00 | 0.75 | 2.00 | 1092.005 | 32 | 62 | 33 | 64 | 1,780 |
| 496 | 2:49:15 PM | 197 | 1,029 | 1091.75 | 1093.00 | 1089.75 | 1090.00 | -1.75 | 3.25 | 1090.753 | 75 | 24 | 79 | 26 | 1,029 |
| 497 | 2:49:16 PM | 97 | 1,300 | 1090.75 | 1090.75 | 1088.50 | 1089.25 | -1.50 | 2.25 | 1089.624 | 42 | 18 | 43 | 18 | 1,300 |
| 498 | 2:49:17 PM | 41 | 275 | 1088.75 | 1089.00 | 1088.50 | 1088.50 | -0.25 | 0.50 | 1088.730 | 19 | 23 | 21 | 24 | 275 |
| 499 | 2:49:18 PM | 47 | 267 | 1088.50 | 1089.50 | 1088.50 | 1089.00 | 0.50 | 1.00 | 1088.874 | 21 | 21 | 22 | 24 | 267 |
| 500 | 2:49:19 PM | 69 | 967 | 1089.00 | 1090.25 | 1088.50 | 1090.25 | 1.25 | 1.75 | 1089.134 | 27 | 30 | 29 | 32 | 967 |
| 501 | 2:49:20 PM | 37 | 387 | 1090.00 | 1090.25 | 1089.00 | 1089.50 | -0.50 | 1.25 | 1089.830 | 15 | 22 | 16 | 22 | 387 |
| 502 | 2:49:21 PM | 99 | 1,230 | 1090.00 | 1090.75 | 1089.25 | 1089.50 | -0.50 | 1.50 | 1090.287 | 18 | 30 | 21 | 34 | 1,230 |
| 503 | 2:49:22 PM | 48 | 265 | 1089.50 | 1090.50 | 1089.50 | 1090.25 | 0.75 | 1.00 | 1089.887 | 17 | 14 | 22 | 17 | 265 |
| 504 | 2:49:23 PM | 71 | 1,046 | 1090.25 | 1090.75 | 1089.50 | 1090.50 | 0.25 | 1.25 | 1089.924 | 36 | 16 | 40 | 17 | 1,046 |
| 505 | 2:49:24 PM | 72 | 876 | 1090.25 | 1090.50 | 1089.25 | 1090.25 | 0.00 | 1.25 | 1089.974 | 27 | 24 | 29 | 27 | 876 |
| 506 | 2:49:25 PM | 51 | 553 | 1090.00 | 1091.00 | 1090.00 | 1091.00 | 1.00 | 1.00 | 1090.397 | 13 | 21 | 15 | 21 | 553 |
| 507 | 2:49:26 PM | 70 | 487 | 1090.50 | 1091.00 | 1089.75 | 1090.00 | -0.50 | 1.25 | 1090.292 | 23 | 17 | 27 | 22 | 487 |
| 508 | 2:49:27 PM | 77 | 660 | 1090.00 | 1090.50 | 1089.25 | 1090.00 | 0.00 | 1.25 | 1089.871 | 34 | 20 | 36 | 23 | 660 |
| 509 | 2:49:28 PM | 68 | 387 | 1089.50 | 1090.00 | 1089.00 | 1089.00 | -0.50 | 1.00 | 1089.464 | 32 | 23 | 34 | 26 | 387 |
| 510 | 2:49:29 PM | 67 | 622 | 1089.25 | 1089.25 | 1088.50 | 1088.75 | -0.50 | 0.75 | 1088.871 | 36 | 18 | 37 | 19 | 622 |
| 511 | 2:49:30 PM | 38 | 618 | 1088.75 | 1089.25 | 1088.50 | 1089.25 | 0.50 | 0.75 | 1088.789 | 14 | 12 | 16 | 13 | 618 |
| 512 | 2:49:31 PM | 89 | 629 | 1089.00 | 1089.50 | 1088.50 | 1088.75 | -0.25 | 1.00 | 1089.168 | 34 | 23 | 34 | 24 | 629 |
| 513 | 2:49:32 PM | 121 | 674 | 1088.50 | 1089.00 | 1088.25 | 1088.25 | -0.25 | 0.75 | 1088.595 | 36 | 26 | 43 | 31 | 674 |
| 514 | 2:49:33 PM | 182 | 1,003 | 1088.25 | 1088.50 | 1087.00 | 1087.25 | -1.00 | 1.50 | 1087.656 | 46 | 39 | 53 | 42 | 1,003 |
| 515 | 2:49:34 PM | 145 | 524 | 1087.25 | 1088.50 | 1086.25 | 1086.75 | -0.50 | 2.25 | 1087.198 | 33 | 30 | 37 | 37 | 524 |
| 516 | 2:49:35 PM | 102 | 962 | 1086.50 | 1087.50 | 1086.00 | 1087.25 | 0.75 | 1.50 | 1086.485 | 34 | 28 | 37 | 32 | 962 |
| 517 | 2:49:36 PM | 59 | 507 | 1087.50 | 1087.50 | 1085.75 | 1086.00 | -1.50 | 1.75 | 1086.810 | 31 | 16 | 33 | 18 | 507 |
| 518 | 2:49:37 PM | 78 | 598 | 1086.00 | 1086.50 | 1085.25 | 1085.50 | -0.50 | 1.25 | 1085.777 | 40 | 15 | 43 | 16 | 598 |
| 519 | 2:49:38 PM | 93 | 1,019 | 1085.25 | 1086.00 | 1084.75 | 1084.75 | -0.50 | 1.25 | 1085.173 | 42 | 26 | 46 | 30 | 1,019 |
| 520 | 2:49:39 PM | 81 | 529 | 1085.00 | 1085.00 | 1083.75 | 1084.50 | -0.50 | 1.25 | 1084.559 | 30 | 23 | 33 | 25 | 529 |
| 521 | 2:49:40 PM | 66 | 501 | 1084.50 | 1084.75 | 1083.25 | 1083.75 | -0.75 | 1.50 | 1084.136 | 24 | 31 | 25 | 31 | 501 |
| 522 | 2:49:41 PM | 59 | 599 | 1084.25 | 1085.00 | 1083.50 | 1085.00 | 0.75 | 1.50 | 1084.521 | 23 | 30 | 25 | 33 | 599 |
| 523 | 2:49:42 PM | 103 | 1,062 | 1084.75 | 1085.75 | 1084.00 | 1085.00 | 0.25 | 1.75 | 1084.917 | 41 | 30 | 47 | 32 | 1,062 |
| 524 | 2:49:43 PM | 74 | 628 | 1085.00 | 1086.50 | 1084.50 | 1085.25 | 0.25 | 2.00 | 1085.522 | 26 | 34 | 29 | 35 | 628 |
| 525 | 2:49:44 PM | 69 | 362 | 1085.25 | 1085.25 | 1084.00 | 1084.25 | -1.00 | 1.25 | 1084.588 | 34 | 17 | 36 | 19 | 362 |
| 526 | 2:49:45 PM | 99 | 839 | 1084.75 | 1085.25 | 1083.25 | 1085.00 | 0.25 | 2.00 | 1084.473 | 26 | 29 | 31 | 30 | 839 |
| 527 | 2:49:46 PM | 78 | 358 | 1084.75 | 1085.00 | 1084.00 | 1085.00 | 0.25 | 1.00 | 1084.633 | 22 | 19 | 25 | 21 | 358 |
| 528 | 2:49:47 PM | 107 | 868 | 1085.00 | 1085.50 | 1084.00 | 1084.75 | -0.25 | 1.50 | 1084.778 | 28 | 29 | 33 | 32 | 868 |
| 529 | 2:49:48 PM | 62 | 564 | 1084.75 | 1085.50 | 1084.75 | 1085.50 | 0.75 | 0.75 | 1085.274 | 19 | 22 | 22 | 24 | 564 |
| 530 | 2:49:49 PM | 123 | 993 | 1085.50 | 1086.75 | 1085.00 | 1086.25 | 0.75 | 1.75 | 1085.900 | 42 | 33 | 48 | 34 | 993 |
| 531 | 2:49:50 PM | 86 | 439 | 1086.00 | 1086.50 | 1085.50 | 1085.75 | -0.25 | 1.00 | 1085.897 | 31 | 20 | 35 | 20 | 439 |
| 532 | 2:49:51 PM | 107 | 734 | 1085.75 | 1086.75 | 1085.50 | 1085.50 | -0.25 | 1.25 | 1086.052 | 25 | 31 | 29 | 34 | 734 |
| 533 | 2:49:52 PM | 129 | 658 | 1085.50 | 1086.25 | 1085.25 | 1086.00 | 0.50 | 1.00 | 1085.795 | 29 | 19 | 33 | 22 | 658 |
| 534 | 2:49:53 PM | 96 | 638 | 1086.00 | 1086.25 | 1085.25 | 1086.25 | 0.25 | 1.00 | 1085.847 | 28 | 27 | 32 | 27 | 638 |
| 535 | 2:49:54 PM | 258 | 1,876 | 1086.00 | 1088.75 | 1085.00 | 1088.25 | 2.25 | 3.75 | 1086.380 | 37 | 56 | 41 | 60 | 1,876 |
| 536 | 2:49:55 PM | 167 | 1,144 | 1088.25 | 1088.75 | 1085.25 | 1088.00 | -0.25 | 3.50 | 1087.939 | 33 | 40 | 35 | 48 | 1,144 |
| 537 | 2:49:56 PM | 80 | 514 | 1088.00 | 1088.25 | 1086.75 | 1087.75 | -0.25 | 1.50 | 1087.744 | 24 | 23 | 27 | 24 | 514 |
| 538 | 2:49:57 PM | 121 | 1,177 | 1087.75 | 1089.25 | 1087.75 | 1088.75 | 1.00 | 1.50 | 1088.525 | 26 | 35 | 31 | 39 | 1,177 |
| 539 | 2:49:58 PM | 59 | 370 | 1089.00 | 1089.50 | 1088.75 | 1089.50 | 0.50 | 0.75 | 1089.114 | 20 | 20 | 22 | 21 | 370 |
| 540 | 2:49:59 PM | 147 | 1,309 | 1089.25 | 1089.50 | 1086.50 | 1088.75 | -0.50 | 3.00 | 1088.258 | 43 | 23 | 45 | 29 | 1,309 |

# End Notes

[1] Joint Report of the SEC and the CFTC on Harmonization of Regulation ,October 16, 2009.

[2] All times in this chapter are EDT.

[3] Statement of Gary Gensler, Chairman, Commodity Futures Trading Commission, Before the House of Representatives Committee on Financial Services, Subcommittee on Capital Markets, Insurance, and

Government Sponsored Enterprises, May 11, 2010, at 8. Except as specifically authorized, Section 8 of the Commodity Exchange Act generally forbids disclosure of additional information regarding such traders.

[4] 17 CFR 18.04.

[5] For example, the same market participant may be known to different broker-dealers by different names making the aggregation of orders for a single participant very difficult. For further details, see the SEC's recent proposal for the Large Trader Reporting System.

[6] Flight to Quality is a term used to describe the movement of capital into asset classes that are perceived to be less risky during times of financial uncertainty.

[7] The three highest single-day increases in the VIX are 10/19/87 (312.95%), 10/13/89 (68.30%), and 2/27/07 (64.22%).

[8] A CDS spread widening means that it will cost more for a company to insure against default, because the market sees default as more likely than it previously did. In other words, someone who wants to buy protection on a risk of default of a debt has to pay a higher premium.

[9] This figure depicts the distribution of returns from the close on May 5 to the lowest transaction price on May 6. The securities included are equity securities (common and preferred) of corporate issuers, exchange-traded products, closed-end funds, and ADRs, traded on major U.S. exchanges, and having in each case, as of the May 5 close, a share price of more than $3.00 and a market capitalization of at least $10 million.

[10] An "out-of-sequence" trade occurs when the TAQ data identifies the posted trade time as incorrect. In this case, the actual time at which the trade was placed is unknown.

[11] Figure 10 depicts the timing of daily lows during the one-hour period from 2:00 p.m. to 3:00 p.m. on May 6. Each point represents the return from the May 5 close to the lowest transaction price on May 6, plotted against the time at which the transaction occurred. Daily lows not occurring during this one-hour interval are not depicted. The figure includes all equity securities (common and preferred) of corporate issuers, exchange-traded products, closed-end funds, and ADRs, traded on major U.S. exchanges, with a share price of more than $3.00 and a market capitalization of at least $10 million as of the May 5 close.

[12] Figure 11 depicts the timing of daily highs during the one-hour period from 2:00 p.m. to 3:00 p.m. on May 6. Each point represents the return from the May 5 close to the highest transaction price on May 6, plotted against the time at which the transaction occurred. Daily highs not occurring during this one-hour interval are not depicted. The figure includes all equity securities (common and preferred) of corporate issuers, exchange-traded products, closed-end funds, and ADRs, traded on major U.S. exchanges, with a share price of more than $3.00 and a market capitalization of at least $10 million as of the May 5 close. For scaling purposes, Figure 11 excludes returns to daily highs on a few equity securities of corporate issuers.

[13] Two other exchanges – BATS and NSX – exercised self-help against NYSE Arca after this time.

[14] All of the equity exchanges provided data on their liquidity providers. Each exchange was requested to identify and provide data on the top ten overall liquidity providers ("Top Ten Providers") on the exchange on May 6. For each of the Top Ten Providers, the exchange was requested to provide (1) the number of trades and share volume of liquidity provided on the exchange from 2:00 p.m. to 3:00 p.m., broken down in 30 second intervals, for all securities traded on the exchange in the aggregate; and (2) the number of trades and share volume of liquidity removed on the exchange from 2:00 p.m. to 3:00 p.m., broken down in 30 second intervals, for all securities traded on the exchange in the aggregate.

[15] The aggregate number of shares taken and provided by each of the top ten liquidity providers for each exchange reported in 30-second intervals.

[16] The percent provided and taken and provided by each of the top ten liquidity providers for each exchange reported in 30-second intervals.

[17] We use 10% as an estimated cutoff for stocks that declined by amounts consistent with the overall market decline because, on any given day with a significant decline in prices, some stocks will decline less and some will decline more. On May 6, for example, 11 DJIA stocks declined by less than 5% from the 2:40 p.m. price, and 26 DJIA stocks declined by less than 10% from the 2:40 p.m. price. (Table 3)

[18] See description of clearly erroneous rules in Appendix A.

[19] Following the wide-scale disruption of May 6, 2010, the exchanges and FINRA settled on the relatively high 60% standard for breaking trades. We understand a substantially lower standard – 10%-20% – typically is selected for the more common discrete erroneous trade events involving one or a few securities. The SEC is working with the exchanges and FINRA to establish more transparent and objective standards for breaking erroneous trades.

[20] The term "broken trades" for these purposes means all trades identified as broken trades by the exchanges and FINRA for May 6, 2010.

[21] From April 1, 2010 to May 5, 2010, the average number of broken trades (excluding FINRA trades) was 118.25.

[22] The total of 326 securities with broken trades is comprised of 227 ETFs, 10 ETPs that are not ETFs and 89 stocks.

[23] The number of broken ADF/TRF trades counts only trades that were not rejected by ACT and that were reported to the tape.

[24] Under Rule 201, trading centers will be required to have and enforce policies and procedures reasonably designed to prevent executions of short sales at or below the national best bid once the stock price has experienced a ten percent decline relative to the prior day's closing price.

[25] This chart and the others below depicting single security price charts plot the second-by-second activity of trades, quotes, and volume for the security indicated. Each thick vertical bar (in black) shows the high/low range of all prices executed for all trades within a given second (scale on left axis). The red line shows the lowest National Best Bid quoted across all exchanges during that second. The green line shows the highest National Best Offer quoted across all exchanges during that second. The thick blue vertical lines indicate the total volume of shares traded each second (scale on right axis).

[26] Figure 15 depicts the distribution of returns from close on May 5 to the lowest transaction price on May 6. The securities included are ETFs trading on major U.S. exchanges, with a share price of more than $3.00 and a market capitalization of at least $10 million as of the May 5 close.

[27] Figure 16 depicts the timing of ETF daily lows during the one-hour period from 2:00 p.m. to 3:00 p.m. on May 6. Each point represents the return from the May 5 close to the lowest transaction price on May 6, plotted against the time at which the transaction occurred. Daily lows not occurring during this one-hour interval are not depicted. The figure includes ETFs trading on major U.S. exchanges with a share price of more than $3.00 and a market capitalization of at least $10 million as of the May 5 close.

[28] Figure 17 depicts the timing of ETF daily highs during the one-hour period from 2:00 p.m. to 3:00 p.m. on May 6. Each point represents the return from the May 5 close to the highest transaction price on May 6, plotted against the time at which the transaction occurred. Daily highs not occurring during this one-hour interval are not depicted. The Figure includes ETFs trading on major U.S. exchanges with a share price of more than $3.00 and a market capitalization of at least $10 million.

[29] Additionally, one fund family appears to account for all five of the commodity-index-related non-ETF ETPs that experienced broken trades

[30] The rate of broken trades for Average Current Net Asset Quartile 1 of 16.3% is computed as 34/(34+175). An analogous calculation is used to compute the average across the other three quartiles.

[31] Table 10 presents the number of ETPs with broken trades on May 6, 2010 by fund family (sponsor).

[32] This presents the number of ETFs by quartile of average current net assets, with broken trades on May 6, 2010 out of all ETFs, the average daily volume for ETFs for May 5, 2010 and May 6, 2010, and the average net assets of registered ETFs.

[33] ETFs in quartile 1 have current net assets less than $16,312,382. Quartile 2 has ETFs with current net assets between $16,312,382 and $75,170,606. Quartile 3 has ETFs with current net assets between $75,170,606 and $351,622,059. Quartile 4 consists of ETFs with current net assets greater than $351,622,059.

[34] In contrast to the stocks that suffered on the downside, the stock of Sotheby's (BID) is notable for displaying aberrant behavior on the upside on May 6 (see Figure 25 and Figure 26).

[35] The"short sale ratio" is defined as the volume of short selling divided by total volume.

[36] For more information on broad-based stock index futures, see Appendix B.

[37] Each of the four dates on which trading volume was greater occurred in September or October 2008, during the financial crisis. During the week of the Lehman bankruptcy filing on September 16, 17 and 18, 2008 trading volumes were 6.1 million contracts, 5.9 million contracts and 6.9 million contracts, respectively. On October 10, 2008 trading volume was 5.9 million contracts.

[38] Open interest means the total number of futures contracts that are not yet liquidated by offsetting transactions or cash settlement.

[39] For more information on electronic trading, order display and order entry, see Appendix B.4, B.5 and B.8.

[40] For more information, see Appendix B.10 and B.11.

[41] If at the end of those five seconds there were no orders that would result in such a transaction, the market would have been held an additional five seconds.

[42] Upon exiting the reserve state, 1,753 contracts were traded at a price of 1056.75. The E-mini S&P 500 began to recover at that point.

[43] Bid/offer spread between 2:30 p.m. and 2:43:10 p.m. and 2:48:10 p.m. and 3:00 p.m. are at their minimums.

[44] These spread measurements are graphed at 10 second intervals, with each data point representing the average of all quotes within a 1 second period.

[45] A side of a transaction means the account was either the buyer or the seller in a transaction. Total volume is equal to half of all transaction sides. To convert transaction sides to volume for a group of accounts, one must also eliminate half of the sides of trades transacted within the group of accounts (that is, not with accounts outside of the group).

[46] For the purposes of this analysis, liquidity providers are defined as follows: from the accounts that were both one of the 10 largest long gross volume accounts and 10 largest short gross volume accounts, CFTC staff selected the accounts that had a net position change of no more than 150 contracts (long or short) during the time period 2:30 p.m. to 2:45 p.m.

[47] CFTC staff confirmed that between 2:42 p.m. and 2:45 p.m. that several additional accounts (belonging to some of the most active traders) ceased trading. Furthermore, CFTC staff confirmed through trader interviews that

several accounts belonging to some of the most active traders ceased trading within seconds after the Stop Logic functionality was triggered and did not return to the market until later. A trader may transact through multiple accounts in Globex.

[48] The numbers reported are the total net volume for accounts with the 10 largest net buy volumes ("top 10 net buying accounts") and, separately, the total net volume for accounts with the 10 largest net sell volumes ("top 10 net selling accounts"). Net volume for an account was calculated as the total buy volume minus the total sell volume in the time period.

[49] The SEC has obtained quotation and last-sale information produced by the Consolidated Tape plans, which cover all executions in NMS stocks, regardless of whether they occurred on an exchange or over-the-counter. The plans information also contains all top-of-book quotations (i.e., the best orders or quotations in each listed equity security at each market at each point in time). However, the Consolidated Tape plans does not include orders that were outside the top of book, which constitute the vast majority of orders placed on any trading day. Most of these orders never execute and are canceled. Under current rules, there is no single record of such orders across the different markets. The relevant sources for this information include:

- ***OATS***. The Order Audit Trail System (OATS) was established by NASD in 1996 and captures information on orders in Nasdaq-listed securities.
- ***OTS***. The Order Tracking System (OTS) was established by the NYSE in 1999 and captures information on orders in equity securities listed on NYSE and NYSE Amex. The OTS is a system for gathering information by a request that can take ten days to fill.
- ***Individual exchanges***. Each exchange has its own systems to record information about orders placed and executed on its market, regardless of which exchange lists the security.

[50] Our initial options analysis suggests that there were not triggers originating from the options markets.

[51] 17 CFR 18.05.

[52] 17 CFR 15.03.

[53] See Securities Exchange Act Release No. 61358 (January 14, 2010), 75 FR 3594 (January 21, 2010).

[54] 17 CFR 18.05.

[55] 17 CFR 15.03.

[56] 17 CFR 18.04.

[57] See Securities Exchange Act Release No. 51808 (June 9, 2005), 70 FR 37496 (June 29, 2005) ("Regulation NMS Release").

[58] 17 CFR 242.611.

[59] Sources of estimated trading volume percentages: NASDAQ; NYSE Group; BATS; Direct Edge; data compiled from Forms ATS for 3d quarter 2009.

[60] See, e.g., BATS Exchange, Inc., http://batstrading.com/resources/features/bats_exchange_Latency.pdf (June 2009) (average latency (time to accept, process, and acknowledge or fill order) of 320 microseconds; NASDAQ, http://www.nasdaqtrader.com/trader.aspx?id=inet (December 12, 2009) (average latency (time to accept, process, and acknowledge or fill order) of 294 microseconds).

[61] See, e.g., BATS Exchange, Inc., Rule 11.12 (equally priced trading interest executed in time priority in the following order: (1) displayed size of limit orders; (2) non-displayed limit orders; (3) pegged orders; (4) mid-point peg orders; (5) reserve size of orders; and (6) discretionary portion of discretionary orders); NASDAQ Rule 4757(a)(1) (book processing algorithm executes trading interest in the following order: (1) displayed orders; (2) non-displayed orders and the reserve portion of quotes and reserve orders (in price/time priority among such interest); and (3) the discretionary portion of discretionary orders.

[62] Data compiled from Forms ATS submitted to Commission for 3d quarter 2009. Some OTC market makers offer dark liquidity primarily in a principal capacity and do not operate as ATSs. For purposes of this chapter, such trading centers are not defined as dark pools because they are not ATSs. They may, however, offer electronic dark liquidity services that are analogous to those offered by dark pools.

[63] See, e.g., http://www.liquidnet.com/about/liquidStats.html (average U.S. execution size in July 2009 was 49,638 shares for manually negotiated trades via Liquidnet's negotiation product); http://www.pipelinetrading.com /AboutPipeline/CompanyInfo.aspx (average trade size of 50,000 shares in Pipeline).

[64] See, e.g., http://www.nasdaqtrader.com/trader/aspx?id=marketshare (average size of NASDAQ matched trades in July 2009 was 228 shares); http://nyxdata.com/nysedata/asp/factbook (NYSE Group average trade size in all stocks traded in July 2009 was 267 shares).

[65] Data compiled from Forms ATS submitted to Commission for 3d quarter 2009.

[66] For example,more than 200 publish execution quality statistics under Rule 605 of Regulation NMS.

[67] An OTC market maker is defined in Rule 600(b)(52) of Regulation NMS as "any dealer that holds itself out as being willing to buy and sell to its customers, or others, in the United States, an NMS stock for its own account on a regular or continuous basis otherwise than on a national securities exchange in amounts of less than block size."

[68] "Block size" is defined in Rule 600(b)(9) of Regulation NMS as an order of at least 10,000 shares or for a quantity of stock having a market value of at least $200,000. A block positioner generally means any broker-dealer in the business of executing, as principal or agent, block size trades for its customers. To facilitate

trades, block positioners often commit their own capital to trade as principal with at least some part of the customer's block order.

[69] For example, a 2nd quarter of 2009 review of the order routing disclosures required by Rule 606 of Regulation NMS of eight broker-dealers with significant retail customer accounts reveals that nearly 100% of their customer market orders are routed to OTC market makers. The review also indicates that most of these retail brokers either receive payment for order flow in connection with the routing of orders or are affiliated with an OTC market maker that executes the orders.

[70] Rule 611(a)(1) requires all trading centers to establish, maintain, and enforce written policies and procedures that are reasonably designed to prevent trade-throughs of protected quotations, subject to certain exceptions set forth in Rule 611(b).

[71] FINRA operates the Alternative Display Facility ("ADF"), a display-only facility that permits its participants to display quotations and report trades, among other things.

[72] 17 CFR 242.600(b)(42).

[73] Technically, the NBBO may include the best bid and best offer of a stock exchange or the ADF even if is non-automated (i.e., manual). In practice, however, all such markets are fully automated with the exception of NYSE (and NYSE Amex, which operates on the same system as NYSE) for which, when it hits a liquidity replenishment point for a given security, its quotation becomes non-firm and thus is not included in the calculation of the NBBO.

[74] Prior to Rule 611, exchanges routed orders through an inflexible, partially manual system called the Intermarket Trading System ("ITS"). See Regulation NMS Release, 70 FR at 37538-37539 ("Although ITS promotes access among participants that is uniform and free, it also is often slow and limited.").

[75] See Regulation NMS Release, 70 FR at 37540 ("[M]any different private firms have entered the business of linking with a wide range of trading centers and then offering their customers access to those trading centers through the private firms' linkages. Competitive forces determine the types and costs of these private linkages.").

[76] In addition, Rule 610(c) limits the fees that a trading center can charge for access to its displayed quotations at the best prices. Rule 611(d) requires SROs to establish, maintain, and enforce rules that restrict their members from displaying quotations that lock or cross previously displayed quotations.

Section 6(a)(2) of the Exchange Act requires registered exchanges to allow any qualified and registered broker-dealer to become a member of the exchange – a key element in assuring fair access to exchange services. In contrast, the access requirements that apply to ATSs are much more limited. Regulation ATS includes two distinct types of access requirements: (1) order display and execution access in Rule 301(b)(3); and (2) fair access to ATS services in general in Rule 301(b)(5). An ATS must meet order display and execution access requirements if it displays orders to more than one person in the ATS and exceeds a 5% trading volume threshold. An ATS must meet the general fair access requirement if it exceeds a 5% trading volume threshold. If an ATS neither displays orders to more than one person in the ATS nor exceeds a 5% trading volume threshold, Regulation ATS does not impose access requirements on the ATS.

[77] See, e.g., Regulation NMS Release, 70 FR at 37537-37538 (discussion of duty of best execution).

[78] In this regard, Rules 605 and 606 of Regulation NMS are designed to support competition by enhancing the transparency of order execution and routing practices. Rule 605 requires market centers to publish monthly reports of statistics on their order execution quality. Rule 606 requires brokers to publish quarterly reports on their routing practices, including the venues to which they route orders for execution.

[79] As noted above, over-the-counter market makers also provide liquidity by trading chiefly with customer orders.

[80] In addition, the Exchange Act does not require a national securities exchange to have market makers. See , e.g. , Securities Exchange Act Release Nos. 61698 (March 12, 2010), 75 FR 13151 (March 18, 2010) (order granting the exchange registration of EDGX Exchange, Inc. and EDGA Exchange, Inc.).

[81] See, e.g. Nasdaq Rule 4613; NYSE Arca Equities Rule 7.23; and BATS Rule 11.8.

[82] See Securities Exchange Act Release No. 56586 (October 1, 2007), 72 FR 57085 (October 5, 2007) (SR-NASDAQ-2007-069).

[83] Id.

[84] Section 11(b) of the Exchange Act allows the rules of a national securities exchange to permit a member to be registered as a specialist and act as both a broker and a dealer. 15 U.S.C. 78k(b).

[85] 17 CFR 240.11b-1.

[86] 17 CFR 240.11b-1(a)(2)(iii).

[87] 17 CFR 240.11b-1(a)(2)(ii).

[88] See, e.g., Jonathan Spicer and Herbert Lash, Who's Afraid of High-Frequency Trading?, Reuters.com, December 2, 2009 (available at http://www.reuters.com/article/idUSN173583920091202) ("High-frequency trading now accounts for 60 percent of total U.S. equity volume, and is spreading overseas and into other markets."); Scott Patterson and Geoffrey Rogow, What's Behind High-Frequency Trading, Wall Street Journal, August 1, 2009 ("High frequency trading now accounts for more than half of all stock-trading volume in the U.S.").

[89] BATS Rule 11.9(a)(2).

[90] See Securities Exchange Act Release No. 34-59258 (January 15, 2009), 74 FR 4788 (January 27, 2009) (SR-BATS-2009-001).

[91] Unpriced Orders would not be Collared Orders for: (1) Market On Open Orders; (2) Market OnClose Orders; (3) Unpriced Orders included in a Nasdaq Halt Cross or Nasdaq Imbalance Cross;or (4) Unpriced Orders that are Reference Price Cross Orders. See Nasdaq Rule 4751(e)(13).

[92] See Securities Exchange Act Release No. 60371 (July 23, 2009), 74 FR 38075 (July 30, 2009) (SR-Nasdaq-2009-070).

[93] Rule 600(b)(3) of Regulation NMS. 17 CFR 242.600(b)(3).

[94] Rule 611(b)(5) of Regulation NMS. 17 CFR 242.611(b)(5).

[95] Rule 611(b)(6) of Regulation NMS. 17 CFR 242.611(b)(6).

To illustrate the operation of intermarket sweep orders, assume that a broker-dealer's customer wished to sell a large amount of a stock. Trading Center A is displaying the national best bid of 500 shares at $10.00, along with quotations in its proprietary depth-of-book data feed of 1500 shares at $9.99, and 5000 shares at $9.97. The customer decides to sweep all liquidity on Trading Center A down to $9.97. Assume also that Trading Center B is displaying a protected bid of 2000 shares at $9.99, Trading Center C is displaying a protected bid of 400 shares at $9.98, and Trading Center D is displaying a protected bid of 200 shares at $9.97. The broker-dealer could execute this trade for its customer, subject to its best execution responsibilities, by simultaneously routing the following orders: (1) an intermarket sweep order to Trading Center A with a limit price of $9.97 and a size of 7000 shares; (2) an intermarket sweep order to Trading Center B with a limit price of $9.99 and a size of 2000 shares; and (3) an intermarket sweep order to Trading Center C with a limit price of $9.98 and a size of 400 shares.

All of these orders would meet the requirements of the definition of intermarket sweep orders because the necessary orders simultaneously were routed to execute against the displayed size of all better-priced protected quotations. Trading Centers A, B, and C all could execute their orders immediately without regard to the protected quotations displayed at other trading centers. No order would need to be routed to Trading Center D because the price of its bid was not superior to the most inferior limit price of the order routed to Trading Center A. Assuming the customer obtained a fill for each of its orders at the displayed prices and sizes, it would have been able to obtain an immediate execution of a 9400-share trade by sweeping through four price levels at Trading Center A, while also honoring the protected quotations at two other trading centers.

[96] For example, if the last sale price in a security is $20 and the LRP value is $0.40, an LRP would be reached at $20.40 on the upside or $19.60 on the downside.

[97] NYSE Rule 1000(a)(iv).

[98] Rule 611(b)(1) of Regulation NMS. 17 CFR 242.611(b)(1).

[99] See Question 4.07 of Responses to Frequently Asked Questions Concerning Rule 611 and Rule 610 of Regulation NMS, available at http://sec.gov/divisions/marketreg/nmsfaq610-11.htm#sec4 (detailing the elements that must be included in a trading center's policies and procedures to implement the self-help exception).

[100] For example, if the last trade in a stock is $20, and a computer malfunction at one firm causes a series of trades to occur on multiple exchanges at prices exceeding $50, the automated systems of other firms may quickly follow, with erroneous trades rapidly impacting multiple markets and market participants.

[101] 17 CFR 242.200(a).

[102] For example, in 2003, the SEC settled a case against certain parties relating to allegations of manipulative short selling in the stock of a corporation. The Commission alleged that the defendants profited from engaging in massive "naked" short selling that flooded the market with the stock, and depressed its price. See Rhino Advisors, Inc. and Thomas Badian, Lit. Rel. No. 18003 (Feb. 27, 2003); SEC v. Rhino Advisors, Inc. and Thomas Badian, Civ. Action No. 03 civ 1310 (RO) (S.D.N.Y); see also U.S. v. Russo, 74 F.3d 1383, 1392 (2d Cir. 1996) (short sales were sufficiently connected to the manipulation scheme as to constitute a violation of Exchange Act Section 10(b) and Rule 10b-5); S.E.C. v. Gardiner, 48 S.E.C. Docket 811, No. 91 Civ. 2091 (S.D.N.Y. Mar. 27, 1991) (alleged manipulation by sales representative by directing or inducing customers to sell stock short in order to depress its price).

[103] A fail to deliver occurs when a seller fails to deliver securities to the buyer when delivery is due.

[104] See Securities Exchange Act Release No. 50103 (July 28, 2004), 69 FR 48008 (August 6, 2004).

[105] See Securities Exchange Act Release No. 58733 (October 14, 2008), 73 FR 61706 (October 17, 2008); see also Securities Exchange Act Release No. 58572 (September 17, 2008), 73 FR 54875 (September 23, 2008).

[106] See Securities Exchange Act Release No. 60388 (July 27, 2009), 74 FR 38266 (July 31, 2009). Under Rule 204, if a firm that clears and settles trades has a fail to deliver position at a registered clearing agency in any equity security for a short sale transaction in that equity security, the firm must, by no later than the beginning of regular trading hours on the settlement day following the settlement date, referred to as T+4, immediately close out the fail to deliver position by borrowing or purchasing securities of like kind and quantity. If the fail to deliver position results from a long sale or bona fide market making activity, the firm must, by no later than the beginning of regular trading hours on the third settlement day following the settlement date, referred to as T+6, immediately close out the fail to deliver position by borrowing or purchasing securities of like kind and quantity. If a firm that clears and settles trades does not purchase or borrow shares, as applicable, to close out a

fail to deliver position in accordance with Rule 204, the firm, and any broker-dealer from which it receives trades for clearance and settlement, must borrow or arrangement to borrow securities prior to accepting or effecting further short sales in that security, until the firm closes out the fail to deliver position by purchasing securities of like kind and quantity and that purchase has cleared and settled at a registered clearing agency.

[107] See Securities Exchange Act Release No. 61595 (February 26, 2010), 75 FR 11232 (March 10, 2010).

[108] See Table 8.

[109] See Securities Exchange Act Release No. 60405 (July 30, 2009), 74 FR 39362 (August 6, 2009) (File No. 4-546).

[110] A "Protected Bid" "Protected Offer" means a bid or offer in an option series that is displayed by an Eligible Exchange, is disseminated pursuant to the Options Price Reporting Authority Plan ("OPRA Plan"), and is the Best Bid or Best Offer of an Eligible Exchange. A "Best Bid" or "Best Offer" means the highest bid price or the lowest offer price communicated by a member of an Eligible Exchange to any broker-dealer or to any customer at which such member is willing to buy or sell, either as principal or agent. "Eligible Exchange" means a national securities exchange registered with the Commission in accordance with Section 6(a) of the Exchange Act that, among other things, is a Participant Exchange in OCC and is a party to the OPRA Plan. See Sections 2(1), 2(2), 2(14), and 2(17) of the Options Plan.
The OPRA Plan is a national market system plan approved by the SEC pursuant to Section 11A of the Exchange Act and Rule 608 thereunder. See Securities Exchange Act Release No. 17638 (March 18, 1981), 22 S.E.C. Docket 484 (March 31, 1981).

[111] See supra note 58.

[112] Prior to the Options Plan, the options exchanges routed specific linkage orders through a stand-alone system, or hub, which acted as a centralized data communications network that electronically linked the options exchanges to one another. See Securities Exchange Act Release No. 60405, supra note 109.

[113] On January 26, 2007, the then-existing six options exchanges implemented a pilot program to quote certain options series in thirteen classes in one-cent increments. Nasdaq became a participant in this program on March 31, 2008, when it commenced trading on NOM, and BATS became a participant on February 26, 2010 when it commenced trading on BATS Options Exchange Market. Since 2007, the pilot program has been extended and expanded several times.

[114] See Securities Exchange Act Release No. 61902 (April 14, 2010), 75 FR 20738 (April 20, 2010).

[115] Exchanges that use the "broker payment" model also generally give priority to customer orders at the best price over other orders or quotations at that price. After customer orders are executed, the rules of "broker payment" options exchanges dictate how the remainder of an incoming order is allocated against resting non-customer orders or quotations. Exchanges that use a "broker payment" model do not give priority to orders from certain customers who are "professional" customers under exchange rules. "Professional" customers are treated on ISE, CBOE, NYSE Amex and Nasdaq OMX Phlx in the same manner as a broker-dealer for purposes of specified order execution rules, including priority rules.

[116] See supra section entitled "Order Types."

[117] See Section 2(9) of the Options Plan. Intermarket sweep orders in the options markets are functionally similarly to the ISO order for NMS stocks. See supra notes 93-95 and accompanying text.

[118] See, e.g., NYSE Arca Options Rule 6.62 (defining NYSE Arca's reserve order as a limit order with a portion of the size displayed and with a reserve portion of the size that is not displayed on NYSE Arca). See also Nasdaq Options Rule Ch. VI. Section 1(e)(6) (defining NOM's price improving order as an order to buy or sell an option at a specified price at an increment smaller than the minimum price variation in the security. Price improving orders that are available for display shall be displayed at the minimum price variation in that security and shall be rounded up for sell orders and rounded down for buy orders); and ISE Rule 715(c) and Supplementary Material .02 to ISE Rule 713 (defining ISE's all-or-none order as a limit or market order that is to be executed in its entirety or not at all. These orders are contingency orders and have no priority on ISE's limit order book. Such orders are not displayed in ISE's best bid or offer but are maintained in the system and remain available for execution after all other trading interest at the same price has been exhausted).

[119] See, e.g., NOM Ch. VI, Section 1(e)(6) (providing that the non-displayed portion of reserve orders are not displayed in the system, and have lower priority within the system than an equally priced order that is displayed within the system, regardless of time stamp); BATS Rule 21.8(a)(2) (generally providing that displayed interest has priority over non-displayed interest at the same price); and Supplementary Material .02 to ISE Rule 713 (all-or-none orders are maintained in the system and remain available for execution after all other trading interest at the same price has been exhausted).

[120] See supra note 77.

[121] Rule 606 of Regulation NMS requires brokers to publish quarterly reports on their routing practices, including the venues to which they route options orders for execution.

[122] Options of the same class that have the same standardized terms ( e.g., strike price) comprise an options series. An options class is an option of the same type (put or call) with the same underlying security.

[123] See, e.g., Nasdaq OMX Phlx Rule 1014(c)(i)(A)(1) and (2).

[124] See supra note 80.

[125] See Securities Exchange Act Release No. 61735 (March 18, 2010), 75 FR 14227 (March 24, 2010).

[126] The theoretical price of an option is, for series that are traded on at least one other exchange, the last national best bid (for erroneous sell transactions) and the last national best offer price (for) erroneous buy transactions) just prior to the trade.

[127] SPDR Trust, Series 1, Investment Company Act Rel. Nos. 18959 (September 17, 1992) (notice) and 19055 (October 26, 1992) (order) and The CountryBaskets Index Fund, Inc., Investment Company Act Rel. Nos. 21736 (February 6, 1996) (notice) and 21802 (March 5, 1996) (order).

[128] Commodity Exchange Act (CEA) Section 3(a), 7 U.S.C. 5(a).

[129] Id.

[130] Id.

[131] See, e.g., CEA Section 5(b)(3), 7 U.S.C. 7(b)(3); CEA Section 5(b)(5), 7 U.S.C. 7(b)(5).

[132] See, e.g., CEA Section 5(b)(2), 7 U.S.C. 7(b)(2); CEA Section 5(b)(5), 7 U.S.C. 7(b)(5); CEA Section 5(d)(4), 7 U.S.C. 7(d)(4); CEA Section 5(d)(11), 7 U.S.C. 7(d)(11); CEA Section 5(d)(12), 7 U.S.C. 7(d)(12).

[133] CEA Section 5, 7 U.S.C. 7.

[134] CEA Section 5(b), 7 U.S.C. 7(b); CEA Section 5(d), 7 U.S.C. 7(d); 17 CFR 38.

[135] CEA Section 5c(c), 7 U.S.C. 7a-2(c); 17 CFR Part 40.

[136] CEA Section 5(b)(5), 7 U.S.C. 7(b)(5).

[137] The DCO functions as the central counterparty and guarantor for the positions that result from all contracts traded on the DCM. This means that the DCO is the long to each short position and the short to each long position in all contracts that it clears. DCOs deal exclusively with clearing participants. Any market participant that is not a clearing member of a particular DCM must have its positions carried by a clearing member. The DCO for CME is the CME Clearing House, while the DCO for ICE Futures US is ICE CLEAR US.

[138] See CEA Section 5(b)(5), 7. U.S.C. 7(b)(5); CEA Section 5(d)(11), 7 U.S.C 7(d)(11).

[139] A broad-based security index means a group or index of securities that does not constitute a narrow-based security index. 17 CFR 41.1(c).

[140] The "Special Opening Quotation" is calculated using normal index calculation procedures except that the values for the respective components are taken as the actual opening values for each of the component equities.

[141] Total trading volume in the E-mini S&P 500 contract exceeded that of the pit-traded contract in 2006. In 2006, total trading volume in the E-mini S&P 500 contract was 257,926,680 contracts compared to 74,221,810 E-mini equivalent contracts for the pit-traded S&P 500 contract.

[142] CEA Section 1a(31), 7 U.S.C. 1a(31); 17 CFR Part 41.

[143] CEA Section 2(a)(1)(C), 7 U.S.C. 2(a)(1)(C); CEA Section 2(a)(1)(D), 7 U.S.C. 2(a)(1)(D).

[144] CEA Section 5f, 7 U.S.C. 7b-1. See also, 17 CFR Part 41.

[145] 15 U.S.C. 78f(g)(2).

[146] The CME Group exchanges include CME, CBOT, NYMEX, and the Commodity Exchange, Inc. (COMEX).

[147] Although all U.S. futures markets trade either exclusively on electronic trading systems or utilize a combination of floor trading and electronic trading, this discussion focuses solely on CME Globex and ICE Trading System, the systems used to trade the E-mini S&P 500 and the Russell 2000 equity index futures contracts.

[148] "Front-end system" refers generally to the technology and infrastructure by which a trader interacts with an exchange's electronic trading system. Front-end systems provide the immediate interface through which orders are entered for transmission to the exchange, and through which market data is received by the trader. Front-end systems can be proprietary to the trader, furnished by third-party providers, or even provided by the exchange itself.

[149] Other characteristics of high frequency trading may also include: (1) the use of computer systems to generate, route and execute orders, (2) short time-frames for establishing and liquidating positions, (3) submission of numerous orders that are cancelled shortly thereafter, and/or (4) ending the trading day in a neutral overall position.

[150] The COT reports provide a breakdown of each Tuesday's open interest for futures markets in which 20 or more traders hold positions equal to or above the reporting levels established by the CFTC. The information is available on the CFTC Website, cftc.gov.

[151] When an individual reportable trader is identified to the CFTC, the trader is classified either as "commercial" or "non-commercial." All of a trader's reported futures positions in a commodity are classified as commercial if the trader uses futures contracts in that particular commodity for hedging as defined in CFTC Regulation 1.3(z), 17 CFR 1.3(z). A trading entity generally gets classified as a "commercial" trader by filing a statement with the CFTC, on CFTC Form 40: Statement of Reporting Trader, that it is commercially "...engaged in business activities hedged by the use of the futures or option markets." To ensure that traders are classified with accuracy and consistency, CFTC staff may exercise judgment in re-classifying a trader if it has additional information about the trader's use of the markets. A trader may be classified as a commercial trader in some commodities and as a non-commercial trader in other commodities. A single trading entity cannot be classified as both a commercial and non-commercial trader in the same commodity. Nonetheless, a multi-functional organization that has more than one trading entity may have each trading entity classified separately in a commodity. For example, a financial organization trading in financial futures may have a banking entity

whose positions are classified as commercial and have a separate money-management entity whose positions are classified as noncommercial.

[152] In the case of the open outcry S&P 500 futures contract, the member firm will transmit the order to CME's trading floor.

[153] In the case of CME, it has market maker programs in the following equity index contracts: E-mini S&P MidCap 400 Futures, E-mini S&P MidCap 600 Futures, S&P 500 Technology Index Futures, S&P 500 Financial Sector Index Futures, E-mini MSCI EAFE Futures, E-mini MSCI Emerging Markets Index Futures, and E-mini Dow Futures (European Hours).

[154] Futures exchanges must also make the terms and conditions of market maker programs publically available. See , Designation Criteria 7, CEA Section 5(b)(7), 7 U.S.C. 7(b)(7); Core Principle 7, CEA Section 5(d)(7), 7 U.S.C. 7(d)(7).

[155] Market maker programs must comply, for example, with Core Principle 2—Compliance with Rules (monitor for trade practice abuses), Core Principle 9—Execution of Transactions (ensuring that the market remains open, competitive and efficient), Core Principle 12—Protection of Market Participants (fiduciary obligations to customers), and Core Principle 18—Antitrust Considerations, as well as Designation Criteria 3—Fair and Equitable Trading. See generally, CEA Section 5(b), 7 U.S.C. 7(b) and CEA Section 5(d), 7 U.S.C. 7(d).

[156] CEA Section 5c(c), 7 U.S.C. 7a-2(c). See also, 17 CFR 40.5; 17 CFR 40.6.

[157] The electronic trading functionality involved is known as "price banding functionality." Generally, the price band is calculated dynamically by the system, based on the last traded price or the best bid or offer, and the price band thus moves dynamically with the market price, with its outer parameters remaining a fixed distance in points (12 in the case of the E-mini) above and below the market price. A "point" on a broad-based equity index, such as the S&P 500, is a concept used to measure the collective value of the securities included in the index.

[158] At CME and ICE Futures US, the number of points involved in the price band is set separately by each exchange for the products they trade.

[159] In the futures markets, however, a stop order as a limit order in the CME Globex and ICE systems. As a limit order, a trade cannot be executed at a price below its limit price.

[160] At CME, a market participant entering a stop loss order can pre-select a limit price only within a 12-point range of reasonability below the stop price. If the participant did not pre-select a limit price, the system defaults to a limit price three points below the stop price. At ICE, the participant can pre-select a limit price only within four points below the stop price, and the system defaults to a limit price four points below the stop price if no limit price is pre-selected.

[161] Absent this Stop Logic functionality, all stop orders at a particular price point would be triggered and traded on a first-in, first-out basis; additional resting stops would be triggered and traded as the market declined, and new orders would continue to be accepted and traded. While the protected range would still be operable, it would continuously adjust downwards with the market until a new equilibrium was reached, including, potentially, the execution of all resting stop orders in the order book.

[162] Globex's Stop Logic functionality was originally developed to address thin markets in back contract months at times of night when open outcry markets were closed. However, it has played a role in volatile markets, such as the May 6 E-mini S&P 500 futures market.

[163] The GCC is the Market Operations and Customer Service desk for electronic trading on the Globex System. The GCC handles inquiries, issues, and support requests for the Globex platform, including electronic trading, order routing and market data interfaces, and network connectivity.

[164] Exchange of Futures for Related Positions includes, among other things. Exchange for Physicals ("EFP"), Exchange of Futures for Swaps ("EFS"), and Exchange of Futures for Risk ("EFR"). An EFP is a transaction in which the buyer of a cash commodity transfers to the seller a corresponding amount of long futures contracts, or receives from the seller a corresponding amount of short futures, at a price difference manually agreed upon. An EFS is a privately negotiated transaction in which a position in a physical delivery futures contract is exchanged for a cash-settled swap position in the same or a related commodity, pursuant to the rules of a futures exchange. An EFR is an exchange of futures for, or in connection with, over-the-counter derivative transactions.

[165] The current reporting levels, in number of contracts, for securities products are as follows: S&P 500 Index, 1,000; Other Broad-Based Securities Indices, 200; Individual Equity Securities, 1,000; and Narrow-Based Security Indices, 200.

[166] 17 CFR 18.05.

[167] While price limits are common in futures contracts, there are no price limits for stocks, equity options or index options.

[168] A futures contract is found to be "locked limit" if exchange officials determine that prices are consistently at the limit price. A price decline that touches a limit but quickly bounces back will not trigger a "locked limit" determination.

[169] See Report of the Presidential Task Force on Market Mechanisms (January 1988) at 66.

[170] The Working Group, established in March 1988, consists of the Secretary of the Treasury and the Chairmen of the SEC, CFTC, and the Board of Governors of the Federal Reserve System.

[171] See Interim Report of the Working Group on Financial Markets (May 1988) at 5.

[172] See Interim Report at 4.

[173] See Interim Report at Appendix A.

[174] See Securities Exchange Act Release Nos. 26198 (Oct. 19, 1988), 53 FR 41637 (October 24, 1988) (Amex, CBOE, NASD, and NYSE) ("1988 Approval Order"); 26218 (October 26, 1988), 53 FR 44137 (Nov. 1, 1988) (CHX); 26357 (December 14, 1988), 53 FR 51182 (December 20, 1988) (BSE); 26368 (December 16, 1988), 53 FR 51942 (Dec. 23, 1988) (PSE); 26386 (December 22, 1988), 53 FR 52904 (December 29, 1988) (PHLX); and 26440 (January 10, 1989), 54 FR 1830 (January 17, 1989) (CSE).

[175] Id.

[176] Id.

[177] See Securities Exchange Act Release No. 37890 (October 29, 1996), 61 FR 56983 (November 5, 1996) (Amex, NYSE, and PHLX).

[178] Id.

[179] See Securities Exchange Act Release No. 38221 (January 31, 1997) 62 FR 5871 (NYSE, Amex, CBOE, CHX, BSE, and PHLX) ("1997 Approval Order").

[180] Id.

[181] See Securities Exchange Act Release No. 39846 (April 9, 1998), 63 FR 18477 (April 15, 1998) (NYSE, Amex, BSE, CHX, NASD, and PHLX) ("April 1998 Approval Order").

[182] In November, 2002, trading in security futures products (SFPs) began. Any NYSE-declared circuit breaker trading halts would apply also to DCMs that trade SFPs including single security and narrow-based security index futures.

[183] The S&P 500 5 percent price limit was hit on October 8, 1988, October 13, 1989, October 27, 1997, April 4, 2000, and April 14, 2000.

[184] CME Group Rule 576 requires that each order entered into CME Globex include the submission of an operator ID, also referred to as the "Tag 50 ID" or "User ID", which is unique to the party who entered the order. For orders entered manually, the Tag 50 ID must be unique to the individual entering the order into CME Globex. For orders entered by an automated trading system ("ATS"), the Tag 50 ID must be unique to the person, or the identified team of persons on the same shift, who are responsible for the operation of the ATS. All Tag 50 IDs must be unique at the level of the clearing member firm. See Market Regulation Advisory Notice RA0915-5, "Operator ID ('Tag 50') Required on All CME Globex Orders," available from CME Group at http://www.cmegroup.com/rulebook/files/CME_Group_RA0915-5.pdf (visited May 15, 2010).

# INDEX

## R



## S



## T